KING COUNTY AND ITS EMERALD CITY:

SEATTLE

I dedicate this book
to my mother, Dorothy Warren,
and to my wife, Gwen Davis Warren.
The first, with patience, interested me in history.
The second, with patience, allows me to pursue
this interest far too much of the time.

Seattle, Washington Territory, 1884. This hand-colored lithograph, made by C.L. Smith from a drawing by A. Burr, depicts Seattle, the Elliott Bay harbor, and Mt. Rainier. Published by the West Shore, Portland, Oregon : Copyright Amon Carter Museum, Fort Worth, Texas. #1967.225

King County and its Emerald City:

Seattle

An Illustrated History by James R. Warren

KING COUNTY AND ITS EMERALD CITY:

SEATTLE

◆

Written by James R. Warren
Picture Research by
Mary-Thadia d'Hondt and Howard Giske

Produced in cooperation with
the Museum of History and Industry

Published 1997
Printed in the United States of America

Library of Congress Card Number: 97-73063
ISBN 0-9654754-2-5

Bibliography p. 286
Includes Index
Refer to p.294 for current attributions for certain
photographs contained in this text.

CONTENTS

Frank Nowell took this aerial photograph of the Alaska-Yukon-Pacific Exposition grounds in 1909 from a balloon hovering about a quarter of a mile above the earth. (MOHAI)

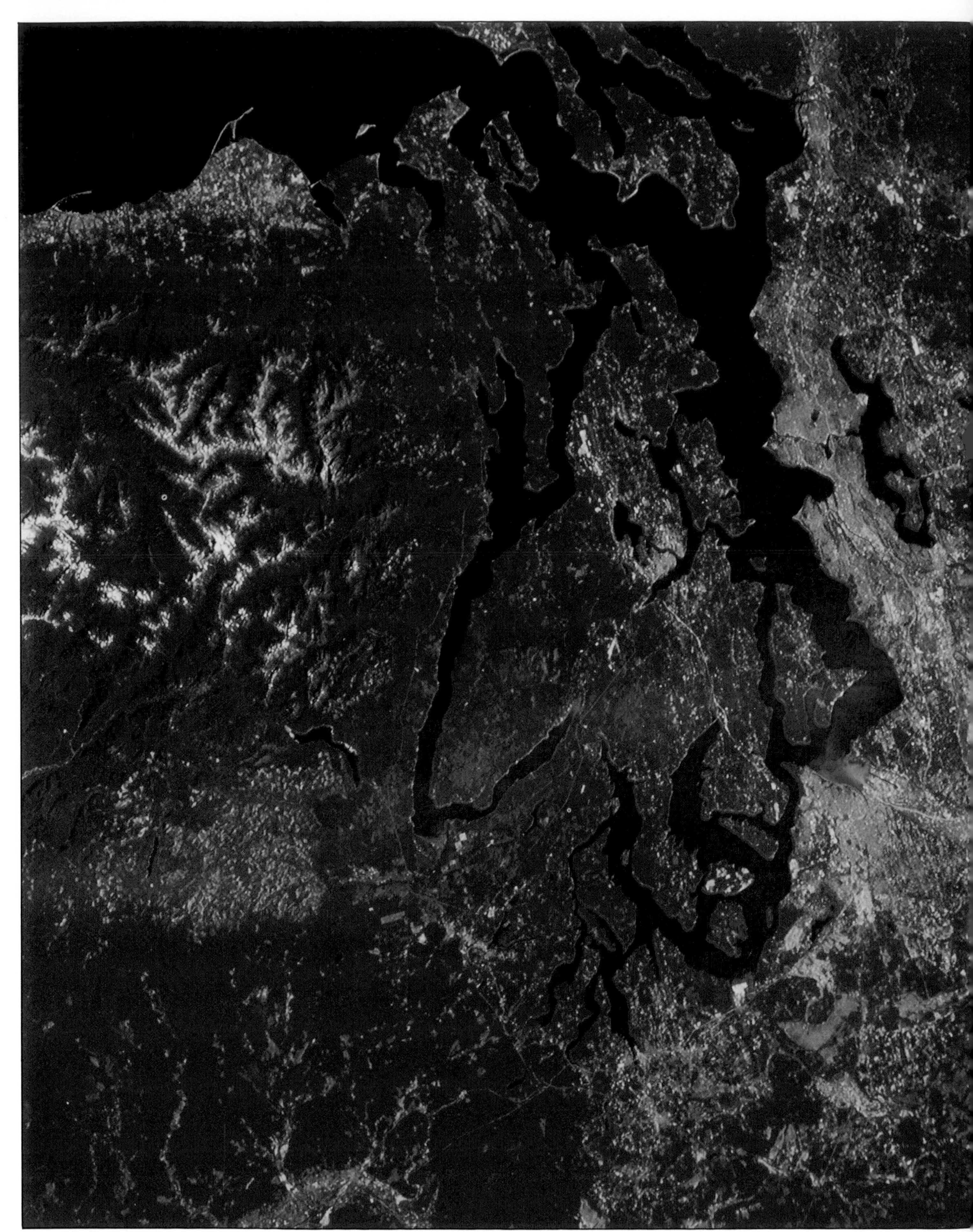
Infra-red satellite photograph of the Puget Sound area. Courtesy, EROS Data Center, U.S. Department of the Interior.

THE CREATION OF PUGET SOUND

◆

Nature was in a generous mood when Puget Sound was created. It ranks among the world's largest and most beautiful inland seas. Yet this beneficent process took hundreds of millions of years to accomplish. Three billion years ago, granite that was slowly separating from the dense rocks of the earth's interior and floating to the surface began to gather together to form continents, and land masses began to emerge and grow from the primordial ocean covering the face of the globe. By half a billion years ago the edge of the North American continent, which had grown slowly westward from a nucleus in eastern Canada, reached the eastern edge of what was to become Puget Sound. For 400 million years thereafter the western half of the continent was alternately crumpled by mountain-building upheavals and then inundated by the sea as the mountains were worn down by erosion.

Some 100 million years ago, an ancestral Cascade Range, crowned with a volcanic chain much like the present one, took form along the western edge of the continent, and began shedding vast quantities of silt, sand, and gravel into the ocean to the west, where it accumulated in a deep trench near the coast. At places along the coast, lush tropical forests grew at times, later to be buried by sediments and compressed into coal seams. Then, about 40 million years ago, the floor of the Pacific Ocean, acting as a huge, rigid plate, began to press slowly but inexorably eastward against the coastal trench, buckling the accumulated pile of sediments upward to form the coast range and Olympic Mountains of western Washington. This uplift along the coast left a lowland trough to the east, between the newly formed coast range on the west and the Cascade Range on the east. The sea, gaining access where the coast range was breached along the Strait of Juan de Fuca, flooded the lowland trough to form Puget Sound. Great volcanic eruptions continued to build the Cascade Range against the eroding forces of rain, flood, wind, and ice; streams of lava and volcanic debris poured down into the Puget Sound trough to the west. With the coming of the Ice Age two million years ago, an immense arm of the continental ice sheet moved down into the Puget Sound lowland from the north, scouring out the trough so that, when at last the ice melted away some 13,000 years ago, the Sound was left enlarged and beautified.

During the Ice Age so much of the earth's water was locked up in glaciers and ice sheets that sea level around the world dropped about 300 feet. As a result, the shallow floor of the Bering Strait emerged from the sea and for several millenia provided a broad avenue of dry land stretching between Siberia and Alaska. Across this land bridge humans crossed from Siberia to Alaska, and then migrated southward into the temperate parts of North America by following an ice-free corridor that existed just east of the Canadian Rockies. Later migrations probably came down along the coast.

A unique network of interconnected waterways, about 2,000 square miles in extent, Puget Sound with its thickly forested land and fertile valleys looked inviting to humans seeking a permanent homeplace. Within this temperate, predominantly moist paradise people gratefully settled. But they were destined to be overwhelmed by incoming groups with more advanced technologies for converting the region's geographical assets and natural resources into economic benefits.—W. Barclay Kamb

FROM COUNTY EXECUTIVE RON SIMS

This pictorial history of Seattle and King County has been out of print for years. Well-worn copies are still found in most local libraries and in the personal libraries of many residents of King County.

This is a book filled with vivid facts and historic photos that illustrate how Seattle and King County developed from the time of the Native Americans to the present.

The author, Dr. James Warren, and the Museum of History and Industry deserve compliments for the original preparation of the book and for this updated second edition.

Ron Sims
King County Executive

FOREWORD

The objective of this book is to use both words and pictures to describe how King County and Seattle developed since their founding. Written for general readership, the history strives to remind readers—both long-time residents and newcomers—of the major events in the social and economic evolution of the area.

Though our history covers a comparatively short period of time, for Seattle is a young city, an abundance of fascinating details exist. And there's the difficulty—for to relate them all would take several books this size. We had to compromise: to select those subjects of greatest importance and to discard many fine historical anecdotes and tales. In so doing, we excised names that we had wanted to include, laid aside intriguing and historically important pictures, and excluded some noteworthy events.

Seattle and King County became the leading metropolitan center in the Pacific Northwest not by gift of nature alone, but also by hard work of many intelligent people, men and women of all races, who labored to make it so. Singly, in groups, and as members of corporate bodies, they developed one of the most livable cities in the world.

Business and industry provided considerable influence in the development of the area. The first settlers welcomed Henry Yesler and his sawmill. They attracted providers of services, developed a mercantile center, secured railroads, discovered coal deposits, outfitted gold rush miners, established the mosquito fleet as a transportation means, built a great port, dug canals, organized banking systems, and founded manufacturing companies. Had they not succeeded, the major Puget Sound metropolis could well have been located elsewhere, for there were many cities competing for the honor.

Likewise, King County's citizens, realizing the value of a good educational system, sought and then constructed the University of Washington and have worked for more than a century to improve both public and private schools. They support the arts, founded libraries, and culturally enrich the society in many ways.

Early in the area's history, the residents began regrading hills and filling tide flats; they developed potable water supplies, laid sewer systems, organized fire and police protection, surveyed street grids, provided utilities and medical services. Neighborhood identities were established and their cultures preserved. Residents helped win wars, overcome disappointments, calm riots, extinguish fires, and lived through financial depressions, utilizing a "Seattle spirit" that became nationally recognized.

As the population increased, county and city citizens voted to tax themselves to relieve the strain on natural resources and the result has been clean lakes and air, and many parks and open green spaces.

We live in one of the world's most scenic areas. Nature has supplied attractive residential environments with views of mountains, forests, lakes and Puget Sound. Human beings have appreciated these aspects of the Northwest since the first Native Americans arrived here thousands of years ago. Our climate is gentle and winter days are frequently misty or rainy, which allows Washington to rightfully be called the Evergreen State.

Nearly every survey of the nation's most livable areas finds Seattle and King County at or near the top of the list. This has resulted in a steady increase in population since the days of the great depression of the 1930s.

We attempt to describe how all this happened in the chapters that follow. We hope you enjoy their perusal.

James R. Warren

CHAPTER 1

IN THE BEGINNING: EARLY INHABITANTS

The first evidence of humankind's presence in western Washington has been carbon-dated to about 12,000 years ago. The earliest archaeological materials were uncovered on private property near Sequim, on the Olympic Peninsula. While Clare and Emanuel Manis were excavating a resting pond for wild fowl in 1977 with a backhoe, mastodon bones and tusks were exposed. They called in Washington State University archaeologists, who discovered a rib from this extinct creature with a spear point embedded. Other bones showed possible marks of butchering.

With few exceptions, the other sites of early human habitation all along the Pacific coastline and its inland seas are dated either more than 10,000 years or less than 5,000 years ago. This time gap may be due to ice melt as the glaciers retreated, which caused the sea levels to rise upward for the next 50 centuries, covering or eroding most signs of human existence on the shorelines.

The later indications of mankind's residence on Puget Sound are quite common in such digs as the Enumclaw Plateau sites, which predate a mudflow from Mt. Rainier that covered the area 6,000 years ago, and Birch Bay, where two digs have dated human presence to 4,000 to 5,000 years ago, a time when the ocean level was stabilizing. About 450 years ago, more than two centuries before the first Europeans explored the Northwest Coast, nature preserved an entire village on the west side of the Olympic Peninsula, near Ozette. A landslide sealed beneath a layer of clay all of the perishable materials of that culture from the deteriorating effects of the air and erosion. Five houses have been located, and more than 42,000 artifacts have been found, preserved, and catalogued. As a result, archaeologists and the Makah Indians, working together, are developing an accurate and detailed record of the life of Native American families, who inhabited the area prior to the influence of the white explorers and settlers. While the culture of these Indians living directly on the Pacific Ocean was not identical to that of their brethren living on the inland sea that became known as Puget Sound, the societies held much in common.

Using the scientific and scholarly processes now standard in paleoanthropology, the life of the early natives in the Northwest Coast is being reconstructed. Similarly, an effort has been made in this century by ethnologists to discover, describe, and comprehend the way of life of the Coast Salish inhabiting the Puget Sound area at the time of white men's arrival.

The first white settlers arrived on the North Pacific Coast with preconceived notions of the Native American cultures mainly based on knowledge of the Eastern Woodland and Midwestern Plains Indians. The Sound Indians in many ways did not fit the already established views. For example, they did *not* build conical tipis of animal hides, ride horses, wear feather headdresses or fringed buckskin, scalp enemies, develop strong intertribal relationships, or elect strong, autocratic chieftains. They were not tall and bronzed, seldom hunted land animals with bow and arrow, and were not ordinarily warlike.

Most of the early pioneers in Puget Sound seemed oblivious to, intolerant of, or unimpressed with the culture of the local Indians, and not until most of the Salish disappeared did trained students or interested amateur observers appear on the scene. As a result, we have lost much information about Native American culture in the Puget Sound region. Furthermore, the Indians on the Sound had felt the effect of the white race even before the settlers arrived. Their population had been decimated by several epidemics, white men's diseases such as smallpox, measles, and syphilis, brought in by early fur traders or exploratory ships' crews. Inevitably, they took a heavy toll among a people that had no built-in immunities.

The local Indians were part of the Northwest Coast culture that extended from the mouth of the Columbia River (or, more loosely, from northern California) to southwestern Alaska. Unlike the great tribes in eastern North America, they were organized in small villages of family-sized groups. The names given them as "tribes" were the white men's way of categorizing them and were not necessarily recognized by the Indians themselves.

The Indians that inhabited present-day King County were of the Coast Salish language group. (Salish was commonly spoken in both western and eastern Washington.) While they had a common basic language, inhabitants of each drainage system had developed subdialects. Sharing

Photograph by Victor Gardaya (MOHAI)

certain physical features, they tended to be of medium stature, averaging about five feet, four inches in height. Usually stocky in build, the men developed broad muscular chests and shoulders from their canoeing and other activities. The hair of both sexes was usually straight or slightly wavy and very dark brown in color. Men had more facial hair than did other North American Indians. Their foreheads were frequently flattened by a pressure board applied to their heads when infants in cradle-carriers.

In the Salish language, a "mish" ending signified "people." The groups in the Puget Sound area were most often named for the river along which they lived. Thus "Duwamish" means people who lived on the banks of the "Duwamps" River.

Modern geographical divisions do not correspond with the loosely defined tribal territories. Seattle and King County today are situated on lands where five different tribes once roamed. The city itself was built on Duwamish tribal lands that included the lower reaches of the Duwamish River, Elliott Bay, and the territory around Lake Washington (originally called Lake Duwamps). The Suquamish lived on the west side of Puget Sound opposite Seattle, and also occupied the islands between. At one time, too, they may have controlled the area directly north of the city. The Duwamish Indians, who lived where the heart of Seattle exists today, were among the first Northwest tribes to be nearly obliterated because their prime location attracted the first white settlements.

The river society created by the Duwamish in some ways set them apart from their more sea-oriented neighbors. Recent excavations of some former living sites have revealed information about these Seattle-area natives. Teams of archaeologists and students from the University of Washington have explored the remains of two winter villages, one near the mouth of the Duwamish River and the other on the former channel of the Black River, within the city of Renton. Traces of several longhouses as well as artifacts reflecting early trade contacts have been found.

At one time, the intersection of First Avenue and Yesler Way was a tidal marsh. Here a low isthmus connected a small island in Elliott Bay with higher ground to the north. It is believed that eight large longhouses stood there, housing as many as 200 people. At one time this island may have been a center of activity among the Indians of the area.

During the Indian War of 1855–1856, most of the Duwamish were forced to leave the Seattle area and move to the Fort Kitsap reservation on the western shore of Puget Sound. Having failed to receive their own tribal reservation lands through treaties, the Duwamish found it difficult to remain together and preserve their own culture. At first, these people tended to return to their old winter villages near the city, even though the law required that they dwell on reservation lands. As Seattle expanded, the Indians were frequently employed as laborers and domestic servants. During the 1860s and '70s, when landfill and sawdust were dumped into the tideland location, near which the Indians camped, the remaining Duwamish moved south to "Ballast Island," near the intersection of First and Washington, where ballast thrown from ships had formed a heap of land. In 1895, when First Hill was regraded, this artificial island was covered, and the Indian encampment moved to the intersection of Utah and Massachusetts streets. Through the early years of this century the Duwamish remained around Seattle, working in local mills, at odd jobs and selling baskets, clams, and firewood—part of the daily scene as well as picturesque or poignant reminders of an earlier era. To this day, there are Duwamish people living in the Seattle and King County area.

Formerly one of the most populous groups on Puget Sound, numbering in the thousands, the Duwamish today can claim perhaps fewer than 300 descendants. Some of their geographical place names exist in anglicized versions, such as Duwamish, Shilshole, and Licton Springs, but most of the hundreds of names they placed on the land they knew have faded into oblivion.

COAST SALISH CULTURE

Through centuries of habitation, the Indians of Puget Sound and their Northwest Coast neighbors created a highly successful fishing and gathering economy. The effects of the Japanese current—moderate temperature and heavy precipitation—resulted in a region that offered a broad array of foodstuffs and substances for domestic use. The clever exploitation of a wealth of natural resources allowed them time to develop and perpetuate a fairly complex society, with a rich material culture. (Later on, many Indians generously showed new white settlers various foods and building procedures they had perfected.) They did not practice agriculture, and the dog was their only domesticated animal. Specialized survival skills were taught so that trained members of each group assumed tasks like fishing, hunting, tool-making, curing hides, shelter-building, and making canoes.

Because of the prevalence of forest lands, plant materials were the main substance used by the local Indians. Red cedar, which splits easily into wide straight planks, became their favorite building material. Yellow cedar and alder, soft woods easily carved without marked cleavage planes, were used for dishes and masks. Bows and harpoon foreshafts were made from tough resilient yew or maple. The inner bark of red cedar and sometimes of yellow cedar was shredded and haggled into soft fiber to be used for swaddling babies, for pillows, and for weaving robes, rain capes, and mats. Checkerwork woven mats of red cedar bark served as floor coverings, interior walls, temporary shelters, tablecloths, and mattresses, and later as sails for canoes.

The utilitarian art of basketry thrived due to the plenti-

Left
These mastodon teeth are among the fossils that have been found in northwest Washington. (MOHAI)

Below
The coiled and twined baskets and various tools pictured were traditionally used by Salish Indians. (MOHAI)

ful plant fibers. Basket styles and shapes varied according to use and were used for most container purposes, including cooking. The Salish did not make pottery.

Like basketry, mat-weaving was a well-developed craft. Mats of red cedar bark were woven in various checkerboard patterns, sometimes with twilled borders. Strips of bark were dyed black by submerging them in mud, or red by boiling them with alder bark. Tules and reeds were also used as mat-weaving materials. Mats were employed for a number of uses, the most spectacular being the feast mats, some 30 feet long.

The Indians were fine woodworkers, using their primitive tools to good advantage. The Indians could split large logs or even standing trees with driving wedges of hardwood, with grommets of tough spruce root wrapped around the butt ends to prevent splitting. Chisels, made of tough stone such as nephrite, of elkhorn, or the dense shell of deepwater clams mounted in hardwood hafts, were in common usage, driven with pear-shaped stone mauls that were unhafted.

For shaping of wood they also used a "D" adze with a handle of wood or whalebone shaped like a saw handle. Some Northwest natives, prior to exposure to whites, had knives and chisels tipped with iron. Prehistoric iron may have come from shipwrecks that washed ashore or from a Siberian iron-age center that supplied Alaskan natives in ancient times.

Wood carving was a distinctive art form among the tribes north of the Puget Sound area. The Coast Salish imitated the more advanced Kwakiutl and Nootka techniques but with a cruder, simplified style. The Puget Sound artisans were not as skilled in ceremonial carving and decoration as were their counterparts to the north in what is now British Columbia. Longhouses sometimes contained lightly carved and painted ceremonial poles, entrances were sometimes decorated, and they did carve miniatures of canoes and other useful items, perhaps as toys for the children or as teaching tools. Often their paddles were decorated as were their rattles and other ceremonial objects. The skill rapidly died out with acculturation and Christianization.

Well-crafted wooden storage boxes made of red cedar planks were highly prized. The wood was steamed and bent, the ends sewn with spruce root withes and pegs were used to secure the bottom. In lieu of sandpaper, the native craftsmen used sandstone and then sharkskin to achieve a smooth finish. Controlled fire was utilized to hollow out canoes and large feasting troughs. The Sound Indians traveled extensively by canoe, though they stuck close to the coastline. Usage dictated the size and conformation of the boats. Saltwater vessels were larger and had tall prows. For river travel, the Indians used shovel-nosed, smaller canoes and notched their paddles for bracing against snags, roots, and boulders. Wooden bailers and well-crafted tackle boxes were often made to fit snugly in bow or stern.

All canoes were made of cedar. The selected log, often a

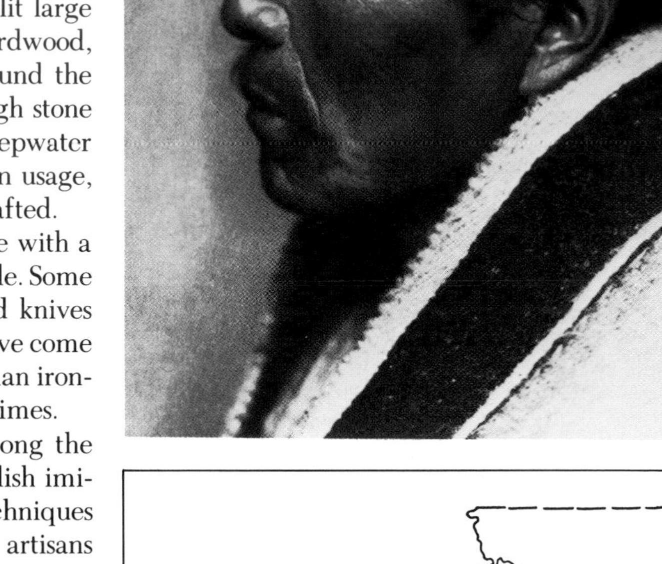

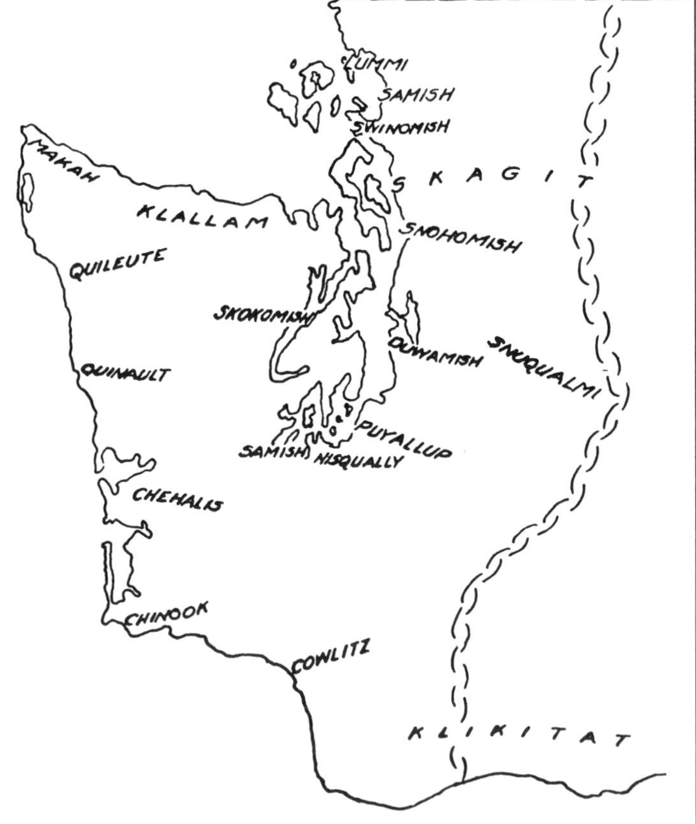

Opposite, top
Taken in the 1890s by Edward S. Curtis, this photo portrays a Snoqualmie man whose forehead was bound to a piece of cedar board when he was a baby. This process, used on both boys and girls, produced a sloping forehead. (MOHAI)

Opposite, bottom
This map indicates the location of some of the Indian tribes of western Washington. Before the mid-19th century, the Duwamish lived where Seattle is located today. Courtesy, Historical Photography Collection, U of W Libraries.

Right
Indian baskets served many purposes and were adapted to carry different loads. Using a tumpline, a headband woven of cedar bark, this woman carries a heavy load of driftwood in a large open basket. Courtesy, Historical Photography Collection, U of W Libraries.

Opposite, top
Edward S. Curtis posed this photograph as realistically as possible, circa 1915, showing this typical Salish portable shelter woven of reeds. The woman in the foreground wears a rain cape of woven cedar, while the person behind her wears a rain hat and cape of animal skins. Shovel-nosed canoes like this one were used for river travel. (MOHAI)

Opposite, bottom
After their traditional lands were taken by the whites, the Indians were given reservations to live on, often far from their customary homes. However, the Indians continued to camp near and work in Seattle as this 1880 photo indicates. (MOHAI)

Above
Tetacu, one of the Indian chiefs who lived at the entrance to the Strait of Juan de Fuca, wears a conical basket-like hat common in the Puget Sound area. Courtesy, Pacific Northwest Collection, U of W Libraries.

tree that had blown down, was trimmed and floated to the village, where it was shaped on the outside and roughed out on the inside by fire. Hot water was poured into the burnt center to soften the wood, and the beam of the canoe was widened by driving thwart-like spreaders between the pliable walls. A shell or stone-tipped adze was the finishing tool. The exterior was charred, then scraped and oiled, giving it a shiny black appearance. The inside was often painted red with color obtained from hematite.

Though the King County Indian tribes were skillful canoists, they were not as noted as such groups as the Chinook. Photographs of Indian canoes with sails are sometimes seen. However, not until after European contact did the Sound Indians begin to use sails of woven cedarbark mats or of canvas traded from the whites.

A water-oriented people, the Salish located their villages on sheltered coves where rivers met salt water. Here they could safely beach their canoes, obtain saltwater fish and shellfish, and drink and bathe in fresh water.

The Puget Sound Indians constructed houses of split cedar planks. Long and narrow, with a shed (one pitch) roof, these structures had large ridgepoles supported by heavy posts. The siding was tied to separate poles, then attached to the framework, allowing it to be removed and transported to new frames when a move was necessary. Often an entire group might live in a single longhouse, each family having its own space curtained off by cattail mats. Bed-platforms, which lined the large room, were built over storage space.

In spring and summer, the Indians left these permanent winter houses to go hunting and fishing, in particular taking advantage of salmon runs. These annual migrations were a pleasant time for the people of Puget Sound. The most energetic left first, usually in April. The old often remained in the longhouses all year round. As they moved about their territory, from two to 10 families would camp together, housed in their easily erected summer shelters of woven mats and of brush.

The Indians altered the environment for their own purposes, mostly with fire. They burned prairies to encourage growth of useful plants like nettles and bracken, and meadows to encourage berries and game. An unintended consequence perhaps, was making Douglas fir the dominant tree. Without this deliberate burning, the climax forest might have been hemlock and cedar. While they altered nature by burning, they knew that they had to live in harmony with all other animals, plants, and even inanimate objects like rocks and mountains. The Indians respected nature and took from it only what they needed.

Fish provided a bountiful food source as well as the basis of the economy. The Indians caught five species of salmon and also smelt, herring, candlefish, cod, halibut, and flounder. Edible shellfish included clams, mussels, oysters, and crab. They used a variety of efficient fish-catching devices: salmon traps, weirs, dip nets, gill nets, spears, harpoons, and baited hooks.

Fish was preserved by drying. After cleaning, it was split, hung on racks and sun-dried, or sometimes smoked over alderwood fires. Dried fish was packed in baskets and canoed to the winter homes. Salmon eggs were dried and the oil base was used in paint for woodworking.

Fishing sites were most valuable if berries, roots, and bulbs could be harvested nearby. Camas bulbs were a major vegetable food. Women and girls would gather in large groups to dig them. Before eating, the bulbs were steamed for a long time in a pit. These bulbs were often used as trading material. The spindly roots of a species of clover and the fibrous roots of bracken fern were also consumed. Berries of several kinds were eaten fresh or mixed with olachen or whale oil. They were also preserved by cooking and drying into cakes. The huckleberry was especially favored since it dried well.

Because of the abundance of seafood, land hunting was infrequent among the Salish living along the Puget Sound waterways. Indians living in the upper valleys used snares, pitfall traps, and bows and arrows. Waterfowl were trapped, netted, and speared.

Food was boiled in watertight baskets and boxes by dropping red-hot stones into the water-filled containers. The Indians also steam-cooked in large shallow pits filled with hot stones covered by leaves and mats, with water poured over all. Fish and meat were often broiled over an open fire or a bed of alder coals. The Puget Sound diet was seldom monotonous. More than 150 different Salish recipes have been collected by anthropologists.

Clothing of the Puget Sound Indians was a simple matter. Men went naked, weather permitting. Women wore a one or two-piece skirt of shredded cedar bark. Buckskin garments were not worn because they tended to shrink in the damp climate. All went barefoot, except in winter, when moccasins were worn when traveling in the higher snowy country.

In rainy weather, people donned flowing conical capes, woven of shredded cedar bark, and tightly woven, wide-brimmed basketry hats. When cold weather prevailed, a robe of twined and stretched shredded yellow cedar bark, sometimes containing dog hair, might be worn under the raincoat.

The chief and wealthier members of the tribe sometimes wore robes of bearskin, sea otter pelts, marmot skins, or other fur, or blankets woven of mountain goat hair. In later years, Hudson's Bay Company blankets were often worn and were a sign of wealth.

All Northwest Coast Indian tribes developed four status levels: chiefs, nobles, commoners, and slaves. The system, based on personal inheritance and economic success, ranged from upper classes to slaves, the latter tradable like material possessions.

Above
Because plant fibers were plentiful, basketry developed into a fine art. The best baskets, made of spruce root and cedar bark cordage, varied in style and shape depending on their function. (MOHAI)

Opposite
This Edward S. Curtis photo from the 1890s depicts a Skokomish chief's daughter in front of a summer mat house. She shows her position in the Indian society by wearing animal skins and sitting on a canoe surrounded by baskets. It is a classic Curtis photo—timeless and natural in its textures. (MOHAI)

The chief, the head of the communal unit, was usually the oldest member of the group descended in the most direct line from a noted ancestor. The power of his leadership derived from his own personality as well as from the large and closely knit lineage that stood behind him. Occasionally more competent junior relatives were allowed to assume leadership roles.

Men of low rank who became skillful craftsmen or valued warriors could be given prerogatives beyond those awarded at birth. The slaves were usually women and children captured from another tribe or received in trade. Having a low social standing, they were expected to perform menial labor.

Compared with other Pacific Northwest tribes, the Coast Salish had few titles, ceremonial privileges, and crests—in other words, they had fewer means of indicating social rank. They did, however, participate in a unique activity that publicly declared and established the social and economic status of an individual.

The famed potlatch ceremony of the Coast Indians of the Pacific Northwest was widely misunderstood by the early white settlers. It was, in effect, a business transaction in a social setting. It allowed the wealthy members of a tribe to redistribute their holdings and in so doing gain recognition for their successes. Families who inherited status maintained that ranking, while a member of the tribe could raise his status through a potlatch. The potlatch also provided group festivities and a means of distributing largesse to the needy in times of scarcity. Convivial feasting, dancing, and singing went on, along with an exchange of food, goods, and sometimes slaves. Gifts went to fellow tribesmen and to invited members of other groups, and at some future date all recipients were expected to return the favor with gifts of greater value. Yet, carefully calculated distribution awarded goods to poorer people who could not possibly ever repay the donor. The potlatch also served as a societal ritual that reaffirmed group affiliations.

The religion of the Northwest Coast Indians differed from those of other Amerindians in their seeming lack of concern for creation, cosmology, and deities. Recognition of a remote Supreme Being was not commonly included in their rituals.

Each kin group adopted an explanation of the origin of their own inception from a rich collection of oral myths and legends. These myths were passed on to younger generations as both education and entertainment. The elders would hold the youth enthralled with lengthy, often humorous adventures of animal characters. These tales were basically serious and communicated important social traditions.

A prevailing Salish ceremony extolled semicompetitive guardian spirit myths told in song. Various individuals—the shaman or a noted hunter or warrior—sang songs taught them by their guardian spirits while the listeners formed a responsive chorus. These songs, highly repetitive, were sung with great enthusiasm, accompanied by percussive rattles and drums.

The Coast Salish believed in the immortality of certain animals. Because of its major role in the culture, the salmon was of special importance. According to their beliefs, the salmon migrated upstream to benefit mankind, died, and later were resurrected. Thus they carefully returned all salmon bones to the water. When the first salmon of the season was caught, a special ceremony was performed. In some tribes these rituals became so complicated that a priesthood of specialists developed. Similar ceremonies were reenacted when game was killed so that the animal's spirit, placated, would return inside a new body.

The Salish believed the future well-being of an individual depended on the intercession of a guardian spirit. This helper was found only after arduous searching, cleansing oneself by fasting, bathing in icy pools, and scrubbing away any traces of human sensuality with bundles of twigs or nettles. Purification rituals sometimes included use of the sweat lodge, a small, mat-covered dome in which water was sprinkled on hot stones. Afterward, the bather raced to the nearby river and plunged into the chilly water.

The maximum gift a human could receive from a spirit-guardian was the ability to affect the well-being of one's friends and neighbors, which made one a shaman. Illness, it was believed, came from small, semianimate objects entering the body or from witchcraft, which could cause one's soul to be lost, stolen, or to go astray. Also, contamination by a ghost or spirit could produce sickness in bodies not ritually clean. The shaman's task was to summon spirit-helpers who would give him the power to extract the diseased object, find the strayed soul, or remove the contamination. Some shamans painted designs or carved replicas to attract these spiritual assistants.

The life cycle was marked in the ceremonies of the tribal groups. Rites of passage marking birth, puberty, marriage, and death were major events. Minor rituals were performed in disposing of the first baby tooth, in celebrating the first game killed by a boy, and the first basket of roots or berries collected by a girl.

Marriage, an occasion for formal and high festivities, was considered a contract not only between bride and groom but their families as well. A bride's father passed on to his new son-in-law various crests and ceremonial privileges to hold for the couple's children. The Salish married within their own social rank. The chief or his son might marry women from other tribes to create useful alliances or they might marry women of approximate rank chosen from the extended family, if the relationship was not too close. Birth of a child triggered rituals to assure long life, health, happiness, and—if a son—success in such skills as canoe-making.

As it does to all peoples, death to the Puget Sound Indi-

Above
The Salish Indians used this roller loom to weave blankets from mountain goat hair and other materials. The heavy blankets were used as bedding and occasionally as clothing.

Right
A Quinault woman wears a cedar skirt woven of inner bark, circa 1890. Men went nude, weather permitting, and all went barefoot, except in winter when they wore moccasins for traveling over the mountains. Photo by Edward S. Curtis. (MOHAI)

Native Americans gamble on the beach in the 1880s. In "Lahal," a favorite game, the challenge was to guess the relative position of marked and unmarked sticks or disks held in the hands of the opposing team members. (MOHAI)

ans brought grief, but for them it also brought fear of the ghost of the dead. The Salish placed the body in a canoe, which was then raised on scaffolding. Personal possessions were placed either in the canoe with the deceased or buried nearby. All kin chopped their hair short as a sign of mourning. After the funeral, the principal mourners and pall bearers bathed to remove the contaminating influences of death. Among the Puget Sound Salish, the dramatization of the journey in a spirit canoe looking for a lost soul was vivid and memorable.

As with other tribal peoples, the Salish had certain recreational diversions. Of the gambling games popular among them, "Lahal" was perhaps the favorite. The challenge was to guess the relative position of marked and unmarked sticks or disks held in the hands of the members of the opposing team. Dice games using four beaver incisors were popular too. The Indians would also bet on wrestling matches, archery, and lance-throwing contests, foot and canoe races, tugs of war, and a variant of the old game called "Shinny."

The Salish were customarily a peaceful people. Any feuds that developed within a group resulted from individual disagreements. The kin of someone slain or injured often tried to retaliate, although payment of indemnities would sometimes suffice. In efforts to prevent open fighting, intermediaries were frequently used, traveling back and forth while attempting to settle the dispute.

Enslavement of a relative was a disgrace to all kin. The family made every effort to secure the person's freedom, usually by paying ransom. If they did not succeed, a cleansing ritual could be performed to allow the family to regain their normal status. Slaves carried great distances from their home territory had little chance for freedom. Occasionally those captured by nearby groups escaped.

Puget Sound Indians sometimes were raided by the Haidas, who raced down from British Columbia waters in their large war canoes to kill the men and enslave women and children. The Coast Salish Indians therefore situated their villages on the shore, where they had sweeping views of the water approaches, and near the forests into which they could escape.

Skirmishes occasionally developed between small groups of Sound Indians representing different tribes. Trespassing on another tribe's territory without permission could bring on war. Before muskets and cutlasses were traded to the Native Americans by Europeans, they used bows and arrows, slings, spears, and pikes, the latter held like a rifle with fixed bayonet. Clubs, some made of whale rib, were employed in combat, and for close attack, daggers were drawn.

The study of Puget Sound's Indian groups and culture is far from complete. However, we do know that these first human inhabitants of this remarkable region revered the terrain and the animal and plant life. While rich in natural resources, the Pacific Northwest was not always an easy place for a nonindustrial people to live. Over the centuries a special material culture was adapted, and each individual had to learn skills of catching fish, digging roots, using materials, and preserving foods in order to survive.

In the 18th century this society would begin to encounter representatives from the "civilization" on the other side of the world. The Salish would swiftly learn that their own rudimentary technology could scarcely compete with that of people who regarded the land, water, and natural resources as commodities to be owned, but their closest contact with free-enterprise capitalism had come with the potlatch ceremonies. However, the Indians soon discovered they could exploit natural resources for profit and could therefore raise their standard of living.

PHOTOGRAPHERS OF THE NORTHWEST INDIANS: THE CURTIS BROTHERS

Indians catching salmon. Photo by Asahel Curtis. Courtesy, Historical Photography Collection, U of W Libraries.

Mussel gatherer. Photo by Edward S. Curtis. (MOHAI)

Edward S. Curtis had already tried photography when he moved with his parents and younger brother Asahel to the Seattle area in 1887 from Minnesota. When the boys' father died, Edward turned his hobby into a profession and later into a partnership with photographer Thomas H. Guptil. Asahel joined the firm as a photo-engraver and soon was promoted to photographer. In 1897 the younger brother was sent to Alaska to record the gold rush. The two worked together until 1901, when Asahel went into business for himself. Although the brothers remained photographers for the rest of their working lives, from this point their careers differed radically.

Before he became a professional, Edward S. Curtis sensed the importance of the camera as a tool to record what was left of the Native American culture, by making exposures of the Duwamish and Suquamish living near Seattle. From the time he joined the Edward Harriman expedition of naturalists and ethnographers to Alaska in 1899, he spent his life pursuing this goal. He was well equipped for the task: he had an ear for language, an educated curiosity about the new science of anthropology, an artistic eye, and a fanatic energy for work. He also had the physical constitution to withstand living in a tent for most of his adult life. After 1904, when Adolph Muhr took over the running of his studio, Edward spent little time in Seattle. His life project, thirty years in the production, was the 20-volume *The North American Indian*. He also produced a semi-fictional motion picture account of precontact Kwakiutl life.

Asahel Curtis went on to produce 60,000 negatives of great importance to the history of the development and growth of his beloved Northwest. His subjects ranged from Native Americans to mountains, local architecture to lumbering, and small businesses to large industries. When he wasn't under the dark cloth making his living, he was an active champion of boosterism. Environmentalists might wince at his schemes to fill the Northwest with people, roads, and hydroelectric projects, but his photographic record, now housed in the Washington State Historical Society Museum in Tacoma, is invaluable. Asahel managed the large studio in Seattle practically until his death in 1941 at the age of 67.

Edward died in 1954 at the age of 84. He achieved some fame but no fortune in his lifetime, but his work with the camera earned him a place in the history of photography. His contribution to anthropology is controversial. He was charged with seeking to recreate a vanished life style for the sake of art. Except for the Eskimos, all of the native peoples he photographed were at least two generations removed from any semblance of their precontact culture. The oral history of these peoples was still very much alive, however, and the books' field notes contain much valuable information in this area.—**Rod Slemmons**

CHAPTER 2

DISCOVERING PUGET SOUND: 16TH CENTURY TO 1850

The long and twisting path through history by which the United States acquired the Pacific Northwest region demonstrates how chance, determination, and persistence aided the Americans, who arrived quite late on the scene. Even the discovery of Puget Sound by European navigators took time—virtually three centuries after Columbus's first trip into the New World.

EARLY EXPLORERS OF THE NORTH PACIFIC

The first Europeans to sail along the Pacific coast of America were Spanish mariners. In 1513 Balboa had claimed possession of the Pacific Ocean and its lands for Spain's monarchs and for two centuries after that, Spain regarded all Pacific shores as hers. Furthermore, through military and commercial ventures in the Americas and on Pacific islands like the Philippines, she exercised her dominion. However, until the late 1700s, the coastline north of San Francisco Bay remained largely unexplored because of its isolation.

During the 16th century, England's best buccaneers raided Spanish galleons in the Pacific, but no firm English territorial rights resulted, even though Drake had proclaimed the region around San Francisco Bay as *Nova Albion* (New England). There is no evidence that these daring freebooters ever ventured into the waters of the North Pacific.

The earliest and most mystifying of all Northwest discovery claims concerns Juan de Fuca, reputedly a Greek sailing for the Spanish. In 1602 Michael Lok recounted De Fuca's story in his book *Purchas, His Pilgrims.* Lok heard from De Fuca how as a pilot he had traveled in the Spanish West Indies and had sailed elsewhere for the Spaniards. He was sent in 1592 by the Viceroy of New Spain (Mexico) to find the legendary waterway that linked the Pacific and Atlantic oceans:

> . . . to follow the said voyage for the discovery of the Strait of Anian, and the passage thereof into the sea, which they called the North Sea, which is our Northwest Sea; and that he followed his course in that voyage, west and northwest in the South Sea, all along the coast in Nova Spania, and California, and the Indies, now called North America, until he came to the latitude of 47 degrees; and that, there finding that the land trended north and northeast, with a broad inlet of sea . . . he entered thereinto, sailing therein more than twenty days . . . and he passed by divers islands in that sailing; and that, at the entrance of this said strait, there is, on the northwest coast thereof, a great headland or island, with an exceeding high pinnacle, or spired rock, like a pillar, thereupon.

De Fuca declared that he had seen people clad in the skin of beasts, a fruitful land rich in gold, silver, pearls, and other valuables as in New Spain. He also claimed to have reached the North Sea; in other words, that he had found the fabled Strait of Anian, and crossed the continent by water—an alleged discovery that would allow Europeans to reach the Orient directly, without going around Cape Horn at the tip of South America. But when De Fuca returned to Mexico to claim his reward, the Viceroy told him to go to Spain and there the authorities refused to recognize De Fuca's discovery.

No proof exists that De Fuca actually voyaged to Northwest waters in the late 16th century. However, a great strait does open eastward just beyond 47 degrees north latitude. It has a wide entrance and on the northwest headland, a pinnacle or spired rock known as Fuca's Pillar does exist.

From the 18th century on, men from many countries became involved in maritime exploration of the Northwest to examine its fur-trading potential. Later explorers came overland from Canada and eastern United States.

As early as 1741, the Russians, through expeditions led by Vitus Bering and Alexis Tchirikoff, staked ownership in the North American continent, mainly in Alaska, and within a few years established fur-trading forts, going as far south as Fort Ross in California by 1812.

In 1774 Juan Perez sailed north from San Blas in northern Mexico, eventually reaching the 54th parallel; then, exploring southward, he touched Queen Charlotte's Island and discovered a harbor on the coast of Vancouver Island. He named this bay Port Lorenzo, but it was eventually called Nootka Sound when the port became the rendezvous for fur-trading vessels.

In 1775 two Spanish captains, Juan Francisco Bodega y Quadra and Bruno Heceta, sailed north to Alaska. On the way, Heceta sent a boat and crew ashore at an island south of Cape Flattery. All hands were captured and murdered by the

Photograph by Victor Gardaya
(MOHAI)

Indians, causing the site to become known as Destruction Island. Heceta afterwards sent the rest of the crew to explore other areas. These men apparently were the first Europeans to walk the beaches of what is now Washington State.

Heceta's ship's log carries an entry which mentions an indentation in the coast, which he named Assumption Inlet. He postulated that a river might be flowing into the sea there. The powerful outflow, however, proved too strong for his ship to stem, and breakers ahead warned of a dangerous barrier. So he sailed on—after almost discovering the Columbia River.

The British arrived on an official expedition into the area in 1778, in a ship captained by James Cook. The geographer and explorer was completing his third circumnavigation of the globe. Cook discovered and named Cape Flattery, one of the headlands at the entrance of the Strait of Juan de Fuca, but did not realize the inlet lay before him.

With Cook was John Ledyard, who, after being discharged from the British Navy, tried to promote other expeditions to the West. Thomas Jefferson may have been influenced later by Ledyard when deciding to send the Lewis and Clark expedition west. Ledyard also probably helped convince Boston merchants to send trading vessels to the Northwest Coast.

After Cook came many English captains, among them James Hanna, who traded off the coast in 1785, and James Strange, following the next year. The French, meanwhile, explored this region too. Jean Galaup, Count de La Perouse, and a staff of scientists in the *Boussole* and *Astrolabe* sailed along the coast, determining the latitude and longitude more accurately than those before them.

In 1787 another Englishman, Captain Charles Barkley, actually found Juan de Fuca's now-mythical strait and named it for its supposed discoverer. Later he sent a boat ashore to investigate the west side of the Olympic Peninsula in the vicinity of the Hoh River. He also brought the first

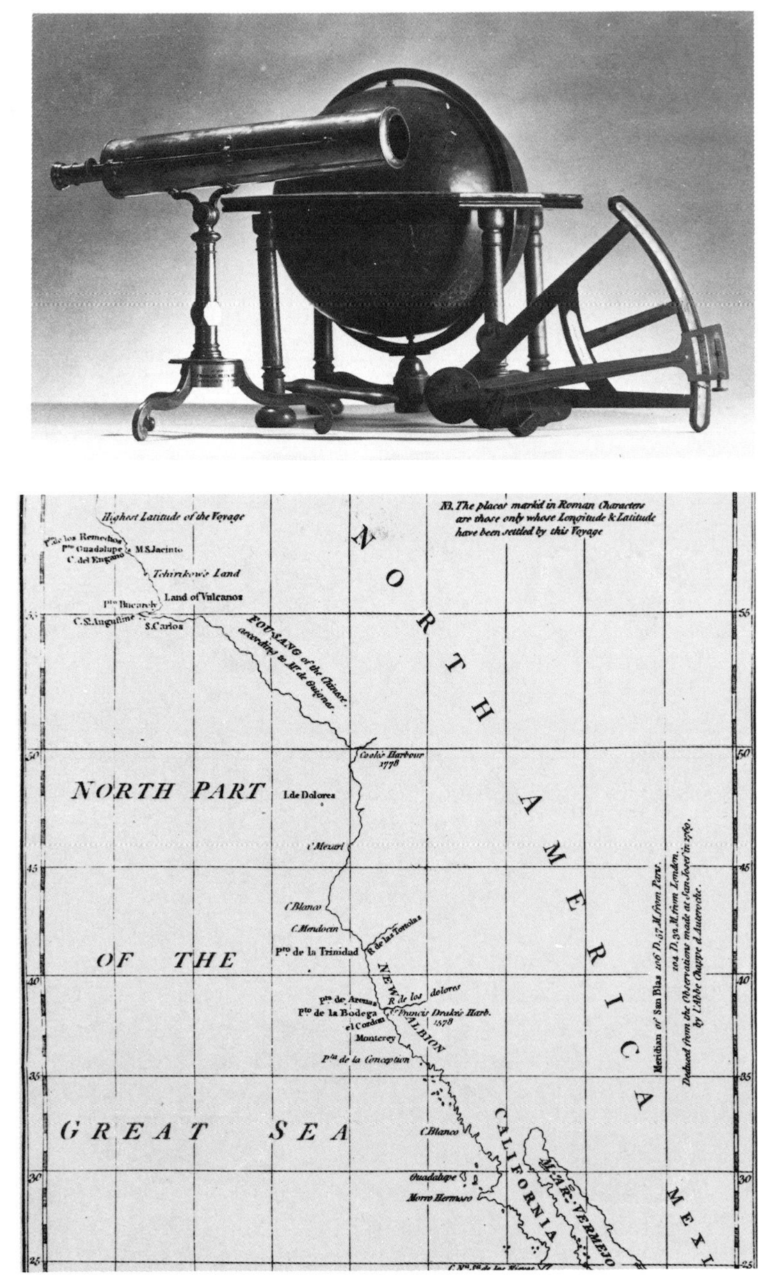

Opposite
The launching of the *North West America* took place in September 1788 at Nootka Sound. A product of cooperative effort between English and American captains and Chinese artisans, the schooner was the first European-style vessel built in the Northwest. Courtesy, Bicentennial Collection. (MOHAI)

Top
The Gregorian reflecting telescope, celestial globe, and Davis quadrant were used in celestial navigation during the late 18th century. Courtesy, McCurdy Marine Collection. (MOHAI)

Above
This map of the 1775 voyage of Spanish Captain Juan Francisco de la Bodega y Quadra was recorded by Maurelle, the pilot. A quarter-century later, Bodega y Quadra represented Spain in resolving the Nootka controversy. (MOHAI)

white woman, his wife, to North Pacific waters. In 1790 the Spanish established at Neah Bay the first white settlement in what is now Washington State.

In 1788 John Meares, a retired British sea captain, crossed from China to Nootka Sound with two vessels registered under the Portuguese flag. He quickly erected some buildings, and members of his crew built a small vessel called the *North West America*—the first one launched on the North Pacific coast. While the vessel was under construction, Meares sailed south in the ship *Felice Adventurer* and entered De Fuca Strait. Afterward, he continued south along the coast, naming Tatoosh Island and Mount Olympus on the way and discovering Willapa Harbor. He then searched for the river indicated on Heceta's chart but without success. He therefore changed the name of Assumption Inlet to Deception Bay and called the north headland Cape Disappointment. Again a sea captain had just missed discovering the Columbia River.

Returning north to Nootka Sound, Meares encountered a Spanish governor who disputed his Portuguese sailing documents and seized his two vessels, as well as the newly built vessel. The governor also took control of Nootka—land Meares claimed to have purchased from Indian chief Maquina for two pistols. The Spanish then established a colony there—the first assertion of national dominion over any part of the Pacific Northwest. Meares retreated to London to lodge his complaints and cause an international crisis.

Oddly, at the time the Spanish at Nootka were troubling Meares and his crew, they permitted the *Lady Washington* and the *Columbia*, two American ships captained by Robert Gray and John Kendrick, to anchor without question.

Captain Robert Gray assumed command of the *Columbia* on her homeward voyage with the furs that had been collected by the two vessels. The ship made history by becoming the first American vessel to circumnavigate the earth, since it had sailed to Nootka from Boston by way of Cape Horn and returned to Boston by way of China and the Cape of Good Hope. Although the journey did not result in a profit, the *Columbia*'s owners sent her on a second venture in the Pacific Northwest, which would bring a further claim to fame.

While based at Nootka awaiting Gray's return, Captain John Kendrick sailed his sloop around Vancouver Island in 1789, proving it was not part of the mainland. When John Meares learned of this exploit, he reported it in London in 1790 and prepared a chart of the *Lady Washington*'s journey around the island. Kendrick explored northern waters until, in the fall of 1791, Gray and the *Columbia* returned on their second voyage to the Northwest.

In March the *Columbia* began her trading expeditions, but Captain Gray, as he cruised up and down the coast, was intent on acquiring more information about harbors and inlets with new opportunities for trade. He took his ship south to Cape Mendocino and then turned northward. On April 27 the *Columbia* met a pair of Vancouver's vessels near the entrance of De Fuca Strait. Captain Gray learned from the British officers that Vancouver had concluded there was no great river near the 46th parallel. Undaunted, Gray sailed southward again, this time making his main discovery. On May 11, 1792, Captain Gray found the Great River of the West, the fabled "Oregon." He named it the Columbia, for his ship. In later negotiations with Britain, his feat was the principal proof that Oregon territory rightly belonged to the United States.

In the meantime, the great "inland sea" north of the Columbia River had received further attention. In 1790, prior to the return of the *Columbia*, the Spanish under Manuel Quimper had explored deep into the Strait of Juan de Fuca, becoming the first Europeans to cruise among its islands. These islands, to which they gave Spanish names, are known today as the San Juans. Some of these Spanish names were later replaced with English names suggested by Vancouver. Quimper, however, failed to note the inlet leading to Puget Sound.

When Captain John Meares told his fellow Englishmen of his mistreatment by the Spaniards in Nootka Sound, the British government, inflamed by his charges, demanded reparations. Spain, whose strength in the New World was declining, decided not to face another international squabble, paid Meares $210,000, released his three vessels, and consented to a restitution of the buildings and land. To execute the agreement Captain George Vancouver—sent off to make an exploratory voyage as well—was to act as British commissioner; Bodega y Quadra would do the same for the Spanish. At Nootka they failed to agree on what was to be restored but, liking each other, named the entire island Quadra and Vancouver's Island—the first name now gone. In 1795 a ceremonial restitution was finally arranged. The Spaniards withdrew, and so the Nootka Controversy ended with the British in official control of that portion of the Northwest.

While on his way north to meet with the Spaniards in 1792, Captain George Vancouver did not want to appear anxious about receiving the Nootka lands, so he leisurely explored Puget Sound. He charted the entire area and provided more than 200 geographical names, among them Bellingham Bay, Vashon Island, Mt. Rainier, Mt. Baker, Port Townsend, and Hood Canal. Puget Sound was named for Lieutenant Peter Puget, who was in charge of one of the survey boats.

THE AMERICANS ENTER OREGON COUNTRY

The second step in American acquisition of Oregon territory was the land exploration of the country drained by the Columbia River. Eleven years after Gray discovered the river, having secured a good share of the continent with the Louisiana Purchase of 1803, President Thomas Jefferson sent Lewis and Clark across the vast land. On November 15, 1805, they faced the Pacific at the mouth of the Columbia. Alexander MacKenzie's expedition in 1793 had earlier crossed the continent but far to the north of the Columbia's drainage basin.

Beaver dress hats such as these were fashionable among men of Europe and America during the 19th century. Because of their popularity, the beaver was nearly trapped to extinction in the Oregon territory by men working for the Hudson's Bay Company. (MOHAI)

American enterprise must also be credited with the first occupancy of the Oregon country. John Jacob Astor of New York developed a joint stock organization, which he called the Pacific Fur Company. Organized in 1810 to engage in the fur trade of the Pacific Northwest, Astor's company planned to locate an American colony at the mouth of the Columbia.

Two expeditions were sent out, an overland group and a group led by Duncan McDougal traveling by sea around Cape Horn. On the 12th of April, McDougal chose Point George on the south side of the Columbia as the site for Fort Astoria. The main body of Astor's overland party arrived at Astoria in early February after a horrendous journey.

The English-owned North West Fur Company had sent an expedition to the mouth of the Columbia attempting to reach the area before the Americans. They arrived in July to find the Astorians already established.

The War of 1812 placed the Pacific Fur Company in a precarious position. McDougal, a Canadian and chief representative of the American company, had permitted a party from the North West Fur Company to maintain a camp near the fort. Knowing that a British warship was en route to seize the fort, the intimidated McDougal sold the American property to the English company for much less than it was worth When the *Raccoon* arrived in November of 1813, in a ceremony of capture, the American flag was hauled down and the British colors hoisted.

At the Treaty of Ghent ending the War of 1812, Great Britain agreed that "all territory, places and possessions what-

MOUNT RAINIER VS. MOUNT TACOMA

In June 1792 a small boat pushed out from shore in the area of Desolation Sound. Aboard were Alexander Menzies and Harry Humphrys. Menzies, the botanist aboard Vancouver's ship *Discovery*, described while midshipman Humphrys sketched the scene that lay before them. Mount Rainier, tall and snow-clad in the morning sunlight.

A month later, Captain Vancouver had named the lofty peak in honor of his friend and fellow British naval captain Peter Rainier. Claiming the discoverer's right to name geographical features, Vancouver was to generate a lively and spirited debate, which persists to this day.

In the 1880s the competition between the two premier cities on Puget Sound, Seattle and Tacoma, was waged with boundless enthusiasm. The geographic designation for the mountain, which looms so large on the skylines of both cities, further fueled this rivalry.

The Tacomans thought that the name for the mountain should reflect the essential Indian character of the Northwest. In 1890 a delegation from the city proposed that the name of the mountain be officially changed to Tacoma. They claimed this was the Indian name for the peak, a Salish word meaning "white mountain." Seattleites, incensed by this provincialism, responded that the name had been Rainier since 1792 and should so remain.

That same year the question was referred to the United States Board on Geographic Names. This august body reflected on the testimony of both sides. The Tacoma delegation even presented Princess Angeline, daughter of Chief Seattle, to testify that her people had always called the mountain "Tacobet." The board decided that "for 100 years the name of Mount Rainier has been used whenever the mountain has been mentioned in the histories, geographies . . . by England, the United States, and even far-off Arabia." The overwhelming general usage favored Rainier.

In 1899 when a resolution of the United States Congress created the nation's fourth national park, the name chosen for the park and surrounding national forest was Mount Rainier.

Undaunted by this act of Congress, in 1924 the forces for Mount Tacoma rallied again around the resolution of Senator Clarence C. Dill, with the support of former President Theodore Roosevelt and others, to pass a bill renaming the mountain Tacoma. Though the bill passed the Senate it was never reported out of a House committee and the name remains Rainier. There has never been any substantiation to a charge made by Senator Dill that the United States Geographic Board was influenced by a "whole car of beer and finer intoxicants" to retain the name of Mount Rainier.

Still, it is possible to walk down the streets of Tacoma today and hear an occasional old-timer refer to the mountain looming on the eastern horizon (clouds willing) as Mount Tacoma.

—William Stannard

This first known picture of Mt. Rainier was drawn by an artist on the Vancouver expedition. (MOHAI) soever, taken by either party from the other during the war shall be restored." As a result, the U.S. claim to the land on which Fort Astoria was built was recognized but the North West Fur Company retained the operations because it had, in fact, purchased the business from McDougal.

After the treaty, a prolonged controversy raged over the Oregon region, but step by step the Americans gained a firmer hold. By the Florida Treaty ratified in 1821, all of Spain's claims with respect to territory north of the 42nd parallel were ceded to the United States, thus transferring all rights of discovery by the early Spanish explorers. By this time the Hudson's Bay Company, taking over the North West Fur Company, was in sole occupation of the Oregon territory. The entire region was nonetheless considered open to joint occupancy by both the United States and Great Britain, a tenantship which was extended indefinitely in 1818 but which could be terminated by either party upon 12 months' notice.

In an effort to solve the dual-ownership confusion, the United States suggested that the boundary be situated at the 49th parallel. Great Britain proposed that the boundary be established at the 49th parallel to the Columbia River and then dip south, with the river serving as the boundary. Meantime, the HBC, with headquarters at Fort Vancouver, was effectively keeping the American settlers, who began arriving in the Northwest in 1834, south of the Columbia.

President Andrew Jackson was suspicious of the British and desired more knowledge of the Puget Sound area, a little-known part of the continent at that time. He appointed Lt. William A. Slacum as special agent, to quietly secure the desired information without exciting suspicions. In his valuable report published in 1838, he argued against relinquishing the American claim to Puget Sound, which he believed militarily important to the protection of the Willamette Valley south of the Columbia being settled by Americans.

During this same period, Lt. Charles Wilkes was placed in command of Pacific and Arctic explorations, which included the Columbia River. At the same time, Lt. John C. Fremont was ordered west on an overland exploration to the coast. Wilkes arrived in 1841 and surveyed the Northwest coast rivers and harbors. In so doing he named many geographical features in the area, including Elliott Bay, Bainbridge Island, Agate Point, and Gig Harbor. Having lost one of his ships on the notorious Columbia bar, Wilkes was unenthusiastic about the Columbia River, but he reported that Puget Sound provided ideal harbors. "Nothing can exceed the beauty of these waters, and their safety," Wilkes wrote; "not a shoal exists within the Straits of Juan de Fuca, Admiralty Inlet, Puget Sound, or Hood's Canal, that can in any way interrupt their navigation by a seventy-four gun ship. I venture nothing in saying, there is no country in the world that possesses waters equal to these."

Wilkes' quickly written report advised that the coastal

Opposite, top
This painting depicts the ship *Columbia* near the mouth of the Columbia River. Captain Robert Gray, the ship's commander, entered the river and laid America's first claim to the land which would later become the Oregon and Washington territories. (MOHAI)

Opposite, bottom
Captain George Vancouver commanded the *Discovery* during the reconnaissance of Puget sound in 1792. The claim that this is his portrait is now in doubt and there may be no extant likeness of this important explorer. (MOHAI)

Above
Captain Robert Gray, American trader and explorer, not only discovered the Columbia River but was also the first American to sail his ship around the world. (MOHAI)

FROM FURS TO FARMING

In the earliest exploratory voyages in the Pacific Northwest, European and American mariners examined the area's potential for exploitation of its rich natural resources. In the first half of the 19th century the region's attraction lay not in the ground, as gold and other mineral deposits, in timber, or in the fertile soil—but in the pelts of animals inhabiting the region's lakes, rivers, and coastline.

The earliest trade in furs was carried on by merchant vessels anchored in the sheltered harbors and inlets which dotted the coast. Indians paddled out in canoes laden with sea otter skins, bartering them on board the traders' ships for metal, cloth, and glass trinkets. The majority of the skins were carried to the Orient, where ships would be loaded with cargoes of spices, silks, and other exotic merchandise worth a fortune in the markets of Europe and on America's eastern seaboard. It is hardly surprising that the sea otter, a rather elusive creature with a thick, shiny black coat prized above all other furs, nearly became extinct. In one year alone (1802), nearly 150,000 skins were traded in Canton, China.

The first white men to actually settle on the land established trading posts in order to trade with the Indians for the pelts of the martin, muskrat, fox, beaver, and sea otter. The largest and best organized of the early commercial fur-trading ventures in the Pacific Northwest was the Hudson's Bay Company, which operated a virtual monopoly after merging in 1821 with its main rival, the North West Company. In the Oregon country, the HBC's headquarters at Fort Vancouver were managed by Dr. John McLoughlin. He was described by George Simpson, head of the company's operations in Canada, as "a figure as I would not like to meet in a dark night . . . dressed in clothes that had once been fashionable, but now covered with a thousand patches of different colors, his beard would do honor to the chin of a Grizzly Bear, his face and hands evidently showing that he had not lost much time at his toilette, loaded with arms and with his own Herculean dimensions forming a stout ensemble that would convey a good idea of the highway men of former days. . . ."

Despite his odd appearance, Dr. McLoughlin gave the HBC firm and farsighted guidance. Realizing that the trade in furs was doomed to end with the fast-declining fur-bearing population, he began to investigate other business ventures. He was impressed with the Mexican rancheros' success in California in raising cattle for hides. McLoughlin persuaded his superiors to establish a farming settlement near the rich fertile land on the Nisqually plain, close to the Fort Nisqually trading post on southeastern Puget Sound. The area around the Sound, anyway, had never been rich in the beaver and sea otter pelts which constituted the bulk of the company's business. Beginning in 1833, the Puget Sound Agricultural Company raised wheat, vegetables, beef, and sheep for use by the company's trappers and their families, and in 1839 it agreed to ship food supplies to the Russian colonies in southeast Alaska.

The first farmers on the Nisqually land (near present-day Tacoma) were trappers and traders retired from the HBC service. Though the settlement took hold quickly and expanded rapidly, the changes did not please all of the company's former employees. Wrote one old trapper: "Do not suppose my friend that I am myself smitten with this colonization mania of ours. That a large population may in course of time spring up over this country I do not at all doubt, but with one eye one can see the motley crew of which it must necessarily be composed. . . . It will be of every cast and hue into which the naturalist has subdivided the three primary branches that first peopled mother earth."

By 1846 the number of immigrants arriving in the Northwest from eastern United States, especially in Olympia and Tumwater, had risen to such a number that it was no longer profitable for the Hudson's Bay Company to operate in the Oregon Country, so its headquarters moved to Fort Victoria. The small agricultural community which had grown up around the old trading post at Fort Nisqually would soon lose much of its importance as other locations on the Sound were settled. Yet Nisqually and its commercial traffic along the Sound had opened the way for the future of the entire Puget Sound area.—**William Stannard**

◆

Hudson's Bay Company trade items—flintlock rifle, glass trade beads, and knife. (MOHAI)

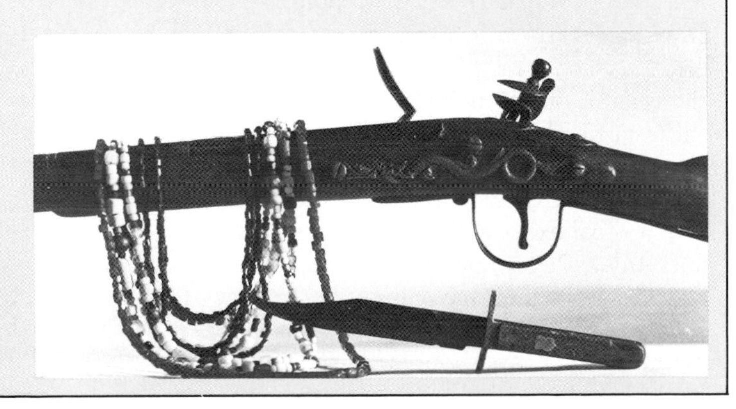

area should not be surrendered in boundary negotiations. He also believed that war would be disastrous to the Hudson's Bay Company. Perhaps because of his chauvinistic opinions, his report was not communicated to Congress, nor published while negotiations were under way.

In 1842 Lord Ashburton (for the British) and Daniel Webster (for the Americans) attempted to adjust all differences between the two nations, but they became deadlocked on the Oregon question. The controversy reached an acute stage as Americans flooded into Oregon. In 1843 more than 1,000 arrived in the Willamette Valley. Two years later, the first Yankees spilled over into territory north of the Columbia River.

With Americans arriving in record number, President James K. Polk was elected on a platform slogan of "Fifty-four/forty or fight!" As the Americans now stridently claimed the Oregon country north to the tip of Alaska, the British stand began to weaken. Congress had long debated the question and remained adamant. Secretary of State James Buchanan steadfastly rejected British proposals to make the Columbia the boundary. The U.S. gave notice that they would end joint occupancy, which meant that at the end of one year, one country must acquiesce or war might develop. In May 1846 Great Britain yielded. Figuring the fur-bearing animals were depleted in the area, the British government submitted to the following proposal: to divide the Oregon country by a line extending westward on the 49th parallel to the middle of the channel that separated the continent from Vancouver Island and thence southerly through the middle of this channel and the Strait of Juan de Fuca to the Pacific Ocean. This gave all of Vancouver Island to the British but otherwise followed the American proposal. The compromise was accepted.

The Puget Sound country, indeed all of the area north and west of the Columbia River to the 49th parallel, now belonged to the United States. Had Britain not compromised, the border might have been at the Columbia River and the area now called King County would have been part of British Columbia or, more likely, with American settlers pouring into the area, British Columbia might be part of the U.S.A.

The first permanent white settlement near Puget Sound was Fort Nisqually, founded by the Hudson's Bay Company. The fort, near the southern end of the Sound, gained importance after the HBC's steamship *Beaver*, the first steamer on the Pacific, began stopping there.

In 1834 Methodist Jason Lee established the first American mission in the Willamette Valley. The American Board of Commissioners for Foreign Missions as well as the American Methodist Society reinforced the effort by sending more Americans to Oregon country in 1836 and 1838.

Meantime, at the behest of the British fur company, Jesuit missionaries, among them two brothers, A.M.A. and Francois Blanchet, were also working the area, serving the

Peter Puget, the 26-year-old lieutenant on the *Discovery,* and Joseph Whidbey, the expedition's master sea surveyor, charted the Sound together in open boats like the one depicted in this 1792 drawing from Vancouver's *Voyages of the Gulph of Georgia.* (MOHAI)

French Canadians and converting the Indians to Catholicism.

Since the American Protestants were strongly anti-Catholic, there was little warmth between the two missionary groups. The Protestants were even less successful in converting the Indians to Christianity, and in 1844 the American mission on the Willamette was closed. However, many of the mission personnel remained as settlers. Like the fur traders, the missionaries, and later the settlers, spoke Chinook, the lingua franca of the Northwest, when conversing with the local Indians. The odd jargon combining French, English, and Indian words was easy to learn. Some proud Indians, however—Chief Seattle among them—refused to communicate in Chinook, considering it demeaning, much as the Salish later objected strongly to being called "Siwash" by the white settlers.

Between 1841 and 1843 hundreds of American settlers traveled the long overland trail to the Willamette Valley. The first wave overwhelmed the British by sheer numbers. Legislation was introduced by Congress to encourage occupation of Oregon by rewarding settlers with free land. Manifest Destiny—expansion as a national purpose—was the constant theme, and the Northwest became to Americans everywhere a frontier both psychologically and geographically. In 1843 a provisional government was established by and for American settlers in Oregon.

In 1845, the year before the boundary settlement, several Americans tried to establish land claims near Fort Vancouver but did not stay on. Later in the year John R. Jackson settled on the Cowlitz plains, and in late summer Michael T. Simmons, George Bush, and others settled near Tumwater at the south end of Puget Sound.

Even after the boundary settlement in 1846, Americans were slow to move into the northern parts of the territory, partly because of its isolation, partly because the Willamette Valley beckoned and the settlers there belittled the lands north of the Columbia. In 1849, when Marshal Joe Meek reported 304 whites settled north of the Columbia, probably the majority were Canadians.

The Donation Land Law enacted by Congress in 1850 encouraged the rapid settlement of newly opened territories in the West, such as Oregon (then containing what is now Washington State) by richly rewarding early pioneers. It gave 320 acres of land to every white or half-breed male U.S. citizen at least 18 years old. To qualify for a final grant, the

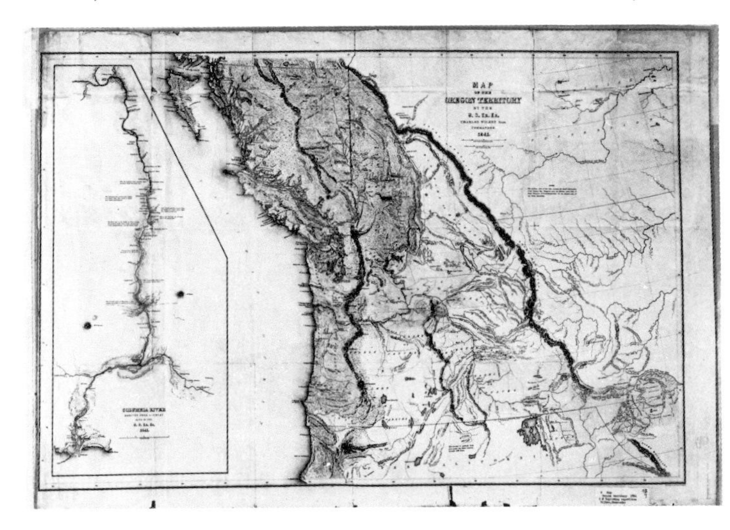

Above
This 1841 map of the Oregon territory belonged to the commander of the United States Naval Exploring Expedition, Charles Wilkes. After completing his survey of the Northwest, Wilkes wrote of Puget Sound: "Nothing can exceed the beauty of these waters and their safety . . ." (MOHAI)

Right
Lieutenant Charles Wilkes commanded the first United States Naval Exploring Expedition. Nine scientists, including naturalists, botanists, and horticulturists, sailed on the four vessels assigned to this voyage: the *Vincennes*, the *Peacock*, the *Porpoise*, and the *Relief*. (MOHAI)

Opposite
This is the last photograph of the Hudson's Bay Company steamship *Beaver*, taken before her wreck in 1883. The *Beaver*, the first steamer to enter the waters of the Pacific Ocean, served along the coast between the Columbia River and Alaska. (MOHAI)

man must occupy and farm the land for at least four consecutive years. It also gave 320 acres of land to the wife of each of the settlers, if the couple were married by December 1, 1851. Thus a man and wife could claim a total of 640 acres, or a square mile of land.

The law also provided 160 acres to each white male over 21 years of age and to the wife of each new settler who came to the territory after 1851 but before December 1, 1853.

During the summer of 1850, a slight, 22-year-old man named John Holgate came to the Puget Sound area. Seeking a site for a donation claim, over a six-week period, on foot and by canoe, he explored from Olympia north to the Snohomish River. Ascending the Duwamish River one day, he spotted a small prairie located about three miles from the mouth of the river and marked it in his mind. In letters to his mother, sister, and brothers in Iowa, he enthusiastically described the area and predicted a city would rise in the vicinity.

In the fall of 1850, after young Holgate had returned to the Willamette, Luther Collins came to the same prairie and staked a legal claim on it. When Holgate returned a few years later and found his chosen residence occupied, he picked a site on what is now Seattle's Beacon Hill.

Holgate was not the first white man to perceive the promise of the area. As far back as 1835, a young sailor from Maine made note of the bay which Vancouver had charted but not named. The whaling ship on which the lad served had anchored in what would be called Elliott Bay. Thirty-two years later, that sailor, D.S. Smith, now past middle age, moved to Seattle to establish a saddle-making shop. On arrival he found not the city he had dreamed of earlier but the tiny Seattle of 1866, a village clinging to stumpy hillsides. Smith served as justice of the peace and lived in Seattle until his death a few years later.

The 1850 census revealed 1,049 white inhabitants living north of the Columbia River, but there were no settlements on Puget Sound except at the southern tip. A tiny settlement was starting up at Tumwater-Olympia, near where the old Hudson's Bay trading and agricultural post and Fort Nisqually were located—not far from the present Fort Lewis. Puget Sound still waited for American settlers to discover its potential. It would not wait long.

CHAPTER 3
THE FOUNDING FAMILIES: 1851-1854

During the late 1840s and early 1850s, the migration of pioneers and gold-seekers from the Eastern and Midwestern states toward the West continued. In the late 1840s most homesteading families seeking donation land grants traveled no further north than the Willamette Valley, the location of several established agricultural settlements by this time.

The land that is now part of Washington State, located south of the newly established boundary at the 49th parallel and north of the Columbia River, had been undisputed American territory only since 1846. By 1850 a few adventuresome Americans had explored the Puget Sound region, where Olympia was becoming a settled town that would gain the customhouse in 1851 and in 1853 the territorial capital. They brought back tales of the beauty and rich possibilities of the inland sea area. This information began to filter eastward along the overland trails that led families to Oregon and California. And some of these men and women decided to travel northward and take a look at Puget Sound before staking a claim anywhere.

A major hindrance to settlement, however, was physical isolation; the region was notoriously difficult to reach. To approach the Puget Sound country directly from the East, travelers would have to cross over Cascade mountain passes on Indian trails, through dense forest often impenetrable to wagons. The route from the south was more accessible. Most of the early arrivals came up from Portland after having traveled down the Columbia River gorge that splits the Cascade range. But the overland trek from Portland to Puget Sound via the Cowlitz portage proved difficult. Ships also carried passengers from Portland by going down the Columbia, over the dangerous bar at the mouth of the river, and up the rugged Pacific coastline, then through the Strait of Juan de Fuca, and finally heading south on Puget Sound.

STAKING CLAIMS AT "DOWN" SOUND

The first four white men actually to settle in the King County area arrived fresh from the gold fields of California. In 1850 Joseph Maple and his son Samuel had taken leave of their family in Iowa and traveled overland to Oregon, then down to the "golden state," where their luck was not good. There they met Luther Collins. Heading back north, these three joined up with Henry Van Asselt in the Willamette Valley, where he too had gone after seeking gold in California.

Collins, the "Daniel Boone" of the first Americans to settle on Puget Sound, was always curious about what lay over the next hill. Prior to his California sojourn in 1850, Collins had chosen a claim on the Nisqually River north of Olympia. He had also explored further north and had been attracted by a piece of bottomland a few miles up from where the Duwamish River emptied into Elliott Bay. He extolled the potential of the Sound country to the other men.

Using Collins' claim on the Nisqually as a home base, the men searched through much of the present Thurston and Pierce counties for claims but found nothing available that was to their liking. When Van Asselt decided to return to Oregon, Collins, remembering the Duwamish River area, assured his friend that the land further north deserved his attention.

The four headed out in early September 1851, and by the 14th were being paddled up the Duwamish by Indians. Exploring the river and its tributaries, they agreed that the best place for their claims was the bottomland, the natural prairie along the river, unwooded and ideal for farming, which Collins had seen earlier. Collins, Van Asselt, and Samuel Maple staked out the corners of their property. Collins then returned southward for his wife, daughter, livestock, and household goods. Ironically, with all the Elliott Bay region to choose from, they had settled on the same site that young John Holgate had selected the previous year but had not legally claimed.

Meanwhile, another group of future King Countians had begun the long journey westward on April 10, 1851. They left from Cherry Grove, Illinois, with Oregon their destination. John Denny, the patriarch of the clan, was married to Sarah Latimer Boren, a widow. Traveling with them was their young daughter, Loretta, John Denny's five adult sons by a previous marriage, and Sarah's two adult daughters and son, Carson. To confuse the genealogy, two of their offspring married. Arthur Denny had wed his stepsister, Mary Boren, and they had already produced two children, with another on the way. (Later, in Seattle, David Denny would marry Louisa Boren.)

Photograph by Victor Gardaya
(MOHAI)

These seven men, four women, and four children started out together in four wagons. Two months later, on the Snake River, they joined with the John Low party of six men and two women. In July they met a man who accompanied the wagon train to The Dalles. En route, he advised his fellow travelers to consider the Puget Sound area as a good place to settle, since the region around the Willamette was already crowded with claims.

In August, the Denny-Boren-Low party reached Portland. Ten days later, Mary Denny gave birth to a son, Rolland. By then about half the party was suffering with malarial fever and chills called "ague."

Two of the healthier males, John Low and 19-year-old David Denny, started north in mid-September to find winter forage for Low's cattle. They ferried the cattle across the Columbia at Fort Vancouver, then drove them over the old Hudson's Bay trail along the Cowlitz across to the lush Chehalis Valley. The two men then hiked on to Olympia, a tiny settlement of about a dozen one-story frame cabins, two dozen Indian huts, and a two-story customhouse. There they met a New Yorker named Leander Terry and an old whaling captain, Robert C. Fay, who was about to head north "down" Sound, seeking salmon to salt for the lucrative San Francisco market that catered to '49ers. (The pioneers referred to the southern end of Puget Sound as "up" Sound and north toward the exit to the Strait of Juan de Fuca and the Pacific Ocean as "down" Sound.) Low, Denny, and Terry, anxious to look the area over, decided to join Fay in his small open sailing vessel.

On September 25, sighting an Indian camp, the four came ashore at Skwudux (an Indian name for clearing on the peninsula), on the eastern side of what is now West Seattle. They were greeted by Chief Seattle of the Duwamish-Suquamish tribes. "I was very favorably impressed with [him] as a man of more than ordinary ability, both physically and mentally," David Denny later wrote. "His head was not flattened by far as much as the ordinary Indians. His chest was full and that gave him considerable lung power. I heard him lecturing his people at a distance of over half a mile." The four travelers slept that night under a giant cedar tree near the Indians' camp. Early the next morning, Captain Fay sailed on to survey the salmon situation, leaving David Denny, John Low, and Lee Terry to explore the Duwamish River that emptied into the bay to the east. Two young Indians with a canoe agreed to paddle them upstream so they could look around.

After spending the night in the wilderness, the three then returned to Skwudux to find Captain Fay waiting for them. As the sun was setting, they heard English-speaking voices over the water and soon sighted a scow being poled around Duwamish Head. After hailing it, they met Luther Collins, his wife, and their daughter Lucinda. Collins had just sold his Nisqually holdings for $525, and the family was moving their household goods from Olympia to their Duwamish claim. The women conversed laughingly with Captain Fay in the Chinook jargon used in Indian trade in the Northwest. As dusk descended, the Collins family poled slowly into the mouth of the river and headed for their new home.

Next day the four men moved camp to an area the Indians called "Smaquamox"—known today as Alki Beach. There a gravelly slope rose between two dense groves of trees, allowing a view both up and down Sound. Terry and Low decided to make their claims there, and Low hired Denny and Terry to build a log cabin for his family. He and Fay sailed for Olympia, after which Low continued on to Portland to rejoin his family. Low carried with him a brief note from David Denny to his older brother, Arthur, urging him to come.

Late in October, the cabin was still without a roof, for want of a frow to split the cedar into shakes. Luther Collins happened by again in his scow, headed for Nisqually; Lee Terry went with him to borrow the needed tool. David Denny was left alone. A few days after Terry left, David's ax slipped and cut a deep gash in his foot. Exposed to the rain and cold, he came down with fever and neuralgia. Then skunks found his food supply. David spent three seemingly interminable weeks wondering when the others would arrive.

THE PIONEERS LAND AT ALKI

In the first light of November 13, 1851, John Low, sighting the tiny clearing at Smaquamox, guided Captain Folger to an anchorage near the shore. The chain rattled as the anchor dropped. David Denny awoke with a start, hearing the clang of chains and voices from afar. With his head and a foot bandaged, with eyes bleary from fatigue, he limped from the partially built cabin to squint through the misty, cold rain, then gave a shout and raced to the beach.

Many of the men and women who were to found Seattle had arrived. Those who disembarked that day from the *Exact* numbered 22: 10 adults and 12 children. The Dennys,

Opposite
Henry Van Asselt settled on the Duwamish River in 1851. In this 1880s photo, the Van Asselt family members, from left to right, are: Henry, Mary Adraan, Nettie, Jacob, Harriet Jane, and Mrs. Van Asselt. (MOHAI)

Above
Paul Morgan Gustin's drawing entitled *The Landing at Alki* depicts the harsh conditions under which the young settlers arrived. From Watt, *The Story of Seattle*. (MOHAI)

Borens, and Lows—joined by Mr. and Mrs. William Bell and Lee Terry's brother, Charles—had reached their destination tired and worn after seven months of grueling travel. To cap their travail, it was a miserable day.

Years later, Arthur Denny recalled it:

> We were landed in the ship's boat when the tide was well out, and while the men of the party were all actively engaged in removing our goods to a point above high tide, the women and children had crawled into the brush, made a fire, and spread a cloth to shelter them from the rain. When the goods were secured I went to look after the women, and found on my approach, that their faces were concealed. On a closer inspection I found that they were in tears having already discovered the gravity of the situation. But I did not, for some time, discover that I had gone a step too far; in fact it was not until I became aware that my wife and helpless children were exposed to the murderous attacks of hostile savages that it dawned upon me that I had made a desperate venture . . .

This momentous yet forlorn occasion was also vividly recollected by "Grandma" Fay, who had been on board the *Exact* that morning:

> I can't never forget when the folks landed at Alki Point. I was sorry for Mrs. Denny with her baby and the rest of the women. You see, it was this way. Mr. Alexander and me went on to Olympia but the rest stopped there. I remember it rained awful hard that last day—and the starch got took out of our bonnets and the wind blew, and when the women got into the rowboat to go ashore they were crying every one of 'em, and their sun bonnets with the starch took out of them went flip flap, flip flap, flip flap, as they rowed off for shore, and the last glimpse I had of them was the women standing under the trees with their wet sun bonnets all lopping down over their faces and their aprons to their eyes.

These pioneers were young. Only two were over 30. The oldest child was nine, several were toddlers, and three were babes in arms. Borrowing Indian mats and using a tent, the resourceful newcomers covered the open roof beams of the single cabin. They moved Mary Denny's cookstove inside, and soon the warmth permeated the room, along with curious but friendly Indians. In days to come, the pioneer women had to get used to Indian visitors who often brought them wild foods or offered information about gathering and using them. But sometimes they helped themselves to foodstuffs. One intrepid housewife learned to spank hands or heads, to good effect.

A log cabin was soon built for the Arthur Denny family, using up all the nearby trees of the right size. The Bell and Boren cabins were constructed of board split from cedar logs, using the Indian style of building.

A short time after the group settled into their new dwellings, the brig *Leonesa* appeared. Captain Daniel S. Howard rowed ashore and contracted with the settlers to harvest a

We have examined the valley of the Duwanish river and find it a fine country. There is plenty of room for one thousand settlers.
Come at once

Above
A note written by young David Denny in 1851 requested that the rest of the Denny party come north to Puget Sound country. (MOHAI)

Above
Captain Robert C. Fay met David Denny, Lee Terry, and John Low in Olympia, offered them a ride in his open boat as he looked for salmon "down Sound," and took them north to the campsite that became Alki. (MOHAI)

Opposite
Nine of the twelve adult founders of Seattle who landed at Alki Point on November 13, 1851, are shown here. Missing are Mrs. Carson Boren, Mrs. William Bell, and Lee Terry. (MOHAI)

W. N. BELL
C. D. BOREN
C. C. TERRY
A. A. DENNY
MRS. A. A. DENNY
D. T. DENNY
LOUISA B. DENNY
MRS. J. N. LOW
J. N. LOW
COPYRIGHT 1914 BY
BENJ. W. PETTIT
THE FOUNDERS OF SEATTLE
WHO LANDED AT ALKI POINT NOV. 13, 1851

load of pilings for him to transport to lumber-scarce San Francisco. Eager to secure cash, the men began chopping down the trees nearest the shore and rolling them to the water. Meanwhile, John Low hurried down to Ford's Prairie to bring up a pair of his oxen; Lee Terry purchased a second pair from settlers on the Puyallup River. With these sturdy draft animals, 13,458 feet of pilings were supplied in 16 working days. Captain Howard was given a pocketful of orders for provisions, including 25 barrels of pork, 3,500 pounds of flour, 150 gallons of molasses, 800 pounds of hard bread, a box of glass, six crosscut saws, a dozen pieces of calico, 400 pounds of soap, and one cask of whiskey. The small group of hopeful settlers intended to log off the forest and make a living at it.

The loading of the *Leonesa* was completed at noon on December 25, 1851. The families then celebrated together with a Christmas dinner featuring wild goose as the main dish. Louisa Boren, always thoughtful, had stored in her trunk and carried across the plains some small seashell boxes and other trinkets, which she distributed as gifts to the delighted children.

As the New Year arrived, Charles C. Terry, dreaming of developing a townsite on this land, named the settlement of four cabins "New York" after his home state and its large seaport city. Noting the irony of the name, someone derisively appended the Chinook-jargon word *alki*—pronounced "Al-key" and meaning "eventually" or "bye and bye." Hence, New York-Alki.

Realizing that their income would depend on timber, the Denny brothers, Carson Boren, and William Bell sought a deep harbor with a heavily forested shore. While Alki was picturesque, it was impractical since ships could not dock there.

Since the weather that first winter was mild, the settlers

began their explorations in January. In February they took soundings in what is now known as Smith Cove. They paddled about in a canoe equipped with a sounding device made from Mary Denny's clothesline weighted with horseshoes. They subsequently discovered in the adjacent waters of Elliott Bay an impressive deep-water harbor surrounded to the water's edge by forests.

On February 15, 1852, Arthur Denny, Boren, and Bell staked their claims. Since each was married, they could claim 320 acres apiece. Arthur Denny, a surveyor by trade, pounded a stake at what is now the foot of Denny Way and another on "The Point," now First and King streets. Bell took the northern section, Denny the middle, and Boren the southern. David Denny, not yet 21 and unmarried, delayed choosing his land until later. Believing that the waterfront obtained was most important, none of the claimants explored the wooded slopes or measured the depth of each claim. The land had not yet been surveyed by the U.S. government, and their holdings would have to be secured later by treaty from the Indians. The U.S. recognized Indian title to land until it was extinguished by treaty. These three claims were the beginning of the city of Seattle.

In March of 1852, Dr. David Swinton Maynard arrived. Maynard had left his family near Cleveland and headed for California. On the way, cholera broke out in a wagon train he had met up with and he ministered to the ill. He helped a widow whose husband had died of the disease to arrive safely in Olympia. There he chopped wood to earn needed cash to open a store in town. He arrived in Elliott Bay hoping to salt salmon for the San Francisco market. Becoming friendly with Chief Seattle of the Duwamish and Suquamish tribes, he was assured by him that salmon were plentiful in the area.

Denny, Boren, and Bell, realizing that enterprising and amiable neighbors were more important than keeping an exclusive hold on the waterfront, allowed Maynard to take a site that seemed the best for salmon salting, and they adjusted

Opposite
Built at Glastonbury, Connecticut in 1830, the *Exact* brought some of Seattle's first settlers to Alki Point on November 13, 1851. It wrecked on Crescent Bay Bar, California, in March 1859. Painting by Hewitt Jackson. (MOHAI)

Right
Among the children who were in the founding party landing at Alki were Olive and Virginia Bell, ages five and four, who "were so wet and cold that not even the knowledge that they would be immortalized side by side in two streets, Olive and Virginia, would have comforted them." From Watt, *Four Wagons West*. (MOHAI)

their water frontages accordingly. It was a wise decision. By most accounts, "Doc" Maynard was the most personable of all the early settlers and among the most influential. He was a generous man who strongly believed in helping others. He also maintained excellent relations with the local Indians.

THE START OF SEATTLE

On April 3, 1852, the Bell and Boren families shifted their possessions from New York-Alki to the eastern shore of Elliott Bay, where they camped until their homes were built. Arthur and Mary Denny stayed at Alki to recover from the ague, which had again struck them. This was the last attack either was to suffer in the mild climate of Puget Sound.

Carson Boren's cabin, the first completed, stood at what is now Second and Cherry. William Bell's home was built in the woods north of the others in an area still referred to as "Belltown." Dr. Maynard's structure stood at First Avenue South and Main Street on the Point, and here in its front half Maynard opened Seattle's first store, where he sold medicine and general merchandise. Since Arthur Denny was still suffering from ague, the men built his cabin for him near the foot of the present Battery Street. A few months later, Denny built another cabin on the southwest corner of his claim at the intersection of First and Marion, where fresh water was readily available.

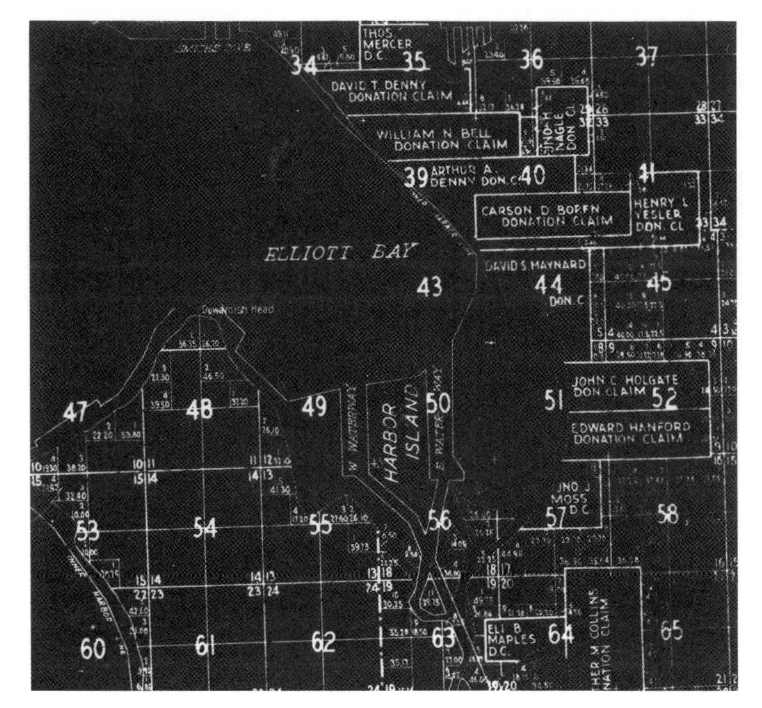

In this map showing the first donation land claims in Seattle, the property of Seattle's founders is at right center and the Duwamish settlers' claims are shown at bottom. (MOHAI)

They were occupying their new homes when the brig *John Davis* arrived. A contract was soon signed to load the ship with timber for San Francisco.

Remaining out on Alki, Charles Terry had opened a store and was doing a brisk business with both settlers and Indians on the west side of Elliott Bay. Lee Terry, who had grown homesick, departed for New York, leaving his claim to his brother. Since the brig *Leonesa* returned to Alki frequently for pilings, Charles Terry hired Indians and itinerant immigrants to fill these contracts, thereby becoming the Seattle area's first employer.

During the settlement's first summer, a few newcomers arrived, looking for a place to settle. Among them were a young lawyer, George N. McConaha, and his wife. Shortly after their arrival, their daughter, Eugenia, appeared—the first white child born in Seattle. Dr. Henry A. Smith, a 22-year-old physician, paddled up from Olympia and nearly passed by the settlement. Finally spotting Dr. Maynard's store, he came ashore. Later he took a claim north of Seattle at what is now called Smith Cove. Dr. Smith brought word that Congress might appropriate funds for a transcontinental railway survey and said he considered Elliott Bay a likely site for a terminus—initiating Seattle's efforts to secure a rail link with the East.

Realizing that the informal name "Duwamps" sounded inelegant for their settlement, the pioneers pondered other possibilities. Dr. Maynard supposedly proposed that they honor his friend Chief Seattle. All seemed to agree it was an

PIONEER DRESS: WHAT PEOPLE WORE

Traveling west by wagon train was difficult at best, but for women, bound in corsets and wearing the long voluminous dress in vogue at the time, it must have been especially uncomfortable and certainly unsuitable for the long journey. The typical pioneer dress was hand sewn calico, usually with a background and a tiny print, sometimes a plaid. It was a simple style though the plain round neckline could be trimmed with a small lace collar to dress it up for church. Sunbonnets, of starched cotton with deep brims and neck ruffles, were worn for protection from the sun as they crossed the prairie—a lady did not have tanned skin or freckles. Little girls wore the same styles as their mothers. And before the trip a cobbler had made shoes for the entire family. The maternity dress of this period was designed for the pregnant woman but also had a double bodice for discreet nursing of the baby. This became almost a uniform for the pioneer woman, as one child followed another in quick succession! Arriving at Puget Sound in a driving rainstorm, imagine the discomfort of soggy skirts flapping about the ankles, petticoats adrip. It must have taken weeks to dry them in the damp air.

Men wore clothing not unlike today's trousers of homespun wool, loosely styled, and a double-breasted shirt of wool that slipped over the head. Leather boots to the knee or a brogan (a heavy-toed short boot), were the typical footcoverings. A heavy coat, sometimes fur-lined, was common. Buckskin clothing was not worn in the Northwest as it tended to shrink and stiffen in the damp climate.

The arrival of the Mercer Girls in 1864 provided a happy social event in the little village of Seattle. Seattle's women must have enjoyed seeing the new styles, especially the innovative steel hoop that allowed them to have the round silhouette, still dictated by European designers, without the bulk of so many petticoats. This also gave women a method to flirt in a very discreet manner, called "swagging." A young woman walking on the street with a chaperone, of course, could sway her hips slightly and the springy hoop would sway in rhythm, perhaps showing a glimpse of a well turned ankle. The townsmen tended to wear apparel similar to the popular statesmen of the time: long coats, low cut vests, and an ascot or black tie tied in a bow.

As the village grew in population, bringing in more people from the East with news of costume changes and especially new materials and trimmings, fashions changed more rapidly. The 1870s and 1880s brought the bustle, with the accent on the rear of the garment, and a long train. Tiny bonnets tied under the chin, with ribbons hanging down the back, called "Follow Me Young Man" ribbons, could be flipped about to entice the interested male.

Women's clothing was still very confining, as if symbolizing their restricted position in social and political affairs. The 1890s, with its coeducational colleges, brought about a breakthrough with competition between young men and women in sports. Since bicycling was impossible to do while in a bustle, a new style was seen—a slim, bell-like skirt with a stock-collared blouse and large "leg o'mutton" sleeves. The turn of the century showed off the wasp waisted, full-bosomed woman with the most elegant fashions yet seen. Then as the Suffrage movement began, women's clothing became simple and more utilitarian as women worked outside the home and fought the battle for equal rights.—**Lois Rayne Bark**

Below, left
Mrs. Caroline McGilvra Burke (wife of Judge Thomas Burke) in a satin brocade evening gown of 1865. (MOHAI)

Below, right
Sarah Yesler (wife of Henry) gowned in the style of the 1860s. (MOHAI)

excellent suggestion.

That summer of 1852 the men filled the holds and decks of several lumber schooners anchored in the bay. Dr. Maynard managed to salt and pack nearly 1,000 barrels of Indian-caught salmon, but when the shipment was unloaded in San Francisco, most of it had spoiled.

Several other milestones occurred that summer. Arthur Denny surveyed several blocks for a seaport city, using his cabin as the starting point. He also was named a commissioner for Thurston County, which had just been created by the Oregon legislature. Its domain encompassed most of what became northwest Washington State. In July, the legislature appointed Dr. Maynard a justice of the peace. That fall, on November 19, Dr. Maynard performed the first wedding ceremony in Seattle and King County when he married John Bradley and Mary Relyea of Steilacoom.

Another important settler arrived in October. Henry Yesler was seeking a waterfront location for the steam sawmill he intended to erect. He had supper with the Arthur Denny family. The next day he staked a waterfront claim in the West Seattle area since the eastern shore of Elliott Bay was taken. Denny talked the matter over with Maynard and Boren. Agreeing that Yesler's enterprise would be an asset to their young community, they offered Yesler any site he wanted on their side of the bay. Yesler chose the "Sag," the low point north of Maynard's claim. Maynard and Boren shifted their corner stakes, allowing Yesler a strip running from the shoreline up the hill where his claim totalled 320 acres. This strip became the "skid road" on which logs were skidded down to Yesler's mill in the Sag. Yesler was then 42 years old and Maynard was 44; since the average age of the settlers was 26, they often acted the role of elder statesmen.

Before Yesler left for San Francisco to obtain the machinery to install in Puget Sound's first steam sawmill, the settlers helped him construct a log cookhouse for his workers. The building, of squared logs with a shake roof, was about 25 square feet and stood one story high. It had an attic above and a shed to the rear, which was used as a kitchen and a bunkhouse. This structure was Seattle's first multi-use building. When Yesler's sawmill began operating on March 28, 1853, before the mill building even had a roof, the first logs came from Dr. Maynard's claim, which he wanted cleared for buildings.

Shortly after Yesler arrived, another man who would have much influence in the area came to the Puget Sound area. Though originally a member of the Bethel Wagon Train Thomas Mercer traveled to the area alone. His wife had died just after they migrated to Oregon. Leaving his four young daughters in Salem with friends, he went to look over the Seattle region. Mercer chose a site on Lake Union's western shore, which included part of Queen Anne Hill.

Seattle's first religious service also occurred that fall of 1852 when Bishop Demers arrived in an Indian canoe. He had been in the Northwest since 1838, and with Fr. Francois Blanchet he had introduced Catholicism to the Oregon country. Before going on to his post at Fort Victoria, he preached a sermon in Yesler's cookhouse. Regardless of the denomination to which they belonged, all Seattleites turned out to hear him.

In October of 1852, the Duwamps precinct was fairly well depleted of leadership. A convention at Monticello (now Longview) had been called to develop a petition for a separate Territory north of the Columbia River, and of the 44 delegates assembled, eight were from the Seattle area. Low and Terry came from Alki, Collins and R. J. White from the Duwamish settlement, and Bell, Arthur Denny, Maynard, and McConaha from Seattle.

After the convention, Dr. Maynard traveled on to Oregon City, where the Oregon Territorial legislature was in session, to obtain a legislative divorce from the wife he had left in Ohio. A month later he married the widow Broshears of Olympia, whom he had helped on the wagon train west. She became the Catherine Maynard of Seattle history. While there, Maynard also apparently influenced decisions about the creation of a new county, to be named King.

SEATTLE AND KING COUNTY GET ON THE MAP

The village called Seattle was hardly noticeable on the timbered shore of Elliott Bay when certain events brought it and King County official recognition.

In the winter of 1852–1853, Colonel Isaac Ebey, the only representative in the Territorial legislature from the region north of the Columbia River, secured a bill to carve four new counties from Thurston County: Island, Jefferson, Pierce, and King. The latter two were named for the nation's newly elected but not yet inaugurated President and Vice-President. The incoming Vice-President, William R. King of Alabama, had been active in the Senate in securing legislation forwarding the U.S. claim to the region north of the Columbia. He was to die before he could assume office.

The new King County was much larger than it is now. Its boundaries at inception included all territory north of Pierce County from the Pacific Ocean to the Cascade summit. The northern boundary was drawn due east and west through Pilot Cove on the west side of Admiralty Inlet.

The county seat was situated by legislation at Seattle, even before the village had been platted. It was located specifically on the land claim of Dr. David S. Maynard. Three county commissioners were named: Arthur A. Denny, Luther M. Collins, and John Low. However, the latter was planning to move to Olympia and refused the appointment. Henry Yesler was named county auditor and Carson D. Boren, sheriff. Furthermore, the area was granted a post office with Arthur Denny as postmaster. Mail was delivered by Robert Moxlie, who paddled down from Olympia once a week. A

Top
Catherine Troutman Simmons was born in Meade County, Kentucky in 1816 and married Israel Broshears in 1832. Left a widow on the trail west, she was escorted to Olympia by Dr. Maynard—her future husband. In September 1853 they traveled up the Duwamish and Black rivers to Lake Washington; she was the first white woman to see or touch the water of that lake. Photo by Sammis. (MOHAI)

Above
Physician Henry A. Smith arrived in Seattle in 1853 after traveling across the continent. He built a cabin on the small cove at the northern arm of Elliott Bay which bears his name. An amateur ethnologist and linguist, he translated Chief Seattle's famous speech. (MOHAI)

Top
Dr. David Swinton Maynard was born in Castleton, Vermont, in 1808. Financial problems in 1837 prompted him to travel to California, and then to Portland in 1851. In 1852 he moved northward, settled with the Denny-Boren party on Elliott Bay, and became Justice of the Peace. By traveling to Olympia, he secured a divorce from his first wife and married Catherine T. Broshears in January 1853. (MOHAI)

Above
Princess Angeline (circa 1820–1896), the daughter of Chief Seattle, was befriended by Yesler and Maynard. In old age she sold clams on street corners. A colorful "character," she was memorialized in tourist souvenirs. Photo by Edward S. Curtis. (MOHAI)

CHIEF SEATTLE

"He was the greatest friend of the whites on this side of the continent," Mrs. Catherine Maynard maintained. She and her husband, Dr. David Maynard, enjoyed the friendship of Chief Seattle, or Sealth, from 1853 until his death in 1866. Unable to pronounce his name in the Salish tongue with its gutteral inflections, the early settlers altered the pronunciation to Seattle.

When residents of the fast-growing settlement on Elliott Bay were searching for a name for their new town—something distinctive that would set it apart from other prospering villages on Puget Sound—"Doc" Maynard supposedly urged them to honor the chief of the local Indians. However, upon hearing that the town was to be given his name, Chief Seattle felt uneasy since the Salish tribes believed that having their names spoken after death would disturb the spirits of the departed. It is said that he used this name-borrowing as grounds for levying a tax upon local citizens, receiving payment now for what he saw as the later unrest of his soul.

There is little documented fact relating to Chief Seattle's early life. Born around 1786 on Blake Island, he claimed that he witnessed the arrival of Vancouver's ships to Puget Sound in 1792. The son of Schweabe, chief of the Suquamish and Scholitza, daughter of the chief of the Duwamish, Seattle assumed leadership sometime around 1810, when he successfully organized the defense of the salt-water tribes against an impending attack by upriver Indians. At a grand council afterward, Seattle became head chief of various local salt-water tribes. Through diplomacy and oratory skills, as well as with a strong party of warriors to back him up, he was able to establish his authority. He was converted to Catholicism in the 1820s by the Jesuit missionaries, along with many of his people.

In 1851 the first whites arrived to establish permanent settlements in the land occupied by Seattle's people. Throughout the Indian wars of 1855–56 Chief Seattle, though frequently distressed, managed to keep his people from entering the fray. This could not have been easily accomplished, for Puget Sound chieftains had little power other than persuasion over individuals.

The last years of Seattle's life were lived on the Port Madison reservation. He died there on June 7, 1866, and was buried after both Catholic and Salish ceremonies. Not until 24 years later did his white friends in the city named for him decide to erect an appropriate marker over his grave. Today the well-marked site in the quiet little Catholic church graveyard in Suquamish stands within viewing distance of the beach where once stood the longhouse in which Chief Seattle had lived for so many years.

—William Stannard

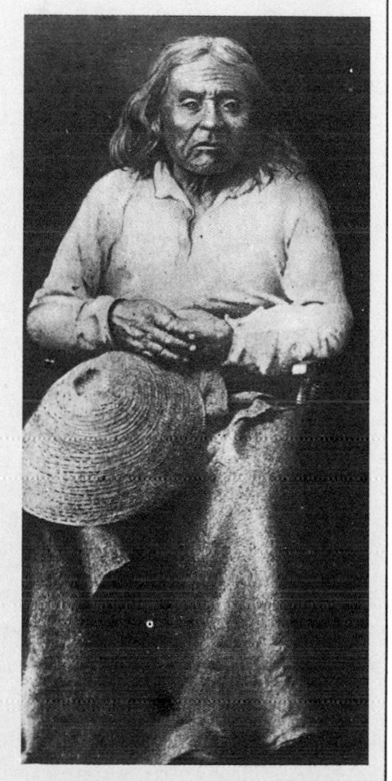

The only known photograph taken of Chief Seattle or Sealth is this one by Sammis in the 1860s. (MOHAI)

Far left
The wooden bench with a hinged back bar was used as a wagon seat by the J.W.H. McCallister family when crossing the plains in the 1850s. An oxen yoke leans against the bench. (MOHAI)

Left
Commemorative Imperial Bone China dinnerware marks the first marriage of Seattleites—that of David T. Denny and Louisa Boren in 1853. (MOHAI).

Middle, far left
Arthur Denny used this desk for sorting mail when he was appointed postmaster in August 1853. The desk was purchased from a sea captain who had brought it around Cape Horn. (MOHAI)

Middle, left
This rawhide-bottom chair was made by Henry Van Asselt, circa 1851. (MOHAI)

Bottom
Emily Inez Denny sketched this scene of bargaining with the Indian traders at Alki Point in the early years of the settlement. (MOHAI)

second post office was established in 1854 at Alki.

The second winter the pioneers spent in Seattle (1852–1853) was unusually cold. Twelve inches of snow lay on the ground for more than two weeks and ice formed on the rivers and lakes. Food grew scarce as storms at sea kept vessels from Elliott Bay. Good hunters, David Denny and Carson Boren furnished game to the small community, and seafood was also available. But after flour ran out, they used up all the hard bread; finally, the last of the potatoes was gone. Arthur Denny, going out in a log canoe paddled by four Indians, managed to purchase 50 bushels of small red potatoes from Indian farmers on the Black River. After the first ship made it into Elliott Bay, bringing in flour, the bread baked by the pioneer women was judged the best ever tasted.

One of Seattle's most famous weddings took place on January 23, 1853, when David Denny married Louisa Boren. Dr. Maynard, as justice of the peace, performed the service at the home of Arthur and Mary Denny. Henry Yesler, county clerk and recorder, issued the first wedding license in King County. Mr. and Mrs. George McConaha and a few curious Indians who managed to crowd into the cabin served as witnesses. Afterward, carrying their few wedding gifts, including an old rooster and hen given them by Dr. Maynard, the couple bundled up warmly, climbed into a canoe, and paddled north to the cabin on their claim at the foot of what became Denny Way. That spring Louisa planted sweetbrier seeds she had brought from Illinois, and the plants soon spread throughout the village. She was thereafter known as "The Sweetbrier Bride."

On May 23, 1853, two plats were filed with county auditor Yesler. Alike in width of thoroughfares and size of blocks, they differed in the direction of the streets. Arthur Denny had developed a plat for his claim and that of his brother-in-law Carson Boren, with the north-south streets running parallel to the shoreline. Dr. Maynard, however, had insisted the streets on his land should run true north and south according to the compass. Denny wrote later: "He [Maynard] had that day taken enough to cause him to feel that he was not only monarch of all he surveyed but what Boren and I surveyed as well."

While it is true that the good doctor enjoyed a drink now and then, it is also true that Arthur Denny was a teetotaler. But clearly Maynard's plan had a distinct advantage. His east-west thoroughfares ascended Seattle's famous hills at an angle, whereas Denny's assumed the steepest grade. The bend in the streets at Yesler Way is the result of their early disagreement.

The first celebration of a national holiday in King County was held at Alki on July 4, 1853. A salute, dinner in a grove, reading of the Declaration of Independence, remarks by several speakers, and a dance in the evening entertained the participants.

Seattle began to grow as men came to work in Yesler's mill and to take up claims. While forest products provided most of the early income for the Seattle area, supporting industries did begin to develop. Barrels were manufactured for the busy salmon trade and various retail shops were opened.

Immigrants and transients, many of them bachelors, were arriving a few at a time. Since they had need of meals and lodging, a small restaurant and lodging house opened in 1852. And Seattle's first hotel opened on Maynard's Point, at what is now Jackson and Western. It was two stories high, lathed and plastered—the first hard-finished structure in town. Known officially as the Felker House, it assumed other names because of the colorful, nasty-tempered, rough-tongued woman who managed it. Mrs. Mary Ann Conklin, sometimes known as Mary Ann Boyer, was famous up and down the coast as "Mother Damnable." As a result her hotel was sometimes called "The Conklin House" or simply "Mother Damnable's." She was noted for her ill temper, and it was said she could outswear any sailor. She was, as well, a dead eye with a rock. Yet she was a good cook, which kept her business booming. Her husband was an old sea captian who, through the years, became ever more mild and inoffensive in contrast to his increasingly termagant wife.

Yesler's cookhouse, as the center of social activity, was the site of the first sermon preached by Seattle's first resident minister, David E. Blaine, who arrived with his wife in 1853. Before he had raised sufficient funds to build Seattle's first church, he preached in Bachelors' Hall, where his wife Catherine conducted the first school.

Important new settlers arrived in 1853. Thomas Mercer returned to Seattle in April, bringing his four motherless daughters. With him traveled Dexter Horton, ailing and broke, who went to work shaving shingles for William Bell at $2.50 a day. Young John C. Holgate returned to find his dream claim site occupied by Luther Collins. He and his brother-in-law, Edward Hanford, settled on Beacon Hill instead. Mr. and Mrs. Hillory Butler and George Frye also became Seattle residents that spring.

By 1853 the population of King County had risen to 170 white settlers, of which 111 were males. Out at Alki, Charles Terry purchased John Low's interests before the latter left for Olympia and became sole owner of the Alki location. Only 22 years old, he started a long but losing campaign to develop a major city on his claim. In 1853 he talked William Renton into joining him in constructing a sawmill there. However, the site was exposed to northerly winds and lacked fresh water, drawbacks which eventually forced them to move the mill to Port Orchard.

On March 2, 1853, President Millard Fillmore signed the organic act establishing the Territory of Washington. (The news did not reach Seattle for many weeks. The May 7 issue of the Olympia *Columbian* reported on the rejoicing, the firing of guns, and other celebrations after word finally reached the territory.) Two days later, Franklin Pierce was inaugurated as President, and shortly thereafter he appointed Isaac I. Stevens as both Governor and Superintendent of Indian Affairs for the new territory. As he traveled westward, Stevens, an engineer by training, surveyed a possible route for a railroad. He also started drawing up treaties with the Indians, clearing the way for the white settlers' claims to be recognized.

Potential new sources of revenue were being discovered in King County. In October of 1853, for example, the Duwamish Coal Company was formed to mine coal, but since capitalization was not available, coal mining had to wait a decade.

Agricultural communities grew along the rivers of King County, with the Duwamish, White, Black, and Green rivers all having settlements such as Mox La Push and a tiny place called Black River, established at the present site of Renton. The Duwamish settlers were raising valuable crops on the bottomlands of their claims. In the fall of 1853, Luther Collins estimated his crops were worth $5,000 and advertised 200,000 fruit trees for sale at $12.50 per hundred. Two years later he raised 300 bushels of peaches.

Local residents began to agitate for a road across the Cascades, so that wagons could travel directly from Fort Walla Walla. They also wanted a road built north from the Willamette Valley, believing that many families would come to the Puget Sound region if access was improved.

By 1854 Seattle boasted a three-block long Commercial Street (now First Avenue South) that extended from Yesler's mill, at what is now Pioneer Square, south to Jackson Street, all of it on Dr. Maynard's plat.

INDIAN TROUBLES

Early in 1854 the engineer for the Alki sawmill hired Snohomish Indians and a canoe to transport him in a claim search. He was never seen again. Two of the Indians were reported in possession of his clothing, watch, and money. The suspects fled and were followed by a sheriff and four deputies. Indians attacked, wounding three of them, one later dying from his wounds. Nine Indians were killed. Pursuing the assailants, the sheriff brought the two culprits back to Seattle, where they pleaded guilty. (The third Indian, they reported, had been killed in the quarrel over division of the spoils.) Confined in Seattle, they were eventually executed by members of their own tribe according to Indian custom. Still, the whole episode made the white settlers uneasy, reminding them of their precarious hold on the Puget Sound area. They depended obviously on the local Indians' forbearance.

While the population was increasing throughout King County, underneath a gnawing concern began to surface. As Governor Isaac Stevens went about the new Washington Territory developing treaties with the Indians, the natives' restlessness and dissatisfaction became ever more apparent. The realization that their land was being taken from them, plus the slowness of the small reparations being paid them and the efforts to keep them on their small reservations, caused continuous problems.

Chief Seattle was a persuasive orator among his own people. As long as he lived, he worked to keep peace between them and the incoming white families. He was perhaps partly influenced by his new religion, Catholicism. But he heeded his own intuition and reason and understood that the Native Americans could only lose in conflicts with the better-armed and innumerable white men. He therefore took the only road which gave his people any chance of survival: removal to a reservation. He was the first to sign the Point Elliot Treaty, negotiated in January of 1855 when Governor Isaac Stevens arrived in the Puget Sound area. Dr. David Maynard, as Indian subagent, arranged for Chief Seattle and some of his tribesmen to meet the governor on the property that was part of Dr. Maynard's claim. And it was there that Chief Seattle made his famous speech.

Dr. Henry A. Smith, a young man who knew both the Salish language and stenography, attempted to record Chief Seattle's words and then translate them. The published document has come down to posterity as one of the most moving and eloquent of Indian utterances that expressed the Native Americans' forced submission to white domination. However, the Victorian-age rhetoric has caused historians to doubt the authenticity of the long speech as Smith translated it. Surely the somber mood with its veiled defiance contains a warning for future Seattleites dwelling in an urban environment far removed from the natural world of the Salish. "It matters little where we pass the remnant of our days," the old chief concluded. "They are not many. . . ."

> . . . A few more moons, a few more winters . . . and not one of all the mighty hosts that once filled this broad land and that now roam in fragmentary bands through these vast solitudes or lived in happy homes, protected by the Great Spirit, will remain to weep over the graves of a people once as powerful and as hopeful as your own. . . .
>
> And when the last Red Man shall have perished from the earth and his memory among the white man shall have become a myth, these shores will swarm with the invisible dead of my tribe; and when your children's children shall think themselves alone in the fields, the store, the shop, upon the highway, or in the silence of the pathless woods, they will not be alone, in all the earth there is no place dedicated to solitude. At night, when the streets of your cities and villages will be silent and you think them deserted, they will throng with the returning hosts that once filled and still love this beautiful land.
>
> The white man will never be alone. Let him be just and deal kindly with my people, for the dead are not powerless . . .

Top
The Felker House, also known as the Conklin House or simply as "Mother Damnable's," was Seattle's first hotel. Built by Captain Leonard Felker, it was the first hard-finished structure in town. Mrs. Mary Ann Conklin, proprietress of the hotel, was notorious for her swearing and bad temper. (MOHAI)

Middle
As one of the first public structures built in Seattle, Yesler's cookhouse was used as courtroom, church, social hall, and election room. It was built in 1853 and stood near First and Yesler. Later, although an eyesore in the business part of town, it held many memories for the first settlers until it was destroyed in the early 1870s. Courtesy, McDonald Collection. (MOHAI)

Bottom
Charles Plummer arrived in Seattle in 1853 and built the second store in the village at Main and First Avenue South. He soon became postmaster and secured the first license to sell liquor. In 1859 the enterprising Plummer added a second story above his store and called it Snoqualmie Hall. Here court sessions, dances, concerts, and lodge meetings were held. The photo shows his store circa 1864, after he had extended a flume out to his wharf so ships could replenish their fresh water supply. (MOHAI)

CHAPTER 4

UNSETTLING TIMES: 1855-1859

Indian unrest flickered along the shores of Puget Sound throughout most of 1855. Late in the year and early in 1856, the frictions were to ignite in several attacks, including a dramatic one-day battle for Seattle.

MOUNTING TENSION WITH THE INDIANS

Seattle, in 1855, was still a small village; in all of King County lived fewer than 200 white settlers. The Indians under the new treaties arranged by Governor Isaac Stevens were given reservations on which they were supposed to live. In agreeing to the Point Elliott Treaty, the local Indian groups had signed over their land in return for certain supplies, a promise of cash and education, a reservation at Port Madison, and a guarantee of fishing rights. However, the Sound Indians continued to freely congregate near the white settlements to work and trade. Some were hired at Yesler's mill, while others worked alongside the settlers in logging and building activities. Many of these Indians sought safety from more warlike northern tribes by camping beside the better-armed whites. The Sound Indians, for the most part, were considered trustworthy by the settlers. The accounts of those times often mention friendships between settler and native.

Rumors of widespread Indian intentions to drive the whites from their ancestral lands became common during 1855. Most of the information concerned the aggressive, horse-riding tribes, the Yakimas and Klickitats east of the Cascades, and was relayed to the Seattle-area residents through local Indians.

In February the territorial legislature petitioned Congress to send a warship to the Puget Sound area—not, however, for protection from local natives but rather from the fierce tribes of British Columbia, whose raids in huge war canoes frightened both the whites and the resident Indians. It was feared that the British might be supporting these Indians, hoping to oust the Americans from the territory lost in the 1846 settlement.

In August two groups of prospectors from the Puget Sound area headed over the mountains toward a new gold strike near Colville in eastern Washington. Joseph Fanjoy and O.M. Eaton, in the first group, were followed by five others. They trespassed on Indian lands, thus breaking promises and treaties signed by Governor Stevens. In the Yakima Valley the second party came across the deserted camp of their predecessors and decided to spend the night. When several Indians wandered by and offered to show them a better route, two men went off. Shortly after they were out of sight, the three in camp heard shots. Scurrying into the brush, they cautiously made their way over the mountains and through the forest back to Seattle. A few days later the deaths of the other prospectors were verified.

Concern over growing Indian hostilities increased when word arrived telling of Colonel Granville Haller's efforts to enter the Yakima Country to arrest Indians accused of killing an Indian agent. The colonel and 100 infantrymen from Fort Dalles, Oregon, were repulsed by a much larger group of Indians, losing several men and most of their equipment.

During August and September there was evidence that eastern Indians were urging Puget Sound tribes to join them in dislodging the white settlers. Also, a few unpleasant local incidents alarmed King Countians. Many settlers in the more remote areas temporarily left their lands and came into Seattle for safety.

Since Governor Isaac Stevens was still in the eastern part of the territory making treaties with tribes, Secretary of State Charles Mason served as acting governor. While traveling from Olympia through the White and Duwamish valleys, he stopped to meet with Indians who assured him that they were friendly toward the settlers. Mason arrived in Seattle early in October. He told the residents that all was peaceful and encouraged the settlers to return to their claims and cabins. Mason also tried to convince Captain Sterrett of the recently arrived sloop-of-war *Decatur* that the ship was not needed in Elliott Bay. He reportedly told the captain that Seattle's merchants wanted the *Decatur* to stay just so they could develop trade with its 140 men and officers. When Sterrett angrily accused Arthur Denny of this charge, Denny earnestly convinced him that the Indian threat was real.

The *Decatur* had been anchored near Honolulu in June 1855, when it was ordered to sail for the Pacific Northwest coast to protect the settlers there. Captain Sterrett had headed for Puget Sound. Arriving at Port Townsend on July 19, he heard of the potential Indian threat to Seattle and

Photograph by Victor Gardaya
(MOHAI)

sailed on to the village. Expecting to furnish protection from the raids of northern Indians, he discovered instead that the danger now came from Indians within the territory. The *Decatur* made a quick voyage to Mare Island near San Francisco for supplies and arms and by early October was again anchored off Seattle.

The settlers remained edgy in spite of the assurances of Acting Governor Mason, partly because friendly tribesmen kept up their warnings. A Seattle volunteer military company of 54 men was organized. Some were stationed on watch in a blockhouse at the confluence of the Green and White rivers. To protect Seattle itself, a log blockhouse was erected near the foot of Cherry Street. Two hundred regulars from Fort Steilacoom were called on to patrol the country between Puget Sound and the Cascade Mountains. In the area west of the Cascades more than 60 blockhouses were speedily constructed. Meanwhile, the *Decatur* traveled up and down the Sound as different locations reported expectations of attack.

THE INDIAN WAR BEGINS

On October 28, 1855, the worst killings of the Indian War in King County occurred in the White River Valley just north of the present city of Auburn. The victims were families who had returned to their farmland after the assurances of Mason but against the advice of many other settlers. Nine men, women, and children were murdered, including Mr. and Mrs. Harvey Jones, whose three young children escaped to Seattle, thanks to seven-year-old Johnny's actions and friendly Indians.

The following day, Captain C. C. Hewitt and 55 volunteers marched over the rough trails to visit the massacre sites and to aid any settlers remaining. After surveying the grisly scene and burying the dead, Hewitt and his men returned to Seattle.

Dr. David S. Maynard, who served as Indian subagent, was ordered by Surveyor-General Tilton to move 434 of Chief Seattle's tribesmen from the Seattle vicinity to the reservation east of the Sound where more than 600 of his people already were living. The Indians already had numerous grievances, for some had virtually been coerced into signing unfair treaties. Two of the Indian leaders, Seattle and Nowchise, became quite agitated. Since the Indians were scattered over a large part of King County, bringing them together for the relocation took considerable time. However, the move was finally completed without incident.

The army tried to stay between the Indians and the militia, and its commander, General Wool, blamed settlers for causing some of the violence. The army began efforts to counter the Indian attacks. Lt. William Slaughter was ordered to follow and capture the murderers of the White River Valley settlers and attack any hostiles. A running battle along the White River ensued, with Indians on one side of the

Above
Isaac I. Stevens was the first governor of Washington Territory. As a reward for his support of General Franklin Pierce for President, Stevens was given three titles in 1853: Governor of Washington Territory, Superintendent of Indian Affairs, and leader of the Northern Pacific Railroad Survey. (MOHAI)

Opposite
In his first known photograph of Seattle (1859) Yesler's house stands on the corner of Front (now First Avenue) and James streets. Mr. and Mrs. Yesler can be seen on the porch. Courtesy, Historical Photography Collection, U. of W Libraries.

SEATTLE.
1859
Boyd

rain-swollen stream and the regulars on the other. In the wet, dense forests the soldiers proved no match for the Indians.

On November 24 Lt. Slaughter with 50 regulars and two companies of volunteers moved over near Puyallup, and as dusk fell they were promptly surrounded by Indians. The Indians fired several shots into the army camp but hit no one, though they did run off several dozen army horses. Next day they again fired into camp, this time wounding one man.

On December 4 Slaughter moved his men to the White River, close to the site of the earlier massacre. Captain Hewitt and Seattle's volunteer company were camped nearby. Young David Denny, one of Hewitt's volunteers, remembered later:

> An Indian guide named Puyallup Tom accompanied Lieut. Slaughter through the Green River country. . . . It was cold and raining nearly all day. When near the spot where they camped they saw an Indian dog skulking along in the underbrush. Puyallup Tom said that the dog's master was not far off and to "Closhe nanatch" (look out).
>
> The Lieutenant found a small cabin in the opening in the woods and here he made camp for the night. They were all drenched to the skin so they stacked their arms and built large fires of fence rails around which the soldiers stood to dry. The Lieutenant did not put out any guards as he had not seen any Indians that day.
>
> He made his quarters in the cabin with his officers where they had a fire on the earth floor. As the night drew on the hooting of owls was heard. The guide told him that it was the Indians signaling to each other but he said, "No, you're mistaken." Puyallup Tom begged that the fire be extinguished but the Lieut. refused. . . . The soldiers were around the bright fire and the Lieut. was sitting in the cabin when the Indians fired a volley into their midst killing Lieut. Slaughter instantly. The bullet came in between logs striking him in the heart. He made no sound save the sharp intaking of his breath and fell over dead. Two of the soldiers were killed and several wounded. The men crowded into the little cabin and Puyallup Tom ran out and kicked the fires apart.
>
> The Indians withdrew for a time. Finally two men who were in a fence corner heard them creeping back and fired on them.

The Seattle volunteers had heard the firing and started toward it, only to meet the regulars who were hurrying to meet them, carrying the wounded and the body of Slaughter on litters. A detachment of soldiers was ordered back the next day to bury the bodies of the two enlisted men killed in the battle.

David Denny helped bring the body of Slaughter and the wounded in canoes to Seattle. A fourth soldier died on the way. Until the bodies could be transferred to Steilacoom, where Slaughter's wife lived, they lay in the new Seattle blockhouse. Gloom pervaded the community on Elliott Bay.

On December 6, Captain Sterrett, at Port Townsend, became aware of the mounting tension. He decided to move the *Decatur* in a position to defend Seattle and its inhabitants from attack. As he explained his actions in a report to the Navy Department:

> Seattle is the nearest point to Snoqualami Pass (sic), and is therefore the most exposed of all settlements on the Sound to incursions of Indians from beyond the mountains. I considered it my duty to remain at that place until the citizens could organize some means of defense, as they were almost destitute of arms and entirely without organization.

On the following day the *Decatur* struck a rocky reef off Bainbridge Island and was stuck high on the rock as the tide fell. Next morning, pulled off at high tide, she limped to Seattle. Because the damage was considerable, the ship's carpenters and crew worked day and night. On January 19, 1856, the ship was refloated at high tide and the battery was

John C. Holgate explored the region around Elliott Bay in a canoe in 1850. In a letter to relatives, he predicted that a glorious city would arise there. (MOHAI)

remounted. She again rode at anchor in Elliott Bay, just in time to take an active role in the Indian attack.

On December 10, however, while the *Decatur* was being repaired, Captain Sterrett was ordered to leave his post. Thomas Phelps, one of his lieutenants, reported that the dismissal had resulted from a false charge. (Sterrett was later "triumphantly vindicated" and returned to active duty.)

The army meantime decided that a winter campaign against the Indians would not be wise, so the troops were garrisoned through the cold winter months. They lived in locations near the settlements and farmlands, which they were called on to protect.

THE ATTACK ON SEATTLE

On January 25 the new commander of the *Decatur*, Captain Gansevoort, received information that a large number of Indians had crossed Lake Washington, north of Seattle. Warned that they were armed and preparing to attack, he quickly evaluated the situation. His report to the Secretary of the Navy describes what happened next:

> Sentries were stationed in the most conspicuous positions, and the several posts visited by me, several times during the night. The next morning at daylight, everything having remained quiet during the night, a little after 6 o'clock I ordered the Divisions to fall back, one on the other, commencing at the outermost post, and move towards the boats, when they embarked, and returned to the ship at about ½ past 7 o'clock A.M. In about half an hour after our return Mr. Gesler [Yesler] came on board, and communicated to me that he had learned from a private source, which was worthy of attention, that the Indians were just in the edge of the woods, close to the Town, and pointed out the positions they had taken up. . . .
>
> Everything being ready, I pointed the Howitzer to a certain point on the opposite side of the marsh, where it was sup-

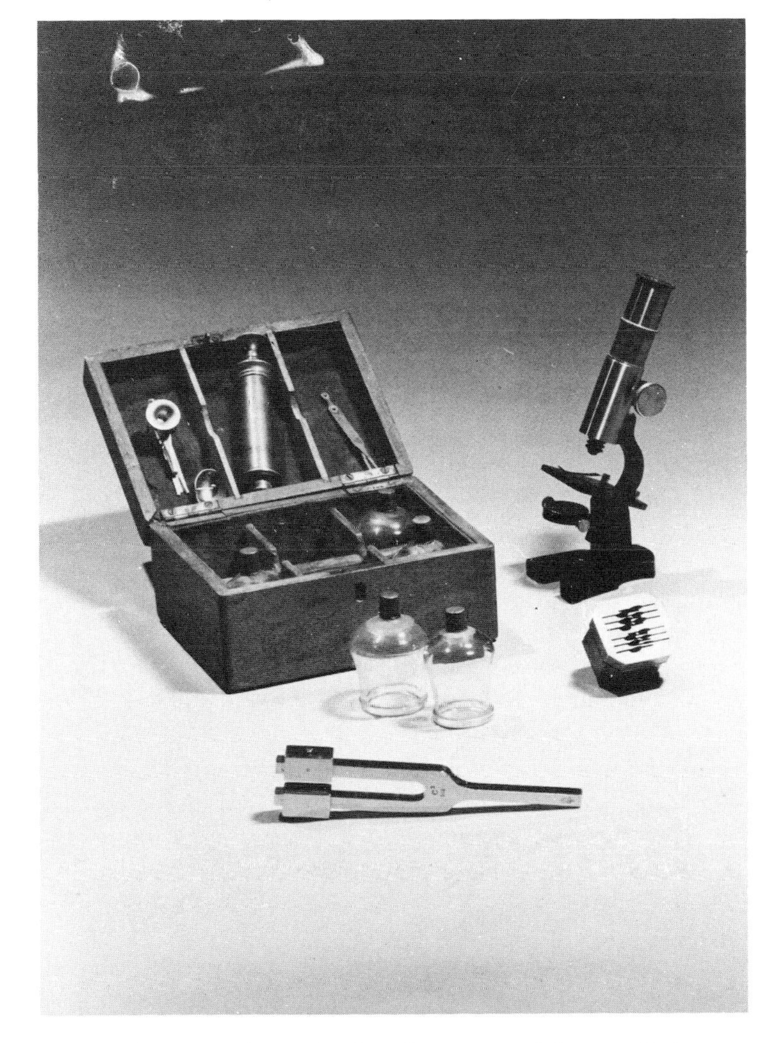

Dr. David S. Maynard, Seattle's first physician, used these medical instruments. They include a microscope, an innoculator, a tuning fork, a medicine chest, and apothecary scales. (MOHAI)

When his mother and stepfather were mortally wounded by renegade Indians in 1855, 7-year-old Johnny King fled his family's White River cabin, which burned, and led his younger sister and baby brother toward Seattle. After travelling a few terrfying miles, they were taken by a friendly Indian to safety. (MOHAI)

Top
This family portrait shows Louisa Boren Denny and David Denny with their first two children Emily Inez, on the right, and Madge Decatur. The latter was born on March 16, 1856, in the Seattle blockhouse named Fort Decatur during the Indian War. (MOHAI)

Above
Edward Hanford, shown here, married Abbie Jane Holgate and moved west at the behest of Mrs. Hanford's brother, John Holgate, the first to choose a claim site in the Seattle area. One of their sons, Cornelius Hanford, became a Chief Justice of Washington Territory and the first United States District Judge for the state. (MOHAI)

> posed the Indians were concealed, and then gave the order to "Fire." This was immediately done, and at once followed by a shell from the Ship's Battery . . . which fell in the same direction. This was followed by a loud howl from the Indians, who rushed to the edge of the Woods, when a general discharge of small arms took place, on both sites. This continued without intermission, for about half an hour, accompanied by frequent discharges from the Howitzer and shells from the Ship.

The Tom Pepper house, reportedly full of Indians, was shelled by the *Decatur,* which served as a warning to all the townspeople, most of whom were in their homes eating breakfast. The fusillade of shots from both sides and the Indian yells that followed left no doubt that this was indeed the long-rumored attack.

Louisa Boren Denny tumbled biscuits fresh from the oven into her apron, grabbed baby Inez with one hand, and raced toward the fort. Her husband David, on guard there, came out to help them. Cornelius Hanford, then seven, recalled his father carrying two of the younger children as they ran to the blockhouse. The lad, turning to close the door of their cabin, glimpsed a hostile Indian peering over a nearby log.

The *Decatur*'s cannon rained ball, shell, and grapeshot on the forest beyond Third Avenue. Volleys from rifles and musketry from sailors and civilians alike whistled about the Indians. In the fort, the women comforted the children and prayed. About noon, Sheriff Thomas Russell, who had been west of the Sound, came paddling home, bringing men from George A. Meigs' sawmill at Port Madison as reinforcements.

During the three o'clock lull in the battle, the Indians retired to feast on the settlers' livestock. Meanwhile the soldiers were called back for repast aboard the *Decatur.* At that time, many of the women and children were paddled over to the warship or to the bark *Brontes,* then laying in harbor awaiting a load of lumber. During the halt in the firing, other pioneers dashed to homes close to the fort to rescue provisions, guns, and valuables left in their hasty flight. The Indians spotted the movement and shot at them, their fire returned by the warship's howitzer.

As the short winter day waned, scouts reported back that the Indians had placed paper and kindling around some deserted homes, preparing to burn them, perhaps as a signal to the Sound Indians to join the fray. The *Decatur* shelled the area around the houses. The pioneers witnessed a tannery and several homes go up in flames.

By ten o'clock all was still. The men had partitioned off the upper part of the blockhouse with blankets for the families staying there, but only the children slept.

Two whites had died in the battle. One was Milton, the 15-year-old brother of John Holgate, who had come to the fort with a shotgun. Wanting to be in the fight—not inside the fort—just as he passed out the door, an Indian's bullet struck him in the forehead. The other was Robert Wilson.

As they left the area, the Indians destroyed every structure they passed, including those of the Duwamish settlers and Plummer's sawmill on the Black River. Nearly every building in King County was destroyed except for those within the protective range of the *Decatur*'s cannonades and those at Alki, which were far out of the way of the retreating warriors.

The only houses in King County outside the village that were not burned belonged to Thomas Mercer and David Denny. The Indians later said they spared them because these two families had been especially kind to them. The Maynards, who stayed at Port Madison during the battle, described Chief Seattle as experiencing great mental distress during the attack. Loving his own race but considering the white men his friends, he prayed the two groups might be reconciled.

The number of Indians involved in the attack on Seattle was comparatively small, perhaps two or three hundred, most from the Yakima and Klickitat areas just east of the Cascades. Yet the town might have been destroyed were it not for three factors: the *Decatur* with its delayed fuse shells and its trained crew that kept the Indians beyond Third Avenue; the friendships that had developed between some settlers and the Sound Indians, so that the former were warned and the latter remained neutral in the battle; and finally the fact that the pioneers took up arms, formed volunteer companies, built blockhouses, and worked together to keep their families and village safe.

Governor Stevens arrived in Seattle on January 29, somewhat chastened by what had happened, for he had stated just days before the attack that there was nothing to fear. He had believed all Indians would be kept on their reservations in spite of the extreme hardships they faced there. (Several settlers, including Doctor Maynard, acting as an assistant Indian agent, tried to help the Indians with food and needed supplies.)

With the coming of spring in 1856, the military authorities sent out hundreds of well-equipped regulars. The volunteers, too, remained active, with the final skirmish with Indians taking place at Connell's Prairie on March 10. But for many months the threat of Indian attack kept the remaining settlers on edge.

Although rumors circulated that the hostile Indians would return and reports abounded that they were prowling about in the vicinity of Seattle, no further trouble occurred in King County. Captain Gansevoort remained in Elliott Bay until the beginning of summer, not leaving with the *Decatur* until all danger of another attack had passed. And she was joined for a few months by the *Massachusetts* and *Active*.

Of the Indian leaders captured during or after the fighting, one was killed trying to escape, others were brought to trial and executed. Leschi and other Indian leaders claimed they should be treated as prisoners-of-war, not murderers, as they were fighting a war for their homeland; many settlers agreed. Nevertheless, Leschi was hanged. Stevens wanted the Indians punished, as they had broken "his" treaty. By 1860, emotions against the Indians had become less volatile. That year, Chief Kitsap was captured, tried, and released. And Chief Wahoolit was pardoned.

Since many pioneers remained anxious, a second blockhouse was erected at Occidental and Jackson Street, and a stockade was built across the front of Seattle from blockhouse to blockhouse. This stockade consisted of two parallel fences between which sawdust was packed to make it bullet-proof. Once the stockade offered protection, for several months settlers who lived nearby returned during the day to their homes and spent their nights in the blockhouse.

Many of the early pioneers had fascinating tales to tell of this tense time. Arthur Denny's granddaughter Roberta Frye Watt recounted some in *The Story of Seattle:*

> Dexter Horton told with a relish how the gunner of the *Decatur* aiming in the direction of the woods, shot through the little lean-to back of his store, and shot a dress of Mrs. Horton's out into the woods. Months afterward the gunner insisted on presenting Mrs. Horton with a new dress.
>
> David Denny told how during the battle he tore a great rent in his trousers; how he tried to get in some corner of the fort away from the eyes of the women in order to repair the damage temporarily, and what big stitches he took in the process.

Stories were also told about life in the blockhouse. During the long days in the fort, the women made an American flag, which was preserved by the David Denny family and eventually donated to Seattle's Museum of History and Industry. Those living in the blockhouse took turns cooking and carrying water from Yesler's mill. The children had little milk to drink since all but one cow had been stolen or killed by the Indians. In March, upstairs in the blockhouse, Louisa Denny gave birth to a second daughter, named Madge Decatur, the middle name honoring the blockhouse called Fort Decatur after the sloop-of-war that had defended Seattle.

In spring the farmers on the Duwamish planted their crops under the protection of the armed volunteers. Since trade on the Sound was largely paralyzed, local produce was of vital importance to the community.

Discouraged and frightened after the Indian attack, many pioneers left the region, moving to more populated areas in Oregon and California. In Grant's *History of Seattle*, Arthur Denny described this economically catastrophic time as:

> . . . a period of pinching want and great privation such as was never experienced here except in the winter of 1852–53.

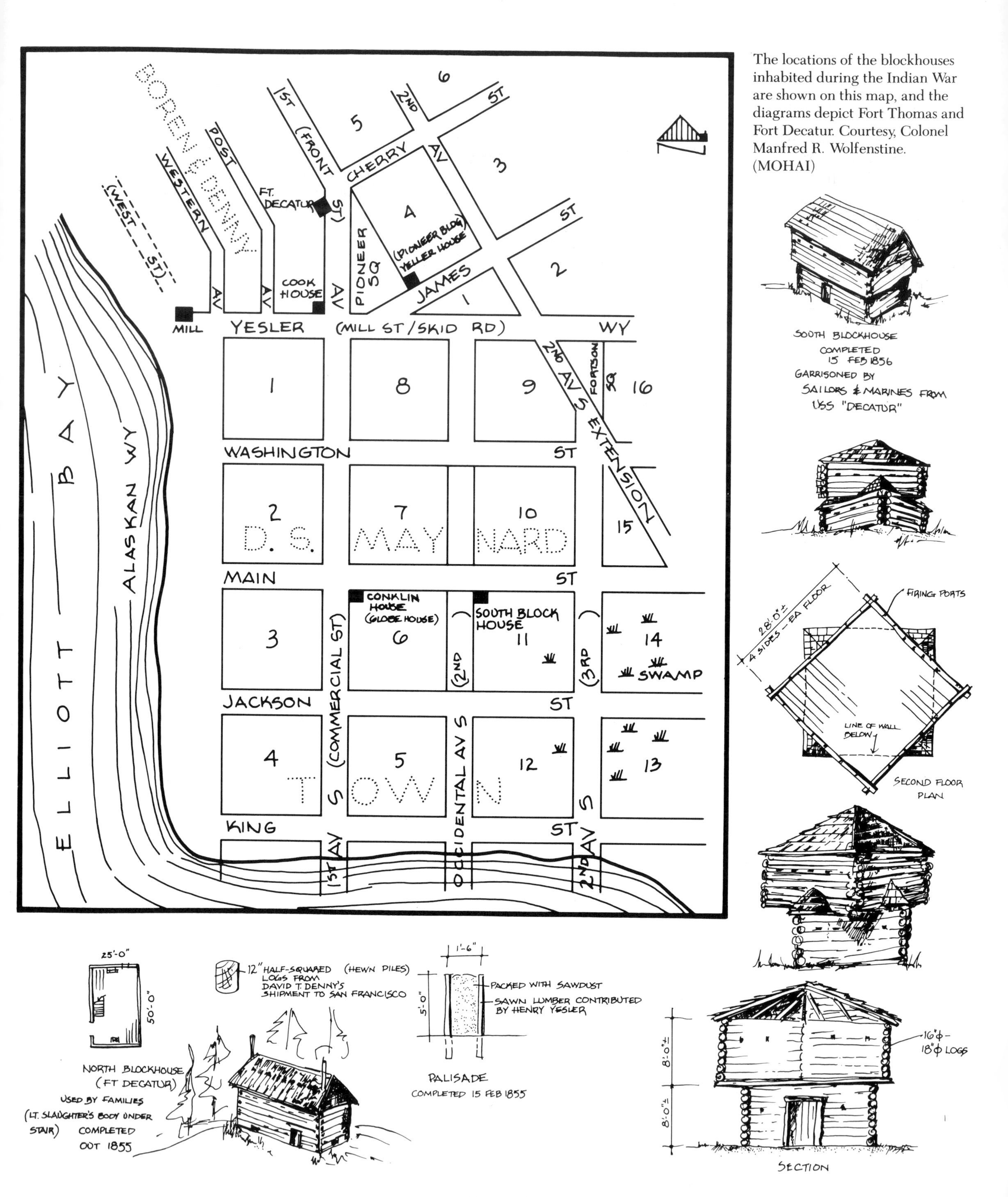

The locations of the blockhouses inhabited during the Indian War are shown on this map, and the diagrams depict Fort Thomas and Fort Decatur. Courtesy, Colonel Manfred R. Wolfenstine. (MOHAI)

> Those who remained until the war closed were so discouraged and so much in dread of another outbreak that they were unwilling to return to their homes in the country and undertake the task of rebuilding them, and in consequence it was years before we recovered our lost ground to any extent. Business was generally stagnant. Little in the way of building or improvement was attempted. Roads that had been opened before the war had most become well nigh impassable, and some of them entirely so, and active efforts were not resumed to improve our roads and open communications with the country east of the mountains until 1865, a period of ten years.

RECOVERY YEARS

After the Indian War, Seattle entered a period of slow growth caused in part by the city's lack of an economic base and by its geographic isolation. Puget Sound was cut off from the rest of the country by the Cascades; until the rails were laid, commerce was severely restricted. The days were long. About 20 men worked the 10-hour shifts at Yesler's mill, still the largest business in Seattle. Every spare hour was given over to grubbing stumps, clearing brush, improving homes, planting gardens and caring for farm animals. It was still very much a frontier economy. To break the monotony, social events such as prayer meetings, spelling contests, debates, and singing schools brought the inhabitants together.

The wedding of Edmund Carr and Olivia Holgate in the summer of 1856 provided the first opportunity after the war for a community feast. The villagers collected milk from the one cow that had escaped the Indians, chickens, eggs, venison, berries, fish, fresh vegetables, sugar, butter, flour, and rice—and started cooking. They found enough ingredients for three wedding cakes, two of which were presented to the commander and crew of the warship *Massachusetts*, which had replaced the *Decatur* in Elliott Bay. The navy men responded with a salute of the ship's cannon to the wedding pair. Since there were no clergymen in the village (the Rev. and Mrs. Blaine had moved to the Willamette Valley after the Indian attack), the ceremony was performed by Justice of the Peace E. A. Clark.

Because there were many more men than women in Seattle at this time—the ratio was about eight to one—single women did not remain so for long. During the years after the Indian attack, many weddings took place.

Though times were tough, school was held in Seattle. Miss Dorcas Phillips took up where Mrs. Blaine had left off, teaching at Bachelor's Hall. School was also scheduled in the Duwamish blockhouse.

Despite the fact that immigration diminished in the five years after the Indian war, newcomers continued to be attracted to the area. Among them were John and Sarah Denny and their eight-year-old daughter, Loretta; and the families of R. J. McMillan, Peter Andrews, Josiah Settle, L.C. Harmon, John Webster, and Samuel Coombs. Bachelors who arrived included Henry A. Atkins, who was to be elected the first mayor of Seattle after its incorporation in 1869. Other single men were Jasper Johnson, Dillis Ward, Hugh McAleer, John Carr, A. S. Pinkham, David Graham, D. K. Baxter, Edwin Richardson, and William Cheney. Manuel Lopes, a black man, worked as a barber and opened a small restaurant. These newcomers opened businesses or worked in the local industries to augment their incomes as they settled in new homes.

On January 16, 1857, the territorial legislature separated off the western portion of King County, naming it "Slaughter" County after the lieutenant killed in the Indian War. Its citizens, however, did not like the name's connotations and later changed it, ironically, to Kitsap, to honor an Indian, who many believed had led his people against the whites. (In 1868 a town in King County was also named to honor Lt. Slaughter, but its residents later changed the name to Auburn.)

In the summer of 1857, horror and dread again swept through Seattle and King County when Indians from Vancouver Island, intent on revenge for the loss of one of their

Mother Joseph (1823–1902) established the first hospital services in Seattle. Altogether she founded 11 hospitals, seven academies, five Indian schools, and two orphanages. Courtesy, Archives of Sisters of Providence, Seattle.

BLACK PIONEERS

John T. Gayton, son of former slaves, came to Seattle in 1899 and became Federal Court Librarian in 1933. Courtesy, Esther Mumford.

The names Manuel Lopes, Big Bill Grose, Matthias F. Monet, Archy Fox, and Thomas Freeman may be unfamiliar to Seattleites, yet each played an important role in the city's history. They were black Seattleites, and they were not written about by early historians.

These pioneers worked to gain equal treatment. When the state constitution was adopted in 1890, a public accommodations act passed at the same time carried fines of $50 to $300 for denying accommodations on the basis of race, color, or nationality. It was amended in 1895 to include eating houses and barbershops, but the penalty clause was omitted. Hence, the law was ineffectual, and local public accommodations were not always open to blacks.

Manuel Lopes, one of Seattle's first pioneers, arrived in 1852. He opened a barbershop on First Avenue South, and later operated a restaurant.

Lopes was Seattle's first black resident, businessman, and property owner. He was noted for his generosity, often furnishing meals to workingmen when they had no money. He also was a snare drummer (Seattle's first) and led each Fourth of July procession. He used the same drum to signal when his restaurant meals were ready. Lopes sold his holding and sometime after 1870 moved to Port Gamble.

Matthias F. Monet arrived in 1864. An excellent cook, he was soon operating the "Seattle Restaurant and Coffee Saloon." He later changed this operation to an oyster house. In that same year Monet opened a barbershop with William Hedges.

Archy Fox arrived in 1866 and opened a barbershop and bathhouse at First and Yesler. Three years later he was associated with Hedges in operating the "Pioneer Bathing and Shaving Saloon."

Thomas P. Freeman and family arrived in 1872 and began making shoes, and in 1876 opened the "Pioneer Variety Store." Three years later he entered the commission and storage business and sold Howe sewing machines. Burned out in the fire of 1889, carrying only $800 insurance, he moved away.

Big Bill Grose (or Gross) stood six foot, four inches tall and weighed about 400 pounds. He arrived in Seattle in 1860, opened "Our House" restaurant and later a hotel, and became an influential black leader. He was active in the western underground railroad that helped blacks escape to Canada.

Robert O. Lee, educated in North Carolina in 1889, was the first black admitted to the Washington State Bar. J. Edward Hawkins was the first locally trained lawyer. He came to Seattle in 1890, worked as a barber, and became acquainted and studied law with several white attorneys.

Black doctors were also practicing in Seattle before the turn of the century: Joshua Rysnowden, Charles Shadd, E.E. Makiell. Veterinarians had practices too.

It is clear that black citizens helped build the frontier town and county. And in many instances, their descendents live in Seattle still.—**condensed by James R. Warren from Esther Mumford's** ***Seattle's Black Victorians, 1852–1901***

high-ranking tribe members, swept down from the north and came ashore at Whidbey Island to murder Colonel Isaac Ebey, one of the best-known pioneer leaders. However, this remained an isolated incident that was not repeated.

In 1858 and 1859, gold was found in the Fraser River Valley in British Columbia, attracting about 30,000 men from California. Almost overnight Victoria changed from a fort to a town and Whatcom (now Bellingham), became a tent city of 10,000. Although a few of the miners went through Seattle, the village did not experience much benefit. The founders themselves were too busy attending to the town's survival to join the gold seekers.

After a while, though, men who had traveled up to the Fraser River gold fields often migrated south to settle in King County. They, along with enterprising men who came west from other parts of the country, became involved in farming, setting up a variety of businesses, opening hotels and saloons, and even establishing a foundry.

Industry struggled along. Yesler's sawmill kept steaming away, but the San Francisco boom was now over. Besides, there were larger mills on the Sound, and only occasionally were shipments of lumber sent out of Seattle. Arthur Denny and George Frye became associated with Yesler's sawmill, and the three men erected a gristmill and a meeting room known as Yesler Hall. When cash grew ever more scarce, the pioneers helped each other. Frye took lumber in lieu of his wages as sawyer at the mill and in this way started construction of business buildings.

Charles Plummer, one of the most energetic businessmen, built a wharf near his mercantile building and then constructed an open-flume water system, which could furnish ships with fresh water. In 1859 he and Charles Terry developed a business, supplying pack trains going east of the Cascades to the newly discovered gold fields in eastern Washington fields, which in 1860 drew so many men from Seattle that for a time Yesler's mill had to close.

Astute Charlie Terry also developed a farm on the Duwamish. In 1857, when Dr. Maynard was figuring that Seattle might never amount to much, he traded his unplatted 260 acres in downtown Seattle for 319 acres Terry had at Alki, now West Seattle. The Maynards moved there to farm, and he and Catherine became renowned for their hospitality. The Indians frequently camped about their simple home, partaking of their generosity.

Dexter Horton, with David Phillips, continued general merchandising at First and Washington. During that time Horton began rudimentary banking services, which consisted of stashing money about the store tied in little bags with the owners' names attached. Finally, Horton bought a safe and would toss the money bags into it. A slip of paper in each bag kept track of deposits and withdrawals. He would eventually open Seattle's first real bank—today's Seattle First National.

Right
In this view down to Yesler's mill on Mill Street (now Yesler Way) from Front Street (now First Avenue), the mill is in operation. People are standing in front of the Pioneer Drug Store. (MOHAI)

Below
Settler women made this "Petticoat Flag" from blouses and petticoats during the 1856 armed conflict with the Indians. Not knowing the current number of stars or their arrangement, they placed 13 from the original states down at random on the blue field. (MOHAI)

LUMBERING

Early Seattle, like all communities on the Puget Sound frontier, depended at first on exploiting the forest. Soon after their landing at Alki Point in 1851, Seattle's founders loaded timber on a vessel bound for California. Unfavorable wind and tide conditions at Alki led the settlers to relocate on the eastern shore of Elliott Bay, where ships could anchor and take on piling for the San Francisco market. In late 1852 Henry L. Yesler built the town's first sawmill. Yesler's mill, the first steam-powered plant on Puget Sound, was for many years the focus of economic life in the community. Settlers worked in the mill and sold timber cut on their claims. Logs arrived at the mill skidded down from the hillside above the bay via the original "skid road"—today's Yesler Way. Lumber cargoes linked Seattle with the bustling port of San Francisco and with the exotic markets of the Pacific Basin.

Seattle, though, never ranked with the major 19th century lumbering ports. Henry Yesler lacked the capital and business skills to expand the mill, to acquire shipping, and to properly exploit markets. The great lumbermen of the era preferred to locate their mills at isolated points on the western shore of Puget Sound and on Hood Canal, where there were no rival land claimants and where timber was free for the taking. Henry Yesler was actually only a minor figure in the lumber industry; his ultimate historical importance rests on the fact that his crude mill allowed the community of Seattle to survive during its initial precarious decades of existence.

The completion of transcontinental railroads and the rapid growth of population in the late 1880s caused Seattle to boom at last. Among the new arrivals, C. D. Stimson, the wealthy and one-armed son of a prominent Michigan lumbering family, reached Seattle just in time to help fight the great fire of 1889. Following the conflagration, the Seattle lumber industry was transferred from the valuable Elliott Bay waterfront to Lake Union and to Ballard, then an independent community north of the city limits. In Ballard, Stimson founded the only major lumbering operation in Seattle's history, the Stimson Mill Company. During the 1890s, with Stimson leading the way, Ballard also became the leading shingle producer in the world. National tariff policies and declining markets, however, sent shingle manufacturing into a permanent decline in the early 20th century, forced the closure of the Stimson mill, and ended the brief period in which Seattle ranked with Tacoma, Everett, and Bellingham as a major source of forest products.

Ironically, the failure of Seattle to become a center of lumber manufacturing was a crucial factor in the city's ultimate success. In the early years, when the economy of western Washington was based almost entirely on lumbering, the town lagged far behind its competitors. Over the long term, however, Seattle avoided dependence on the economically unstable industry and developed a diversified economy based on trade and such services as banking. During the severe depression of the mid-1890s, Tacoma and other mill towns failed to grow in population. Seattle, though, continued to expand and established permanently its dominant position on Puget Sound.

—Robert E. Ficken

Top: The first load of logs arrives in Seattle on the Columbia and Puget Sound Railroad. Middle: The first Shay locomotive to come to the Pacific Northwest hauled logs. Bottom: Western Mill, founded by David T. Denny, operated at the south end of Lake Union, circa 1909. (MOHAI)

Chief Leschi, the son of a Nisqually chief, was accused by Governor Stevens of playing a leading role in the Battle of Seattle. Leschi was tried for the deaths of two federal volunteers at Connell's Prairie in 1855, during his role in the uprising. Hanged on February 18, 1858, he was buried on the Nisqually Reservation. (MOHAI)

George Frye, a German immigrant, arrived in Seattle in 1853 and began to work as a sawyer in Yesler's mill. Frye established several of Seattle's firsts: a meat market, a grist mill, and a brass band. He also acted as the town's first Santa Claus. He built and managed the Frye Opera House, which burned in the 1889 fire, and completed the Frye Hotel before he died in 1912. (MOHAI)

After Henry Van Asselt opened a cabinet shop, his curly maple furniture was much in demand. E.A. Clark became Seattle's first photographer, his specialty being "ambrotypes." Lewis Wyckoff ran the village livery stable. Captain John S. Hill, in his little sternwheeler *Ranger*, jobbed up and down the Sound. Dr. Josiah Settle acted as a nurse as well as a doctor and later went into the clothing business. David Denny farmed and logged on his land north of the village, though he, Louisa, and their children lived in their home at Second and Seneca.

While Seattle and King County had been set back financially and psychologically by the Indian attack, the rest of the Puget Sound district was busily exploiting its products. In 1857 exports worth $543,000 were carried away on 171 ships. Of this, $261,000 was for sawed rough lumber and $55,000 for dressed lumber. Also exported in some quantity were whale and fish oil, potatoes, cattle, horses, onions, cranberries, coal, animal skins, salmon, and flour. As a sign of the times, in 1858 the Southworth Company of San Francisco sent the first McCormick reapers to Puget Sound.

That same year, Dr. Maynard, out on his Alki farm, harvested and chopped kelp and spread it on his vegetable garden as fertilizer. He reported that it increased his potato crop tremendously. The area was becoming known for its enormous fruits and vegetables. (Two heads of cabbage weighing 59 pounds and two beets weighing 24 pounds were recorded by Luther Collins on his Duwamish farm.) After awhile, however, Maynard—missing the active social life in Seattle—grew tired of farming and began trying to sell his Alki holdings. It took a few years for him to sell his 314 remaining acreage for $450, enabling the Maynards to move back to the village.

Frederick Grant, an early Seattle historian, referred to those "dull and quiet times" of the late 1850s and early '60s as actually a period of accomplishment for the city. In this era the dream was formed for securing a railroad, that all-important transportation and communication system that sped up the pace of the Industrial Revolution and greatly accelerated the settlement of previously isolated regions. During the first legislative session after the Indian War, the ambitious young lawmakers of Washington Territory organized the "Northern Pacific Railroad Company," which was to extend from Puget Sound to the Rocky Mountains (then the eastern border of the territory). But being all talk and no capital, nothing came of it. Later, a different Northern Pacific would bring iron rails to the region.

In the decade to come, Seattleites would begin to concentrate on improving, by various means, the accessibility of their chosen place. Railroad or no railroad, whether connected by land or sea, their town's future prospects depended on linking a still-remote region with other markets and with centers of population that could send families to help build their city.

CHAPTER 5

CITY IN THE MAKING: 1860 - 1869

The year 1860 was launched in Seattle with a New Year's Ball organized by the young people. They invited "all creation" but commented afterward that the journey was too far for most people.

The 1860 census showed King County's population at 303, with 179 of this number men over 21 years of age. Real estate was evaluated at $71,300, personal property at $175,580. In all of the county there were 287 milk cows, 55 horses, 40 work cattle, and 230 swine. The farms produced 1,395 bushels of wheat, 920 of oats, 773 of peas, and 14,282 of potatoes; they also yielded 99 tons of hay and 2,655 pounds of butter.

ROAD BUILDING

The push continued for roads to connect towns within the Pacific Northwest and the Puget Sound region with other areas. A wagon road through the Cascades was being planned, especially after a gold find in eastern Washington again demonstrated that Puget Sound was cut off from the lands east of the mountains rich in farmlands and now, apparently, gold. In August 1859 Maynard, Yesler, and Arthur Denny were appointed a committee to solicit funds for a road through Snoqualmie Pass. They raised $1,050 and requested legislative help but, impatient to begin, they hired T.D. Hinckley as superintendent. Soon the part of the road between North Bend and Snoqualmie Falls was surveyed and cleared, with some grading done.

The legislature memorialized Congress for two roads: one that would connect eastern Washington with the seaports on Puget Sound and a military route to Walla Walla through Snoqualmie Pass. When Congress responded favorably, a bill appropriating $75,000 was introduced, but the Civil War interfered, so it was never enacted.

In July of 1859 a contract had been let by the territory to clear the road between Steilacoom and Bellingham Bay. By October 1860 the road was completed as far as Lewis's Ferry, and two months later the first mail to come overland from Steilacoom to Seattle arrived, though the service was soon discontinued. In the same year the Reverend Daniel Bagley, his wife Susannah, and son Clarence became the first family to arrive in Seattle on wheels. They drove from Salem in a buggy drawn by two horses.

In 1865 the citizens of King County, still wanting to build a wagon road across the Cascades, held a mass meeting. While John Denny and Henry Yesler went about securing funds, Lewis Wyckoff, Arthur Denny, John Ross, and William Perkins explored the passes through the Cascades, intent on finding the most favorable route. With Indian guides, they discovered the lower Snoqualmie Pass. (An earlier pass called that was nearby but at a higher elevation.) The solicitors raised $2,500, and a contract was given to William Perkins to build the new road. By November he and his 20 workers had opened 25 miles. In the following spring and summer they finished the road. Though it had steep grades, it was passable. In October a train of six wagons arrived in Seattle over Snoqualmie Pass.

That little road over the pass, however, proved horrendous to maintain. Trees fell across it, bridges were washed away, and grades were gullied. It also terminated at Lake Keechelus, where wagons had to be loaded on log rafts and poled to the other end. On stormy days, which came often, it made a fearful trip. In 1867, with $2,000 in matching money from the territorial legislature, the road was continued past the lake to the Cedar River pack trail.

In spite of its problems, that road broke the barrier between eastern Washington and the Puget Sound country. When J.E. Wyche, a district judge, traveled the road in the fall of 1867 on his way from Walla Walla to Port Townsend, he told of meeting Northern Pacific Railroad surveyors in the mountains. Seattle really sparked at that news, since a railway by now meant prosperity to a town along its route, especially to a terminus on a waterway.

During the next two decades, there would be more surveying, legislation, and hard labor, for the pioneers not only built the road through the Cascades but also kept it open.

THE CIVIL WAR

Indirectly, Washingtonians witnessed the growing dispute elsewhere over the institution of slavery, which would soon convulse the nation after Lincoln's election to the Presidency in November 1860. Many of the settlers had moved to

Photograph by Victor Gardaya
(MOHAI)

In 1860 a flume carried fresh water past Henry Yesler's house to his mill from a spring at Third Avenue. Courtesy, Historical Photography Collection, U of W Libraries.

the Pacific Northwest from the political crucible of the Midwest and brought with them strong feelings for independence from external authority and devotion to the principle of local self-government. During the early territorial period, the Democrats were in control because the Whigs were considered by many frontiersmen as the party of aristocracy and wealth.

King County settlers felt a strong kinship with the national government, for land grants, military protection, and road building were largely federal activities. As a group they tended to develop a conservative attitude toward the slavery issue. Most were opposed to the militant antislavery position of the more radical Republicans as well as to the adamant stand of the secessionists in the South. The majority seemed willing for slavery to exist in order to save the Union.

Oregon Territory, at the time, was home to a small number of slaves, tolerated in spite of the slavery prohibition in the Territorial Organic Act. Fearing the region might become a refuge for "free Negroes" early in the governmental development, blacks were prohibited from settling in Oregon Territory. Keeping blacks from the territory, it was hoped, would also prevent the agitation sweeping the rest of the nation from flaring locally. When Oregon was admitted to the Union as a free state in 1859, much of the controversy dissipated, although slavery did remain a political issue until the end of the Civil War.

News of the lead-up to the War Between the States and then of the battles and other events took several months to arrive in Puget Sound. Since the community was still recovering from its own Indian War, at first it believed that the Union was in no real danger. With the battles being fought a continent's breadth away, Seattle residents did not fully comprehend the seriousness of the crisis. However, the pioneers, somewhat passive at first, gradually became more vocal as accounts of the tremendous struggle and its casualties filtered west. Emotion increased further when rumors were circulated of possible Southern attempts to seize ships and recruit soldiers on the West Coast.

Union clubs were organized in towns and the anti-Union stance, which at first was popular, gradually lost favor with the citizenry. In December 1862 the legislature, largely made up of outspoken Union supporters, adopted resolutions against secession and strongly supporting the Union.

In Seattle, political partisanship increased tremendously. At one time, the opposing factions almost refused to trade with one another. The Republicans—Mercer, Bagley, the Dennys, and Dexter Horton—actively opposed Yesler, Maynard, Terry, and Plummer, who were accused of being Copperheads, or Southern sympathizers. The partisanship, however, was largely a party feeling rather than a fundamental difference of belief concerning slavery. The Democrats were not proslavery Democrats. Besides, all were too far from the national struggle to become personally involved. As the war progressed, the Democrats, under the leadership of Terry, Plummer, Joe Foster, and Thomas Russell, formed a Union branch, held a convention, and strongly denounced slavery. Common local problems inevitably drew the settlers together again, and during the Civil War years they accomplished some of their most important community projects.

President Lincoln appointed Arthur Denny to the land office and Christopher Hewitt as Chief Justice of Washington Territory. He also appointed John J. McGilvra of Illinois as U.S. Attorney for the territory. When McGilvra came to the territory he cracked down on land frauds and timber cutting on federal lands co-opted by timber companies.

In the spring of 1861, Acting Governor Henry McGill called upon all citizens capable of bearing arms and of age for military duty to organize by counties and regiments in order to be ready to meet any call by President Lincoln. In November the King County Rifles organized as a private, independent organization, which was self-armed and self-governed. Their primary purposes were to admonish Southern sympathizers and to foster Union sentiment. They met and marched, but did little else.

During this period, old John Denny, who had served with Lincoln in the Illinois legislature, made a trip back to Washington, D.C., to help Daniel Bagley gain support for locating the new territorial university in Seattle. Thinking to test Lincoln's memory, Denny joined the reception line at the White House. When it came his turn, he simply shook hands with the President and was passing on when his old friend called out, "No you don't, John Denny! You come around here and we'll have a talk after a while." They later visited and laughed over old times.

One of the saddest days in the territory was when the news arrived of Major General Isaac Stevens' death at the Battle of Chantilly. This first governor of the territory had earned the respect of even some of his political foes. "He was a Democrat and I was a Whig," Arthur Denny wrote, "but he paid the supreme sacrifice and I have only praise for his memory." However, others, including pioneer Ezra Meeker, were not so kind.

Seattleites read the latest, delayed news—relayed up the coast by ships from San Francisco, which now had the transcontinental telegraph—in their very own newspaper, the *Gazette*. By the fall of 1864, when telegraph lines had stretched up to Seattle from San Francisco, the final war dispatches arrived over the wire. So did word of Lincoln's assassination. Bells were tolled, flags hung at half-staff, and a memorial service was held. In the ensuing election, Republicans in Washington Territory won their first big victory and Arthur Denny was elected King County's delegate to Congress.

FOUNDING THE UNIVERSITY OF WASHINGTON

Shortly after Washington became a territory, Governor Isaac Stevens proposed that the legislative assembly petition Congress for a university grant. The suggestion was adopted, and on March 22, 1854, a memorial was sent to the national capital asking Congress to donate two townships to Washington Territory in order to support a university. Within a year Congress acted, and on July 17, 1854, President Franklin Pierce signed the bill stating that: "There shall be reserved to each of the territories of Washington and Oregon two Townships of land of thirty-six sections each, to be selected in legal subdivisions for the universities' purposes under the direction of the legislatures of said Territories respectively."

The location of this university immediately became a political exercise that found the legislators changing the location of the institution at almost every session. In 1861, when the legislators finally assigned the territorial university to Seattle, Arthur Denny decided to take the matter seriously.

Daniel Bagley, John Webster, and Edmund Carr were named commissioners, with Bagley elected president. In Seattle the project lacked monetary support. The acreages intended to support the university were located far from the settlement and priced above the going rate by the legislature. There was also a requirement that the local citizens provide matching acreage for the campus itself. The problems seemed unsolvable. Arthur Denny first offered a 10-acre campus for the university at the northern edge of his property, but when attempting to survey the area, he found it an impossible tangle of brush and trees. He decided instead to provide eight and one half acres on his knoll above the town. The additional acre and a half was provided by C.C. Terry and Ed Lander. Even that knoll was forested with giant firs. Seattle's male population was soon earning $2.50 to $4.50 per day in clearing the area.

George A. Meigs' Port Madison mill and Yesler's Seattle mill provided most of the lumber for the buildings; Meigs was sold a large tract of university-owned land for $25,000. Carpenters and workmen sometimes, in lieu of pay, received a receipt in the value of the work. For this receipt they could select land in like value from the support tracts.

In the construction, foundation stone came from a Port Orchard quarry, and brick and lime from Bellingham; glass and hardware were imported from Victoria. Forty-eight men were employed in the construction and before winter the university building, its boardinghouse, and the president's home stood white and imposing atop the hill. A white picket fence was placed around the campus and the whole institution was turned over to the regents. Total cost: $35,000.

Daniel Bagley sold additional university reserve lands to raise funds for furniture and supplies. He gave $23,000 to the regents as an endowment, but the fund was soon expended. Other towns, realizing Seattle meant to keep the university, charged misuse of funds, but several investigations over ensuing years showed that the Reverend Mr. Bagley's books were essentially in order. Though some of the processes might be questioned, no funds had been diverted nor was there undue personal gain for anyone involved. To this day, Bagley is often referred to as the "father" of the University of Washington, a title he shares with Arthur Denny.

The first classes met on November 4, 1861. Not until 1877, however, would direct legislative aid be provided to Seattle's new educational institution. Operational funds depended principally on tuition. Whatever the problems the young university had, those buildings on the hill served as a constant reminder that Seattle was the home of the territorial

Opposite, top
The south side of the Territorial University building as it appeared circa 1875. It was erected in 1861 on Arthur Denny's Knoll, now the site of the Olympic Hotel. The columns stand preserved in a sylvan setting on the present University of Washington campus. (MOHAI)

Opposite, bottom
An imposing structure, Seattle's first large centralized school stood on Seventh between Madison and Marion. It was also the first school of more than two rooms to be built in the town. The school opened in 1883, only to be destroyed by fire in 1888. (MOHAI)

PUBLISHING THE NEWS

The *Intelligencer* was published in this building between 1876 and 1881, before it merged with the *Post* to become the *Post-Intelligencer.* (MOHAI)

This printing press, made by Adam Ramage in the early 1800s, printed Seattle's first newspaper, the *Gazette*, in 1863. (MOHAI)

The frontier editor of the 1860s was a "capable printer who could set type, run a press, make up the forms, make a roller and wash it if need be. He was editorial writer, local reporter, business manager, and mailing clerk. A 'job office' was usually part of the printing establishment and he had to be his own job printer and pressman as well." So wrote Clarence Bagley of a field he knew intimately as a youth.

James R. Watson was just such a man. After printing a few sample newspapers on the old Ramage press in Olympia and trying them out with some success on Seattleites, he commenced printing the *Seattle Gazette* in December of 1863.

Watson, always broke, gathered quarters from several friends in order to pay the "collect" costs on war dispatches before the telegraph office would let him have them. He then would repay his friends by revealing the contents of the dispatch before distributing the *Gazette*.

The paper was issued spasmodically, as the news collected. Watson was described as full of humor, the central figure of a coterie of jovial spirits that congregated nightly in the editor's sanctum or at a place with a bar, a stove, a score of rawhide-bottomed chairs, and sawdust-covered floors.

Gazette offices were in the Gem Saloon building at First Avenue South near Yesler Way, in space provided by Henry Yesler. Watson, a colorful character, was a bachelor who arranged his kitchen, parlor, and bedroom in one half of the print shop. Because sweeping raised dust, which he claimed was bad for his printing, he seldom swept. For food, he had the run of Yesler's cellar, where the millman kept a supply of apples, potatoes, and other vegetables. If Yesler allowed the store to run low, Watson would soon reprove him for this neglect.

The rollers for the press were homemade, a combination of glue and molasses boiled down to a rubber-like consistency. Watson hired an Indian boy to ink his presses. Since the lad loved molasses, one day he ate a discarded roller and became wretchedly ill. Clarence Bagley had to substitute as roller boy that day.

Watson severed his connection with the paper in 1865 and its new owners suspended publication in March of 1866. Next year, Samuel Maxwell came to town from San Francisco and soon founded the *Weekly Intelligencer*, the first paper to survive and a forerunner of today's *Post-Intelligencer*. David Higgins, from Victoria, bought the paper in 1874 but sold out to Thaddeus Hanford. After having several different owners, the *Intelligencer* became a daily in 1876. In 1878 the *Post* was established but after a fitful existence it merged with the *Intelligencer*. In 1886 following the anti-Chinese riots, a group from the Law and Order party purchased the *Post-Intelligencer* to communicate their side of that divisive episode.

In the '80s, several journals started up, and merged into the *Times* in 1887. At about the same time a paper called *The Press* was founded. Soon thereafter, W.E. Bailey bought the *Times* and consolidated the two papers as the *Press-Times*. Just as the paper ran into financial difficulties, Colonel Alden J. Blethen, an experienced newspaperman, appeared on the scene. He bought the *Press-Times* which became a great success as the *Seattle Times*.

The first issue of the *Argus*, Seattle's oldest weekly newspaper appeared on February 17, 1894. Other papers too were sprouting up and merging. *The Daily Bulletin* in 1916 was sold to the *Seattle Daily Record*, which in 1919 changed its name to the *Seattle Daily Journal of Commerce*.—**James R. Warren** university—a portent, perhaps, of intellectual accomplishments to come. During those early years it was used as a tuition school for all levels and for public meetings. From 1863 to 1877 the university saw a succession of presidents but there was little interest on the community's part in providing serious scholars. In some years, no college-level classes were conducted, and not until 1876 did the university grant its first degree—to Clara McCarty.

Asa Shinn Mercer, only 23 years of age, was selected the first president of the university. A graduate of Franklin College in New Athens, Ohio, he had joined elder brother Thomas in Seattle in 1861 and during preparation of the campus he worked as a laborer. After him came a series of short-term presidents. Professor Alexander J. Anderson assumed the presidency in 1877, and in the following year the legislature appropriated $1,500 in the form of scholarships. Now students began to be attracted and the curriculum was enlarged. Though it still faced many lean years ahead, the university was deepening its roots.

MERCER GIRLS

Seattle and King County in the early 1860s had a shortage of the "fair sex." This was thought "most bothersome," for women were considered to be agents of civilization on the frontier. Not only did bachelors miss the cooking, sewing, and companionship provided by a "good wife"; the community itself missed the teaching, morality, and civic good works that womenfolk traditionally offered.

Moreover, a frequent embarrassment to the community was the practice of single men forming common-law marriages or alliances with Indian women. What was standard and acceptable among fur traders was beyond the pale of proper society in a town. Inevitably, the whites would be called "squaw men," and they, their wives, and their children were often ostracized by both townspeople and Indians.

The absence of women was a common topic for conversation among the residents. Charles Prosch, editor of the *Puget Sound Herald*, wrote on this subject. His articles encouraged the single males of the area to meet in Steilacoom to address the problem. This public advertisement, written by Prosch, appeared in his paper on February 24, 1860:

> Attention, Bachelors: Believing that our only chance of a realization of the benefits and early attainments of matrimonial alliances depends upon the arrival in our midst of a number of the fair sex from the Atlantic States, and that, to bring about such an arrival a united effort and action are called for on our part, we respectfully request a full attendance of all eligible and sincerely desirous bachelors in this community to assemble on Tuesday evening next in DeLin and Shorey's building to devise ways and means to secure this much needed and desirable emigration to our shores.

A few years after the first "bachelor's meeting" was called, Asa Mercer became interested in this situation. Asa had served as the university's first president and was well-known in the community. His personal interest in the project probably was due to the fact that he was himself one of the community's single young men. Full of vitality and imagination, he conceived of a unique plan to solve the local "problem." His plan was to travel to New England, home to many widows and orphans of the ongoing Civil War, and to a disproportionate number of marriageable spinsters. He hoped to convince young women of the East to emigrate West. Asa spoke of his plan with Governor William Pickering and with legislators. Receiving hearty official approval but no financial backing, he proceeded to seek private contributions sufficient to pay his expenses to Boston.

Once in the East, Asa, a charming and well-educated fellow, explained his proposition to many a young woman. He did not mention matrimony, only Seattle's salubrious cli-

The Reverend Daniel Bagley brought his family to Seattle from Salem, Oregon, in 1860. He was instrumental in securing the University of Washington for Seattle. (MOHAI)

mate, the natural beauty of the area, and the good livings that would be earned by women who could teach, sew, cook, and provide other "womanly" labors. The sheer adventure of the trip, as well as the independence it would bring to the young women, was undoubtedly attractive.

Eleven young women finally agreed to make the trip. Considering this mid-Victorian era, it was quite remarkable that this group of refined Eastern women agreed to journey to the rough-and-ready frontier. Daniel Pearson, father of two young travelers, came along with Asa to act as a chaperon. The passengers left New York in March 1864, bound for Washington Territory via the Isthmus of Panama and San Francisco. They arrived in Seattle at midnight on May 16. No one had known when to expect them, and at that late hour the newcomers were led up the dark wharf to the DeLin House on the corner of Commercial and Main streets and given rooms. The next morning the word spread quickly that Asa and his "girls" had arrived. Socials were arranged for the group, and since many of the young women were musical, song soon filled the air.

Before the summer was over, most of the new arrivals had found jobs, several as teachers. They settled in various communities in the Puget Sound area. Daniel Pearson and his two daughters went to Whidbey Island, where he sold shoes brought from Massachusetts. He then became the lighthouse keeper at Fort Casey. Both daughters worked as teachers. One young woman stayed only a short time and then apparently moved to San Francisco. The rest of the original group stayed in the area, and all but one married. Only Lizzie Ordway, the oldest of the group, remained single. She taught school at Whidbey Island and then Port Madison, and later became Superintendent of Schools in Kitsap County.

The success of Mercer's plan resulted in his nomination for the position of territorial senator; without campaigning he

Clara McCarty received the first college diploma from the University of Washington when she earned her Bachelor of Science degree in 1876. A women's dormitory has been named in her honor. Courtesy, Special Collections, University of Washington Libraries (UW 3269)

Asa Mercer was the first "principal" of the Territorial University, holding the office from 1861–1863 while still a young man in his twenties. He and Mrs. Virginia Calhoun taught all primary, grammar, and high school grades, as there were no college-level students during those first years. He later brought the "Mercer Girls" to Seattle, married one of them, and moved to Wyoming in 1883. (MOHAI) won the election. He also decided to try again with a grander scheme, planning this time to transport several hundred young women to the Northwest. Mercer relied once more on the fact that many young women with little chance of marriage resided in New England. He also knew that, since the war would soon be ending, many government ships would be lying idle while thousands of seamen were still on government payrolls.

Mercer had known President Lincoln, and indeed as a child had sat on his lap and listened to his stories. He was confident the President would back his scheme, so he sailed East again. His ship arrived in New York about noon and he entrained for the nation's capital that evening. As he entered his hotel at dawn, he noted crepe draped across the door and upon inquiry learned that the President had been assassinated the night before.

Convinced that there would be no help in Washington now, young Mercer decided to call on the Massachusetts Governor John A. Andrew, a popular and influential man. Andrew appreciated his plan and introduced Mercer to Edward Everett Hale, who in turn provided connections. Mercer developed much moral support but no one seemed willing to aid him financially. Finally, Mercer called on General Ulysses S. Grant, who had once served at Fort Vancouver and knew Washington Territory well. Grant promptly wrote an order for a steamship to be coaled and manned to transport up to

PUBLIC SCHOOLS BEGIN

Catherine and David Blaine. (MOHAI)

Mrs. David E. (Catherine) Blaine, Seattle's first schoolteacher, held classes in Bachelors' Hall, which had been built as a single men's boardinghouse. This tuition school opened in 1854, with fees paid by parents. After the university building was completed in 1861, classes for school-age children were conducted on the premises, again at a fee. By 1865 the need for a free common school in Seattle became apparent. New families, it was argued, would not move there unless educational services were provided. The population included at least 75 children, many roaming the streets. Since the territorial legislature had passed a law providing for the establishment and maintenance of county schools, parents asked King County to pay the university to provide free schooling.

At a meeting in Yesler's Hall in 1867, a school board was elected and the citizens decided to erect a school. Taxes were voted for in 1869 to pay for land and construction. In the summer of 1870 the city's first school building was finished at a total cost of $2,500. On August 15, Miss Lizzie Ordway, one of the Mercer Girls, rang the bell that opened that first "Central School." So many students showed up that she sent the younger ones home "to ripen a little," and until accommodations were ready and more teachers were hired. On that day, Seattle School District No. 1 began a century of almost constant growth. Following Seattle's example, in the succeeding years other settlements in King County built public schools, some starting as cabins made of logs or split cedar.

In 1871, 295 schoolchildren were counted in the district, but only 130 were in classes. Since more classrooms were needed, North and South Schools were built, simple one-story structures located at Third and Pine and Sixth and Main. In 1874 Professor John H. Hall, formerly president of the university, became superintendent. He implemented many changes: he restricted the social life of teachers, developed honor rolls and blacklists, and segregated students into grades for the first time.

In periods of overcrowding and for purposes of dispensing special education, private schools helped to fill educational needs. By 1880 Seattle had five public and three private schools serving between 700 and 800 students. From time to time, space for classes was leased from the university. In 1882 citizens agreed to tax themselves $24,000 to build a large new Central School building at the Sixth and Madison site. As the city spread, each neighborhood was provided with educational facilities.

By 1890 Seattle boasted 12 schools with a registration of 4,374; the high school curriculum was given an independent existence and took over part of the Central School. Not until 1886 had there been high-school graduates, and at the first commencement exercises in Frye's Opera House, the governor and various other dignitaries and most of the townspeople crowded in to witness the occasion.

In 1912 Seattle's school district had 66 public school buildings and 31,624 pupils. Three years later, the number had grown to 80 schools, to eventually reach 112 after World War II. The demand for more schools did not slacken until the 1970s. Then as enrollment dropped, the district entered a period in which fewer and fewer schools were needed.—**James R. Warren**

Central School, 1891. Courtesy, Northwest Collection, U of W Libraries.

500 women from New York to Seattle. President Andrew Johnson and his cabinet approved the plan. However, Quartermaster General M.C. Meigs would not honor the order. Weeks later, Meigs offered Mercer the ship *Continental* for $80,000. Mercer was crestfallen; he would never be able to raise that much money.

Financier Ben Holladay, however, heard of the offer and agreed to prepare the *Continental* for the trip and to carry the cargo of women to Seattle at a nominal fare, providing he could have the ship. Mercer later wrote: "Mr. Holladay had two good lawyers pitted against an inexperienced youth, over-anxious and ready to be sacrificed. Result—a contract to carry 500 passengers to Seattle for a minimum, in consideration of turning over the ship to him."

Mercer notified all the young women he had managed to interest in his proposition of the time of departure and issued free tickets to each. He financed the tickets in part from money solicited from Seattle's young bachelors.

But before the scheduled departure, a long and scurrilous article appeared in the *New York Herald*. It stated that the men on Puget Sound were "rotten" and "profligate," and that the girls would be used in houses of ill-fame. The article was copied by other newspapers across the country. Before Asa could counter this charge, two-thirds of his potential passengers had written to decline his invitation to go West.

When Mercer approached Holladay to say that he could not provide 500 female passengers but perhaps 200, Mercer was told the contract had been abrogated. Since the ship would be sent to the Pacific anyway, Holladay said that he would take such passengers as Mercer would present, but at the regular fares.

The ship finally sailed on January 16, 1866, with 100 passengers. Only 36 were unmarried women and 10 were widows. The rest were families. Among these were the remaining members of the Pearson family: Flora, age 15, the youngest girl in the family (who later became the assistant lighthouse keeper), her young brother, and their mother. The expedition received national coverage in a supportive article in the *Harper's Weekly* of January 6.

The *Continental* sailed around the Horn of South America and reached San Francisco on April 24. The *Herald*'s notorious attack had reached the Bay City before the Mercer party arrived, and well-intentioned citizens greeted the ship, prepared to save the women from an unkind fate. Though the women of the city offered this second batch of Mercer girls homes and protection, the passengers trusted Asa Mercer and all continued on to Seattle. But not before Mercer had solved another financial crisis. He was penniless and needed fare from the city for his charges. He sent a telegram over the wires to the territorial governor asking for $2,000. In return, he received 100 words of congratulations but no money. While in New York, Mercer had purchased $2,000 worth of agricultural machinery, mostly wagons, to be

Top
Lizzie Ordway, the only "Mercer girl" to remain single, was in her thirties when she arrived in Seattle in 1864. She opened Seattle's first public school in 1870 and later served as Kitsap County Superintendent of Schools. Involved with the Women's Suffrage Movement, she signed her letters "L.M. Ordway" in case the recipient held women administrators in low esteem. She died in Seattle in 1897 and is buried in Lakeview Cemetery. (MOHAI)

Above
This hand-carved wooden box was made for Lizzie Ordway by a sailor—one of her male admirers. (MOHAI)

shipped to San Francisco, then on to Seattle. Rushing to the shipping office, he found the wagons and machinery stored in a warehouse. Mercer sold them to Californians to raise the funds necessary to transport the women to Seattle.

Since the ships that plied between California and Puget Sound ports were small and equipped to carry only a few passengers, the party divided up, sailing northward a few at a time. The first group of the second Mercer expedition arrived in Seattle on May 11. Immediately a gala social party was arranged at Yesler's Hall. News of the "States" was eagerly received. By then the newspaper criticism of Asa Mercer had arrived on Puget Sound, so a general meeting was scheduled at Yesler's Hall to allow Mercer to respond. Most of the young women who had accompanied him turned out publicly to support him.

Some time after this event, on July 15, 1866, notice was carried in the Seattle paper of a marriage performed by the Reverend Daniel Bagley. Asa had married Miss Annie E. Stephens of Baltimore—one of "his girls."

These educated New England women brought culture and education to Puget Sound, and from these "Mercer Girls" descend many of Washington's most substantial families.

INCORPORATION

In 1869 Seattle was granted a city charter by the territorial legislature. This charter was largely experimental, for the legislators had no experience in such matters. The act was needed principally to allow the city to tax the citizens for street improvements. The townsite was very hilly, full of gullies, and indented with tideflats. A good share of the waterfront was framed by a cliff of varying heights, making wharfing difficult. As the hillsides were gradually denuded of the forests, giant stumps remained everywhere. Streets meandered around them, buildings were built on both sides, and cows pastured about them. Furthermore, the streets had been platted by surveyors without any study or design by an engineer.

King County had a road fund disbursed by its commissioners, but most of it was spent in a vain attempt to maintain a wagon passage from Seattle south around the edge of the tidelands at the base of Beacon Hill to the Duwamish farms. Every rainy season a layer of blue clay under the topsoil played havoc with the road base. It simply slid away. A better road climbed over the top of the hill, but its steep slopes at both ends discouraged wagoneers. Eventually, the city built a plank road across the mudflats. The county also hacked out trails through the woods from Seattle to Lake Washington and to Salmon Bay.

Under the new city charter, each property owner was charged for improving all streets conterminous with frontage of his property. In other words, the adjacent landowners were to pay all costs for the excavating, filling, and grading of the streets. Henry Yesler refused to pay his assessment and won a court case on this issue. For several years the new city sought legal ways to tax for general improvements. Meantime, the streets were graded and most landowners voluntarily paid their share. Not until after statehood came in 1889 was the matter finally cleared up, allowing the city to tax the general citizenry to fund specific improvements.

The taxation problem arose because Seattleites were dis-

covering that it was necessary to develop complex laws in order to build the city. Complications would become ever more intricate and controversial as debates over public ownership of water, electricity, transportation, and other utilities were introduced. But some of the founders weren't going to pay more than they believed was their fair share, especially ones with large property holdings. So as they left behind the era of the Civil War, the pioneers faced two decades of trial and travail, which would be met by the now acknowledged "Seattle spirit"; two decades in which both their city and county would become the most populous in the territory.

The exploits of Asa Mercer in securing women to marry Puget Sound bachelors received national attention. His second effort was described in *Harper's Weekly* in January 1866, accompanied by these sketches. (MOHAI)

CHAPTER 6

MOVING AHEAD: 1870-1888

In spite of its recent incorporation as a city, Seattle in early 1870 was still a village with dwellings and small enterprises scattered among stump-studded hills—home to 1,107 people.

The pioneer settlers in King County always seemed willing to try a new business venture, but they did not always meet with success. For instance, in 1870, three hopeful entrepreneurs planted 1,000 bushels of oysters on the flats of Elliott Bay. They planned to commercially harvest the succulent shellfish, but silt that washed into the bay from rivers and creeks smothered the seed and they lost their total investment.

King County's progress posed certain limitations. A growing center of population traditionally must produce surplus food. The county's fertile river valleys were intensively cultivated. Much of the area around Seattle, which had been covered with evergreen forests, was cleared and planted, but the soil was not ideal for agriculture. Unlike Oregon's Willamette Valley with its rich acreage, King County's tillable land was limited and as a result was unable to produce exportable foodstuffs in great quantity.

However, other natural resources—timber, coal, clay, fish and other seafoods—were available in abundant supply to help the pioneers through the final, lean frontier years. The greatest source of income, however, soon developed through mercantile and service establishments. During the 1870s and '80s, as Seattle became the major supply center for the area, it also became the transportation hub. This in turn accelerated the growth of smaller towns along the transportation routes—the rivers, roads, and railroad tracks—which further increased the commerce through Seattle.

By the early 1880s, Seattle would surpass all other communities in the Territory in population, assessed valuations, and other measures of metropolitan size. The details in the picture of a growing Seattle indicate how business and the service industries diversified, how a thriving transportation network assisted commerce, and how a developing cosmopolitan city sent roots deep into the steep hills to which it clung.

Undoubtedly Seattle's central location on the Sound contributed greatly to its growth, as did its deep-water harbor. In addition, the leading citizens of the city and county deserve special commendation, for they had worked hard—not just in making use of the region's geographical assets and natural resources, but also in asserting their determination to achieve success for both themselves and their city. These were the years when the grit of the pioneers began to pay dividends.

THE RAILROAD RUMOR

The decade of the 1870s commenced with good news. Jay Cook and Company, America's most prominent banking firm, agreed to finance the building of the Northern Pacific Railroad. The plan proposed building a railway west from Duluth, to meet tracks laid eastward from Puget Sound through the Cascades. The rails would be extended north to whichever Puget Sound town was named the terminus.

Seattle swiftly became a boom town. Newcomers flocked to it. Surveyors working in the Cascade range made Seattle their headquarters. Hotels changed names to "Western Terminus" and "The Railroad House."

The *Intelligencer*, the Seattle paper founded in 1867, featured railroad articles in nearly every issue, along with reports of buildings, housing shortages, and other indications of rapid growth.

Real-estate values were escalating. Yesler, Bell, and the Denny brothers platted and sold lots on their claims at a rate that surprised and pleased them. Yesler was on his way to becoming a millionaire. He constructed buildings and warehouses which he rented out, he owned the major wharf, and his mill provided much of the lumber for new construction.

Not all of King County's pioneers had taken donation claims; some who did sold out before land values began climbing. Carson Boren, who had domestic problems and was not much interested in commerce, had parted with most of his holdings. George Frye had not taken a claim but grew wealthy in the construction and rental business. Likewise, Dexter Horton as the town's first banker became rich. However, Charles Terry, who had accumulated more acreage than any of the other early settlers, did not live to enjoy his rewards.

The promise of the railroad during the early '70s at-

Photograph by Victor Gardaya (MOHAI)

HENRY YESLER

Henry Leiter Yesler (1810–1892), Seattle's first industrialist, built the first steam sawmill on Puget Sound in the village of Seattle in 1852. (MOHAI)

◆

One could usually find Henry Yesler looking over his holdings or sitting on a log whittling a piece of white pine. Laconic, often humorous, hardworking, he was a man who hated to let loose of a dollar. Known as Seattle's first industrialist, he built the first steam sawmill on Puget Sound. Had he not located that mill on Seattle's waterfront, the founders might have been hard put to start the city.

Yesler was born in 1810 in Leitersburg, Maryland, a town his mother's family had founded. He was largely self-educated. He spent most of his youth working on his father's farm.

At age 17 he became a house joiner apprentice. At 22, seeking opportunities, he began five years of travel. In 1837 he found himself in Massillon, Ohio, where he established a partnership in house carpentry and mill building. And there he married. After 14 years, feeling restless, Yesler decided to visit the Pacific Coast.

He found work in Portland. He had earlier met a sea captain who told him of Puget Sound, so he decided to see the area for himself. In the fall of 1852 he arrived at Alki and eventually took a claim on Elliott Bay and installed his sawmill in what is now Pioneer Square.

Yesler built a wharf and commercial space to lease, both of which attracted settlers. He suffered severe losses in the great Seattle fire, but immediately rebuilt. The first structure completed was his Pioneer Building, still very much in use today.

In 1885, Yesler, by then one of Seattle's wealthiest men, constructed a spacious 40-room residence, using all native woods. He held many public offices, including those of auditor, county commissioner, and mayor (twice).

His wife, Sarah Burgert, came west as soon as he was settled. The loss of both their children in early childhood was the tragedy of their lives. In 1887 Sarah died and three years later Henry married Minnie Gagle, a woman from his hometown. He was then 77 and this marriage to a much younger woman caused considerable gossip.

After selling his first mill, he built a second on Union Bay, and a village grew up around it called Yesler. Many years ago it was absorbed into the city. In 1892 Yesler endowed a home for young women and named it for his first wife. On December 15 of that year he died.

Yesler probably was mentioned in more law suits than any other of the founders. On the other hand, Roberta Frye Watt wrote of him in her book *The Story of Seattle*:

> Even though Henry Yesler's sawmill had been a moneymaker from the first, somehow or other, the genial mill owner was always hard up—perhaps because he was too easy going. Later he became rich, not from the mill but from the sale of his property as it increased in value.

There can be no doubt this controversial industrialist, realtor, and financier greatly influenced the creation of the Queen City of the Northwest.

—**James R. Warren**

tracted hundreds of new citizens, among them men who became leaders in the years that followed, like James Colman, Orange Jacobs, John Leary, Thomas Burke, Robert Moran, and John McGraw.

The town was spreading northward. David Denny and Thomas Mercer were selling lots at the base of Queen Anne Hill. Denny called his area "North Seattle" and there he and Louisa built a larger home on Lake Union. Thomas Mercer also cleared and platted; soon the forest that had stood between the Denny and Mercer homes was gone and they could wave to one another from their yards.

Out on the land between Lakes Washington and Union, Harvey Pike planned a settlement he called "Union City." Dreaming of a canal that would cut through his property to connect the two lakes, he reserved a 200-foot-wide strip for it. At the same time, Edward Hanford was platting his donation claim on Beacon Hill south of town.

Even the suburbs were expanding. After the Indian War, William Bell had taken his wife to California for health reasons. After she died, he returned to Seattle in 1870 to find his land claim far more valuable. Soon a village called "Belltown," but never platted as such, was a settlement in itself.

During the summer of 1872, a committee of Northern Pacific directors visited Puget Sound to look the prospects over and decide on the terminus location. On arriving in Seattle, they asked the citizens to pledge a subsidy should their city be chosen. Seattleites strained every purse in a major effort to affect the choice. After a large sum was privately raised, a public meeting came up with these contributions: 7,500 town lots, 3,000 acres of land, $50,000 in cash, $200,000 in bonds, and the use of part of the waterfront for terminal and depot purposes—in all amounting in value to more than $700,000, an enormous pledge for a village with a permanent population of about 1,500.

At the end of the week, the committee left for the East Coast, the choice of the terminus reportedly narrowed to three possible sites: Tacoma, Mukilteo, and Seattle.

The matter was not resolved for a year. All that time Seattle waited expectantly. On July 14, 1873, Arthur Denny received a terse telegram from the N.P. railroad commissioners: "We have located the terminus on Commencement Bay." Tacoma won the prize.

Seattle was stunned. Its business halted. Some merchants closed up shop and moved away quickly. After the anguish had slightly subsided, a town meeting was called. There the townspeople decided to build their own railroad—a line through Snoqualmie Pass to Walla Walla. The Seattle and Walla Walla Railroad and Transportation Company was formed, and initial stock was quickly subscribed. Estimated costs ran from $3 to $4 million, a sum the citizens could not raise themselves. They decided to build the road with their own labor.

On May 1, 1874, actual preparation of the roadbed be-

Top
This hand-forged felling ax and peavey were typical of those used in logging camps. (MOHAI)

Above
Early Seattle is depicted in this front-page drawing from *West Shore*, June 1884. (MOHAI)

Right
The cover of a Northern Pacific booklet promotes emigration to Washington Territory in 1883. (MOHAI)

Top
Artist W. Fife painted Seattle in 1871, showing the Territorial University on the hill and the sidewheeler *Olympia*. (MOHAI)

Bottom
Mill Street (circa 1876), now Yesler Way, was the original Skid Road. The trail led to the hilltop where most of Yesler's land claim was located. Using oxen, he skidded the logs down to his mill located at what is now Pioneer Square. (MOHAI)

gan. All the wagons in town carried food and families to the location. Others came in boats, on horseback, and on foot. The town was emptied as the citizens began preparing the grade for the tracks, which commenced at the present Spokane and Grant streets. At a stream where the Lucile Street bridge stands today, the women laid out a picnic dinner. After the repast, the orators of the day were called on to speak. First came John Denny, then Judge Orange Jacobs. Finally, Henry Yesler, a man of few words, was summoned. He stopped his interminable whittling, threw down the stick and pocketed his knife, stepped onto the wagon bed, and said: "Time to quit foolin' and go to work!" That they did.

By October the volunteers had built 12 miles of railroad. The town with no high-finance or potent political connections, and no representation in Congress, was fighting a giant combine, asserting its right to be Puget Sound's major city. Then construction lagged. Three years passed. Realizing action was at a standstill, the directors of the Seattle and Walla Walla Railroad set a new goal: to build as far as the coal mines which Captain William Renton had developed at the town named for him. This decision led the way to securing Seattle's economic future, first through coal exports and then through transportation and commerce.

COAL IN KING COUNTY

During their early years Seattle and King County were economically dependent on California markets, which fortunately had an insatiable hunger for lumber, pilings, fish, and coal. The latter sent coal prospectors searching throughout western Washington.

Dr. R.M. Bigelow discovered the first King County coal in 1853 while clearing land on his donation claim near Black River, not far from the present Renton. He and several others worked the mine in a small way, barging the fuel downriver to Elliott Bay.

L.B. Andrews carried a flour sack full of coal out of the Squak Valley during 1862, and a blacksmith and a foundry owner both pronounced the coal of excellent quality. A year later Edwin Richardson, while surveying a township on the eastern shore of Lake Washington, came across a coal bed on the north bank of what is now known as Coal Creek. In those days coal was not counted as a mineral and could be included as part of a donation claim. Once word was out about Richardson's find, a small coal rush resulted, with prospectors filing a number of claims, and the Seattle *Gazette* printed maps of the finds.

More than 20 years would elapse between the time coal was discovered and the first major coal-mining developments. With the coal deposits miles from salt water, transportation systems demanded major investments in roads, railroads, and mine equipment. No pioneer could raise that kind of funding, so they attempted in the '60s and early '70s to interest California financiers. But about that time, the Mount Diablo field close to San Francisco was opened. Though the California coal was low grade, it cost much less because of cheaper transportation. King Countians, however, continued to explore the possibilities in their local coal fields.

On January 24, 1867, the territorial legislature passed an act incorporating the Coal Creek Road Company and giving it authority to build a rail or tram road from a point on Lake Washington to a point three miles eastward. The company, with what amounted to an exclusive franchise at the Coal Creek Valley, spent considerable money building a road and brought out some coal, but by the winter of 1867–68 it was in bad financial shape and was sold to a San Francisco company. This proved to be a brokerage deal with no money behind it, so that the Coal Creek stockholders lost all their money.

The Lake Washington Coal Company opened the first tunnel on the hillside above Coal Creek. At first the fuel was carried out in sacks. The company then built a light draft barge on the Black River. Coal was delivered from the mine by wagon, loaded on the barge, floated down the Black to the Duwamish, then down the Duwamish to a dock at Elliott Bay. Eventually the company was sold to San Francisco financiers.

In 1868 T.A. Blake, a young mining engineer from California, was sent to the Puget Sound area to investigate the coalfields. He reported on the importance to Seattle of the coal but also mentioned the heavy financing necessary to open the mines at a proper scale. Since no California assistance came through, a new local mining company was incorporated in 1870. The Seattle Coal Company was associated with the coal-handling Seattle Coal and Transportation Company. The coal was mined, loaded on small cars, pulled by a small engine on rails to Lake Washington, then on barges, towed across the lake to the portage, taken on tracks across to Lake Union, loaded again onto barges that were towed across Lake Union; there at the south shore, the engine pulled its load to the Pike Street bunkers on Elliott Bay.

Coal money in the last quarter of the 19th century provided employment for many men, especially to those idled by the Panic of 1873. By the close of 1875 Seattle's waterfront was a busy place. Once the production increased, the facilities for handling coal were enlarged. As a better grade fuel, even with higher transportation costs, it quickly overtook the California product.

Soon a long trestle to deep water allowed the coal to be dumped directly from the cars into ships' holds. The 60 men in the mines and 15 in the transportation department were delivering up to 100 tons of coal a day to the waterfront bunkers.

When the stalled, Seattle-directed Seattle and Walla Walla Railroad needed money and the right man to lead the way toward the Renton coal fields, they found both in one of their own members—James M. Colman, a young engineer. Although not wealthy, he offered to give $20,000 of his savings if the community would add $40,000.

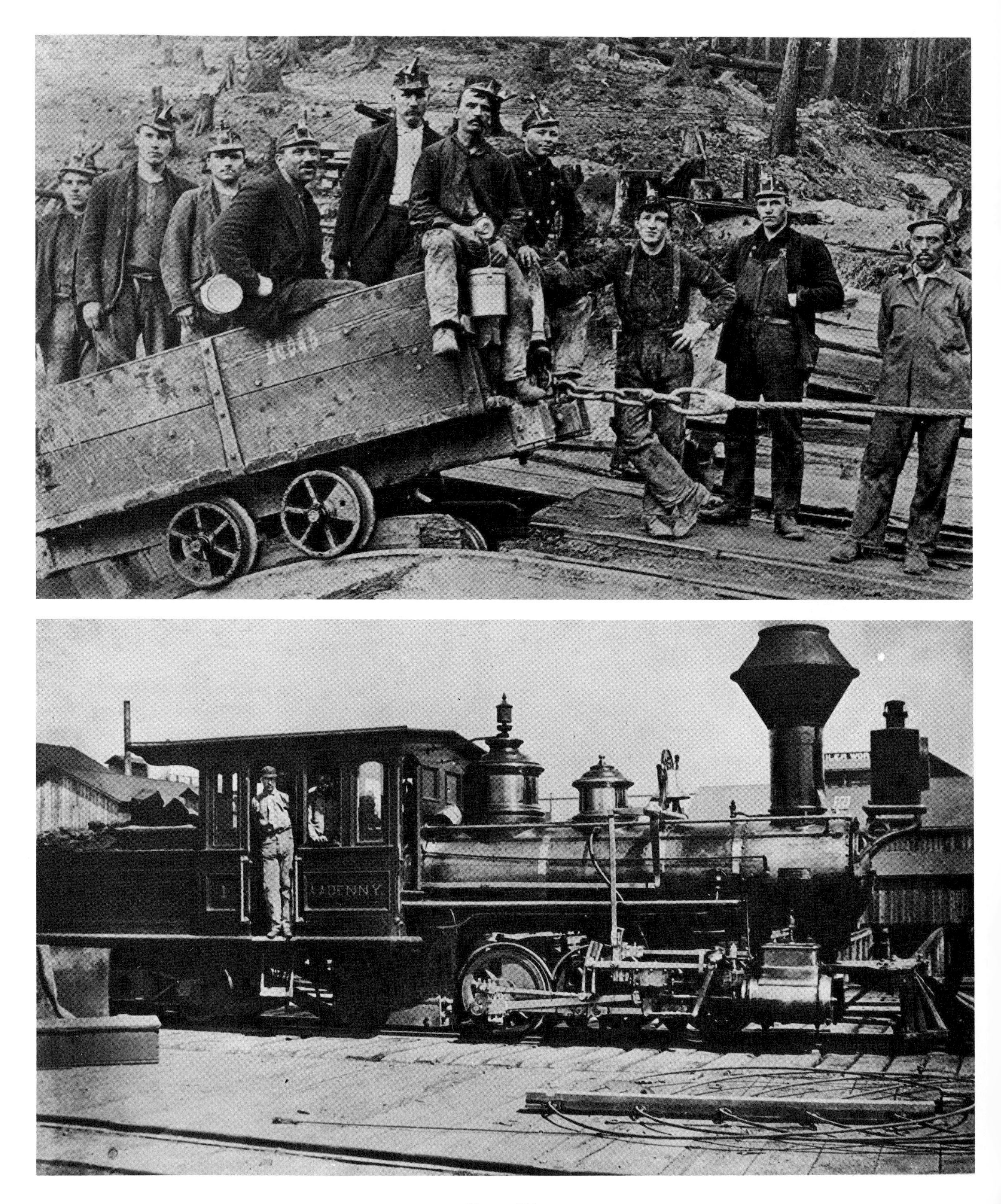
1
A.A.DENNY.

Opposite, top
Coal miners at the Newcastle mine take time out for a photograph. Courtesy, Bicentennial Collection, Renton Historical Society.

Opposite, bottom
Seattle's first locomotive, the "A.A. Denny," operated for the Seattle and Walla Walla Railroad & Transportation Company, which became the Columbia and Puget Sound Railway from Seattle to Renton. Courtesy, McDonald Collection. (MOHAI)

Top
This miniature resembles the coal wagons used by Henry Heckman in his fuel and transfer business in 1895. It was made by Joseph Hardwiger, who made all of Heckman's full-sized vehicles, as a gift to Heckman's children. (MOHAI)

Above
Miner's tools, a lunch box, a canvas hat with a lantern, and a candle holder were all implements used in the extraction of Washington soft coal, circa 1880. (MOHAI)

By 1876 the railroad had made considerable progress in laying track. The first locomotive, the "A.A. Denny," so named because Arthur Denny was one of the trustees of the Seattle and Walla Walla, started operations. A large number of cars were built in Seattle, their cast-iron wheels and woodwork the product of local shops and mechanics. In March 1877 the railway was opened to Renton. Excursion trains were scheduled to carry everyone free on opening day.

Soon coal trains began delivering loads to Seattle. During the rest of the year, the company extended the tracks toward Newcastle, reaching its destination in February 1878. Now the cross-lake barges were abandoned. One of the most lucrative and promising railroad ventures in the Territory, the railroad company lengthened its wharf to accommodate four vessels at a time, ran four engines and 50 coal cars, moved from 400 to 800 tons of coal a day, and carried mail and passengers. The Seattle and Walla Walla Railroad proved that Seattle deserved to be connected with a major national railroad.

In July of 1880 Victor E. Tull of the California-based Black Diamond Coal Company found the beds that underlie the Black Diamond, Franklin, and Ravensdale area. By January of 1882, a crew of men was building houses, cutting trails to the river, and opening veins of coal. Soon an extension of the Columbia and Puget Sound Railroad (the old Seattle and Walla Walla RR) from Renton to the area was completed.

Through the years and into the mid-20th century coal was mined in King County. The business had terrific ups and downs. Labor troubles in 1886 reduced the coal output considerably, and the following year the hoists at the mouth of the Newcastle mine caught fire. The flames spread into the mine and burned for several months, closing the operations.

Old-timers often bemoaned the fact that outsiders mostly had gained control and took the profits.

By 1907, nearly 1.5 million tons were mined annually. But when fuel oil began to arrive from California's oil fields, coal production gradually decreased. To this day, there are untold tons of coal below the surface of King County—potentially of great value in light of the present scarcity of fossil fuels.

BUSINESS IN THE '70S AND '80S

The number of businesses in Seattle had increased by 1876 to the point where B.L. Northup figured he could earn some income from a Directory. That first little book, invaluable to historians, listed 1,015 names of Seattle residents and families and reported that the town had 1,013 buildings, 3,700 inhabitants, and 479 pupils in the public schools. But Northup lost money on the publication.

In April of 1877 William Hammond began construction of a shipyard and marine railway just north of Yesler's mill. Eventually several small steamboats and schooners were built there—a harbinger of King County's future prominence in the shipbuilding industry.

As commerce within the Sound communities and to the outside world increased, waterfront traffic was constant. Foreign ships began to visit Seattle. But the major activities involved the ubiquitous "Mosquito Fleet," dozens of sail- and steam-propelled boats, large and small, that played a huge role in Seattle's first half-century of effort to become the dominant trade center of the Northwest. In his *History of King County*, Clarence Bagley states:

> The early mosquito fleet were [sic] the miniature mail order houses which supplied the settlers with their conveniences and small luxuries. Their masters were the friends of the village people. They carried with them a store of pithy yarns, a large fund of the latest gossip and a good word for old and young.

Seattle's greatest fire thus far burned a score of businesses on July 26, 1879. The fire originated in the American House, and even though the fire department (organized in 1870) responded quickly, the city's predominantly wooden structures on the waterfront burned fiercely, including Yesler's mill, leased to J.M. Colman. Seattle's ability to regenerate—to be tested more severely 10 years later—was evidenced by the middle of September, when seven new buildings had replaced those burned and Colman was busy rebuilding his mill.

The 1880 census counted 3,533 inhabitants in Seattle and 29 manufacturing establishments, which employed 174 people and paid wages of $102,891. The value of products produced in Seattle that year totaled $464,000. During this decade new business and institutional construction increased in value and volume. Card and Lair's sawmill was built on the beach between Marion and Madison. The Sisters of Charity bought four lots at Fifth and Madison and built Providence Hospital, Seattle's first major health-care facility. The fishing industry was bolstered by the opening of the first salmon-canning company within the city.

The Seattle Chamber of Commerce was organized in 1882 to fight high-handed monopolistic practices that aided business in other communities. It aimed to foster and develop the resources and services of the Northwest, in spite of the predatory aggressions of railroad magnates, Eastern financiers, California corporations, and in a few instances local businessmen. In 1890, with more than 300 members, it incor-

A typical miner's cabin at Carbonado, Washington, in 1908 consisted of one small front room, bedroom, pantry, and kitchen, and was built of shiplap with wallpaper on the inside walls and tarpaper on the outside. The residents left southern Belgium in 1902, came first to Nova Scotia, and then to Washington. Courtesy, Bicentennial Collection, Renton Historical Society.

Denny Hill looms over the Seattle of 1878. The scene is Front Street between Columbia and Madison.

porated and in 1910 reorganized and broadened its scope by furthering trade with countries on the Pacific Rim.

Financial problems emanating in the East caused a national recession in 1884 but Seattle hardly noticed. The building business boomed with the Frye Opera House and dozens of other major institutional and business structures going up, as well as large homes, water and river improvements, street planking, and railways being built.

New technology began to surface in Seattle by the late '70s. In September 1879 Seattle was awed by the Edison phonograph, which was exhibited for the first time at Yesler's Hall. About the same time, the first bicycle was imported to Seattle from San Francisco. And on the night of July 31, 1882, most Seattleites visited the steamship *Willamette* to view bright new electric lights for the first time.

In 1886, the Pacific Postal Telegraph Company was given permission to use street rights-of-way for its lines. Real estate was accelerating in value and several new realty companies formed. Land values doubled and trebled in price, and several additions were platted in and about the city. Seattle's population soared to 20,000. The following year, Thomas Burke, William R. Ballard, John Leary, and Boyd Tallman formed the West Coast Improvement Company and secured 800 acres on the north side of Shilshole Bay and platted the Gilman Addition, later called Ballard.

As Seattle and King County grew, they attracted not only the desirable kind of settler but some unsavory types as well. And still retaining the frontier mentality, Seattleites delivered retribution swiftly to certain perpetrators of the worst crimes.

THE LYNCHING IN 1882

In the early 1880s, King County and Seattle experienced many robberies, and more often than not the culprits escaped. Courts were charged with leniency. The assassination of President Garfield fueled the public's indignation. Increasingly, citizens felt inclined to emulate the Vigilance Committee of San Francisco.

On January 17, 1882, in the midst of this intense feeling, a couple of "footpads," as they were known in those days, accosted a popular merchant, George B. Reynolds, as he walked back to his store in the early evening after dining at home. The two stopped him near Third and Marion, ordered him to put his hands up and pushed a pistol at him. Instead,

Frye's Opera House was erected in 1884 on First Avenue between Madison and Marion streets as the largest theater north of San Francisco. John Nester, the architect, patterned it after the old Baldwin Theater in San Francisco. Built and owned by George Frye, the Opera House was one of the first major structures to be devastated in the great fire of 1889. Courtesy, Northwest Collection, U of W Libraries.

Frank Osgood came to Seattle in 1883 from Boston. He acquired the franchise earlier taken out by George Kinnear and David Denny and organized the Seattle Street Railway, the first streetcar line in town, which ran from Main Street to Pike on Second Avenue. (MOHAI)

Top
The three officials who tried to stop the lynching in 1882 of three murder suspects were Chief Justice Roger S. Greene, Sheriff Louis V. Wyckoff, and Justice Samuel Coombs. (MOHAI)

Bottom
An 1882 newspaper sketch depicts the lynching of the three men accused of murder. They were hanged by vigilantes without proper trials. (MOHAI)

Reynolds reached for his own revolver. One of his assailants fired, wounding Reynolds in the chest. He died two hours later.

After someone rang the fire bell, some 200 enraged citizens congregated at the engine house to form a vigilance committee. They sent out squads of men to patrol the streets and to block means of escape from the city. About ten o'clock, four hours after the shooting, two men were found hiding in hay stored on Harrington and Smith's wharf. A one-armed man had a revolver with four unspent cartridges and an empty chamber. His companion had about a hundred bullets for the revolver. The committee delivered the prisoners to a police officer, who took them to the county jail. Soon the vigilantes arrived at the jail, where the prisoners were being guarded by Sheriff L.V. Wyckoff, Chief of Police J.H. McGraw, and others. The hall leading to the sheriff's office filled with angry men bent on vengeance. They demanded that the two prisoners be turned over, but Sheriff Wyckoff, with drawn revolver, asked them to desist from violence and announced his intention to protect the men in his charge. The crowd hesitated and finally left after the sheriff promised the two suspects would be produced in court the next morning.

By nine o'clock the streets were thronged with anxious people. During the night, the citizens' committee had collected evidence against the accused, including shoe prints from the mud. At 9:30 a.m. Justice S.F. Coombs opened court in Yesler's Hall and the prisoners James Sullivan and William Howard, were brought in. After the testimony of both sides was heard, Justice Coombs stood up and said: "I am convinced that the evidence is sufficient to hold these men without bail for their appearance to wait the action of the grand jury, and they are now turned over to the officers and remanded back to jail."

A deafening shout arose from the courtroom crowd. Men rushed forward, then seized and overpowered the officers. The prisoners were shoved out a back door into the alley. On the street two scantlings had been placed between the forks of trees to the south of Henry Yesler's residence (now the site of the Pioneer Building). Ropes were slung over the bars and fastened about the neck of each suspect. Many hands pulled the other ends to hang the men.

Chief Justice Greene rushed out of the crowd and with his pocketknife tried to cut the hanging ropes, but vigilantes wrestled him aside. About 20 minutes later someone in the throng suggested they go after Benjamin Payne, who was confined in the jail, charged with murder of Police Officer David Sires. As the fire bell rang again, about 500 men marched on the jail. They tore down tall fencing south of the building, chopped down the heavy outside wooden doors, and battered two iron doors to pieces with sledges. They grabbed Payne and pushed him at the head of the crowd toward those same trees. When asked to confess the killing of Sires, Payne replied, "You hang me, and you will hang an innocent man." Payne was strung up with the other two.

At the time the illegal act was stoutly defended by the participants and observers. Most citizens and the public press agreed. But when the reaction came from other communities and the deed was calmly reviewed, many of those who took part admitted their grave error. Seattle had learned a lesson. Maintaining law and order should be applied, not only to criminals but also to those irate citizens who react outside the law. This attitude would re-emerge three years later during another wave of public hostility—this time not against criminals but against a racial minority.

ANTI-CHINESE AGITATION

Many Chinese men had been brought to the West Coast of North America to help build the transcontinental railroads. On completion of their work elsewhere, many Chinese emigrated to Washington Territory, congregating principally in Seattle, Tacoma, and Olympia. In the late 1870s Seattle's "Chinatown" had developed on Washington Street around the store of Wa Chung, the first Chinese-owned Seattle retail establishment. Gum King had opened a similar store in Renton to supply the needs of about 320 Chinese laborers who were building the Seattle and Walla Walla extension to Newcastle. At this time, the newspapers carried the first articles warning of potential conflicts between the white race and the Asians or "yellow peril."

The territorial census of 1885 counted 3,276 persons of Chinese extraction. Mostly males, they were employed as servants, miners, and construction and public-works laborers. Contract labor was arranged through Chinese merchants. The Chinese also did "women's work" (laundry and cooking) on the frontier, possibly to avoid competition with whites. The latter part of 1885 witnessed much labor agitation across the country. In western Washington, this took the form of anti-Chinese agitation brought on by racial antagonism, poor enforcement of the Exclusion Act enacted in 1880 to restrict Chinese from entering the country, and by distress caused by a prolonged business depression. With times hard, the unemployed whites tended to blame the Chinese, whom they claimed were "cheap labor."

A massacre of Chinese laborers at Rock Springs, Wyoming, in the summer of 1885 was the first overt action. That September, in the Squak Valley 15 miles east of Seattle, shots were fired into tents where hop pickers were sleeping, and three Chinese were killed. A number of alleged participants were arrested and brought to trial, but none was convicted.

Violent speeches were made in towns up and down the Sound. "The Chinese must go!" was the common cry. On September 25, an anti-Chinese congress was held in Seattle. Delegates from eight communities and seven labor unions voted on resolutions claiming that most of the Chinese had entered the territory illegally. They issued an edict demanding that the Chinese leave western Washington by November

THE BEST, CHEAPEST, AND MOST FASHIONABLE STOCK OF DRY GOODS AND CLOTHING ON PUGET SOUND AT THE ARCADE, BOYD, PONCIN & YOUNG, SEATTLE, W. T.

20 *DIRECTORY OF THE CITY OF SEATTLE.*

AMERICAN HOUSE,

GEO. W. WALSH, Proprietor.

MILL STREET, - - - SEATTLE, W. T

Board per day $1, Board per Week, $5, $6 & $7 according to room. Meals, 25 cts. Beds 25 to 50 cts.

Baggage conveyed to and from the house free of chagre.

NO CHINAMEN EMPLOYED.

WA CHONG & CO.,

China Tea Store,

Brick Store, Corner of Washington and Third Sts., Seattle.

DEALERS IN

RICE, OPIUM AND ALL KINDS OF CHINESE GOODS,

Chinese Landscape Pictures, Oil Paintings, also for Sale

Contractors, Mill Owners and others requiring Chinese help will be furnished at short notice.

THE HIGHEST PRICE PAID FOR LIVE HOGS.

SEATTLE RESTAURANT

Under New Management.

The Traveling Public will find this the Cheapest and Best House in Town.

No Chinese Employed About the House.

Meals, 25c.
Single Rooms, 25c.

A. J. TICE, Proprietor,

No. 8 Mill Street, SEATTLE, W. T.

OAK RESTAURANT,

SHORT & STEVENS, PROPRIETORS,

Washington Street, Near Commercial,

(Opp. Judge Lyon's Court.)

EMPLOYS WHITE HELP ONLY.

Table Always Supplied with the Best that the Market can Afford.

Twenty-one Meal Tickets for $4.50.

In 1886 mobs of anti-Chinese citizens attempted to evict the Chinese from Seattle. Brutal conflicts arose between vigilantes who wanted to force the Chinese out and citizens who,backed by militia,wanted to preserve law and order. (MOHAI)

Above
Both the Seattle Restaurant and the Oak Restaurant promoted their establishments in this circa 1885 ad by noting, respectively, "No Chinese employed about the house" and "Employs white help only." Courtesy, Historical Photography Collection, U of W Libraries.

Top
An ad in the city directory of 1879 shows the coexistence of American and Asian businesses. Wa Chong & Company is a dealer in several Asian goods, including "Chinese help." However the American House notes that one of its attractions is "No Chinamen Employed." Courtesy, Historical Photography Collection, U of W Libraries.

1. And they absolved themselves of responsibility "for any acts of violence which may arise from the non-compliance with these resolutions." On October 3, a Tacoma mass meeting issued the same decree, but allowed the Chinese 30 days to leave. A month later, with various leading citizens helping propagate the sentiment, the Chinese were forcibly removed from Tacoma. Neither the sheriff nor any city officials made an attempt to protect them, and the Chinese did not resist. They and their possessions were taken to a railroad station, placed in boxcars, and sent south to Portland.

Later, people were arrested and charged with denying Chinese rights, and with insurrection. But they never came to trial and the indictments lapsed. Since those who had forced the Chinese out were never punished, the agitators elsewhere in Washington Territory, believing they were sustained by public approval, forced the Chinese to leave the smaller towns in Pierce, King, Kitsap, Snohomish, Skagit, and Whatcom counties.

On November 4, Governor Watson Squire issued a proclamation in which he warned all citizens to refrain from participating in acts of violence and asked them to maintain law and order. The next night a Seattle meeting advocated the expulsion of the Chinese, but differing views on law and order resulted in a split between the two groups in attendance. Henceforth the law-and-order group and the anti-Chinese elements would hold separate meetings.

By Saturday, November 7, agitation had become intense. Sheriff John H. McGraw assembled several hundred citizens who had previously been sworn as deputy sheriffs. The revenue cutter *Oliver Wolcott* lay all day off Yesler's wharf with her guns pointing toward the city center. The two companies of territorial militia stationed in Seattle were held in readiness. President Cleveland, kept apprised of the situation, issued a proclamation stating that military force would be deployed if necessary to maintain faithful execution of the laws of the United States. Since 10 companies of federal troops were dispatched from Fort Vancouver barracks to Seattle, the disturbance temporarily subsided. During November, 15 persons were indicted in Seattle for conspiracy to deprive the Chinese of equal protection of the law. The trial lasted until January 16, 1886, when all charged were acquitted.

After the regular troops were withdrawn, a false calm pervaded Seattle and King County. However, the agitators continued to meet and lay plans. On February 6 an anti-Chinese mass meeting was held. A committee of 15 was appointed to visit Chinatown, ostensibly to inspect the sanitary facilities for possible health violations. This was only cover for a raid on the Asian population—the goal being to drive them from the city. As one of the committee men knocked on a door to conduct the "inspection," others forced their way into the homes and carried the people's personal belongings to waiting wagons. The Chinese and their baggage were delivered to the dock, where the steamer *Queen of the Pacific* was preparing to sail for San Francisco.

Many from the police force reportedly took part in this anti-Chinese activity. When Sheriff McGraw arrived at dockside, he ordered the mob to disperse, but they ignored him. Judge Greene, Mayor Yesler, U.S. Attorney W. H. White, and others vainly attempted to stop the forced removal of the Chinese. Meantime the fire bells clanged as a signal to rally the citizens and the deputy sheriffs.

Governor Squire, who happened to be in the city, issued a proclamation ordering the unlawful actions to cease, warning that all lawbreakers would be punished, and calling for the militia to assist the sheriff in maintaining the law. The proclamation, when read to the crowd, raised shouts of defiance.

Meanwhile, about 350 of the Chinese had been herded into a warehouse on the dock. Their captors now attempted to force them aboard the *Queen of the Pacific*. Captain Alexander refused to accept them until their fares were paid. A collection was taken, which totaled enough to pay passage for about 100 persons. Judge Greene now prepared a writ of *habeas corpus* charging that the Chinese were illegally restrained of liberty on board the *Queen*. This writ was served on Captain Alexander, enjoining the steamer from sailing. The captain was also ordered to produce the Chinese in court at eight o'clock the next morning, where they would be questioned about their desire to leave. The other Chinese remained in a warehouse on the dock.

The anti-Chinese group busily collected donations to fund the fares of all the Chinese. By 3 p.m., rain had dispersed most of the mob. Governor Squire telegraphed the Secretaries of War and the Interior to request that U.S. troops be sent immediately.

About midnight, an attempt was made to load the Chinese on a train scheduled to leave at 4 a.m., for Tacoma, but the militia intervened. The Home Guards moved to the warehouse, forced the few anti-Chinese guards away, and gained control of the building and its inhabitants.

Warrants were issued for the arrest of eight of the leading agitators and were served the next morning by the militia, who marched the men to jail. All, however, quickly furnished bail and were soon on the streets again.

At 8 a.m., the Chinese aboard the *Queen* were escorted by two militia companies and the Home Guard to Judge Greene's court. Though hoots and yells were heard from passersby, no one interfered. Judge Greene addressed the Chinese through an interpreter, acknowledging that they were perhaps kept aboard the steamer against their will. He told them frankly that public sentiment strongly favored their leaving but assured them that they would be protected should they stay. Each person was then asked to choose. Sixteen of 89 in the courtroom indicated they wished to remain.

At 11:30 the *Queen* left the dock with 197 Chinese

aboard. The remaining hundred were told they could board a steamer, expected to arrive the next day. They were then escorted toward their houses by the Home Guards. At the corner of Main and Commercial a hostile crowd had gathered. As the Chinese and the guardsmen appeared, the mob attempted to turn them down Commercial Street toward the depot. When a few rowdies rushed for the Chinese, the Guards beat them back with the butts of their rifles. The crowd would not heed repeated orders to disperse. A large and angry logger named Charles G. Stewart rushed forward, attempting to wrest the guards' weapons from them and calling for others to follow him. Stewart's voice rang sharply over the melee. Suddenly, without any orders being given, shots rang out. The crowd now retreated to the side, leaving four men writhing on the muddy street—one of them Stewart.

At this moment the Seattle Rifles, a local volunteer group, came running up from the wharf and formed a line to support the Home Guards. Shortly thereafter, Company D hurried down from the courthouse and formed another battle line. Within the square of these armed military protectors, the Chinese had thrown themselves to the ground for safety.

The crowd milled about until their four casualties were placed in express wagons and taken to the hospital, where Stewart died the following day. For 45 minutes the crowd shouted and threatened but at last began to disperse. The Chinese, uninjured physically, were escorted to their homes.

Now denunciations and threats of hanging fell on the Home Guard leaders. Five Home Guardsmen were charged with shooting with intent to kill. However, before the warrants were served, Judge Greene declared that the accused were officers of his court and could not be arrested. Meanwhile, Governor Squire declared martial law. He appointed a staff, ordered all saloons closed, and called for a curfew between 7 p.m. and 6 a.m. Patrols were provided with rifles and ammunition and vigorous measures were adopted to preserve peace and order.

On February 9 President Cleveland issued a proclamation of martial law. Next day, U.S. troops arrived. While federal troops patrolled the town, the governor posted notices calling for the arrest of vagrants.

On February 11, the Home Guards, the Seattle Rifles, Company D, the University Cadets, and the members of Governor Squire's staff met at the courthouse to receive final orders. The governor recited the valuable services all had rendered, thanked them, and temporarily relieved them from duty. The Home Guards held a meeting a few days later to form a permanent organization for the protection of Seattle.

Nine men, alleged to be the leading instigators of the movement to expel the Chinese, were arrested and tried. When the cases came to court some months later, all were acquitted.

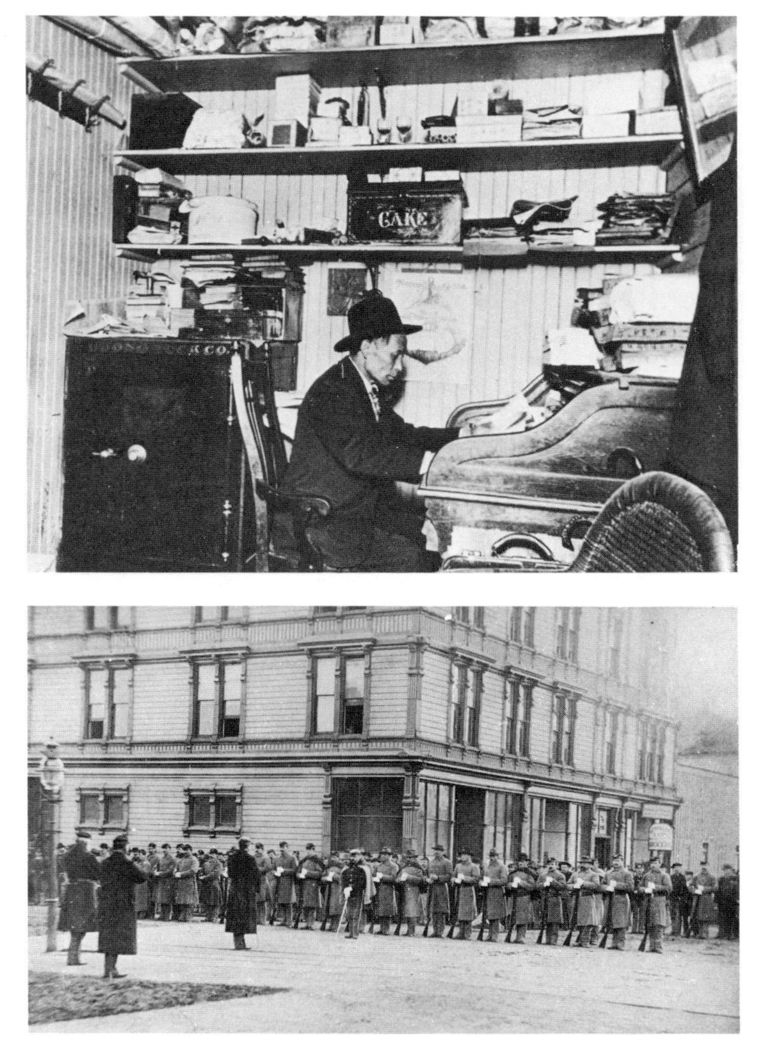

Top
This portrait by Asahel Curtis shows Chin Gee Hee at his desk. As a labor contractor, he employed hundreds of his countrymen from China to help build railroads in the West. These workers were usually paid 75 cents per day. Courtesy, McDonald Collection. (MOHAI)

Above
During the anti-Chinese riots of 1886, Governor Watson Squire called out the state militia to help Sheriff John H. McGraw maintain law and order and to prevent bloodshed. They experienced a few active days in Seattle, and when martial law was declared, they helped patrol the streets and enforce curfews. (MOHAI)

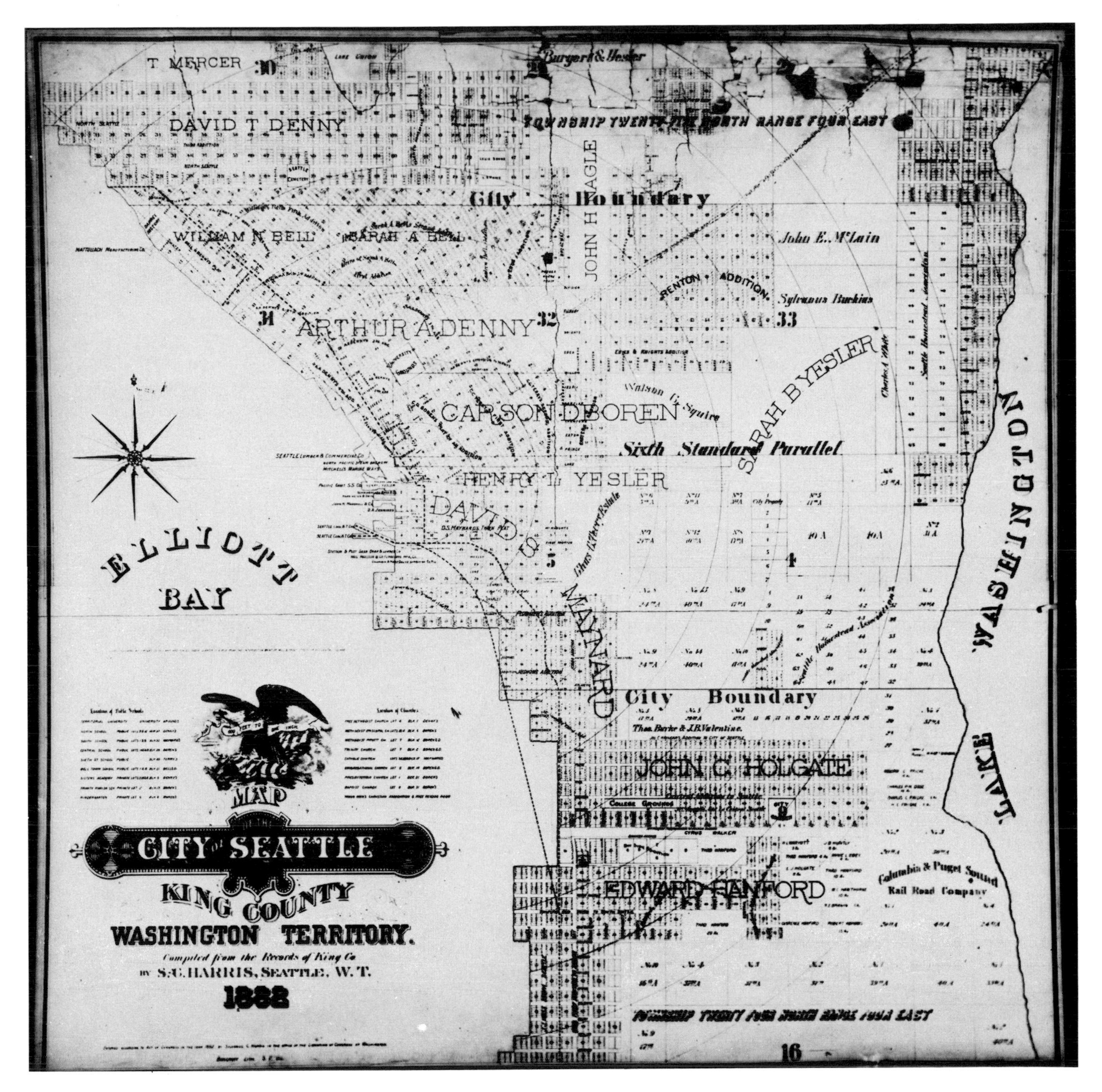

This map shows the city of Seattle, King County, Washington Territory, in 1882. (MOHAI)

Additional money was raised to send away those Chinese who wished to leave. Governor Squire revoked his order of martial law and the city quieted down. Many of the men responsible for the trouble left Seattle. Some time later, Congress appropriated over $276,000 to pay for the losses and injuries sustained by the Chinese. The money was paid to the Chinese government as the representative of these Chinese workers.

By 1886, when the business recession seemed over, new arrivals again began to increase the city and county population. Word spread across the country that Seattle had maintained itself admirably in trying times, and this reputation attracted many progressive-minded families to the area. Old animosities were lost in the new interests as the city reentered the era of prosperity, which was ushered in and sustained by railroads.

SEATTLE GETS ITS MAJOR RAILROADS

By 1880 Seattle had become a business center of such magnitude that again it had to be considered a prime railroad terminus prospect. Henry Villard came to realize that fact as he was acquiring control of the transportation business in the Northwest. He had already purchased the Oregon Steam Navigation Company and holdings along the Columbia River and amalgamated them into a new corporation called the Oregon Railway and Navigation Company. He planned railroad extensions from Portland into eastern Washington, Idaho, and other parts of Oregon. He also conceived a plan connecting his holdings with the Northern Pacific at a point on the Columbia River.

To accomplish his aims, he obtained some $8 million from Eastern capitalists without divulging the intended use of it. With this money he gained control and assumed the presidency of the Northern Pacific. Realizing that the narrow-gauge Seattle and Walla Walla Railroad had the potential of reaching the inland empire and was therefore a threat, he purchased the line in 1880 and renamed it the Columbia and Puget Sound Railroad Company.

Villard then informed Seattle that he did not intend to tie Seattle direclty to the major line. He explained that construction of the Northern Pacific branch from Puget Sound over the Cascades was being postponed indefinitely. But he proposed extending the existing standard-gauge track from Tacoma to Puyallup and then north to meet the Columbia and Puget Sound at Black River. Thus Seattle would be connected by rail to Tacoma, Portland, and thence to the transcontinental line.

As a condition for building this new track, Villard demanded from Seattle a free right-of-way along the waterfront northward to the land he had purchased from the Seattle and Walla Walla Railroad. The city council granted as much of the required right-of-way as it controlled. The remainder was acquired from individuals who decided whether to grant right-of-way on the land or water side of their property. The result was a wandering track referred to as the "Ram's Horn."

Villard built the standard gauge track as promised by adding a third rail. Service to Seattle commenced in the summer of 1883. It lasted one month and was stopped. Ever after, that connection between Black River and Puyallup was referred to as "The Orphan Railroad."

A new corporation named the Puget Sound Shore Railroad Company was organized by several prominent King County residents to reestablish service but, even so, trains traveled infrequently over the Orphan Railroad tracks. In 1885 "Foghorn" Green, so called on account of his deep bass voice, arranged a mass meeting in Kent to devise a plan whereby the tracks might be put to use. He advertised the meeting widely and requested members of the legislature, of Villard's corporations, county officers, and others to attend. Representatives from several groups appeared. John L. Howard, an agent of Villard's corporations, explained that a stub railroad could not be operated profitably except as a feeder to bring traffic to a main line. Cornelius Hanford, pioneer lawyer and later state supreme court judge, responded that since railroads are primarily for public use, a railroad franchise imposes a duty to serve that public. If whoever had proprietary rights to the railroad did not operate it, he said, the farmers whose land it went through could acquire possession of it and put it to work. Hanford, who had access to information, revealed that figures showed that the one month of operation had earned a healthy profit. About that time in the proceedings, a telegram from New York was received which announced that the road would be restored to operation within two weeks—and it was.

Villard now ran into trouble. The company was having financial problems and his enemies successfully convinced his investors that he had squandered their money, and the board of directors demanded his resignation. Villard was shorn of power and all service to Seattle was again terminated.

The large land claims set aside for the Northern Pacific for building the railroad had taken some of the best acreage in the territory. Settlers in eastern Washington who had claims on sections within the lieu limits were challenged by railroad lawyers. These settlers, who had occupied and improved their holdings, gained support from King County citizens in general as public sentiment swung strongly against the railroad.

The N.P. officers sought expressions of public support opposing any forfeiture of its land grant. Appeals to the Seattle Chamber of Commerce resulted in a call for a general meeting to consider the matter. A committee drafted a resolution opposed to forfeiture, which the chamber adopted.

Top
The Territorial University was decorated for Seattle's reception for Villard in September 1883. (MOHAI)

Bottom
Henry Villard, elected president of the Northern Pacific Railroad in 1881, is remembered for being more sympathetic than other company officers to Seattle's efforts to become a rail terminus. He purchased the Seattle and Walla Walla Railroad and renamed it the Columbia and Puget Sound. He later took on other interests and purchased the *New York Evening Post* and the weekly *The Nation*. In 1889 Villard organized the Edison General Electric Company. (MOHAI)

The antiforfeiture resolution was soon regretted by those who signed it, and the newspapers vigorously denounced it. In the territorial election of 1884 it became a political issue, and candidates debated for or against the actions of the Northern Pacific. But by now the branch line was being rapidly built across the Cascades. The first train came over the mountains on temporary switchbacks into Tacoma on July 3, 1887. Seattleites joined with Tacomans in a Fourth of July celebration on Commencement Bay—one of the rare occasions when the normally feuding communities socialized.

While Seattle was being snubbed by the Northern Pacific, the Canadian Pacific Railway was completed with a terminal in Vancouver, B.C. Since the Canadian line provided water transportation to Vancouver, Seattleites often used the C.P.R. for eastward transportation in preference to the N.P. at Tacoma.

In 1883 Daniel Hunt Gilman had arrived in Seattle and conceived the need for a rail line from Seattle north to a junction with the C.P.R. He interested Thomas Burke, John Leary, and J.R. McDonald in the project, and they organized the Seattle, Lake Shore and Eastern Railway Company. Eastern investors added to local money. The road was built in sections, eventually with the rails extending through King, Snohomish, Skagit, and Whatcom counties to Sumas on the Canadian border. Since most of the timber had previously been cut from the shores of navigable water, now a means of transporting logs from inland forests was supplied. Small lumber towns developed along the railway.

In order to extend the tracks to a location convenient for a passenger depot in Seattle, the city council adopted an ordinance creating Railroad Avenue, a necessary move since the Northern Pacific controlled the "Ram's Horn" right-of-way. The eastern half was granted to the Seattle, Lake Shore and Eastern for its right-of-way. The Northern Pacific was offered a 30-foot thoroughfare but refused the gift. (Later this was used by the Great Northern Railway tracks, which arrived in 1893.) In 1896 the Seattle, Lake Shore and Eastern would be purchased by the Northern Pacific, after it finally recognized Seattle's successes. However, through the 1890s, there was no covered depot for N.P. passengers, who were discharged unceremoniously in the Ram's Horn right-of-way.

In the 1880s news reached Seattle concerning the Great Northern Railroad, which James J. Hill was pushing across the northern states. Numerous survey parties were reported in the mountains. Eventually Hill himself came to Seattle and looked around. Shortly thereafter his attorney arrived quietly in Judge Thomas Burke's office. Telling him that Hill had decided Seattle would be his terminus because of its position as the port most accessible to Pacific Rim trade, he asked Burke to be the Great Northern's local representative.

Hill asked for unobstructed entrance to the city for his tracks and no legislative difficulties. Terminal space was offered to him on a strip of land south of Dearborn Street. Thinking that this was too far from the wholesale district, Hill purchased more land between these holdings and Jackson Street. The first Great Northern depot at the foot of Columbia Street, used after the railway's completion in 1893, was a ramshackle structure, but it would remain until 1905, when a tunnel was constructed beneath the city and tracks were built through to the tide flats south of town. There Hill erected his terminal, the King Street Station. Across Fourth Avenue South from the King Street terminal stands the Union Depot, erect-

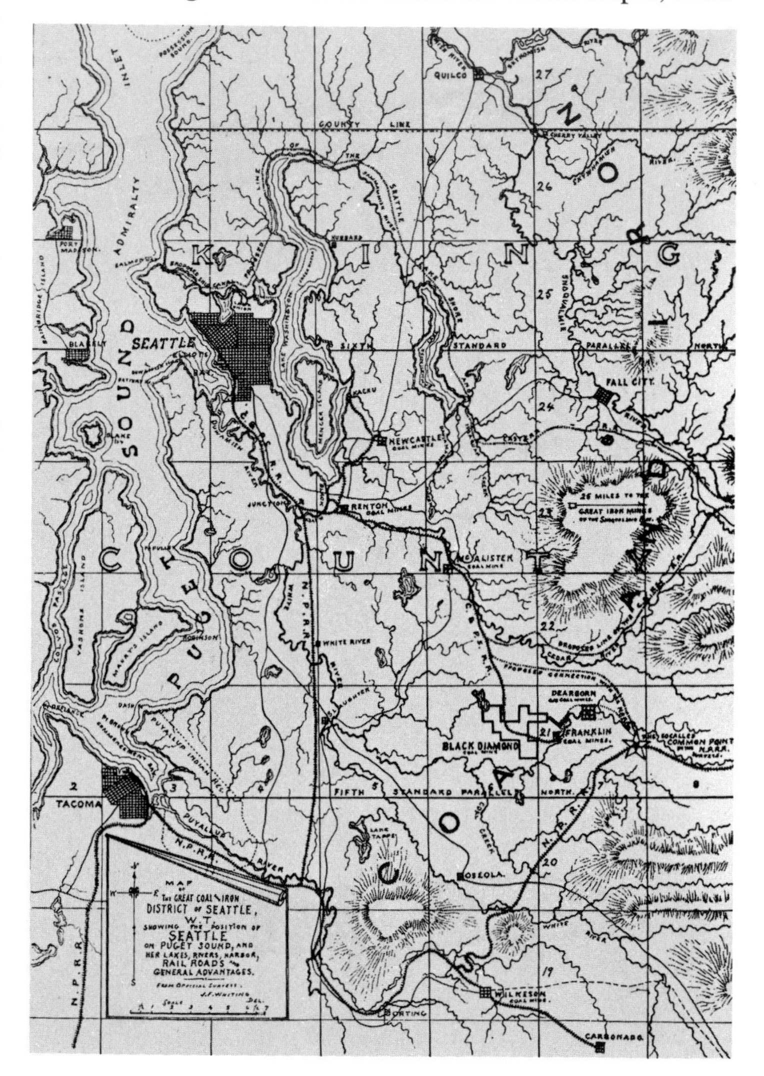

This "Map of the Great Coal and Iron District of Seattle" ran in *Northwest Magazine* May 1886. It shows the railroad lines of the Seattle, Lake Shore and Eastern Railway going north out of the city, the Columbia and Puget Sound heading south to Franklin after a junction with the Northern Pacific which goes down to Tacoma, and the original shape of the Duwamish River. Courtesy, Northwest Collection, U of W Libraries.

ed in 1911 by the Union Pacific Railroad which reached Seattle in 1910.

In 1909 the Chicago, Milwaukee and St. Paul line was completed, the first railway routed over Snoqualmie Pass. That little Seattle and Walla Walla Railway, which the determined city fathers had started to build over Snoqualmie Pass, was leased by the C.M. and St. P. and tied to their rails over the pass.

Now all the fond dreams of the early settlers were coming true. The selection of Seattle as the Great Northern's terminus-port on the Pacific guaranteed a solid future. After two decades of stubborn, grueling, constant efforts to become the railroad center on Puget Sound, Seattle was succeeding in that endeavor by the late 1880s. The city's citizens were intent on building and benefiting from a prosperous and livable city. They had finally turned the territorial university into an institution providing higher education and developed a public school system, library, and other viable municipal services. Seattleites had earned national respect for maintaining law and order in a burgeoning frontier town. Now they would have to confront another crisis: the devastation of a great fire. ◆

Above
The engine "J.R. McDonald" was named for one of the founders of the Seattle, Lake Shore and Eastern Railway. This circa 1888 photo was taken at 34th Avenue North and Stoneway in the Fremont/Wallingford neighborhood. (MOHAI)

Left
Thomas Burke was born in New York in 1849. In 1875 he came west to Seattle, entered law practice, and soon became known as an eloquent speaker. In 1889 Burke was appointed Chief Justice of the Washington Supreme Court. He died while speaking before the Board of the Carnegie Endowment for International Peace in New York on December 4, 1925. (MOHAI)

CHAPTER 7
FIRE AND GOLD: 1889-1899

During the 1890s, Seattle acquired the status of a major metropolis. The decade was ushered in by the great fire, and then, as the old century turned into new, the area bathed in the glow of gold rushes, railroad activity, regrades, and the culmination of an important military endeavor.

THE GREAT SEATTLE FIRE

The spring of 1889 saw little rain. By early June, Seattleites, unaccustomed to drought, were remarking about how dry things were. At 2:30 in the afternoon of June 6, in a building on the southwest corner of Front and Madison streets, a newly arrived Swedish immigrant named John E. Back was melting glue on an iron stove in Victor Clairmont's basement woodworking shop. The gluepot overheated and exploded into flame. When Back attempted to douse the flames with a bucket of water, burning glue scattered over shavings on the floor, setting them on fire. The dilapidated frame building was soon burning fiercely.

Engine Company No. 1 raced to the scene and laid two lines of hose from the hydrant at the corner of First and Columbia. However, the fire burned so hotly that the water had little effect. Persons in adjoining structures began to remove their goods. As the flames leaped higher, a bucket brigade was formed to wet down roofs of buildings on the east side of First Avenue.

The fire moved southward down Front to George Frye's Opera House. This brick structure was expected to act as a fire stop, but its mansard roof ignited. The finest of Seattle's buildings was soon gutted. Next the long wooden Denny Block burst into flame.

Because Fire Chief Josiah Collins was away, his assistant, James Murphy, took charge. As the fire area enlarged, he seemed unable to make proper decisions. Mayor Robert Moran organized the men who were standing around watching the fire into teams, to carry merchandise from the stores to the docks.

The fire jumped Madison to the Colman Block, which was soon ashes. The heat and firebrands were endangering the east side of Front Street. Eventually the heat and wind-blown firebrands caused the fire to jump the street and burn down both sides.

As more hoses were hooked to hydrants, water pressure began to fail. When the wind shifted to blow from the south, the situation eased, but then it shifted again and blew even stronger, this time from the northwest. Now the fire expanded rapidly. The Safe Deposit building began to glow from the inside, then flames shot from all windows. (In spite of the heat, the vault preserved most of the valuables therein.) The next building to burn was a hardware store, where 20 tons of cartridges started popping, punctuated by the roar of exploding drums of oil, paint, and alcohol.

The fire leaped Cherry Street and in 20 minutes consumed the entire block to James Street. Then the flames came against the new Yesler-Leary Building, built of stone, iron, and brick, and the sturdy Occidental Hotel. When the walls of buildings to the north collapsed, the heat was so great that both the Yesler-Leary and the Occidental began burning from the inside. Having crossed Yesler Way now, the flames licked hungrily at the old wooden heart of Seattle. On the waterfront the conflagration burned its way under the planking, consuming every wharf and pier.

Around the periphery of the fire, valiant efforts were made to save structures and goods. Some buildings were blown up in an attempt to build a fire break. Volunteers saved the Boston Block, the Colonial Building, and Yesler's mansion. The courthouse did not burn, even though at times it smoked from the heat. The Catholic Church was also saved. Such efforts prevented the fire from advancing eastward into the hillside residential areas. In several instances the mature shade trees fringing the streets helped to halt the advancing wall of flames.

Attempts to save personal property met with only partial success. If piled in the streets, it was usually consumed by the flames. Goods transported to the wharves were also burned except for what little was loaded on two steamships and moved out into Elliott Bay. By sunset the fire had reached its ultimate boundaries but flames continued to light the sky. The coal bunkers containing about 300 tons of coal burned for days.

Miraculously, as far as could be determined, no one had died in the fire. A citizens' committee was appointed to look after the people's welfare and to help the regular police and

Photograph by Victor Gardaya (MOHAI)

Above
Robert Patton, the "Umbrella Man," modeled for a popular weather report cartoon. "You can only understand this peculiar Puget Sound climate by actual experience; no amount of reading about it will make an adequate impression on your mind of its novel features . . . In fact there are only two seasons on the Pacific Coast—the wet and the dry." From *Northwest Magazine*, February 1891.

Below
This photo was taken of Mill Street (Yesler Way), then the center of town, a few days before the 1889 fire. James Street goes to the left and the Occidental Hotel stands in the center. Pioneer Square later developed around the site of the Yesler-Leary Building, on the left, after it burned. Photo by Warner and Randolph. (MOHAI)

militia. Mayor Moran ordered the arrest of all persons found on the streets after the 8 p.m. curfew. All saloons were closed. Company C of Tacoma and Company G from Port Blakely were called up by the National Guard and sent to Seattle.

The mayor requested that the women of the town render assistance in preparing meals for the military and the destitute, and the city supplied the provisions. Those with arms in their homes were asked to lend them to the police.The Armory became headquarters of the military and relief efforts. In one day volunteer women there served an estimated 10,000 meals.

The city of Tacoma not only sent its firefighters; it also brought up three boatloads and a train full of food, erected a large tent, and began serving meals, prepared to serve 6,000 persons a day for as long as necessary. Tacomans had donated nearly $20,000 for the relief efforts. Among the many cities that sent liberal amounts were San Francisco, Olympia, Virginia City, and Portland. Telegrams arrived from the East and from San Francisco, offering merchants liberal credit in restocking their stores and extending credit on previous obligations.

At a meeting on June 7, Mayor Moran spoke to nearly 600 businessmen and asked their opinions on reconstruction. Unanimously they agreed that no wooden buildings should be erected in the burned area. They also thought this was the time to widen and straighten the streets. Jacob Furth spoke for those present when he said: "The time is not far distant when we shall look upon the fire as an actual benefit. I say we shall have a finer city than before, not within five years, but in eighteen months."

City officials agreed that in the interim businesses might operate from tents. Within five days canvas billowed on the streets in the blackened blocks, and within a fortnight customers again crowded the streets. These tents housed businesses through the succeeding winter while the burned area was rebuilt.

Seattleites again demonstrated their indomitable spirit. With its commercial section burned to the ground, Seattle rose from its ashes in less than two years. The city expanded with new enterprises, and its population increased more rapidly than ever before.

The fire was given credit for clearing the decks so that the city could usher in the '90s with a modern business district. Thousands of people were attracted to Seattle and King County in this period of the city's rebuilding. According to the census of 1890, Seattle was home to 42,837 individuals—11 times the population of 1880.

STATEHOOD AND THE CITY

Late in 1889 Washington became a state. The first legislature was scheduled to convene on November 6, but President Benjamin Harrison refused to sign the proclamation of admission until he had a copy of the state constitution authorized by Governor Miles C. Moore. The first copy sent him had not been certified. This oversight remedied, on November 11, 1889, Washington gained statehood. But this delay resulted in Washington's becoming the 42nd state of the Union, with North Dakota, South Dakota, and Montana admitted just ahead of it.

After statehood, the issues of women's suffrage and prohibition were presented as separate riders to the constitution. The people turned down both. Elisha P. Ferry of Seattle was elected governor and the legislators chose ex-governor Watson C. Squire and John B. Allen as the state's first senators.

The constitution contained a provision permitting cities having 20,000 or more inhabitants to frame and adopt their own charters. Since Seattle had outgrown its original charter, the city leaders began the process of developing a new one. Fifteen freeholders were chosen, and the charter they wrote was adopted at an election in 1890, but it proved unwieldy, with its large bodies of aldermen and councilmen. After 1895 the city's governance was concentrated in one body of 13 members.

Seattleites from the outset demonstrated their enlightened approach to government. The right of initiative and referendum was included. The city council was charged with much of the responsibility for operations of the city. The

THE DENNY BROTHERS

The names of Arthur and David Denny will always remain premier among Seattle's founders. And rightly so, for they were hardworking, God-fearing men whose contributions were mighty.

In many ways the brothers were alike, but in certain key aspects of character, they differed. Arthur, ten years older, was more influential in the early stages of the city's history. The more taciturn of the two, he was constant and energetic in building his city, yet prudent and thrifty. A strict prohibitionist, he refused to see liquor in his store even though it might bring more profit than any other merchandise. However, he seemed willing to forgive those who did not abide by his standards—since forgiveness is a Christian ethic and Arthur Denny strove to live an upright Christian life. He was a good family man and loved his wife, but these were private matters of which he did not write and seldom spoke. He wished the Indians to be treated fairly and attempted to so treat them himself, feeling that others often mistreated them. But he wanted to make them over into Christians, so did not truly understand them.

While not a warm, outgoing individual, Arthur was trusted. He did not shirk his civic duties when called upon. While involved in establishing the village, he served as King County Commissioner, territorial representative in the first Olympia legislative session, and as a delegate to Congress.

Arthur Denny acted with caution. His holdings in Seattle were not to be gambled with, just as the success of the growing town was not for speculation.

David Denny was much like his older brother: strong in Protestant belief, hard-working, a prohibitionist, and a family man. Like Arthur, he was concerned about relations with the natives. David was one of the few pioneers to learn Indian dialects and to build personal friendships with the Indians.

Where the two brothers differed the most, perhaps, was in their approach to business. David was the more expansive, and as Seattle burgeoned in the '80s he was far less conservative than Arthur in handling his finances. David—whose claim, farther north than Arthur's, did not become valuable until just before he lost it—made a fortune from business ventures. His was the respected name and he the willing investor in many schemes he believed would help the city grow and prosper. But he overextended himself, and during the 1893 panic he went almost overnight from being one of the richest men in Seattle to complete destitution.

When David died, C.B. Bagley said of him:

> Mr. Denny was one of the best men Seattle ever had. Next to Henry Yesler, he was perhaps the most progressive of all the old timers whose lives form a part of the early history of this city.

He was called "Honest Dave." And honest he was, to the end of his life, even after events broke him. Dexter Horton's bank finally foreclosed after David Denny had over-extended himself in financing streetcar lines. One of the bank's vice presidents at the time was Arthur Denny, then over 70, semiretired and in no position to dictate bank policy.

David Denny died in 1903 at Licton Springs, about a mile north of Green Lake. His last years were spent mining in the Cascades and working on the Snoqualmie Pass road. Arthur had died four years previously in his home on First Avenue. The newspapers estimated Arthur's wealth at from one to three million dollars.

The Denny brothers, from the start, did more than any of the founders in establishing the character of Seattle and the basis of its livelihoods.

—James R. Warren

Far left
David Thomas Denny (1832–1903) came to the Seattle area with 25 cents in his pocket and eventually became a multimillionaire, but was reduced to poverty in the Panic of 1893. Photo by Peterson and Brothers. (MOHAI)

Left
Arthur Armstrong Denny (1822–1899) participated in Seattle and King County affairs as postmaster, county commissioner, and member of the legislature for nine sessions. (MOHAI)

Clockwise from top left:
The great fire was sweeping south down Front Street (First Avenue) within an hour, June 6, 1889. This photo looking north shows flames on both sides of the street. (MOHAI)

The morning after the fire of June 6, 1889, the left side of Mill Street (Yesler Way) was scattered with remains of the Post-Intelligencer Building, the Yesler-Leary Building, and the Occidental Hotel. (MOHAI)

After the fire, Tacomans sent food and volunteers to Seattle. In this large tent they prepared thousands of meals a day for diners who stood while they ate. At night the tent was cleared and portable cots were brought in for the homeless to sleep on. (MOHAI)

A cable car travels along Yesler Way, on the right, in a view looking east in 1891. On the left is Jefferson Street, and the new county courthouse stands on Profanity Hill, with the "Hair Store" in the foreground. (MOHAI)

The Queen City Cycle Club poses in front of and atop the Van de Venter home, circa 1896. (MOHAI)

The women of the Seattle Athletic Club pose with their trainer, circa 1893. Photo by Braas. (MOHAI)

Seattle Electric Company employees string wires from a horse drawn wagon, circa 1900. Electric lights were turned on for a demonstration at the company's headquarters on March 22, 1886. (MOHAI)

The City Council voted to allow businesses to operate from tents after the fire leveled the heart of the city. Soon a joke was repeated over and over: "Our business is intense." (MOHAI) charter also stated that eight hours of labor comprised a full day's work for the city.

During the opening years of the "Gay '90s," Seattle gained the reputation of an immoral town. Many West Coast towns were fairly "open" to vice activities during this period, but Seattle earned an especially colorful notoriety. An open town was considered good for business, and was therefore supported by many businessmen, with reform movements attempting to stem the leniency.

Signals of an impending depression had arrived in 1890 when some major financial institutions in the East failed. The city, still raising itself from the ashes, was strapped for cash, but the planning and building had progressed so rapidly that most of the development moved ahead.

At a cost of $125,000 the city purchased the triangular piece of ground now called Pioneer Square and removed the jog at First Avenue. With a slanted connection, Front Street (renamed First Avenue) now met Commercial Street (renamed First Avenue South).

There were moves now to increase the size of the city by extending its boundaries through annexation. At the 1891 election Seattle acquired such regions as the area north of Smith Cove, West Point, the west side of Shilshole Bay, the north shore of Lake Union, the Green Lake area, and the west shores of Lake Washington.

In efforts to improve streets, install sidewalks, build sewers, and in other ways improve the city, Seattle built up a debt burden to its limit (which could amount to no more than 10 percent of the value of all taxable property in the city). At the time of the fire, the city owed a little more than $44,000; a year later that amount was increased to $311,000 and in 1893 to $3,535,000. Until that time, the cost of water mains and sewers was charged to the city, but now the burden was shifted to property owners. The cost of those utilities was paid by a system of local assessments against those benefiting. To add to the confusion, the school district erected buildings with money from city bonds, and King County was deriving revenue from taxes on Seattle property.

Part of the money raised by the county was used to build the new courthouse in 1890 on the brow of the hill some 400 feet above the business district. The county owned that land and, rather than purchase a more convenient site, insisted the building go there. The area soon was nicknamed "Profanity Hill" for the oaths uttered by those people who trudged up the steep stairs to perform their duties.

Also in the early 1890s the school district built three large brick schoolhouses to meet the demands of a surging school-age population. The city also focused on improving the water supply, a concern naturally heightened by experiences during the fire, when water pressure failed. In January 1890 the city purchased the Spring Hill Water Company for $352,000 from its private owners. Municipal utilities were a focus of the Populist movement, which held that "natural monopolies" should belong to the government.

HARD TIMES

For several months in 1891, violence erupted in the county's coal mines. A disagreement between the miners at Franklin and Newcastle and the officers of the Oregon Improvement Company resulted in a strike. The company sent an agent to the Midwest where he recruited several hundred black miners to be used in the effort to divide labor. (Once the blacks were allowed to join the miners' union, they became its supporters.) This move was kept quiet until the train arrived at Palmer Junction, where the blacks got off and marched into Franklin.

Within a few days the blacks were working the mines and living in company cabins. Sympathy strikes broke out at other mines. On June 8, 60 blacks took over the Newcastle mine. Armed by the company, when attacked, they returned the gunfire. No one, however, was hurt.

Shortly after this confrontation, Park Robinson, the mine boss, shot and killed two men near his home. Two white women were slightly wounded though it was not known by whom. When the state militia was called out, two Seattle companies were sent to Gilman. One of the Tacoma companies went to Black Diamond, a second to Newcastle, and the third to Gilman. The Port Townsend Company occupied Franklin. While martial law was not declared, meetings were discouraged and violent talk repressed. Governor Ferry commanded that all arms be taken from the coal companies' private guards, the numerous deputy sheriffs, the black miners, and the white striking miners. Most turned in their firearms. New men were brought in to work the mines. Even those men who struck in sympathy found that they returned on even poorer terms than before. Park Robinson, accused of manslaughter, was acquitted on a plea of self-defense.

When state authorities were requested to pay the militia, the Adjutant General refused, asserting that King County should pay the bill. Suits on the part of the militia resulted in the Supreme Court's decision that the state was responsible for the costs of the state militia.

The recession that swept the country hit Seattle hard in 1893, forcing many corporations and several streetcar lines into bankruptcy. (These lines were tied to real-estate promotion, considered bad business by some.) David Denny, who owned several lines, was one of the city's wealthiest capitalists one day and destitute the next.

The depression lasted until 1897. In this period, the problem of deflation was very serious. The value of the dollar had increased by 50 percent since the Civil War. Cash was short, especially in an isolated city like Seattle.

During this period of severe unemployment, roving bands of desperate men took to riding freight trains. The hardship for the unemployed and their families was considerable as there was no government aid to help them. A movement called Coxey's Army planned to assemble a host of unemployed at the nation's capital to influence legislation. Calling themselves the Commonweal Army, 1,500 local persons showed up at Puyallup and insisted the Northern Pacific provide them free transportation to Washington, D.C. A corps of several hundred deputies prevented the seizure of the train. Shortly thereafter, a strike sympathetic to Coxey's Army of jobless was called by Eugene V. Debs, and the deputies continued to guard the trains until the strike ended.

CITY IMPROVEMENTS

Before the fire, the sidewalk on the north side of James Street had been two feet below grade because Henry Yesler, who lived on that corner, refused to allow the sidewalk to be raised higher than his doorstep. The sidewalk on the east side of Second Avenue was five feet higher than the grade of the street and stairs had been constructed at each corner and in front of some businesses. Along with correcting such situations, the width of the principal streets was now increased from 66 to 90 feet. Prior to 1893, if paved at all, streets were surfaced with creosoted fir planks, which wore out quickly under the heavy traffic of wagons and carriages. Graveling and even macadamizing were tried.

The Denny Clay Company, wishing to demonstrate the practicality of paving with vitrified brick, paved a strip on First Avenue South from the sidewalk to the streetcar line. An auspicious experiment, it later resulted in the company's becoming the world's largest producer of paving brick.

The turn of the century serves as a dividing line between Seattle, the western town, and Seattle, the modern city. Until 1900, muddy streets and wooden sidewalks were acceptable, but after that even the planking used on streets in

ENTERTAINMENT

The development of early Seattle theater is largely the story of the remarkable entrepreneurs who were willing to gamble their skills and daring in untested waters. The foresight of such men as John Considine, John Cort, and Alexander Pantages made Seattle, in spite of its being one of America's youngest cities, a trend-setter and a leader in the entertainment world of the early 20th century.

As Americans moved westward in the 19th century, they brought with them not only their household goods and tools, but their needs and desires for diversion from their hard life.

Seattle's first theatrical performance, a Shakespearean piece, took place on April 23, 1864, in the hall above Charles Plummer's store. Squire's Opera House, named for Watson C. Squire (former territorial governor and later a senator), was recognized to be the first real theater in Seattle. This building, which had served as a landmark in Seattle's downtown district was burned during the fire of 1889 and was not rebuilt.

When Seattle's citizens started to rebuild their civic buildings after the fire, fire prevention was very much on their minds. Theaters, banks, stores, and office buildings were constructed of brick or stone, and incorporated as many fire preventive precautions as possible.

John Cort's New Standard, located at Washington and Occidental, was typical of the evolution of Seattle's live theater. Built after the 1889 fire the two story building's theater originally occupied both floors, but modifications were soon made to provide a lower floor, housing a saloon and gambling establishment. Until 1894 the theater presented stock and variety shows. From 1894 until 1907 the Standard provided a place for many non-theatrical uses. In 1907, it reopened as the Lyric, a popular location for stock companies, then burlesque, variety, and (until 1925) even motion pictures. By this time the major theaters had moved uptown and the houses south of Yesler Way were disappearing. Those which continued fell into less respectable entertainments. Henry Broderick recollected that in later years the Lyric was only a shell of its former self ". . . it was patronized by loggers, stevedores, carnies, pimps, parasites, con men and lower types. The elite of the town were seen there occasionally on slumming tours in order to get a glimpse of authentic underworld . . . it was the only place in town where one could be in a theater and a bordello at the same time."

It was during the latter part of the 19th century that a city ordinance restricted Seattle's entertainment district to an area south of Yesler Way along south Washington and Main streets and on Commercial Avenue. It was upon this unsteady and less than respectable foundation of raucous, skid road variety halls, that vaudeville and its late-found partner, the moving picture, started out in Seattle. In the 1890s and early 1900s theaters like the New Standard, Grand Opera House, Coliseum, and others played an important role in establishing Seattle as the home base for some of the leading vaudeville and motion picture circuits.—**William Stannard**

◆

The Orpheum, located at Fifth and Stewart, served as one of Seattle's primary theaters for 40 years. (MOHAI)

Top
During the 1890s the tideflats south of the city center were reclaimed. Photo by Anders B. Wilse. (MOHAI)

Middle
James Hill, president of the Great Northern Railway, dreamed of a Pacific-wide transportation network feeding into Seattle. He built these docks at Smith Cove complete with warehouses. Soon his "silk trains" were speeding Oriental merchandise eastward along with trainloads of lumber and passengers, to return westward with manufactured goods, produce, and passengers. The Great Northern Dock, shown here in the 1890s, is now Piers 90 and 91. Courtesy, Williamson Collection, Puget Sound Maritime Historical Society.

Bottom
The northeast shore of Green Lake, circa 1900. The Green Lake Library and the Green Lake Fieldhouse are now located in the area to the right. Photo by Anders B. Wilse. (MOHAI)

Top
After City Engineer Reginald H. Thomson was appointed in 1892, he worked on the water supply and sewer systems. He was responsible for most of the regrading done in Seattle. Courtesy, Historical Photography Collection, U of W Libraries.

Above
James J. Hill worked his way up from clerk on a steamboat to railroad magnate. He eventually built the transcontinental Great Northern Railroad from St. Paul, Minnesota to Seattle. (MOHAI)

the business district no longer seemed sufficient. Cement replaced wooden sidewalks. Streets which were level or where the grade did not exceed 5 percent were paved with asphalt laid on concrete.

Seattle's business section in the mid-1890s was hemmed in by hills and tideflats into a small area along the waterfront between Main and Pike streets. A few hurriedly built wharves extended into Elliott Bay, their pilings requiring constant replacement because the unprotected wood was liable to damage from shipworms. These piers extended out over tideflats. The shoreline meandered, so the length of piers and pilings differed, resulting in an irregular harbor line. Ships found it difficult to maneuver.

The filling of tidal lands that prevented southward expansion of the business section had been considered as early as 1868. Cornelius H. Hanford, then carrying mail between Seattle and Puyallup, came up with the idea of removing part of Beacon Hill in order to reclaim the huge tidal area at the south end of the city, but he was 30 years ahead of his time.

Down in the old part of town, Doc Maynard's original plat included an area of tide marsh. The south part of the bay included nearly 3,000 acres of mudflats.

Owners of the waterfront properties on tidelands fought a long, hard battle to prevent all properties from becoming vested in the state. But the legislators decreed that all shoreline belonged to the state and created a Harbor Line Commission. This commission acted to protect public interest on state-owned tidelands and harbors, and was upheld by all port experts and every court. Yet private interests were able to block proposed Seattle harbor lines by injunction until John McGraw was elected governor and appointed a new commission, which redrew the line to the liking of private interests. Later the Port of Seattle had to buy back what could have been public property.

More than 2,000 acres about Seattle were swept by tidal waters twice a day. Eugene Semple, a commission member and former governor, proposed to fill in the tideflats with earth removed by digging a canal that would connect Lake Washington and Elliott Bay through Beacon Hill. This proposal was contrary to previous plans to connect Lakes Washington and Union and the Sound to the north of downtown.

The state legislature in 1893 passed an act authorizing any person or company to excavate waterways through the tide or shore lands belonging to the state. With the material excavated, they could fill in any tide and shore lands above high tide adjacent to, or in front of, any incorporated towns or cities. As reimbursement the individuals or companies undertaking the task received first lien on all such lands plus an additional 15 percent.

Eugene Semple resigned from the Harbor Commission and filed an application to fill in the tidelands of Elliott Bay at the confluence of the Duwamish River. For almost a year, Governor John H. McGraw withheld action on Semple's application, but the Chamber of Commerce put pressure on him and the newspapers publicized the fill idea. Finally McGraw was satisfied that it was a legitimate application.

On June 22, 1894, the Seattle and Lake Washington Waterways Company was organized with ex-governors Ferry as president and Semple as vice-president. A St. Louis organization agreed to finance the undertaking if local citizens could raise a subsidy of half a million dollars. This was pledged within one week. Over the next two years, the company reclaimed about 175 acres of tideflats and lined 1,000 feet of the East Waterway with bulkheads. Then they ran out of money.

Because many people disagreed with the Beacon Hill canal scheme, additional financing was difficult to find. The proponents of the "northern canal" included property holders around Lake Union and Salmon Bay. Three years of inactivity followed, during which those who had purchased tidelands refused to pay assessments for work done. In 1900 the State Supreme Court found the agreement between the company and the state was binding. Again interest in filling the flats was revived, financial assistance was secured, and the tidelands' fill was again under way. Eventually 1,400 acres were reclaimed, and the sale of the newly created properties paid for the dredging of waterways and for a large portion of the embankments constructed at the mouth of the Duwamish River.

In the decades to follow, the heart of the waterfront slowly moved southward onto the reclaimed acres. Indeed, that area played a major role in Seattle's success as a major Pacific port. Shipyards and loading docks developed on Harbor Island, which today is a major container cargo handling area. Furthermore, an important Seattle industrial and commerical area developed on those former mudflats. Sears, Roebuck and Company's regional headquarters is located there, as are several foundries, a brewery, the railroad marshaling yards, military shipping areas, and many other industries.

RAILROADS

On February 14, 1891, the last spike was driven in the railroad connecting British Columbia with King County. The road was called the New Westminster Southern to the border and the Fairhaven and Southern from Bellingham Bay south.

In 1893 the first cross-country Great Northern train arrived in Seattle. Among the railroad builders, James Hill probably did the most for Seattle. Hill was responsible for building the King Street station, improving the service and the terminal grounds, and constructing a large dock, ample freight warehouses, and switch tracks. Under his leadership, the corporation also bored the tunnel under Seattle to relieve congestion of traffic in Railroad Avenue. Partly through his efforts Seattle became recognized as the gateway to the Orient, a battle long fought with San Francisco and other port cities. The battle for preeminence continues and Seattle's modern port facilities and proximity via the northern route keep it in contention.

Before building the Great Northern, Hill recognized that the success of his enterprise depended on having loaded cars traveling both ways. He therefore decided that he must develop trade with Pacific Rim countries and chose Seattle as the most logical seaport at the end of the line.

To assure permanence of the trans-Pacific Ocean commerce of Seattle, Hill built the *Minnesota* and *Dakota*, two palatial passenger liners and the largest cargo carriers then existing, and put them into service from Seattle traveling to Asian countries. These steamers provided the first direct passenger service between the U.S. and Asia.

In 1896, Seattle gained a major trans-Pacific shipping line when the Japan Steamship Company signed a contract with the Great Northern Railway Company for the exchange of freight and passengers. In August the *Miiki Maru* arrived from Yokohama, the first ship to arrive under the contract. For a time Seattle was the only western port they visited. The first vessels were lightly loaded with tea, curios, matting, paper, and silk; on the return their holds were full of lumber, fish, raw cotton, tobacco, and manufactured goods. The incoming cargoes gradually increased, with the Great Northern "silk trains" speeding the raw product to New England mills.

As for the financially troubled Northern Pacific, beset by the business recession of the early 1890s, it was placed in receivership. Service improved markedly, including scheduling a profitable night train service between Seattle and Portland. In 1896 a new corporation took control of the Northern Pacific Railroad Company and purchased the Seattle, Lake Shore and Eastern Railway, improving service from Seattle to Sumas and to Snoqualmie Falls. Later the N.P. became joint user with the Great Northern of the King Street station. In 1922, when the Northern Pacific moved its general offices from Tacoma to Seattle, the Queen City would finally win the battle of the railroads.

THE REGRADING OF SEATTLE'S HILLS

Considerable assistance in the alteration of the city's contours was provided by City Engineer Reginald H. Thomson, an educated, experienced engineer who possessed great vision and energy. Though his projects often raised animosity among property owners and taxpayers, for they did cost dearly, his name is today recognized as a mover of hills and a builder extraordinaire.

In 1892, when it was discovered that a sewer trench dug on First Avenue had been installed running uphill, the city council realized it needed a competent civil engineer. Thomson was appointed to the position, and during the next 20

years he changed the face of Seattle. He was largely responsible for Seattle's excellent water supply, its sewer system, its paved and lighted streets, and—most notably—its "regrades."

Thomson's first assignment was to secure a permanent supply of pure water for the city; through his efforts the Cedar River was reserved for Seattleites. Then he undertook to build proper sewers and improve transportation in the city. He also proposed that all wharves and piers jutting in the Sound be realigned and rebuilt along lines extended northwest from the shore, thereby affording vessels entering the harbor a course along a direct line from Elliott Bay's entrance to alongside each dock. He assigned George Cotterill, then assistant engineer, later mayor, the task of drawing up the proposed alignment. The plan was adopted by the legislature and put into effect.

In 1898 Thomson opened First Avenue as far north as Denny Way. Next Thomson regraded Pike from Fifth Avenue and Pine from Second Avenue as far east as Broadway. In 1903 Second Avenue would be regraded from Pike Street to Denny Way, which called for removing a portion of Denny Hill. (This hill was chewed on for three decades before it vanished completely.) Thomson then turned to the southern end of the city and started the Jackson Street project, which involved the lowering of nearly 50 city blocks lying between Main Street and Judkins and extending from 12th Avenue to Fourth. He afterward attacked the Dearborn Street cut and excavated there, and as a result the $60,000 12th Street Bridge was constructed to give access to Beacon Hill.

The regrading was continued at various locations all over the city. Mechanization increasingly made the work easier. The earliest process involved plowing the ground so that a gang of men with shovels could load wagons, which carted the earth away. Afterward, small railroads were used, then the hydraulic sluicing methods of literally "washing down" a hill. Finally, endless belt systems loaded by giant

Opposite, top left
Seattle outfitting businesses gained from the Alaska Gold Rush. Merchandise flowed through in such quantities that it was piled on sidewalks to await transport to ships heading north. (MOHAI)

Opposite, bottom left
These Laplanders, helping in the effort to introduce reindeer to Alaska, came through Seattle at the turn of the century. Photo by Curtis. (MOHAI)

Opposite, top right
Passengers with "Klondike fever" board the *Queen*, bound for Alaska, on March 6, 1898. Photo by Anders B. Wilse. (MOHAI)

Opposite, bottom right
A stilt-man and chicken advertise Lamont's crystallized eggs during the Alaska Gold Rush, circa 1898. This was one of various enterprises whereby Seattle merchants who could not mine the gold mines in Alaska learned how to "mine the miners." (MOHAI)

Top, right
Pioneer Square was decorated for the return of the Spanish-American War veterans. The portraits may be of local boys killed in battle. Company B of the Washington Volunteers lost five men, and Company D lost three. Photo by Anders B. Wilse. (MOHAI)

Bottom, right
This mining pan was used by "Skagway" Bill Fonda, who built the first log cabin in Skagway. The leather poke was the common way to transport gold dust. (MOHAI)

steam shovels were developed. This ambitious regrading helped to release Seattle from its restricting topography. The slopes still remain, but they are tame compared to the early steep hillsides.

ALASKA GOLD RUSH

THE STEAMSHIP PORTLAND HAS JUST ARRIVED IN SEATTLE WITH A TON OF GOLD ON BOARD.

The telegram announcing the *Portland*'s arrival in Seattle on July 17, 1897, was read all over the country. Space on board for its return voyage was immediately booked by local residents eager to earn fortunes.

The fortunate ones among the miners of 1897 verified the find and returned to Seattle with individual fortunes ranging from $50,000 to $300,000 in gold. Hopefuls streamed to Seattle from every part of the United States, Europe, and indeed the world, with money to pay for transportation and for the purchase of supplies.

Vessels of all descriptions sailed into Elliott Bay and soon headed for Alaska loaded with paying customers. As Clarence Bagley observed: "Everything that would float and some that would not was immediately put into service and new construction at every available shipyard was rushed feverishly day and night."

Some ships on the way to Alaska never made it. The coast and shores of interior waters became strewn with wrecks and debris.

Several new industries swiftly developed. Preserved foodstuffs in compact form were processed, among them crystalized eggs, dried potatoes, onions, and fruit. Seattle outfitting stores such as Cooper and Levy processed food and sold it under their own labels. Sled dogs and horses were trained and sold. Horses were in demand to pack goods over Chilkoot Pass, many to be worked to death in the fierce cold of the North.

Before the Klondike excitement had ended, rich depos-

its of gold were discovered in the tundra along the shore at Nome. Gold mines elsewhere in Alaska were exploited, and during the prospecting other minerals were discovered, including several coalfields.

In July 1898 a government assay office was established in Seattle, and during the first four years gold bullion worth more than $174 million passed over the scales. Seattle grew rich as the supplier of prospectors. It was advertised as the jumping off place to the Yukon.

While gold was flowing from Alaska and northern Canada, one commodity moved the other way—a herd of reindeer. Scheduled for delivery to the Eskimo of northwestern Alaska, the animals passed through Seattle under the care of U.S. officers. The herd, brought from the north of Europe, quickly multiplied on the tundra lands of the North.

Seattle is to this day the major port for Alaska. Geographically it is the closest U.S. city; furthermore, the route to Alaska using the inland passage, though it requires experienced navigation, avoids much of the turbulence of Pacific storms.

A NEW MILITARY BASE

When the U.S. Army began considering establishment of an army post on Magnolia Bluff on the northern side of Elliott Bay, Seattleites became excited. An army post meant good business. Army officials agreed that it was an ideal location but requested that instead of the government's preempting the land, the citizens make a gift of it. Very quickly the title was acquired after most of the land was donated by its owners and the rest bought with a fund made up of voluntary contributions. The 640-acre post, established in 1897, was later named Fort Lawton after a general who was killed in battle in the Philippines during the Spanish-American War. Hundreds of thousands of men were shipped through the fort on their way to fight in various wars. No longer an active military post, most of Fort Lawton has become a city park.

The faraway Spanish-American War begun in 1898 affected Seattle and King County primarily because the National Guard of Washington State was one of the best-prepared units in the country. After President McKinley proclaimed the blockage of Cuban ports, a telegram arrived in Seattle stating the Guard would soon be called up. Next day the Secretary of War ordered preparations to ship out a 12-company regiment of infantry. Before the war ended, the Washington regiment went through 35 battles in the Philippines.

During the 1890s, in spite of the recession early in the decade, Seattle's population increased every year. By 1900 the population numbered 80,761, a figure nearly double that of 10 years earlier.

A major change had also taken place in the city. Individual effort and enterprise had given way to community and corporation activities. The grand old men who had been leaders and active workers in the development of the village and town were now mostly dead or retired. Among those who died during this decade were Henry Yesler, Thomas Mercer, Arthur Denny, and William Renton. They and dozens of other pioneers had seen Seattle become the largest city and King County the leading county in the state. Henceforth, the complications of a large population and involved government would make individual accomplishment more difficult. Nonetheless, new leaders would emerge and the area would proceed to even greater successes. In the next years, the activity would center upon Seattle as a prime port city on the Pacific. ◆

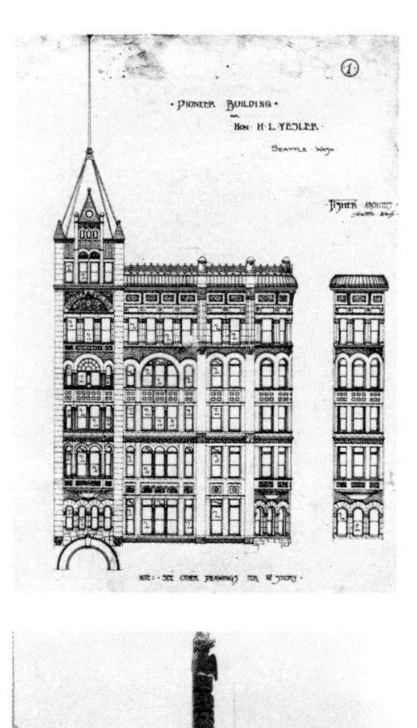

Opposite
The Jackson Street regrade, looking east from Weller Street and Maynard Avenue, was in progress in 1908. People lived in the houses as the earth was removed around them, and large pipes carried the slurry (soil and water) to the tideflats. (MOHAI)

Top
Henry Yesler's Pioneer Building had been planned before the fire by architect Elmer Fisher. Although excavation had begun, fortunately the building had not been started when the conflagration leveled the area. Courtesy, Architectural History Collection, U of W Libraries.

Above
The original totem pole in Pioneer Square, shown here in 1900, was taken from an Indian village by a touring group of businessmen on a return trip from Alaska. It was destroyed by fire in 1932. Photo by Anders B. Wilse. (MOHAI)

HOW SEATTLE GETS ITS WATER

Seattle and King County, blessed with a plentiful supply of soft, fresh water, has guarded this natural resource with great caution and foresight.

Two years after Seattle's founding, Henry Yesler built the first water tank in what is now the lawn of the old county-city building. Using V-shaped flumes, he tapped one of numerous springs on the hillside, carried the water to the tank, and from there down the hill to his steam sawmill. Later he and others extended the flumes to the end of their docks so ships could fill their casks and reservoirs with fresh water.

The Spring Hill and Union Water companies, organized in the early '80s, served some of Seattle's population through hollowed log pipes connected with wooden spigots. The major source of water in those days was Lake Washington. A reservoir holding 4.28 million gallons was erected on Beacon Hill in 1886 by the Spring Hill Company.

After the great fire of 1889 demonstrated the deficient water supply, the citizens voted to acquire the two major water systems that served one-quarter of the population, the rest using springs and private wells. A nationally known hydraulic engineer was hired by the city to study its water needs. He recommended use of Cedar River water, but no action was taken until City Engineer R. H. Thomson requested authorization to complete the survey and build a pipeline.

In February 1901, with the population now over 80,000, Cedar River Pipeline No. 1 was completed, carrying water through 28 miles of 42-inch steel and wood stave pipeline, delivering 23.5 million gallons per day by gravity from the intake at Landsburg on the Cedar. In 1909 a second pipeline was installed, and a third one in 1922. A fourth was added in 1954, bringing 205 million gallons a day to the city from Cedar River.

In 1904 the Cedar Lake waters were tapped for electric power, when the first generators were installed by City Light in a powerhouse below Cedar Falls. In 1918 a masonry dam was built to increase storage, raising the lake elevation by 30 feet.

A short and modest stream, only 40 miles in length and with an average yearly flow of nearly 700 second feet, the Cedar has several advantages. Its waters are clear and soft. The watershed contains 143 square miles of timbered valleys, foothills, and mountains. Precipitation varies considerably in the area but even in dry years was sufficient to satisfy Seattle's needs through the 1960s.

To deliver gravity-flow water north and south of the central city, tunnels were dug under the ship canal and under the Duwamish River. Because of Seattle's hills, pressures vary from 35 pounds per square inch to 130 pounds per square inch.

Lake Youngs, the primary storage reservoir, serves as a settling basin during the occasional periods of turbidity on the Cedar. But the water is usually clear and can be taken directly from the river. The entire watershed area is carefully patrolled to prevent contamination by the public. All swampy areas around the lake have been drained and dikes built to prevent taste and odor problems. The lake is occasionally treated with copper sulphate.

In 1970 the city began development of the Tolt River watershed some 23 miles north of Cedar River. This river water is slightly softer even than Cedar River water. With the combined resources of these rivers, Seattle is able to meet most of its water needs from nearby resources.

—**James R. Warren**

Wooden pipes and spigots like these were used in early water systems. (MOHAI)

CHAPTER 8

STARTING THE NEW CENTURY: 1900-1913

The arrival of the 20th century found Seattle an exciting, boom city with new businesses starting up and old ones expanding. Much of this activity came from the commercial stimulation of the Alaska-Yukon gold rush, the Spanish-American War, the improvements of the port facilities, and an increase in shipbuilding.

Shipbuilding was not new to Seattle. Back in the late 1870s and early '80s, increasing activity in the yards resulted in a larger number of ships being launched. These shipyards were small businesses with no machinery or tools other than what millwrights and carpenters carried in their tool chests.

The man who did the most for shipbuilding was Robert Moran. He arrived in Seattle in 1875 at age 18 with his brothers, Peter and William. The three New Yorkers were natural mechanics, and within the next few years Robert mastered the science of marine architecture.

After they had saved $1,500, the brothers opened a small machine shop which began turning a profit just before the fire of 1889 burned them out. Robert Moran was Seattle's mayor that year. In December 1889 a new Moran Brothers Corporation was organized with stock of $250,000. In 1895 the corporation contracted to supply the steam plant for the dry dock at the naval shipyard at Bremerton. The boilers, engines, and pumps were manufactured in Seattle using Robert Moran's designs.

In 1900 the company made a successful bid for construction of the *Nebraska*, a battleship for the U.S. Navy. There was some union picketing and a boycott because Moran insisted on using electrically powered cranes, mechanical hoists and hammers, and other modern devices. On October 7, 1904, the ship was launched from the Moran yards with viewers present from all over the state. Known as one of the country's best ships, the *Nebraska* symbolized Seattle's past and future prominence in shipbuilding.

Seattle's emergence as a major world port was verified by the discovery in 1908 of several cases of bubonic plague, already an epidemic taking a terrible toll of lives in the Far East. News of its outbreak in Seattle caused grave concern. The town was preparing for the Alaska-Yukon-Pacific Exposition, and the presence of the plague would cause the fair's cancellation. Mayor William Hickman Moore took the lead in adopting strenuous measures to prevent the disease from spreading. Quietly a campaign was planned. Women's clubs distributed information. There was a general cleaning of back yards and buildings that might harbor the rats and fleas that carried the disease. No more than three dozen of the rats were found to be infected. Soon all vestiges of the disease were eradicated.

THE ALASKA-YUKON-PACIFIC EXPOSITION

In late 1905 Godfrey Chealander returned to Seattle from the Lewis and Clark Exposition in Portland, where he had directed a small Alaska exhibit. Chealander, who had lived for some years in Alaska, was grand secretary of the Arctic Brotherhood. After the exhibit closed, he determined to preserve the Alaska exhibit. He talked with William Sheffield, secretary of the Alaska Club (later the Arctic Club), and the two discussed developing a permanent Alaska exhibit in Seattle. Sheffield took Chealander to see James A. Wood, city editor of the *Seattle Times*, and Wood decided to gain the public approval of the project. After interviewing the most influential business and professional men of the city, the three developed the plan for an Alaskan exposition. In 1906 the concept grew into a major exhibition and fair.

After the articles of incorporation were filed, the *Post-Intelligencer* joined its rival the *Times* in promoting the endeavor. The problem of a site for the exposition was solved when Professor Edmond S. Meany suggested locating it on the university grounds. At the time, the small educational institution consisted of three permanent buildings hidden in a forest on the shores of Lake Washington. This way, the campus could be cleared, and new buildings would be erected, so the fair would permanently benefit the university. The plan also would encourage state support for the buildings.

The state legislature agreed to prepare the fairgrounds and to allow use of the university's existing permanent buildings for fair purposes. In addition they agreed that most of the money spent on the exposition by the state would be used to erect four permanent buildings, which would eventually belong to the university.

At first the fair was called the Alaska Exposition, but the enthusiastic response to the plan enlarged its scope to include

Photograph by Victor Gardaya
(MOHAI)

the Yukon Territory in British Columbia. Then Meany suggested that the exposition include all countries bordering on the North Pacific Ocean. Emissaries were sent to China, Japan, Hawaii, California, and to Canada. Soon all of the coast states had agreed to participate and the name became the Alaska-Yukon-Pacific Exposition, commonly called "the A-Y-P."

Originally the schedule called for the fair to open in 1907, the 10th anniversary of the discovery of gold in the Klondike, but this interfered with the Jamestown Exposition at Norfolk, Virginia, so the A-Y-P directors agreed to delay until 1909. In 1907 a widespread financial panic struck the country. In an extraordinary effort, Will H. Parry managed to lead the campaign to sell the total capital stock of the exposition in one day. Seattle citizens purchased it all.

The groundbreaking ceremony occurred in June 1907, and the mammoth task of converting forest to park commenced. Bids for the agricultural building and three state buildings were let. The King County commissioners agreed to erect a forestry building that would cost $300,000 and to pay $78,000 for a county exhibit. Congress agreed to donate $600,000 if the citizens of Seattle would raise $1 million, which they did by June 1908.

By January 1909 most of the buildings were nearing completion. By the end of March, many of the exhibits were in place. In mid-April the two-story King County Building was finished. On its first floor were various exhibits, including a reproduction of the Newcastle coal mine and other Seattle-area scenes in miniature.

The university campus was laid out as a beautiful park—planned by the Olmsted Brothers, a firm founded by the sons of famed landscape designer Frederick Olmsted. About 20 new buildings had been erected, including Meany Hall, which would become the auditorium of the university when the fair was over. It was named for Professor Edmond Meany in 1914 by the Board of Regents in appreciation for his constructive work.

C.J. Smith, chairman of the building committee, was a hard driver who kept the construction on schedule. "The Fair That Will Be Ready" was his slogan. Mayor John F. Miller declared its opening day, June 1, 1909, a holiday. At 10 a.m., the President of the United States, William Howard Taft, at the nation's capital, pressed the Alaskan gold-nugget key that sent the telegraphic signal across the country. More than 80,000 spectators attended the fair's first day.

The directors had planned to bring as many conventions and public assemblies to the fairgrounds as possible. Nearly every day was dedicated to a special city, county or state occasion. There were Seattle, Norway, Chinese, Iowa, Swedish and Strawberry days, among others. Good days saw an attendance ranging from 34,000 to 60,000, and on Seattle Day a record-breaking 117,013 people passed through the gates.

The Alaska Building was one of the chief attractions, and the Oregon, Japanese, and Hawaiian buildings were rated among the finest. The Washington State Woman's Building was conspicuous and popular. "Pay Streak" was the name given the popular amusement section fashioned after Chicago's "Midway."

A statue of William Henry Seward was unveiled on September 10, honoring the man credited with purchasing Alaska from the Russians. On September 29, President Taft and a party of national officials arrived. William Jennings Bryan visited the fair on October 10, drawing a crowd who heard the popular Democrat speak.

When the fair closed on the appointed day, October 16, it was free of debt. During the 138 days it had been open, the total attendance was 3,740,551, with paid admissions aggregating $1,096,475.64. It had accomplished its two major purposes: to prove to the the people of the world the enormous value of Alaska and the greatness of its main entry port, Seattle.

After the exposition closed, a Chamber of Commerce banquet paid tribute to the hardworking volunteers. W.A. Peters, a Seattle lawyer, praised those who had dedicated themselves to make the A-Y-P a success. "Such men are the proudest possession of any community and the surest guaranty of its prosperity and greatness. Thus may your chil-

Top
These performers represented different countries for the Alaska-Yukon-Pacific Exposition in 1909. They stand in the Oriental Village on the "Pay Streak" the popular amusement section. (MOHAI)

Above
Edmond S. Meany, known primarily for his historical work, was a professor at the University of Washington. He was one of the prime movers in the Mountaineers and a great naturalist. It was he who suggested that the Alaska-Yukon-Pacific Exposition be held on university grounds. (MOHAI)

Above
The billikens, a design patented in 1908 by Florence Pretz, an art teacher from Kansas City, Missouri, represented "the God of Things as They Ought to Be." It was adopted as a mascot for the A-Y-P. The first ivory billiken was made by Happy Jack, an Eskimo. (MOHAI)

Opposite
This view facing southeast toward Mt. Rainier shows the main thoroughfare at the Alaska-Yukon-Pacific Exposition. In 1981 one of the few remnants of the Exposition on the university campus is the pond, renamed "Frosh Pond." Courtesy, Nowell Collection. (MOHAI)

This panorama was taken by the Seattle Photographic Company, circa 1900. (MOHAI)

dren's children, and generations on the heel of these, made mindful of our measure of your worth, themselves add honor to a noble heritage."

CITY BUSINESS

In the 1910 census the population of Seattle was counted at 237,194, an increase of 194 percent over the decade. This astounding increase, however, was partly due to Seattle's penchant for annexation. That year Hiram C. Gill, a member of the city council for 10 years, was elected mayor. A small, thin man, he was a blunt but fluent speaker. His abrasive personality became a major issue during the campaign. The direct primary system had just been instituted, resulting in his name being on the ballot. In the bitter speeches that followed, he was denounced and maligned in a manner that caused a good share of the voters to support him. He appointed C.W. Wappenstein as the new chief of police. Though Wappenstein was active against thieves, burglars, and bandits, he apparently made no effort to close down gambling dens or the red-light district—which were among the most lucrative attractions offered to both transients and denizens.

That summer, while Gill was out of the city on vacation, acting Mayor Wardall suspended the chief of police and moved to "clean up the city." Revelations of underworld activities such as gambling and prostitution were headlined in the papers. At a special election held early in 1911, Gill was recalled and George W. Dilling was elected in his stead. Gill did not give up easily, and in 1912 he again was on the ballot. He was defeated by engineer George F. Cotterill, a prohibitionist. However, in 1914, Gill was reelected mayor.

In November 1915 residents of the state of Washington voted to go dry. Seattle's majority, however, was against prohibition. Robert T. Hodge, the sheriff of King County, and Charles L. Beckingham, the chief of police, worked with Mayor Gill in vigorous enforcement. Gill was antiprohibition, but when the initiative was approved by the state's citizens, he vigorously enforced it, personally leading raids on establishments where liquor was sold—and made new enemies. On testimony of bootleggers, a federal grand jury rendered an indictment against Gill, Hodge, and Beckingham, charging them with conspiring to violate the interstate commerce law. They were found not guilty. Nonetheless, there was a second recall petition against the mayor. This was dropped in favor of the less expensive method of impeachment, but the city council refused to remove the mayor.

In spite of animosity against him, Gill was elected mayor for a third time in 1916, the first Seattle mayor to serve three terms. He worked to remove the stigma cast on Seattle that came as a result of criticism of him for failing to enforce the laws. He closed bawdy houses as well as saloons. He ran again in 1918, but was defeated by Ole Hanson, a former legislator and shipyard laborer. Gill died within the year, a victim of Spanish influenza.

Ten years in advance of most other states, the state constitution was amended in 1910 to allow women the right to

vote. Washington was also the first state to enact a worker's compensation law. Injured workers were henceforth paid from a state insurance fund.

In 1913 the legislature adopted the initiative and referendum method of enacting laws by direct vote of the people; again Washington was one of the first states to do so. By this method, prohibition was voted into effect in 1916, to be superseded by a more drastic state law in 1917. Then the 18th Amendment to the Constitution (backed up by the Volstead Act) became the law of the land, prohibiting consumption of intoxicating liquor in any form. Seattle and King County, located on Puget Sound and within easy sailing or driving distance of British Columbia, were the scene of constant battles with smugglers all through the prohibition years.

In 1911, the voters of Seattle and King County established a port commission with jurisdiction over the harbors and waterways of the county. This populist progressive reform act, it was hoped, would correct a chaotic waterfront criss-crossed with railroads and piers. Within a decade, Seattle became a major port. The first port commissioners, General Hiram M. Chittenden, Robert Bridges, and C.E. Remsberg, accomplished much. On November 8 the voters authorized a bond issue of $1.75 million for excavating the Lake Washington Canal, providing dollars for public docks and wharves, aid for Duwamish Waterway, and for diverting the Cedar River.

The commissioners next developed a comprehensive general plan of port improvement costing $3 million. To this was added the costs for the "Bush Terminal Scheme," a possible scam involving $5 million in bonds to buy 147 acres of filled land (Harbor Island) and then to lease it to the Pacific Coast Terminals Company, which was to construct an extensive system of wharves and railway terminals patterned after the Bush Terminals at South Brooklyn, New York. The terms of the lease were to extend over 30 years. The voters approved the entire package totaling more than $8 million. However, Pacific Coast Terminals began delaying and tried to change provisions in the initial agreement. Eventually, the commission requested the $5 million be rescinded but asked for $3 million to purchase the West Seattle ferry and its terminals and to build a turning basin in the West Waterway. Again, the voters backed the commission.

Voter support of the port commission permitted purchase of the Smith Cove terminals and construction there of the largest pier on the Pacific Coast. The Bell Street Terminals were erected, Stacy and Lander Street and East Waterway Terminals were built and the Salmon Bay Terminals improved and enlarged. The port commission then acquired the ferry landing on Elliott Bay and authorized construction and operation of a ferry on Lake Washington between Leschi Park and Mercer Island, Bellevue, and Medina. The ferryboat *Leschi*, launched in 1913, could carry as many as 30 vehicles and 1,000 passengers. While the waterfront around Elliott Bay was developing, the dream of building a canal to permit large ships to enter the sheltered fresh water of Lakes Washington and Union began to move toward reality.

SHIPBUILDING

Seattle's location on the tidewater margin of the Pacific Northwest forest and its dependence on maritime trade made the community an early center of shipbuilding. Because of the economic importance of lumbering, 19th-century shipbuilding focused on the construction of schooners and other sailing vessels for the lumber trade. Featuring special ports and holds to facilitate loading of cumbersome lumber, these vessels were an essential component of the trade prior to the completion of transcontinental railroads and the opening of markets east of the Cascades. Shipyards were located in most of the Puget Sound lumber ports; the best-known was the Hall Brothers operation at Port Blakely on Bainbridge Island opposite Seattle. However, the decline of the so-called cargo mills—those shipping lumber by sea—at the end of the century meant a corresponding end to the early shipbuilding era.

The Mosquito Fleet vessels, too, which transported passengers and small freight items, had been refurbished and replaced in the early shipyards.

In the 20th century, military needs replaced civilian and commercial ones as the principal source of business, imparting a distinctive boom-and-bust aspect to the Puget Sound shipbuilding industry. The harbinger of this change was the launching of the battleship *Nebraska* in 1904 by the Moran Brothers' shipyard in Seattle. With the aid of a large subscription from the public, Robert Moran had secured the contract and achieved what he claimed was his boyhood dream of building a giant warship.

During World War I, the demand for naval and civilian vessels brought an incredible boom to the Seattle waterfront. Attracted by unprecedented rates of pay, over 35,000 persons were employed in the city's yards and related industries manufacturing steel freighters and small wooden support vessels. Ninety-six ships were produced in 1918 alone and, over the course of the war, Seattle supplied a fourth of the federal government's shipping requirements. The armistice of November 1918, of course, brought the boom to a sudden and troubling end. Among other difficult peacetime adjustments, the effort to reduce wages by the Skinner and Eddy Corporation, the city's largest yard, resulted in the famed Seattle General Strike of early 1919.

Two decades later, war again produced a dramatic and short-lived expansion of activity. The percentage of industrial employees engaged in shipbuilding in Washington State mounted from 2 percent in 1940 to 38 percent in 1943, before falling with peace to 10 percent in 1946 and 2 percent in 1948. In the postwar era, Seattle shipbuilders remained dependent on a limited number of government orders. The city's yards turned out an occasional cutter for the coast guard, support ship for the navy, or war vessel for an allied nation. At last, the long hoped for revision of American laws stifling the domestic construction of civilian vessels enabled Seattle and other Puget Sound ports to again boast of a sustained boat-building industry of the 19th century variety.—**Robert E. Ficken**

The U.S.S. *Nebraska* is shown here near completion in the Moran Brothers Company shipyard. Photograph by Webster and Stevens. Courtesy, Williamson Collection, Puget Sound Maritime Historical Society.

Opposite, top
This view looking north shows the dredged East Waterway of the Duwamish River, with Harbor Island to the left. The old tideflats area is located to the right, circa 1915. Courtesy, James P. Lee Collection. (MOHAI)

Middle
Virgil Bogue, a civil engineer, was employed by the Municipal Plans Commission to create a plan for Seattle's development. This is a diagram of the civic center group that he wanted to build near Fourth and Blanchard. The voters turned his plan down two to one. (MOHAI)

Bottom
Hiram C. Gill, elected mayor of Seattle in 1910, was recalled, and then reelected in 1914. He had served on the city council for 10 years before he became mayor after a campaign in which his abrasive personality developed into an issue. (MOHAI)

BUILDING THE SHIP CANAL AND LOCKS

Thomas Mercer had predicted in 1854 that someday a canal would link the waters of Lakes Washington and Union with Puget Sound. Soon afterward, George B. McClellan, a captain of engineers at that time, reported that such a canal would create "the finest naval resort in the world." Through the years that followed, government engineers continuously investigated the possibilities.

When Harvey Pike filed his Union City plat in 1869, he reserved a strip 200 feet wide between the two lakes for the canal. He stubbornly attacked the portage with a pick and shovel but finally decided his back couldn't take it. In 1871 he and several others incorporated the Lake Washington Canal Association. They petitioned Congress for a grant of land to support the construction of the canal, but Congress took no notice.

Also in 1871, another government report recommended two feasible canal routes: the first to proceed from the southern end of Lake Union southwesterly, to reach Elliott Bay at the foot of Battery Street; the second to follow present Westlake Avenue to Pike Street, then down to Elliott Bay. Congress again took no action.

Nine years later delegate Thomas H. Brents introduced a bill in the House of Representatives requesting $15,000 to start the process, but Washington Territory still did not command much recognition in Congress, so the bill was ignored.

Henry Villard, while president of the Northern Pacific Railroad, had a renowned naval engineer examine the physical conditions of the canal right-of-way. The report favorably impressed Villard, who undoubtedly was dreaming of tolls that could be earned. He believed that ultimately the United States would purchase the canal, so there was little chance of losing the investment. However, Villard lost the presidency of the railroad; the company became insolvent; and when it reorganized, the canal interest died.

Then, in 1883, the Lake Washington Improvement Company—incorporated by David T. Denny, J.W. George, C.P. Stone, Thomas Burke, F.H. Whitworth, H.B. Bagley, and others—was capitalized for $50,000. It proposed to construct a canal with locks. Their plan called for the excavation to be located a few hundred feet south of the present canal. But first they planned to link the two lakes.

The surface of Lake Washington was from 15 to 20 feet above the high tide mark of Puget Sound. The natural lake outlet was the Black River, narrow and rapid except when high water in the White and Cedar rivers backed it up. During heavy rains or rapid snow melt, Lake Washington would rise as much as six or seven feet, flooding surrounding acreage. The Improvement Company planned for the link with Lake Union to relieve this situation, serving as a drain in times of high water. Work started on the interlake canal in June 1883 with a force of 50 men. But the contractor, J.J. Cummings, claimed he hit hardpan and demanded more than the 27 cents per yard of earth provided in the contract. He was dismissed, and a new agreement was signed with the Wa Chong Company, which hired Chinese workers to dig north of Queen Anne Hill and excavate a canal between Lake Union and Salmon Bay, a distance of three-quarters of a mile.

The 25 Chinese laborers, digging away, by 1885 had cut through from lake to bay and had erected a small wooden lock, which permitted the passage of logs from Lake Union to salt water on the Sound. Under the leadership of Frank H. Osgood a small ditch across the portage between the two lakes was opened, large enough to deliver logs, but too small for vessels of any size.

Between 1876 and 1890, six different canal routes were proposed by the U.S. Army Corps of Engineers, and some of them were surveyed. After Washington became a state in 1889, the legislature requested the appointment of a congressional commission to study the canal situation. In 1890 Congress passed an act authorizing the survey of a ship canal by the most feasible route. The report filed on December 15, 1891, estimated the cost of a canal to Shilshole Bay at $2.9 million and to Smith Cove at $3.5 million. They also estimated the cost of linking Lake Sammamish to Lake Washington at nearly $5 million. Congress voted to pay for the surveys but extended no aid for the construction of the waterway.

Though public opinion seemed to swing toward the south canal route through Beacon Hill, the prominent Judges John J. McGilvra, Thomas Burke, and Roger S. Greene, all refused to endorse it. In 1894 the Rivers and Harbors Committee of Congress endorsed the Shilshole Bay route, but former Governor Semple and his company, already busily filling the tideflats, proceeded to plan "an entirely Seattle- and Washington-built canal." In July 1895 they began to dredge, dig, and fill. When they ran out of funds and lost local support, a timely Supreme Court decision ordered the payment of fees owed to the company by property owners benefiting from the fill. Will H. Parry took over direction of the company, with financial backing of $4 million arranged out of New York. The sluicing of the canal through Beacon Hill was started. The tideflats were being filled. Now a joint committee was formed to promote construction of the north canal. The Seattle and Ballard Chambers of Commerce, the county commissioners, and the city councils of each city each provided three representatives.

In 1898 still another engineering commission surveyed and again recommended the Shilshole Bay route. King County, at an expense of $250,000, secured the right-of-way for the north canal, with property deeded to the United States. Early the next year bids were asked for construction

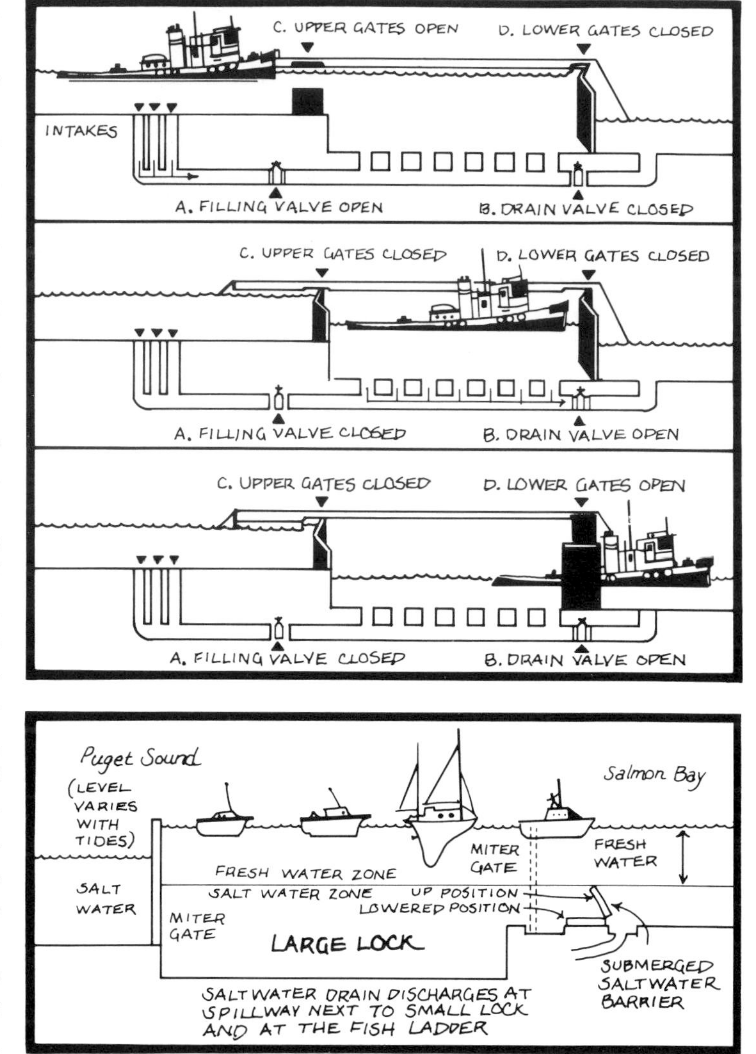

Lakes Union and Washington would have become saltwater reservoirs if a way had not been found to return saltwater to Puget Sound. The problem was solved by dredging a basin immediately above the large lock and extending a discharge pipe to the downstream side of the spillway dam. In January 1975 the discharge was partially diverted to the fish ladder through a six-foot diameter pipe, creating a flow of water to attract fish up the ladder. The Chittenden Locks are operated from a control tower. From there the lock and spillway gates and saltwater barrier are regulated, and directions are flashed to boaters. Drawing by Sandra Lee Bell, based on diagrams provided by the United States Army Corps of Engineers.

Top, left
Horse-drawn delivery wagons crowd Western Avenue, circa 1904. At the turn of the century, the city was booming and had a population of 80,671. The next decade that figure would nearly triple to more than 237,000. (MOHAI)

Top, right
In this view of Seattle in the 1880s, a lumber schooner is tied to Yesler's Wharf. To the right of its rigging, the university building stands on the hill. Courtesy, Historical Photography Collection, U of W Libraries.

Middle
This scene shows the original log canal dug through the portage area between Lakes Washington and Union. The Lake Washington Ship Canal was excavated to the left of the old canal. (MOHAI)

Bottom
King County was responsible for excavating the Montlake cut of the Lake Washington Ship Canal. This view looks west toward Lake Union. (MOHAI)

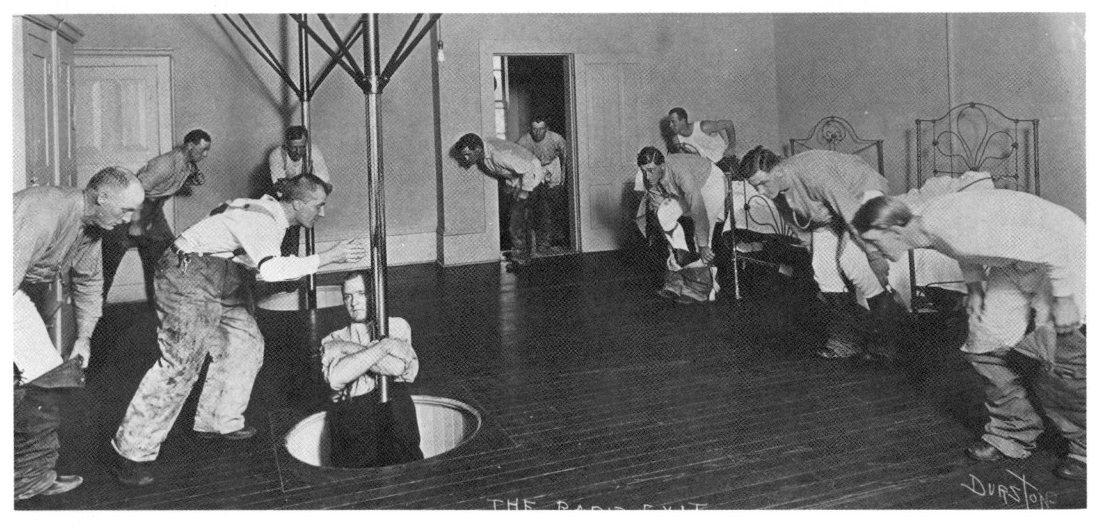

Top, left
The Pacific Great White Fleet enters Elliott Bay in 1908. Courtesy, Wilcox Collection. (MOHAI)

Middle, left
Engine Company Number Six responds to an alarm in Seattle on August 6, 1916. (MOHAI)

Bottom, left
The Pike Place Market, shown here in 1912, was started in 1907 as a way for farmers to sell their produce directly to consumers. It became a market for meat, fish, and produce from western and eastern Washington. Photo by Asahel Curtis. Courtesy, Historical Photography Collection, U of W Libraries.

Opposite, top
The old Fire Station dock, located at the foot of Madison Street, was torn down in 1912. The fireboats *Snoqualmie* and *Duwamish* were anchored at the dock, circa 1911. (MOHAI)

Opposite, bottom
In 1911 engineer Hiram Chittenden became one of the three port commissioners in King County and worked diligently to develop the Port of Seattle. His most notable feat, however, was supervising the construction of the Lake Washington Ship Canal and the locks, which bear his name. Courtesy, Historical Photography Collection, U of W Libraries.

work. The contract was awarded to the Puget Sound Bridge and Dredging Company to begin deepening the channel at the west end of the canal.

In 1902 Congress, looking for a fresh water basin for the U.S. Navy, ordered yet another survey. The army engineers reported that the south canal was feasible but the cost prohibitive, and favored the north canal as the most practical route. At the hearings that followed, the engineers recommended against building either canal, since neither was needed at the time.

This report brought the differing Seattle factions together. For the first time all canal proponents in King County backed a single plan of action. The Chamber of Commerce agreed to the filling of the tidelands by the Seattle and Lake Washington Waterways Company while that corporation agreed to drop all plans for a south canal.

Meantime, the government continued dredging Shilshole Bay as far east as the Ballard wharves. The millmen of Salmon Bay, with some help from Elliott Bay wharf owners, for a time fought the location of the locks at the mouth of the bay because it would raise the waters in front of the Ballard holdings. This further delayed congressional appropriations.

In 1905 General Hiram M. Chittenden, then a lieutenant colonel in the U.S. Army Corps of Engineers, was asked to take charge of the Seattle office.

In March 1907 the Lake Washington Canal Association was formed to raise additional funds for excavating of various units of the canal, as stipulated by government engineers. The Canal Assessment Act of 1907, passed by the state legislature, provided for a commission of 11 members to designate an assessment district to raise necessary funds in cooperation with the United States in the construction of the north canal.

Congress, approached again in 1908, sent more government engineers to investigate and report. The engineers recommended a canal 75 feet wide, at a minimum depth of 25 feet, with a lock 825 feet long by 80 feet wide and 36 feet deep. Cost was estimated at $3,554,932. The engineers also recommended that King County excavate the canal (at an estimated cost of $1,064,000) and that the government furnish the locks.

Major Chittenden himself estimated the total cost of the canal at $4,358,229. He submitted extensive maps and drawings showing how the Cedar River could be diverted into Lake Washington to provide a constant water flow through the locks.

The legislature had platted and sold certain shore lands on Lakes Union and Washington to support the A-Y-P Exposition and to establish permanent buildings for the University of Washington. The funds raised exceeded what was needed by $250,000. This sum was turned over to the canal fund. A special election appropriated the remaining $750,000. On June 25, 1910, the construction of the Lake Washington Canal was authorized in the Rivers and Harbors Act passed by Congress. An appropriation of $2,275,000 for the building of the locks by the government was contingent upon the construction of the canal by King County. This contingency was assured, and one year later, in June of 1911, the Secretary of War ordered commencement of the work by the U.S. Army Corps of Engineers. In accordance with provisions of the new act, a larger and smaller lock, side by side, designed to prevent saltwater intrusion, were to be constructed by the government at Salmon Bay.

While the U.S. government was constructing the locks and the county was excavating the channel, agitations for numerous bridges over the canal were started by residents and real-estate dealers concerned with the different communities adjoining the canal route on the north, which would now be separated by water from the main part of Seattle. In 1913 citizens voted down a bond issue to build 13 bridges. Instead, the city leaders developed a more reasonable plan for four bridges—Fremont, Ballard, and University bridges, to be later joined by Montlake. These the citizens approved.

Here is the timetable of progress in building the canal:

November 10, 1911: ground was broken for construction of the lock.
February 26, 1913: the first concrete was poured in the lock.
February 7, 1916: the first boat passed through the lock, but the gates were not yet closed.
July 12, 1916: the lock gates were closed and the water of Salmon Bay raised.
July 19, 1916: the waters of Lake Washington were released and by October 21, the waters of Lake Washington were lowered to the level of Lake Union.
October 12, 1916: the canal was opened into Lake Union.
May 8, 1917: the canal was opened for navigation into Lake Washington.

The ceremonial dedication of the Lake Washington Ship Canal took place on July 4, 1917. On that sunny day, multitudes viewed the oncoming fleet of vessels from Puget Sound. Decked out in all their colors, the ships proceeded in groups through the lock and Lake Union and on through the cut into Lake Washington, convoyed by an airplane overhead. At a point off Leschi Park, the boats circled and returned. That evening the canal was lit with fireworks and Judge Thomas Burke, as master of ceremonies at the locks, told of the history of the canal, using material written by General Hiram M. Chittenden.

After the canal opened in 1917, Seattleites hardly had time to sit back and contemplate the progress they had witnessed—growth of the port, the building of the canal, and the A-Y-P Exposition. Their city was now home to more than 250,000 people. Automobiles were chugging up the hills; women were voting. But dwelling on past accomplishments had ceased as the United States entered, belatedly, the "war to end all wars."

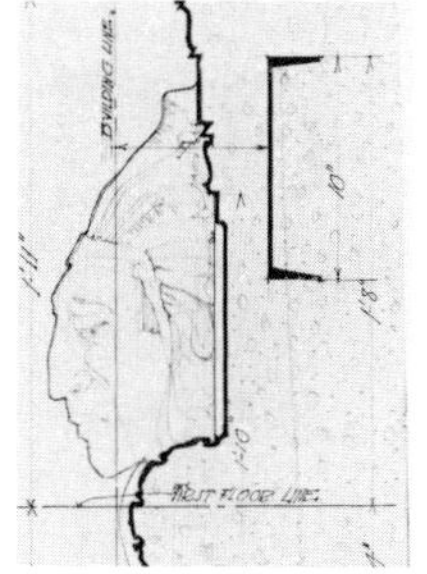

Top
This view looking west from the Fremont Bridge shows the construction of the Lake Washington Ship Canal on May 4, 1916. (MOHAI)

Middle
The *Roosevelt*, the ship that brought Admiral Peary home from the North Pole, passes under the new Fremont Bridge on the opening day of the Lake Washington Ship Canal, July 4, 1917. Photograph by Webster and Stevens. Courtesy, Williamson Collection, Puget Sound Maritime Historical Society.

Above, left
The original St. Marks Episcopal Church was located at Harvard and Spring, circa 1910. (MOHAI)

Above
Here the side view of the "Terra Cotta Indian" drawing by architects Howells and Stokes is shown. It was used as a detail on the Henry Building, built in 1908 and replaced in the 1970s by the Rainier Tower complex. Courtesy, Architectural History Collection, U of W Libraries.

WOMEN'S SUFFRAGE

Three women hang posters in 1910 during a suffrage campaign. Courtesy, Asahel Curtis Collection, Washington State Historical Society.

◆

Women got the vote in Washington State in 1910, a decade ahead of their sisters in most other states. The struggle for that right had begun many years before.

In 1854 the first territorial legislature voted on the issue of women's suffrage. The bill failed by one vote. After the passage of the 14th and 15th Amendments to the Constitution, a Washington woman named Mary Olney Brown challenged the existing laws. Women she had organized to vote were turned away from the polls. Yet on the same election day, in a precinct near Centralia, a group of women brought lunch to the men at the polls. After all had eaten, the women proclaimed, "Now we're going to vote." And they did.

Susan B. Anthony and Abigail Scott Duniway, leaders in the national women's suffrage movement, spoke to the territorial legislature in Olympia in 1871 to discuss women's right to vote. Again the measure met defeat—as it did 10 years later.

Duniway, a feminist from Portland, published a newspaper called the *New Northwest* which advocated women's rights issues. She was strongly criticized by Anthony and others because she called for the separation of the temperance and the suffrage issues. Linking them eventually proved disadvantageous to the suffragists' cause.

In 1883 the legislature finally awarded Washington women the right to vote, but four years later the territorial court declared women's suffrage unconstitutional—which happened three more times when suffragists challenged the decision. In 1890 women at least won the right to vote in school elections.

Washington suffragists introduced a legislative bill in 1908 to amend the State Constitution by striking the word "male" from the clause relating to qualifications for voters, but their bid was not successful.

Emma Smith De Voe was a prominent leader in the Washington suffrage movement. An astute political organizer, while seeking support for the cause, she often traveled alone in unsettled parts of the west. De Voe advised her followers to "avoid big meetings" and to "avoid antagonizing big business, but get the labor vote quietly." In this way, suffragists would not reveal their real strength.

In the summer of 1909, a group of women planted a Votes-for-Women banner on the topmost peak of Mount Rainier. Among them was Dr. Cora Smith Eaton, the treasurer of the Washington State Woman Suffrage Association, a practicing physician, and one of the early leaders of the Mountaineers.

The "poster brigade" was an effective tactic used by the suffragists. This campaign, launched in 1910, was organized by Adella Parker. An article in *Colliers* on "Women's Political Methods," by Francis M. Björkman describes the effort, reporting: "It has been said by some of the British suffragettes that the worst difficulty they had to overcome was their own inbred reluctance for going out into the public streets." One suffragist wrote: "I went calling last night and took with me a can of paste and a wad of cloth, and as I went along I put up posters on telephone posts and fences."

Very aware of the fears that women's suffrage stirred up in the minds of many men, De Voe worked to diminish them. Other Washington figures involved in the movement included Sarah and Henry Yesler, Lizzie Ordway, and a Spokane millionairess, May Arkwright Hutton.

In their campaign, the Washington suffragists emphasized justice and the need to "clean house" in politics. As De Voe wrote in a 1910 article: "Shall a human soul, whether in male or female form, have an equal opportunity with every other soul to express an opinion (for voting is simply an expression of an opinion) or shall physiological structure determine the capacity of human intelligence to life, liberty, or self-government?"

In November of 1910, Washington women permanently gained the right to vote. In 1920 the United States Constitution was amended so that all women citizens were granted entry at the election polls.—**Carol V. Davis**

◆

These women hold *Suffragist* magazine, circa 1910–1915. Suffragists employed a variety of tactics. The Washington Equal Suffrage Association sold 3,000 cookbooks with the twin mottos "Votes for Women" and "Good Things to Eat" in which suffragist messages were interspersed among the recipes. (MOHAI)

CHAPTER 9

WORLD WAR I AND THE '20'S: 1914 - 1929

The year 1913 arrived for many Seattleites as they stood in front of the Bon Marche at Second and Union singing "Auld Lang Syne." The Bon had erected a gaily decorated bandstand and lighted it with "electric bulbs."

A few blocks to the south, silhouetted against the sky, rose the skeleton of the new, partially built Smith Tower—touted to be, when finished, the tallest building west of New York. To the southeast the Yesler Regrade was under way; by the time of its completion in 1914, it would have supplied five million cubic yards of earth fill for the Elliott Bay tideflats south of town, gaining hundreds of acres for industrial sites.

During 1914 major fires destroyed two landmarks in Seattle—the Madison Park Pavilion and the Grand Trunk Dock. The major international headline of 1914 reported the assassination on June 23 of Archduke Francis Ferdinand, heir to the Austrian throne. In November the distant war hit close to home when the four-masted bark *William P. Frye*, bound from Puget Sound for Great Britain with a load of lumber, was sunk in the Atlantic by a German U-boat. The following year, in May, a German submarine sent the *Lusitania* to the bottom, taking 1,198 men, women, and children, including 124 Americans, to their deaths. Of the five Washington State residents aboard the *Lusitania*, four lost their lives. Then on May 30 a barge loaded with dynamite for transshipment to Russia exploded in Elliott Bay near Harbor Island, destroying $75,000 in property. Sabotage was suspected but never proven.

On January 26, 1916, cold weather pushed the thermometer down to a record 17 degrees and Green Lake froze over. A great storm moved in on February 2, piling up 29 inches of snow, causing property damage, broken communication wires, and even death to some residents of King County and Seattle. But the intense cold soon vanished, as it always does in King County.

By July, the townspeople talked of the new Aero Products Company, which was building "aeroplanes" in a little shop on the east shore of Lake Union, directed by a man named William E. Boeing, a young scion of a timber- and mineral-rich Minnesota family.

In 1917 the navy ordered 50 Boeing Model C's to be used as trainers. Soon thereafter they contracted with the company to build 50 Curtiss HS-2L flying boats. As they started to manufacture the Curtiss plane, the armistice was signed, and soon the navy cancelled half the order.

(In 1920 Boeing secured the bids to build 20 GAX attack planes for the army, and three experimental armored planes called the GA-2S. Then in 1921 Boeing was awarded the nation's largest plane order since the war—200 Thomas Morse type MB-3A pursuit planes. The Boeing Company work force escalated to 300. The company was on its way.)

For Americans, the war flared up in 1917 when on February 1 Germany declared unrestricted submarine warfare. A few weeks later the United States began to arm merchant ships. On April 6 America entered the war officially. President Wilson signed the Selective Military Conscription Bill on May 18 and the first American troops landed in France on June 26.

Pierce County citizens made national news when they voted to bond themselves for $2 million to purchase 70,000 acres south of Tacoma, which they donated to the government for an army post. Construction of Camp Lewis started in June, to become the first and largest of 16 national army cantonments built to train World War I soldiers.

For a time, Camp Lewis officials marked Seattle as off-limits because of purported prostitution and other vices. Mayor Hiram Gill and Chief of Police Joseph F. Warren resorted to drastic measures to clean up the town, after which restrictions were eased.

After the Lake Washington Ship Canal was completed in 1917, the county commissioners spent more than $10,000 dredging a canal from the University of Washington campus to the waterway, which allowed naval training ships to dock at the campus on training missions. More than 6,000 men were trained there for the U.S. Navy.

Since the outbreak of war in Europe, industrial activities had been increasing in Seattle. The shipyards were busy day and night producing both wooden and steel ships. During the war, an estimated 40,000 men worked there. This employment potential brought many new families to Seattle. The pay, $5 a day, was good for the time and enticed many professional men to give up their practice to help build ships and construct machinery. Skinner and Eddy, the largest shipyard during the war, completed and delivered 75 ships, the largest with a capacity of 10,000 tons.

Photograph by Victor Gardaya
(MOHAI)

Left
H.W. McCurdy, after joining the navy, held the position of chief engineer aboard the yacht *Anemone*, which sailed back and forth between Seattle and Bremerton. Requesting a transfer, he was sent to the Brooklyn Naval Yard for duty on a troop carrier. Later he attended M.I.T. and eventually took charge of Puget Sound Bridge and Dredge, which during World War II employed up to 40,000 people and built many important projects (MOHAI)

Opposite
Top, left
Enlisted men march down Fourth Avenue at Columbia Street, their destination—Fort Lewis, to join the First World War effort. (MOHAI)

Top, right
Red Cross drivers, in about 1916, stand in front of the O'Leary Apartments at 2125 Western Avenue as World War I approaches. Photo by Jacobs. (MOHAI)

Middle, left
Employees and the public attended a launching at Skinner and Eddy Shipyard on July 17, 1918. During World War I Seattle's 20 shipyards employed 40,000 workers. Courtesy, Williamson Collection, Puget Sound Maritime Historical Society.

Middle, right
Volunteer Park was covered with a white blanket during the great snow of 1916, before the Seattle Art Museum was built there. Seattle residents used Alaskan-style dog teams during the storm. (MOHAI)

Bottom
The vast surplus of wooden hulled freighters created as a result of World War I, often referred to as "Wilson's Wood Row," were lined up on Lake Union and other backwaters of Puget Sound. (MOHAI)

Above, left
As part of the home front war effort, this poster asks Seattleites to conserve food. Courtesy, Sophie Frye Bass Collection. (MOHAI)

Washington State supplied most of the spruce lumber used in constructing airplanes. The government established a logging camp and built a railroad to transport the logs to the mill.

After the country was at war, more than 3,000 of King County's young people enlisted or were drafted. C.H. Hanford lists 837 who died in battle or of disease, especially the Spanish influenza epidemic that afflicted other Americans as well toward the end of the war. The exploits of King Countians in the armed forces were reported in the daily press, and those who came home brought back vivid memories of their experiences.

Many things changed as a result of the war. Local organizations were formed to provide whatever service was needed. The King County Council of Patriotic Service, later the King County Council of Defense, acted as a supervisory agency in directing war work. Unions were efficient supporters. As mirrored in other parts of the country, local people of German extraction became suspect as aliens and potential saboteurs. Persons accused of disloyalty were investigated by the council. Conservation of food received much attention. Seattleites initiated meatless Tuesdays, wheatless Wednesdays, and porkless Saturdays. Money was raised in Seattle for such organizations as the Red Cross, the YMCA, YWCA, Salvation Army, and Jewish Relief and Community Service. The people of Washington State invested more than $227 million in Liberty Bonds.

During and after the war, Seattle citizens extended aid to stricken towns in France and Belgium. Horace C. Henry, the leader of this effort, was awarded France's Legion of Honor medal.

The county purchased ferries with 2,000 passenger capacity to carry shipyard workers to Harbor Island and paved a 60-mile boulevard around Lake Washington, enabling residents of Renton and Bothell to reach Seattle quickly.

The virulent influenza epidemic circling the globe struck viciously in Seattle late in 1918–1919. In 1918, at a rate of 252 per 100,000 population, it killed more Seattleites than any other illness. Public assemblages were prohibited, and the Health Department ordered all citizens to wear flu masks.

On November 10, the armistice was signed. The following day was declared a holiday, with the "flu ban" lifted so people could congregate to celebrate.

GENERAL STRIKE OF 1919

Seattle holds the dubious "honor" of having been the site of the nation's first general strike. At 10 a.m., on February 6, 1919, the city became ominously quiet as 60,000 organized workers walked off the job. The reporters on all the wire services branded the strike a "revolution."

The causes of the strike are complex. Those first months after World War I ended launched an era of general instability around the world: the Kapp Putsch in Berlin, the general strike in Argentina, the Bela Kun revolution in Hungary, and above all the Bolshevik Revolution in Russia. In this country, several blacks were lynched in the South, the prohibition amendment had dried up the country's liquor supplies, and influenza was still taking its toll of lives. Serious confrontations between American labor and capital occurred in areas across the country and often the "Wobblies" were blamed.

During the last stages of the war, the activities of the Industrial Workers of the World, known as the IWWs or the "Wobblies," began gaining attention. Founded in 1905 by a heterogeneous group of radicals, the IWW attracted mostly transient laborers from Western mines and forests who had not been drawn to the American Federation of Labor. Seattle's Local 432 was especially active at times.

The Industrial Workers of the World had opposed American participation in what they called the "Capitalist War." On the opposite side, the American Protective League developed "Minutemen" to suppress "anarchy, sedition, and sabotage," and they infiltrated labor organizations. Louise Olivereau, a secretary of an IWW local, was sentenced to 10 years in prison for distributing antiwar leaflets. Hulet Wells and Sam Sadler, two local Socialists, were given two-year prison terms for agitating against conscription. In effect the IWW was crushed during and after the war, with some of their members incarcerated, others deported, and many in hiding or joined to other unions. The "Wobbly" spirit, however, lingered among the workers of Washington and nationwide progressives.

With the Bolshevik Revolution underway in Russia, and with American labor unions gaining influence over the workers, conservative Americans grew increasingly fearful. Both union and management knew that the war would not last forever. The war had brought high profits for capitalists and increasing possibilities for the unions' bargaining power. A confrontation between the two sides was perhaps inevitable once the war ended. Less than three months after Armistice Day, an already volatile situation erupted.

The strife had spread to Elliott Bay from fierce labor-management battles in the mining states of the Rockies. Blood was shed in nearby Everett (the "Everett Massacre") and later in Centralia. The warfare between the IWW members and the lumber companies and their supporters resulted in innumerable beatings and at Everett on November 5, 1916, at least seven men died, five of them union men, shot as their boat moored to the dock. In addition, 31 other persons were wounded by the rifle fire.

The Seattle labor movement also had its differences with Samuel Gompers, national leader of the A.F. of L. Local unions felt the national body was insufficiently militant. The radicals included free-wheeling A.F. of L. members and some IWW members who had infiltrated other unions with their own A.F. of L. cards. Some visionaries among them believed strongly that the labor movement should be broader than

Top
During the 1918–1919 influenza epidemic, the Seattle Health Department ordered all citizens to wear flu masks and prohibited all public assemblages. This newspaper boy wears a protective mask as he stands in front of a closed theater, circa 1918. (MOHAI)

Bottom
The "Wobblies" or Industrial Workers of the World (IWW) held beliefs antithetical to the capitalistic system as it was then understood. They were generally working people like John Henry Smith, shown here proudly displaying his IWW card, circa 1920.

efforts to increase wages, reduce hours, and improve working conditions. They had a vision of "a more equitable society." But since they could not agree, no organized faction was developed.

At the outset, the progressives became the dominant force, led by James A. Duncan, secretary of the Central Labor Council. Duncan believed the best way to control the radicals was to develop a strong, united, active, and fairly militant A.F. of L. He was backed by the labor-owned Seattle *Union Record*, where Anna Louise Strong was feature editor.

Negotiations for all craft unions were carried on by the Seattle Metal Trades Council presided over by James A. Taylor. He was sent to Washington, D.C., to appeal to the board of the Emergency Fleet Corporation to settle the threatened shipyard strike, the most pressing labor-management disagreement. He was rebuffed, and before the Metal Trades unions could strike or management could make a firm offer, the director of the Emergency Fleet Corporation, Charles Piez, sent a telegram to the employers, which was misdelivered to the Metal Trades Council. In it Piez threatened to cut off the supply of steel if the employers acceded to labor's demands. This infuriated the labor leaders. On January 21, 1919, the shipyards were struck.

Piez continued to bombard shipyard owners with telegrams ordering them to stand fast; management complied. A proposal to call a general strike was suggested at a meeting of the Central Labor Council. A resolution was passed requesting local unions to vote on whether to walk out in sympathy with the shipyard workers. Wobblies packed the galleries and applauded after radicals' speeches. Union leaders, meeting on January 27, agreed that if by February 2 a majority of the unions voted for the general strike, a mass meeting of workers would be scheduled at which a final decision could be made.

On January 28 the Central Labor Council heard 23 locals report that their members were willing to strike. Although the lack of enthusiasm for a general strike was apparent among the leaders, the Labor Council did not bid strongly to regain leadership; instead, they acted as informal advisors to the elected strike leaders.

Now new mediation efforts began, but a mediator named Henry White was quoted as saying that the strike vote was not an honest one. He claimed that he was misquoted. The newspapers editorialized that a general strike would be disastrous. A hastily conceived Industrial Relations Committee began negotiations to settle the shipyard strike, but to no avail. More than 300 delegates attended the mass meeting held on February 2, setting a February 6 date for the general walkout.

Labor elected an Executive Committee of Fifteen to be responsible for the strike effort. They made plans for cafeterias to feed those without food; they would arrange to make fuel and laundry deliveries to hospitals, deliver mail, operate milk stations, and unload government cargo. They also set up emergency transportation and fire protection, and established a law-and-order subcommittee. Supportive war veterans were asked to volunteer for guard duty to prevent any clashes.

On February 4 James Duncan and others urged the Executive Committee to set a time limit on the strike so that the general public would not consider it a revolution. The request lost by one vote.

One individual whose name became prominent during the strike was Anna Louise Strong, daughter of a pacifist Seattle minister. In her thirties, she had been elected to the school board with the support of conservatives, but during the war she had issued pamphlets urging young men not to volunteer. A petition demanding her recall was circulated, and she was thrown out of office in the ensuing election, an action that hardened her conviction that America was on the wrong track.

Strong became a reporter on a left-wing newspaper, *The Call*. It was about to fold from lack of advertisers when a mob broke into the plant and smashed the old flatbed press. *The Call* was subsumed under the *Union Record* with Miss Strong as one of its editors. In Chicago, while attending a rally for convicted labor leader Tom Mooney, she received a telegram informing her of the imminent strike. Boarding the first train headed for Seattle, she wrote an editorial for the *Union Record* in support of the General Strike.

Strong's editorial explained how labor would feed the people and maintain order, and how the power of the workers to manage would win the strike. She predicted that labor would shut down vital industries, then reopen them under management of appropriate tradesmen who would provide all services needed to preserve public health and peace. If the strike demands were not met, these workers would reopen more and more activities under their own management. She concluded: "And this is why we say we are starting on a road that leads to no one knows where."

Businessmen read this as a call for socialism even though Miss Strong had not mentioned the word. Mayor Ole Hanson, who previously had been sympathetic to labor, read the article and went over to the side of business. He called for an immediate meeting with the chief of police and promised to call the militia and troops from the regular army at Camp Lewis, if necessary.

Certain business leaders suggested bringing in strikebreakers and Burns detectives, even mounting machine guns on downtown roofs, but none of this was done. Mayor Hanson fanned Easterners' fears of revolution by giving interviews to the press and writing articles for national magazines. "The anarchists in this community shall not rule its affairs," he boasted. Hanson clearly saw his strong stand against the strike as an entry into national politics, perhaps to the presidency.

The general strike was called for 10 a.m., on Thursday,

Top
In President Wilson's 1919 visit to Seattle, at a scheduled parade, Wilson received a friendly welcome in the downtown area. But as the dignitaries approached an area on north Second Avenue, they were met by a street lined with solemn-faced Wobblies and pacifist laborites. At Virginia Street on Second Avenue, Wilson encountered a "human canyon of silence." He continued to smile and wave for a few minutes before finally slumping in his seat, visibly shaken. (MOHAI)

Middle
The labor conflicts which culminated in the 1919 Seattle General Strike pitted laboring men and women against their employers, many of whom had profited from the recent war. To raise funds, "Class War Picnics" were organized. Courtesy, Historical Photography Collection, U of W Libraries.

Bottom
"Hello Girls"—members of the Telephone Operators' Local 42A—went on strike for better wages and working conditions. They are holding up the issue of the Seattle *Union Record* in which they received front-page coverage, circa 1917. (MOHAI)

to be signaled by whistles from sawmills and ships at the wharves. At that time, the city of a quarter of a million people fell silent. Most services stopped. But there was no trouble. Troops from Camp Lewis were stationed in the new brick Armory but kept out of sight. The 1,500 policemen, many of them temporary deputies, appeared in small, non-belligerent groups. Labor kept its head and order was preserved. The Committee of Fifteen, organized by the union members, delivered milk to hospitals, to the ill, and to families with babies. Light, power, and gas services continued, though not for private businesses.

The second day of the strike passed with no picketing, no marching, no rousing soapbox orations. Yet rumors ran rife through the town. The police switchboard constantly rang with calls from hysterical citizens, who were assured everything was quiet.

By the third day the strike began to waver. Union leaders were coming in droves from East Coast headquarters to cool tempers. The war had ended and a recession was setting in, they said.

Some workers began to return to their jobs. Mayor Hanson continued his interviews, explaining how he had "smashed" the general strike. By the fourth day his office was loaded with flowers and other tributes sent by businessmen across the country.

The Committee of Fifteen now voted 13 to 2 to return to work, with the provision that the strike be extended one more day to include Lincoln's birthday.

Since Mayor Hanson was receiving lucrative offers to join the lecture circuit, he resigned as mayor, turned Republican, and traveled. He attended the national presidential convention as a "dark horse," but his fame was not influential in Republican circles; the nomination went to Warren G. Harding. Hanson, who returned to Seattle, soon disappeared

Anna Louise Strong (1885–1970) began her Seattle social involvement in child welfare and other social welfare efforts. Becoming an editor of the *Union Record* was the turning point of her life, and her role in the General Strike was crucial. Courtesy, Historical Photography Collection, U of W Libraries.

Ole Hanson was the mayor of Seattle during the General Strike of 1919. He won the favor of businessmen across the country in response to his anti-labor stance during that strike. (MOHAI)

from the scene. He later sold real estate in California, where he helped found a new town, San Clemente.

Anna Louise Strong, depressed and confused, found little warmth among her labor associates, now more divided than ever. In 1928 the *Union Record* went out of business. When the famous socialist Lincoln Steffens came to Seattle, he suggested that Miss Strong visit Moscow. She took his advice, leaving her beloved Northwest. She lived for nearly 30 years in Russia, was finally expelled as a traitor, and in her sixties returned to Seattle to find it had grown into a strong union town. After a flurry of publicity, she moved to Communist China and died there.

Immediately after the strike, laboring men came upon hard times. Jobs were hard to find. Police raided the Socialist and IWW halls. However, indictments were later dropped or the people acquitted. The Associated Industries of Seattle was developed to promote the open shop.

The very complexity of the general strike's causes prevented it from having a successful conclusion. It served as a vehicle through which the strikers could vent their frustration and perhaps some fears. But it had no defined goals, no stipulated duration, and the dominant leaders were not strong supporters.

Two decades and more of turmoil highlighted by the IWW, the Everett and Centralia massacres, and the Seattle General Strike have caused more than one scholar to ask: Was Washington a liberal state that attracted more than its share of radical movements?

True, Washington was and is a progressive state. Earlier than most, it voted in reforms like women's suffrage, industrial compensation, and direct legislation measures such as the initiative and referendum. During the two decades 1920 to 1940, strong labor organizations developed in the state as did organizations such as the Washington Pension Union and the Washington Commonwealth Federation.

Novelist John Dos Passos mentioned Washington's radicalism in his famous book *Nineteen Nineteen.* And in the mid-'30s, Postmaster-General James A. Farley, when visiting Seattle, supposedly offered a toast: "To the 47 states and the Soviet of Washington."

On the other hand, the IWW practically ceased to exist after the bloody confrontations it faced. After the strike of 1919, labor's strength was greatly diminished. But 20 years later, the state was again one of the most unionized in the nation.

Some call the state progressive; some call it radical. But to this day it is one of the "bellwether" states of the union. Consulting firms who predict the future use it as a guide. They say that most new concepts develop in nine or 10 of the 50 states, and Washington is one of them.

PROHIBITION AND OLMSTEAD

In 1916, after the citizens of Washington State had voted in a referendum to make the sale or consumption of intoxicating beverages unlawful, bootlegging and rum-running swiftly became profitable and popular. But competition between two rival bootlegging groups soon turned vicious. Jack Marquett, a former policeman, headed one group; the brothers Logan and Fred Billingsley the other. The brothers developed a network extending from Cuba to Canada, and Marquett, unable to meet their successes, took to hijacking their boats, which led to a shooting fray and several deaths. Members of both gangs were jailed, and the supply of liquor in Seattle became erratic. Small marginal operations were not reliable.

When the National Prohibition Act (the famed Volstead Act) turned the whole nation dry in January 1920, the Treasury Department was given the responsibility of enforcing the law. A 34-year-old Seattle policeman, the youngest lieutenant in the department, intelligent and respected, had discovered that he could sell this respectability to those who faced incarceration. As a result of the reputation he had earned among Seattle's judges, in many cases the lieutenant's recommendations were accepted for probation. Often he was rewarded by the accused and sought a means of investing this ill-gained bankroll. Having experienced four years in the dry state of Washington and having learned from the mistakes of rumrunners before him, Roy Olmstead decided to enter the game.

On March 22, 1920, at 2 a.m., shortly after beginning his activities, Olmstead was caught with several of his men while unloading cases of liquor on a Meadowdale beach. Prohibition agents, firing from behind a roadblock, allowed Olmstead to escape in his automobile, but he was picked up at his home that afternoon. Summarily he was dismissed from the Police Department. Arraigned on a federal charge, he was released on bail, entered a plea of guilty, paid $500 in fines, and became a folk hero. He immediately went full time into serious bootlegging.

Puget Sound with its bays and inlets, its forests, its islands, and its extension into Canadian-controlled waters, was a rumrunner's paradise.

With 11 backers, who each staked $1,000, Olmstead began a vigorous campaign to supply liquor, and eventually almost monopolized the King County market. He developed a means of avoiding the $20 a case excise duty imposed by Canada on liquor exported to the United States and thereby undercut his competition.

By 1924 Olmstead was almost entirely engaged in wholesaling. He divorced his wife, married young Elsie Campbell, and bought a colonial residence in the Mt. Baker section of town, where he and his wife established Seattle's first radio station.

His prestige mounted with each daring maneuver. He often unloaded cases of liquor at downtown Seattle docks in broad daylight. He never diluted his product, never allowed his men to bear arms, and followed respectable business practices. His gross exceeded $200,000 a month for several years.

To avoid police and pirates, Olmstead developed a fleet of fast boats and relied on shrewd planning and tight control to escape capture. Only the prohibition administrator proved a relentless enemy. The chief administrator, Roy Lyle, and his legal advisor, William Whitney, were political appointees. Whitney handled the agents. Whitney and Lyle were friends of Wesley L. Jones, the state's senior senator, a staunch supporter of prohibition. Jones, when informed of Olmstead's fame, ordered Lyle and Whitney to stop him at all costs.

Soon the agents had chartered the fastest boats they could find. Olmstead shifted deliveries to stormy nights. The agents hired a free-lance wire tapper and began listening in on Olmstead's phone calls. After this initial tap was discovered, others were installed.

In November 1924 Whitney led a raid on Olmstead's home and arrested him, his wife, and more than a dozen guests. The following January a federal grand jury indicted Olmstead and 90 other defendants for violating the Volstead Act. Olmstead posted bail, went back to work, tightened his organization, and continued rum-running.

Some of the defendants in the Olmstead organization became concerned; a few scattered to Canada, but others offered to testify for the government in exchange for leniency. During the 1926 trial, witnesses for the government, in order to refresh their memories, were provided with transcripts of Olmstead's tapped telephone conversations. The defense was not allowed access to these notes. George Vanderveer, an Olmstead lawyer, quickly cited the Washington State statute of 1909 that made wiretapping illegal.

At the time, public sentiment was not disposed toward mercy. After all, the citizens had elected as their mayor a prohibitionist and strict moralist, Bertha Landes. Twenty-three of the defendants were convicted and sentenced. Roy Olmstead received four years at hard labor and an $8,000

Above
Roy Olmstead, a former police lieutenant, was the "king" of Puget Sound rumrunners. He and his wife operated one of Seattle's earliest radio stations until federal "dry agents" arrested him. From David Richardson, *Puget Sounds*.

Right
Lyman Cornelius Smith, typewriter and firearms manufacturer, began construction of a skyscraper on his property at the corner of Second and Yesler in 1911. The 42-story Smith Tower was opened on July 4, 1914. At one time the Smith Tower housed a Chinese temple on its top floor and for many years was the tallest building west of the Mississippi. (MOHAI)

fine. The case was referred to the Circuit Court of Appeals in San Francisco, which found no cause to reverse the lower court. But a dissenting opinion by Circuit Judge Frank Rudkin questioned the use of the transcript of the tapped phone calls. Olmstead's attorneys petitioned the Supreme Court to review the case, but the Court refused. Returning to the McNeil Island prison, Olmstead commented to a reporter, "I'm not complaining. I violated the law." But he was soon bailed out again when the Supreme Court reconsidered and decided to review the case.

In February 1928 the case was heard and the majority of justices denied the defense contention. Olmstead remained in prison. Then in 1929, the newspapers carried stories of a delegation from McNeil that would testify against those who sent them to prison. The front pages again carried Roy Olmstead's name. Whitney, Lyle, and others were charged with bribery and cooperation with bootleggers. Olmstead swore he had been promised a presidential pardon in return for testimony against city and county officials. The jury found the defendants Whitney, Lyle, and the others not guilty, a decision not popular with many citizens.

In May 1931 Roy Olmstead was released after serving 35 months of his four-year term. Having found religion, when he left prison he dedicated himself to Christian Science. Prohibition came to an official end in 1934. On Christmas Day 1935, Olmstead received a pardon from President Franklin D. Roosevelt. Olmstead, shortly after, began visiting McNeil Island to carry the word of his church to the prisoners.

The effects of prohibition only gradually faded away. For years sale of liquor was prohibited on Sundays. By-the-drink sales were forbidden for years, but wine and beer could

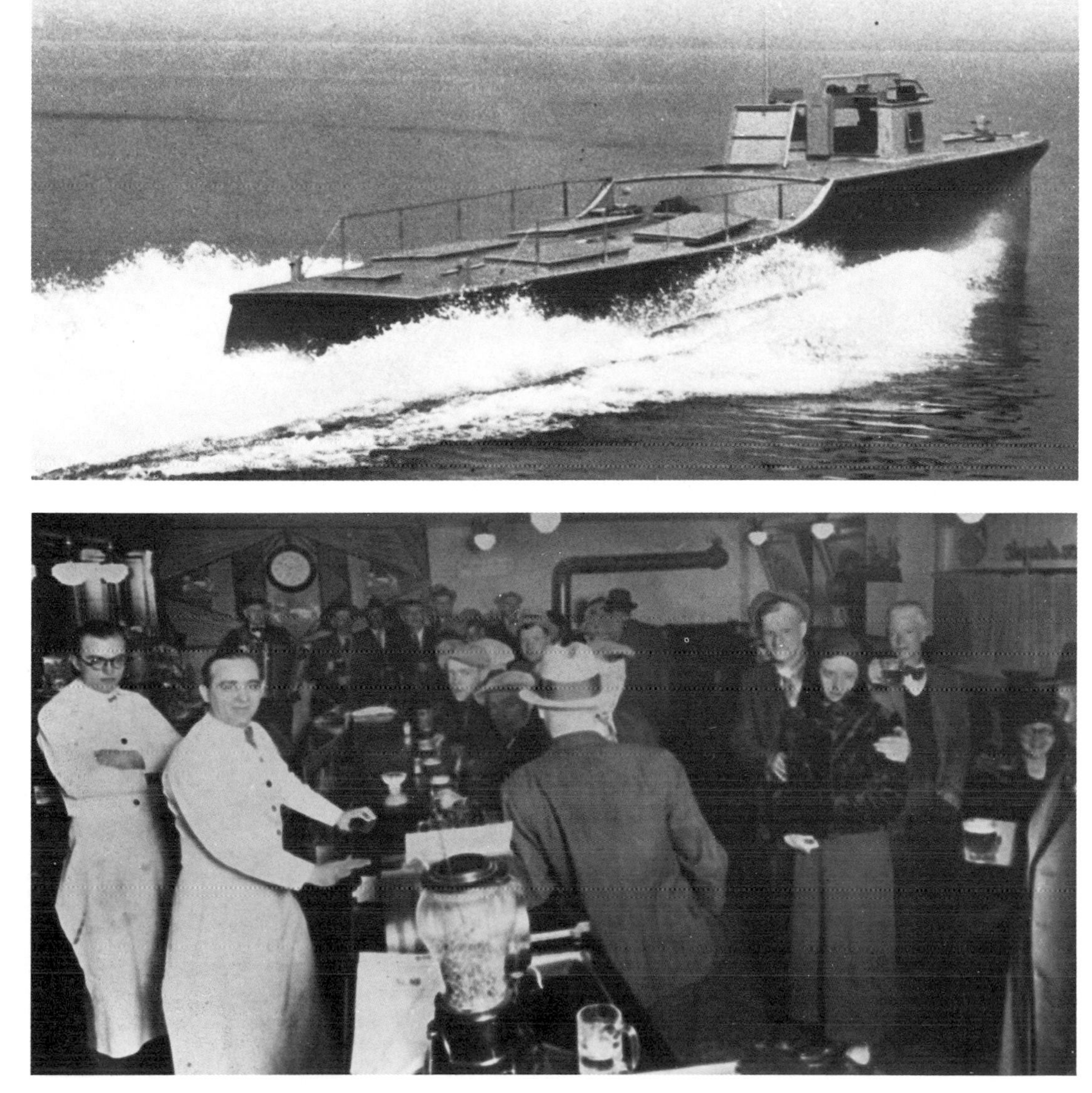

Top
A fast rum-running craft of the 1920s is shown taking a speed test. Boats such as this, used by Olmstead's men, could outrun any federal or police boat of the time. Courtesy, Puget Sound Maritime Historical Society.

Bottom
Patrons at 94 Pine Street enjoyed drinking beer. Although the sale of alcoholic beverages was illegal, "speakeasies" were popular throughout King County in the 1920s. (MOHAI)

be consumed in taverns. Eventually, most of these restrictions were wiped from the books. However, to this day, only state-controlled liquor stores can retail hard liquor by the bottle.

AVIATION IN THE 1920s

After World War I, the importance of aviation became apparent to King County Commissioners. They all strived to improve Seattle's potential as a center of air transport. Local pilots, government experts, army and navy fliers, and others all cooperated in the effort to find the proper site for a military airfield. In 1926 Carkeek Park on the point east of the University of Washington was purchased from the city and a new Carkeek Park was developed north of town.

Sand Point, being on Lake Washington, made an ideal location for both land and sea planes. It was deeded to the government with the stipulation that it be maintained as a naval air base. For many years Congress hesitated. Seven years later the appropriations bill finally passed. Meanwhile, the county commissioners had developed a small airfield at Sand Point, from which the army fliers (who first flew around the world), left in March and returned in September of 1924. This also provided a field for the Boeing factory to test-fly its planes.

Though the county commissioners were criticized for buying Sand Point and deeding it free of charge to the government, they proceeded to place on the ballot a $2 million bond issue to be used to purchase a large tract near Georgetown for a commercial airport. After voter approval, the Commissioners, aided by a citizen's committee, planned the field, which they named for William E. Boeing. This served as Seattle's major commercial field until Seattle–Tacoma International Airport opened in 1949.

This northwest corner of the country in the 1920s became more closely linked to the other 47 states. Radio was a popular pastime. Air travel was developing. The automobile had become reliable for long trips. All of the major railroads were accessible, the majority using Seattle as a terminus. Passenger liners docked at Elliott Bay piers. Entertainment "palaces" provided both live and filmed dramas.

But the boom of the '20s had seemed to pass the area by. Manufacturing in the state had declined and so had the number of wage earners. Many families had migrated to California or other boom areas. The population of King County increased during those 10 years by only 74,000 or 19 percent, from 389,000 to 463,000. These were comparatively stagnant years when compared to the boom decades between 1890 and 1920.

However, the next decade—the down-and-out '30s—would bring even less development, as well as some old and new problems to test the "Seattle Spirit."

Opposite

Top
William Boeing (right) with pilot Eddie Hubbard posed in front of a Boeing "C" Seaplane on Lake Union in 1918. Boeing holds a bag of mail from Canada. (MOHAI)

Middle
This view shows the interior of the assembly floor at the Boeing Airplane Company, circa 1927. After the war, airplanes proved to be a feasible form of rapid transportation. (MOHAI)

Bottom
President Harding visited Seattle shortly before his death in 1923. H.C. Henry, a prominent Seattle businessman, stands at top of steps. (MOHAI)

SEATTLE'S WOMAN MAYOR

When Bertha Knight Landes became the mayor of Seattle in March 1926, she was the first woman to be elected mayor of a major American city. Born in Massachusetts in 1868, she was a descendant of two New England colonial families. While earning a degree in history from the University of Indiana, she met fellow student Henry Landes. Married in 1894, they came to Seattle in the following year, when Henry was appointed professor of geology at the University of Washington. He later served there as acting president and as dean of the College of Science.

Mrs. Landes was devoted primarily to her family life prior to 1920. The Landeses had three children. Her outside activities related to a variety of community affairs and social services. While president of the Seattle Federation of Women's Clubs, in 1921 she gained city-wide attention as a driving force behind the Women's Exhibit for Washington Manufacturers. This highly successful venture impressed the business community at a time when the region was experiencing economic depression. Later that year, when Mrs. Landes was the only woman appointed to the mayor's commission on unemployment, a fellow commissioner urged her to run for the city council.

During her council campaign, which was organized and run by her women's club colleagues, she said, "It is not only the right but the privilege and duty of women to take part in the administration of public affairs." She continually stressed the right of 40 percent of the voters to representation on the council. Elected by an unprecedented 22,000 vote plurality, she was made council president, then reelected to the council in 1924.

Her boldest move in public office doubtless came in 1924 when, as acting mayor, she fired the chief of police for his alleged refusal to clean out corruption in the department and to strengthen vice and prohibition law enforcement. In 1926 she became a reluctant candidate for mayor, since she realized that no other candidate could defeat the incumbent, Edwin J. (Doc) Brown. Her campaign against Brown stressed law enforcement and occurred at the same time as the "Rum Trial" of policeman-turned-bootlegger Roy Olmsted—a coincidence that kept her concern for morality before the public.

An avowed prohibitionist, she favored expanded and regulated opportunities for wholesome recreation. She supported municipal ownership of utilities, and brought about not only stricter law enforcement but also sound management for City Light, profitable operation for the streetcar system, improved traffic safety, enhanced Park Department programs, and appointments based on merit. Although her administration was generally considered effective, when she sought reelection in 1928 with the same support that had won in the past, she was defeated by a political unknown. Reasons for her defeat were the pervasive issue of her sex, the public vs. private utilities questions, city employee dissatisfaction with personnel cuts, and her failure to broaden her power base through a strong organization.

Bertha Landes lacked personal political ambition. She undertook her public career as a duty and as a civic service, fashioning her political philosophy within the context of woman's "proper sphere," as an enlargement of her family role. Toward the end of her term, she characterized her role:

> Municipal housekeeping means adventure and romance and accomplishment to me. To be in some degree a guiding force in the destiny of a city, to help lay the foundation stones for making it good and great, to aid in advancing the political position of women . . . to spread the political philosophy that the city is only a larger home—I find it richly worthwhile.

—Doris Pieroth

Mayor Bertha Landes bids farewell to Arctic explorer Amundsen on his departure from Seattle in 1926. Photo by Asahel Curtis. (MOHAI)

CHAPTER 10

THE DEPRESSED ERA: 1930-1940

Trepidation over the dismal financial situation was foremost in the minds of many at the close of the decade of the '20s. In the 1930s King Countians endured a decade of economic depression, the worst and longest ever suffered, a time of lost fortunes, foreclosed mortgages, bankrupt companies, radical movements, delayed weddings, and broken dreams.

Efforts by federal, state, and local governments to feed the hungry, doctor the ill, make jobs for the unemployed simply could not reach everyone in need. There were some who escaped the worst effects of the Great Depression, but everyone recognized the suffering, turmoil, and tragedy that struck the vast majority of American families. Seattle and King County residents were no exception.

THE STOCK MARKET CRASH

The financial boom of 1922–29, fed by unprecedented speculation in securities, involved Seattle investors as it did others across the nation. During September 1929 the New York Stock Exchange seemed healthy enough. In fact, brokers' loans increased by nearly $670 million, the largest increase of any month in the history of the stock market. On October 18 a weak market was reported with the New York Times Industrial Average down 7 points. The next day, nearly 3.5 million shares changed hands with Industrials down 12 points. When the market opened on Monday, October 21, sales totaled in excess of 6 million and the ticker was an hour and a half late. The market rallied slightly at day's end.

Thursday, October 24, was disastrous. Nearly 13 million shares were traded, prices dropped precipitously, and the tape was hours late. In New York the panic was over by noon, when organized support from bankers arrived, but outside New York, with the late tape, nobody knew what was happening. In the closing hours, selling orders streamed in from across the country. Even so, the Industrials finished only 12 points down, a little over a third of the loss of the previous day.

On Monday, October 28, the possibility of a major market crash began to be discussed in the investment world. Industrials fell 49 points that day. More than 9.25 million shares were sold.

The next day, Tuesday, October 29, proved the most devastating day in the history of the stock exchange. Selling in huge volume began when the market opened. Industrial averages were down 43 points, and 16.5 million shares were sold. Investment trusts failed at a rapid rate.

Because of the lagging tape, few traders outside of New York knew whether their orders to buy or sell had been completed. Meantime, the *Post-Intelligencer* reported, "business outside the financial district of the city appeared unruffled as merchants prepared for the coming Christmas trade."

The market stabilized for a few days, then continued its downward plunge. On November 11, 12, and 13, Industrials lost another 50 points. President Hoover ordered a small cut in income taxes to stimulate the economy. During the first three months of 1930, the stock market showed some recovery but by June the momentum had been lost; prices slid day after day, month after month. On November 13, 1929, the New York Times Industrial Average had closed at 224; a year later, on November 13, it was at 180. On July 8, 1932, it stood at 58.

The crash blighted the fortunes of several hundred thousand Americans—among them some well-to-do Seattle and King County citizens—and threw many others, wholly unconnected with stock speculation, into abject poverty. Bankers, along with other business leaders, lost their formerly healthy reputation, as did politicians. Among those to quickly lose support was President Hoover.

While the full winds of the Depression took longer to reach Seattle than Eastern cities, the collapse of the building industry, added to the weakened condition of the state's agriculture and lumber industries, soon plunged the local economy into deep distress. The city council moved to increase its program of public works. In September of 1931 the District Relief Organization was created. The Unemployed Citizens' League was incorporated to establish food depots and supply workers for local relief efforts; in 1932, with the city almost bankrupt, help from the county was arranged and volunteer League members were replaced with a paid staff.

In the 1932 presidential election, President Hoover was defeated when Franklin D. Roosevelt was given a strong majority—including that of King County voters. Under Roosevelt, the federal government quickly began to share responsibility with both city and county for the indigent and unemployed.

Photograph by Victor Gardaya (MOHAI)

Top, left
The Coliseum Theatre at the corner of Fifth and Pike was built in 1929. (MOHAI)

Bottom, left
In the early and mid-1930s, hungry unemployed men flocked to Seattle hunting for work. Some of President Roosevelt's New Deal efforts to feed the hungry began to take effect, as with this WPA food line. Courtesy, Post-Intelligencer Collection. (MOHAI)

Opposite, top
The Fourteen-Eleven Fourth-Avenue Building was designed by architect Robert C. Reamer of the Metropolitan Building Company. Ready for occupancy on January 1, 1929, it epitomized the optimism of the 1920s. Courtesy, Architectural History Collection, U of W Libraries.

Opposite, bottom
This Western Union telegraph ticker tape machine was used during the stock market activities in the late 1920s. (MOHAI)

The ensuing years would bring local programs that implemented the New Deal's efforts to put the nation back on its feet by relieving the unemployed and revitalizing business and industry. There were the Civilian Conservation Corps, the Agricultural Adjustment Act, the Public Works Administration, the National Industrial Recovery Act, the Rural Electrification Act, the Social Security Act, the Works Progress Administration, and dozens of other agencies and programs.

Surely the most pathetic yet colorful indicator of the hard times was the nine-acre shacktown where many unemployed settled in 1931. The impromptu village was situated on the property of the Seattle Port Commission between Railroad, Dearborn, and Connecticut streets and the waterfront.

Seattle health officials soon decided the shacks were unfit for human habitation and ordered them burned. The inhabitants, whose average age ran to 50, salvaged their belongings and in a driving rain left the area just as uniformed officers set the town ablaze. The inhabitants promptly returned and rebuilt their shacks, only to be run out again when this "Hooverville," as it was called, was burned a second time. The people again came back, this time building underground and using noncombustible materials. In June 1932, with a new municipal administration in office, the city relented and called the inhabitants together to suggest they rebuild on top of the ground. Local businesses contributed cast-off materials and foodstuffs. Soon a hundred rough shelters were being built of discarded materials, some as small as large wooden crates and some with as many as five rooms.

A commission composed of various ethnic backgrounds formed to govern the shacktown. The houses were given numbers, a mayor was elected and a post office established. Medical care was provided at Harborview Hospital or, for veterans or seamen, at Marine Hospital. This "Hooverville," one of many in the Seattle area, tended to be the abode of the forgotten man. In midwinter the population was at its peak; in summer many left for eastern Washington to work in the harvest. Most of the residents were unemployed seamen, lumberjacks, fishermen, and miners, with a sprinkling of tradesmen among them. Many of the men built pushcarts, collected waste material, sorted and bailed it, then sold it as salvage. People fished in Elliott Bay, gathered driftwood to be sold as firewood, and picked berries.

It was a town inhabited mostly by men (women were supposedly not allowed but a few wives lived there anyway). At a time when the economic situation kept them from rejoining the mainstream of society, they were dedicated to their own independence and self-sufficiency.

During the New Deal years, the states, like the federal government, increased their responsibilities, especially in the areas of pensions and unemployment relief. But these actions, even when combined with federal programs, often proved inadequate for the jobless and the aged. Because of this, sev-

Opposite, top
In 1934 a County Works Project hired men to clean used brick. These men worked at South Alaskan Way and Connecticut Street. (MOHAI)

Opposite, bottom
The unemployed used discarded materials to build structures in "Hoovervilles." Shacks like this one were home to the displaced, unemployed, and mostly penniless inhabitants. Courtesy, James P. Lee Collection. (MOHAI)

Top, right
This post office sign hung during the early 1930s in one of Seattle's shack towns located at 929 Charles Street, circa 1933. (MOHAI)

Bottom, right
Looking north from Atlantic Street, this view shows a Seattle "Hooverville," circa 1937. These shack towns sprang up during the Depression to house the homeless unemployed. Courtesy, James P. Lee Collection. (MOHAI)

eral left-wing movements took root, ranging from self-help groups at the beginning of the Depression to popular-front organizations dedicated to social and economic change, such as the Washington Commonwealth Federation.

CINCINNATUS

On an August evening in 1933, six young men sat in a law office in the Fourth and Pike Building discussing graft and corruption in city government. They agreed to recruit other young men into an organization that would pursue certain objectives: to bring about a renaissance in politics, clean out graft and corruption in public offices, modernize government, and eliminate governmental waste. They chose Cincinnatus as the name for their organization, commemorating Lucius Quintus Cincinnatus, who fought for Rome but refused honors.

None of the six had political ambitions; they sought candidates willing to reveal their assets and who would pledge to accept no more than $50 from any firm or individual. At their next meeting 16 more members were accepted. Each succeeding meeting grew in size, until late in September when nearly 400 men crowded into the room. They agreed to run a full slate of city council candidates in the primary for the 1934 elections.

David Lockwood, Lloyd Johnson, and Wellington Rhinehart were drafted to run. Campaign funds were not available in that deep Depression year, but mass meetings, parades, and door-to-door canvasses resulted in Lockwood's winning sixth place and surviving the primary. Though the other two candidates were eliminated, in the general election, Lockwood received more votes than any other candidate.

Lockwood, shunted by the older council members to the "efficiency committee," began investigating possible graft in a garbage contract; as a result, a city employee and two contractors were eventually sentenced to the penitentiary.

Charles L. Smith, the 42-year-old mayor, asked Cincinnatus to help him revive "Potlatch," Seattle's once popular summer celebration, which they did. (Potlatch, begun as a civic celebration in 1911, had been discontinued after 1914. It was revived for one year, in 1934, and in 1938 it was reintroduced and was popular each summer until World War II prevented all such celebrations. Based around maritime activities and parades, it was the forerunner of Seafair, which has been scheduled annually since 1950.)

Now the newspapers picked up the Cincinnatus story. Soon others wanted to know about Cincinnatus and the organization went statewide. Cincinnatus held its own state convention and decided to run a third party ticket in the November elections of 1934.

They selected Mrs. F. F. Powell, Frederick Hamley, and Leo Mortland to run for the three city council positions. But Mortland revealed after his selection that the 36th District Republican Club, to which he belonged, had voted to endorse him. For the first time disharmony was heard at a Cincinnatus meeting. The young Democrats of the organization protested. After a wrangle, the chairman of the meeting opened the slate again. The nominating committee found a young attorney, Arthur B. Langlie, who agreed to replace Mortland, who seconded his nomination.

As was expected, Hamley, Langlie, and Mrs. Powell defeated the incumbents, so Seattle had a new city council. Now politically alert citizens in other cities outside the state wanted information on how to effect similar changes. Members of Cincinnatus helped San Francisco get started; the president of the chapter there was Edmund ("Pat") Brown, later governor, and still later father of another governor of California.

During 1935 Cincinnatus was instrumental in combining all different city purchasing agencies into one office.

They worked to merge the Department of Streets and Sewers with Engineering, to start a police-training academy, and to cut the city budget by $2 million.

The city council also moved to stamp out vice in Seattle. Mrs. Powell and a young attorney, William F. Devin, displayed maps at a hearing showing the locations of gambling dens and houses of prostitution. When the chief of police still refused to acknowledge their existence, Councilman Hamley asked that the chief follow him from the courtroom and promptly escorted him to a gambling den.

In 1936 Cincinnatus supported Arthur Langlie for mayor, but he was beaten by John Dore, who had been backed by the head of the Teamsters' Union, Dave Beck. In 1938, however, Langlie defeated Vic Meyers, the state's lieutenant-governor. A major issue in the race was whether trackless trollies and buses should replace the worn-out streetcar system. Langlie supported the plan—and won. Langlie resigned during his second term as mayor to become the first man to serve three terms as state governor.

DEPRESSION STRIKES

In the middle of the Depression, Seattle again entered a period of labor unrest and political confusion. The Pacific Coast Waterfront strike of 1934 was the most divisive event to occur during the early Depression years and resulted in considerable bloodshed in Seattle.

The National Industrial Recovery Act, passed by Congress in 1933, gave unions the right to organize and bargain with employers. The International Longshoremen's Association, led by Alfred Renton ("Harry") Bridges of San Francisco, took advantage of the new rights. In Seattle, Local 38-12 sprang to life with three major objectives—a union-run hiring hall, a coast-wide agreement that would recognize the ILA as the waterfront workers' official union, and an end to Depression-induced speedups, which forced some gangs to work twice as fast if they were to keep their jobs.

The Waterfront Employers Association (W.E.A.) refused to recognize Local 38-12. The entire membership of the West Coast union voted to strike on March 23, 1934. Two days later, the W.E.A. brought in 150 strikebreakers. The longshoremen raided several piers, beat up the strikebreakers, and tossed a foreman into Elliott Bay. The employers demanded protection from the National Guard and Seattle police.

Governor Clarence Martin ordered State Patrol members to the waterfront. Mayor John Dore accused the longshoremen of letting Communists infiltrate their union.

As the strike tied up the waterfront for the second month, the effects were causing severe economic hardship. The lumber and flour mills shut down and some companies threatened to move to other cities. The new mayor of Seattle, Charles Smith, first tried to mediate, then to toughen his stand.

On June 14 a striker was run over by a truck trying to cross the picket line. Police seized 49 baseball bats at the hall of the Sailors' Union. The Chamber of Commerce organized a "Council of War" and took over policing the neighborhoods to allow police to travel en masse to Smith Cove, where the employers would try to break the strike. On June 19, a police force of 400, including those mounted and armed with sawed-off baseball bats and tear gas, assembled at the Cove as 225 guards with shotguns escorted 150 strikebreakers via boat

This panoramic view of Seattle was taken around 1931. Courtesy, McDonald Collection. (MOHAI)

to the terminal.

The longshoremen, now 2,000 strong, massed outside the terminal and stopped all trains and trucks from moving. For the next month daily violent confrontations sent men to the hospitals. For every longshoreman beaten by the police, the union attempted to send three strikebreakers to medical centers. On June 30 a striker was shot dead by a company guard at Point Wells. The longshoremen used this martyred death to considerable propaganda advantage. Three days later a special deputy was disarmed by a large crowd at Third and Seneca and killed with his own revolver. On July 19 Mayor Smith fired the police chief for being too lenient with strikers. The mayor took over, ordering machine guns placed at strategic locations. When 2,000 strikers blocked a train at Smith Cove, police clubbed so many to the ground that reporters were unable to keep count. Tear gas filled the area and even the mayor had to be treated for gas inhalation.

This was the final bloodletting, and five days later both sides accepted the arbitration of President Franklin D. Roosevelt's National Longshoremen's Board. In the end, they granted the union a coast-wide agreement, but stipulated that hiring halls would be jointly operated by management and union though allowing the ILA to select the dispatcher. This almost guaranteed only ILA members would be sent to work on the ships.

The 98-day strike cost untold millions at the deepest part of the Depression and created lasting bitterness that resulted in more strikes in the years that followed. The worst ones were precipitated in the late '30s by the Teamsters Union and its West Coast organizer, Dave Beck, when they fought with Bridges and the ILA over organizing and controlling the warehouse workers.

Beck had begun to establish a reputation, and even a certain rapport, with the Seattle business community by helping to settle the *Post-Intelligencer* strike in the fall of 1936. The *P-I* had been struck by the Newspaper Guild, becoming the first large newspaper in the world to have publication suspended by a dispute with its editorial staff. Dave Beck moved in by lending his support for the strike to show union solidarity. When the *Seattle Times* accused him of actually causing the strike, Beck retaliated with a libel suit, and Mayor John F. Dore came to his defense. When no one else could settle the dispute and it dragged on for several months, Beck called Harvey Kelley, a top labor-relations official for the Hearst organization and asked for a partnership between management and labor, with labor getting a better cut of the profits. This move was necessary, Beck argued, to keep radicals out of the picture. They flew to Miami to meet William Green, president of the A.F. of L., and the strike was settled. Now Beck's image took a different turn. Businessmen said he had mellowed, and obviously favored him over radical union leaders like Bridges, whom they suspected of being a Communist.

Above
During the Depression, Hitler's Nazis, by backing Franco, tested their war machine in Spain's Civil War. Pickets gathered on June 1, 1937, in front of the German Consulate in Seattle at Fourth and Union to protest German and Italian involvement. Courtesy, Post-Intelligencer Collection. (MOHAI)

Opposite
Clockwise from top, left
In an effort to end the longshoremen's strike of 1934, on July 19 Mayor Charles Smith ordered police, armed with machine guns, to strategic locations near Smith Cove. Courtesy, Post-Intelligencer Collection. (MOHAI)

Before the Aurora Bridge barred high mast ships from passing under it, ships such as the *Monographela* passed through. The Aurora, or George Washington Bridge, was completed in 1931 and carried traffic northward from downtown Seattle. Courtesy, Williamson Collection, Puget Sound Maritime Historical Society.

This map of Seattle, the product of a 1938 WPA project, shows the original incorporation and annexations. Courtesy, Historical Photography Collection, U of W Libraries.

This view, circa 1940, faces west across the first Lake Washington Floating Bridge. Constructed by the Washington Toll Bridge Authority and the WPA at a cost of nearly nine million dollars, it opened in 1939. It was the first floating bridge in the world. (MOHAI)

Seattle police standing among striking longshoremen outside Smith Cove during the summer of 1934. A few days later, bloody confrontations took place and continued almost daily until the conflict was taken to national arbitration. Courtesy, Post-Intelligencer Collection. (MOHAI)

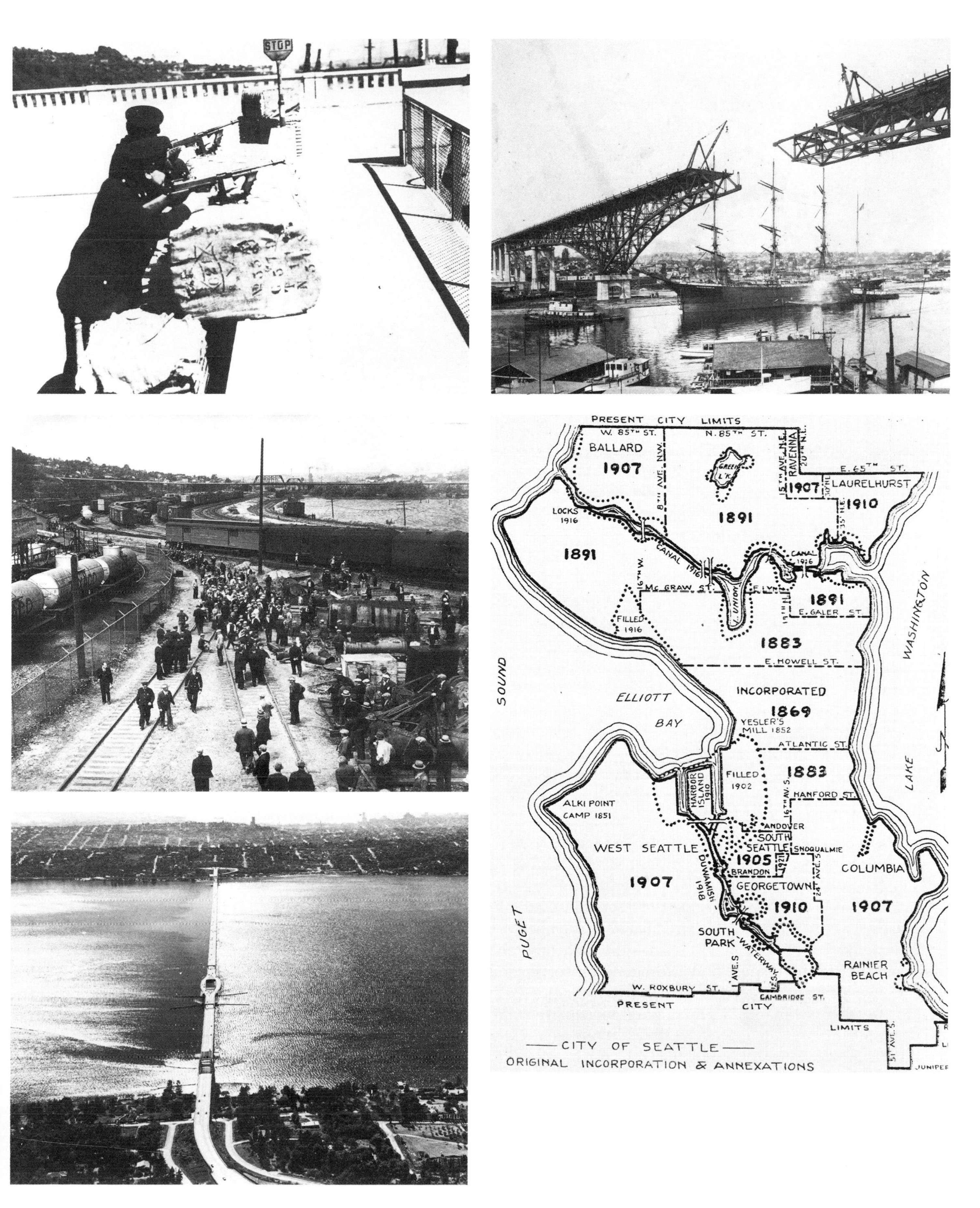
STOP
PRESENT CITY LIMITS
W. 85TH ST.
N. 85TH ST.
BALLARD
1907
8TH AVE. N.W.
15TH AVE. N.E.
RAVENNA
20TH N.E.
E. 65TH ST.
1907
LAURELHURST
1910
1891
LOCKS 1916
CANAL 1916
CANAL 1916
1891
16TH W.
MC GRAW ST.
L. UNION
E. LYN
11TH N.E.
1891
E. GALER ST.
FILLED 1916
1883
WASHINGTON
E. HOWELL ST.
SOUND
ELLIOTT
BAY
INCORPORATED
1869
YESLER'S MILL 1852
ATLANTIC ST.
1883
LAKE
HARBOR ISLAND 1910
FILLED 1902
HANFORD ST.
ALKI POINT CAMP 1851
ANDOVER
SOUTH SEATTLE
SNOQUALMIE
WEST SEATTLE
1905
BRANDON
COLUMBIA
1907
DUWAMISH 1918
GEORGETOWN
1910
1907
PUGET
SOUTH PARK
WATERWAY
RAINIER BEACH
W. ROXBURY ST.
CAMBRIDGE ST.
PRESENT
CITY
LIMITS
JUNIPER
—CITY OF SEATTLE—
ORIGINAL INCORPORATION & ANNEXATIONS

As Beck began to fight Bridges and the ILA for control of Seattle's warehouses, he attempted to confine his opponents to the waterfront. He accused Bridges' men of beating up his Teamsters, who then retaliated.

Bridges closed the port of San Francisco and called for a sympathy strike in Seattle. Seattle businessmen, who increasingly favored Beck, formed the "Industrial Council" to fight back.

Mayor Charles L. Smith led an assault on Bridges' pickets at Pier 41, and after a few gas shells had been fired and the police lines forced their way in, the port was opened. After a series of strikes broke out, the Labor Relations Board as arbitrator essentially confined Bridges and the ILA to the waterfront area.

Dave Beck found that through the rapidly growing Teamsters' Union he could influence much of the Seattle business world. He was adept at conciliation and considered strikes a last resort. By the end of World War II, Seattle workers were more than 90 percent organized, and Beck could claim much of the credit. And some businesses actually solicited his advice on labor matters.

Now Beck had begun to look beyond the state of Washington. He created a Western Conference of 240 locals and became its president. Though realizing the Teamsters with a million members were already the largest union in the country, Beck nevertheless planned to increase Teamster membership fourfold. He established a national organizing headquarters in Washington, D.C. Then in 1952, he took over as Teamsters president at the request of old Dan Tobin who was retiring from the job. Beck continued to live in Seattle and bought a big Sheridan Beach home with a pool and guardhouses. Beck's stature as a respectable citizen of the Seattle community was confirmed by his appointment to the board of regents of the University of Washington. He invested his money while Teamster funds paid for many of his expenses. When Treasury Department men were ordered to look at his financial records, they found he was no bookkeeper. They dug through his records for many months, and in 1957 Beck was charged with personal income tax evasion but was declared innocent. He was convicted of filing fraudulent union tax forms and of keeping the cash from the sale of a used Cadillac belonging to the union. Later in Tacoma, after his income tax trial, he was found guilty on six counts. He was sent to McNeil Island Federal Penitentiary. After serving two and a half years, Dave Beck was paroled, returned to Seattle, was accepted back as a citizen of importance but no longer did he dominate the scene.

During the '30s when his power was increasing, Beck had seen Seattle change greatly. Now the city faced even greater challenges as World War II loomed on the horizon. Almost overnight it seemed the Depression had ended and Seattle and King County were deeply involved in manufacturing,building,and shipping.

Dave Beck, known for his presidency of the International Teamsters Union, grew to national stature as a controversial figure. Courtesy, Historical Photography Collection, U of W Libraries.

THE LABOR MOVEMENT IN WASHINGTON STATE

Organized labor arose in Washington as a consequence of the industrialization of the 1870s and 1880s. At first it was a highly heterogeneous movement, which included a few scattered locals of international craft unions, such as the Bricklayers and Iron Molders, as well as an odd assemblage of political radicals. All these groups, however, were outnumbered by the Knights of Labor, a body that accepted farmers, housewives, the unemployed, and even small businessmen, in addition to wage earners. Labor's first unified action came in the mid-1880s, when laid-off railroad workers found themselves competing with imported Chinese laborers for the few remaining jobs. In both Tacoma and Seattle, workers organized to expel the Chinese by force. Out of these efforts grew the Seattle Central Labor Council. For the next 50 years Washington labor was in the forefront of the anti-immigration movement.

As time went on, the craft union locals began to grow. By the turn of the century they dominated the labor movement while the Knights fell into decline. In 1902 labor began to organize statewide, forming the State Federation of Labor and affiliating with the American Federation of Labor. Many of those disappointed by the decision to affiliate with the AFL reacted in 1905 by forming the Industrial Workers of the World (IWW or "Wobblies"), which preached class war and industrial union doctrines and criticized the AFL.

The struggle between the IWW and the AFL went on for 20 years. The AFL unions successfully organized among the native-born workers who held the skilled and better-paying jobs. They also achieved some notable political successes, such as the State Workmen's Compensation Act in 1911. Meanwhile, the IWW achieved its greatest popularity among immigrant groups, who were often unskilled and unemployed. The IWW won worldwide notoriety with its "Free Speech Fights" which publicized the plight of these workers. By World War I, however, the AFL had clearly won the struggle. The IWW faded away, and the immigrants remained unorganized until the 1930s.

During the 1920s Washington State labor was in eclipse and isolated, as business-oriented administrations ran the state. Membership fell, and the unions spent their meager resources battling one another over ideological and factional issues. Meanwhile, labor leadership grew more and more conservative. When the Depression struck, labor was thus ill-prepared to respond. Membership declined further and conditions worsened until the national economic policies of the New Deal began to take effect. Radical union leaders and activist rank-and-file members, irritated at the lack of union militancy, responded on their own. This resulted in the formation in 1935 of the Congress of Industrial Organizations, which reached out to the unorganized workers and actively recruited among the immigrant groups. By the late 1930s the threat of the CIO so alarmed the AFL that it too began to organize and compete for new members. The result was rapid growth for both branches of the labor movement and the achievement of numerous economic and political gains. By the end of the 1930s, despite its internal divisions, the state labor movement was at the height of its power and influence.

The rapid economic growth caused by World War II further encouraged union growth and began to reduce tensions between the AFL and CIO. This trend toward reconciliation was aided when the CIO began expelling its Communist leaders in the late 1940s and culminated in the reunification of the labor movement in 1955 with the formation of the AFL-CIO.

Since World War II the growth of the labor movement has slowed nearly to a halt. The organized percentage of the labor force has declined as new industries sprang up without unions and old, organized industries declined. As workers that fought the labor battles of the 1930s retire, younger, less disciplined members have taken their places. New questions of a broader nature have complicated the simple labor-management disputes of the past: civil rights, affirmative action, sexual equality, and environmental protection. Labor is still a powerful element in the society of Washington State, but if recent trends continue, it may find this position threatened in the days and years ahead.—**Jonathan Dembo**

The Labor Day Parade of 1945 marched down Second Avenue at Union. Courtesy, Post-Intelligencer Collection. (MOHAI)

Unemployed masses rallied in City Hall Park in February 1931. (MOHAI)

CHAPTER 11

WAR AND PEACE--AGAIN: 1941-1960

The Seattle Sunday newspapers for December 7, 1941, were full of war news, but it was a war being fought by countries in Europe and Asia. The reports of lend-lease, consultation with Japanese ambassadors, and ship sinkings near the American coast line brought the war closer. But while people listened to Edward R. Murrow, a local boy who had graduated from Washington State College, speaking all the way from London, it remained someone else's war.

By mid-afternoon that Sunday, though, telephones began ringing, and radios were switched on. The Japanese, the reports said, had attacked Pearl Harbor in Hawaii. The United States was at war! People felt fear as well as anger. Many scanned the skies for possible Japanese bombers. The military services went on full alert. And all of King County joined the rest of America to hear President Roosevelt talk about the "day that will live in infamy."

In spite of the feeling that something momentous was happening, residents of King County could not have foreseen the dramatic effects the war would have on the area over the next four years.

KING COUNTY IN THE WAR

City and county populations increased sharply as people were hired to build airplanes, ships, and materials needed by the military. Within three years, from 1940 to 1943, Seattle's residents grew in number from 368,302 to an approximate 480,000. Outlying communities involved in war production had commensurate expansions. Many new arrivals moved into unincorporated areas of King County, especially around Kirkland, Renton, and Seattle.

The large war plants on Puget Sound—notably Boeing Aircraft Company, the Puget Sound Navy Yard at Bremerton, the Seattle-Tacoma Shipbuilding Corporation, Associate Shipbuilders in Seattle, and Pacific Car and Foundry—attracted new workers. Western Washington's four basic industries—lumbering, agriculture, fishing, and mining—all showed marked expansion. The unprecedented demand for wood products and paper stimulated the lumber industry. Increased war needs for aluminum, magnesium, copper, and coal gave an impetus to the mining and metallurgical industries throughout the state. The big food processing plants located in or near Seattle, Auburn, and Kent employed an ever-growing number of workers.

The military bases themselves, which ringed Seattle, further swelled the population boom, albeit in part with transient servicemen and women.

Fort Lewis, 50 miles to the south, was one of the largest active army bases in the country. Sand Point Naval Air Station on Lake Washington was within the city limits as was Fort Lawton. Soon an Army Port of Embarkation was in operation and many piers were taken over by the military. Across Puget Sound were the Bremerton Navy Yard, the Keyport Naval Torpedo Station, and the Bangor Naval Station. The Coast Guard already had headquarters in Seattle and its activities were greatly enlarged. The Naval Station at the south end of Lake Union was activated. A new Army Air Force installation was built at Paine Field between Seattle and Everett, and McChord Air Field just north of Fort Lewis was very busy. Smaller installations seemed to spring up overnight within the city and county.

Business picked up, too, along the waterfront. Beginning as early as 1939, non-strategic shipments to Japan and renewed trade with the Soviet Union dominated Seattle exports. By September 1940, outgoing shipments were up 25 percent over the previous year.

Anticipating greater American involvement in the war, the navy in March 1941 took over the country's longest earth-filled piers at Smith Cove, for which they paid the Port of Seattle $3 million. After the Japanese attack on Pearl Harbor, the navy controlled most Puget Sound shipping and the army leased for the duration piers 36 through 39 as a Port of Embarkation. Seattle also became a major port for the Army Transport Service.

The Port Commissioners, now short of pier space, bought the East Waterway Dock on Harbor Island in 1942, built the Hanford Street Grain elevator, and began work on rebuilding Pier 42 at a cost of nearly $3 million. In 1943 the Port broke ground for the Seattle-Tacoma airport at Bow Lake.

Also in 1943, grim evidence of the Pacific combat came to Seattle with the first trainload of casualties to be treated at Seattle hospitals. Dimouts were common as fear rose that the

Photograph by Victor Gardaya (MOHAI)

Japanese might bomb the city or send a submarine into Puget Sound. Reducing the light level was intended to keep key targets from being silhouetted. On February 18, 1943, the first B-29 bomber, being test-flown by Boeing, crashed into the Frye Packing Company plant on Airport Way, killing 11 aboard and 21 in the plant. Because of wartime restrictions on the news, the public didn't learn of the details until after the war.

When the war erupted in Europe in 1939, Boeing was building planes on subcontract to the Douglas Company in California. But the company during the '30s had developed the Flying Fortress. After Europe was in German hands, the British Royal Air Force decided that the Boeing version of the B-17 was the best means of striking back at the Germans. Almost immediately the company was seeking workers and the number of employees grew to 30,000 by the time America entered the war. The B-17 didn't take long to prove its worth.

In 1942, President Roosevelt said the country would build 50,000 planes a year, more than had been built since the Wright brothers flew. Working on a cost plus fixed fee basis and with government capital, Boeing built huge structures in which to house assembly lines. A larger, longer-range plane, the B-29, was operational in 1943. (It was, of course the B-29, the *Enola Gay*, that carried the first atomic bomb to Hiroshima in 1945; another B-29 took a second nuclear bomb to Nagasaki.) The peak year for Boeing employment was 1944, when the company had 50,000 employees in Seattle and total sales topped $600 million.

With the induction of men and women into the armed services (eventually 89,000 King County residents would serve), an acute shortage of labor developed in King County. As factories competed for manpower, advertisements were published nationwide to attract additional labor to the Seattle area. Retail stores, restaurants, and the service industry all felt the strain.

A campaign was launched to utilize the work potential within the whole community. Public policy and public-opinion networks enticed workers, especially women and youths, into war-production jobs. Many women who had never worked outside the home were employed. By 1943 nearly half the employees at Boeing were women. These former housewives often earned from $200 to $250 a month, sometimes as much as $400 a month once they acquired particular job skills. The wage contrast with the Depression era of four or five years earlier, when WPA jobs paid employees $40 a month or less, was tremendous.

Labor priorities were established, depending on the importance of the service or material produced. Boeing had the highest urgency rating and labor priority.

Newcomers to King County sometimes found the older residents less than cordial, and many stayed only a short time after encountering the drastic housing shortage and other problems. However, determined minorities seeking new homes arrived. From 1910 to 1940, blacks made up only 1.0 percent of the Seattle population. In 1940 there were 3,789 blacks in the area. Three years later that number had doubled, though blacks were not hired at many major indus-

Looking north on Seattle in the 1940s, this aerial view shows the business district in the foreground and Lake Union in the distance. Note that the Alaskan Way viaduct—Highway 99—is not yet built. (MOHAI)

The Boeing industrial plant was camouflaged against enemy air attack during World War II by an entire artificial village built above it. Courtesy, Boeing Historical Services.

tries until 1942, and then ony under pressure. Signs saying, "We Cater to White Trade Only" appeared in a few stores, and some restaurants refused to serve blacks, and many recreational facilities barred their entrance. White workers in a war-industry plant in Seattle demanded that blacks have separate toilet facilities. One city official voiced the opinion that as long as the Army followed a policy of segregation, it was an impertinence to expect civilians to integrate.

Lack of adequate housing and recreational facilities for blacks precipitated several conflicts. As an example, one unpleasant incident involved a group of black soldiers and members of a young people's church society who were refused admittance to two skating rinks.

Some citizens of King County worked to ease the tensions between old and new residents and to help the minorities and other newcomers adjust; unfortunately, their number proved far short of the need.

For one minority group that had long lived in King County, a very different form of rejection took place.

THE JAPANESE-AMERICAN EXPERIENCE

By the turn of the century, Japanese-Americans made up Seattle's largest minority population, developing a community reaching from Second to Twelfth streets, and from Yesler Way to Jackson Street. They had immigrated to Seattle beginning in 1879, and had increased in number after the anti-Chinese riots had driven many Chinese from the city.

Above
A Landing Ship Tank docks at Seattle's Port of Embarkation on February 3, 1945. During World War II many Seattle piers were taken over by the military. (MOHAI)

Top, right
"Rosie the Riveter" works at Boeing during the war. By 1943 nearly half of the employees at Boeing were women, many of whom had never worked outside the home. Courtesy, Boeing Historical Services.

Above
Women working at Boeing during World War II read a sign that ironically cautions them to avoid indecorous language. Courtesy, Boeing Historical Services.

They were prominent in King County agriculture, in Seattle hotels, and as operators of grocery stores and florist shops. In those years, the United States was developing trade with Japan; therefore it was decided that the Chinese Exclusion Act of 1882 did not apply to the Japanese.

In the 1920s, a resurgence of racism had surfaced; in 1924 Congress voted to apply the exclusion act to the Japanese. From the beginning, Japanese immigrants were ineligible for naturalization. Furthermore, state laws passed in 1921 and 1923 prohibited land ownership by aliens. Some Japanese turned their property over to their American-born children, others to trusted white supporters. But many lost title to their property holdings on which they had usually made considerable improvements.

In 1939 an area, part of which included, "Japantown" or "Little Tokyo," was selected as the first site for public housing. Twelve city blocks of dilapidated buildings became Yesler Terrace Housing Project. But Pearl Harbor was attacked later that year, and not long after that the Japanese-Americans were sent to internment camps.

Three months after the Japanese bombed Pearl Harbor, President Roosevelt signed Executive Order 9066, which instructed military commanders to evacuate any persons of Japanese ancestry from designated military areas. On March 2, 1942, the Western Defense Command declared the three Far-Western states a military area in which all Japanese must be confined. A nervous officer, fearing that the Japanese living on Bainbridge Island might damage Bremerton Navy Yard, immediately posted notices demanding that Japanese-American families prepare to evacuate in eight days. These Bainbridge Japanese were the first to be interned.

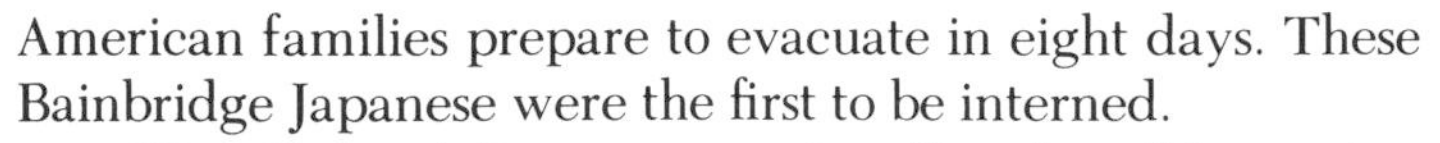

King County's Japanese people suffered terrible psychological and economic hardships when they were forced to move. Some sold their belongings at far below actual value; others tried to lease or leave their property in the hands of friends. The Japanese could take with them only what they could carry. Most lost treasured family possessions, property, businesses, and assets—in short, nearly everything they had accrued through years of hard work. Two-thirds of those forced from Seattle were American-born and therefore U.S. citizens. In the Northwest, as elsewhere, the same treatment was not given the German- and Italian-Americans whose countries of origin were counted with Japan as the enemy Axis.

The Japanese-Americans from King County were temporarily housed in the stables and other buildings at the Puyallup Fairgrounds. From there they were taken to Camp Minidoka near Hunt, Idaho. As the months went by, the government gradually relented in its extreme stand. Because of the labor shortage, Japanese workers were recruited to help in the sugar beet fields; later, some of the younger people were allowed to leave, to work at jobs in the Midwest and East or attend college. When finally allowed to enlist, thousands of young Japanese-American men served in the United States Army, many in the famed 442nd Combat Team, the most highly decorated unit of the war. Others served in the war's Pacific theater, decoding Japanese messages, interrogating prisoners, even flushing the enemy from island caves.

The Buddhist Church, located at 1427 Main Street, was completed in 1941, just before the Japanese attack on Pearl Harbor. The war with Japan would seriously disrupt the lives of all Seattle-area Japanese-Americans. Photo by Depue and Morgan. (MOHAI)

Guards and a crowd of Japanese civilians on their way to internment stand at Eagle Harbor dock on May 25, 1942 during the expulsion of Japanese from Bainbridge Island. Courtesy, Post-Intelligencer Collection. (MOHAI)

While their sons were suffering casualties and their daughters worked in the war effort, parents remained incarcerated. Not until 1950 were the citizenship laws changed so that native Japanese could apply for citizenship. And not until 1966 was the alien land law repealed.

As the war was ending, a few Japanese began to return to their former hometowns and received a mixed reception. A White River Valley newspaper editorialized that the Japanese should never be allowed to return. On the other hand, some families were warmly welcomed by their old neighbors.

Today, third and fourth generation Japanese-Americans are part of the mainstream of life in King County. Of those who did not return permanently after the war, many settled elsewhere, away from reminders of a bitter past. Most importantly, the younger Nisei realized they could succeed anywhere in this country by applying themselves to a variety of endeavors. As a result, instead of concentrating in the West, they scattered far and wide.

Now many years after that period, older King Countians will remember those dark days of 1942. As Morton Grodzins wrote in his book *Americans Betrayed:*

> No charges were ever filed against these persons, and no guilt was ever attributed to them. . . . Evacuation swept into guarded camps orphans, foster children in white homes, Japanese married to Caucasians, the offspring of such marriages, persons who were unaware of their Japanese ancestry, and American citizens with as little as one-sixteenth Japanese blood.

Today the wartime evacuation is commonly condemned as an act of racial injustice perpetrated during strained and fearful times.

ON THE HOME FRONT

During the war, family life generally altered. Fathers, away in the service or else working long hours, were seldom home. Often the mother in a family also found employment. Some children spent hours without supervision, frequently suffering from neglect.

Marriage and divorce rates soared during the early years of the war, along with the birth rate. Then marriage rates leveled off, and by 1943 actually decreased because there were fewer eligible men available.

Schools, especially at the grade-school level, became crowded. At junior and senior high schools, attendance was spotty as more and more young people found war work or entered the military services. To take care of fluctuating increases, staggered school hours were scheduled and double shifting began. Churches and other buildings were utilized as classrooms. The shortage of teachers forced school boards to issue War Emergency teaching certificates to persons who would not ordinarily meet state requirements.

Because housing too was in short supply throughout King County, obsolete and even condemned buildings were patched up. Chicken coops, sheds, lodge halls, empty service stations, and offices became dwelling units. In September 1943 the National Housing Agency programmed approximately 45,500 new family dwelling units to be built in the

When the Japanese were sent from King County to internment camps in 1942, they could take only what they could carry. These businesses on Jackson Street were boarded up when their owners were forced to leave. Courtesy, Post-Intelligencer Collection. (MOHAI)

These Civil Defense and Home Defense paraphernalia were used during World War II. (MOHAI)

Puget Sound area, two-thirds of them funded by the federal government; accommodations for 6,500 single persons were also built. Public housing projects were erected in Seattle, Kirkland, Auburn, and elsewhere.

Health problems grew with the increase in population. Physicians and dentists were in short supply because of the armed forces' recruitment policies. In Seattle the prewar ratio of one physician per 600 people slipped in 1943 to one per 1,300. Hospital facilities were seriously overtaxed. Sewage dumped into Lake Washington from the shipyards at Kirkland polluted large areas. And garbage disposal became a serious problem in all parts of the Puget Sound region.

Typical of war-congested cities, the cost of living in Seattle rose precipitously. By September 1943 it cost 27.8 percent more to live in Seattle than it had before the war. Food costs soared 142.2 percent.

Retailers, indeed businesses of all kinds, served an increased population with greater buying power; yet government restrictions and regulations added to their problems with inexperienced clerks and a shortage of consumer goods. Food, shoes, gas, tires, and other merchandise were rationed. Some foods, clothing, and household supplies were difficult to obtain. Sudden shortages appeared, then vanished, without warning. Sliced bread was banned for the duration. The li-

Above
Poster on the home front effort encourages conservation of gasoline during World War II. Actually, gasoline, like many consumer goods, was strictly rationed as part of the war effort. (MOHAI)

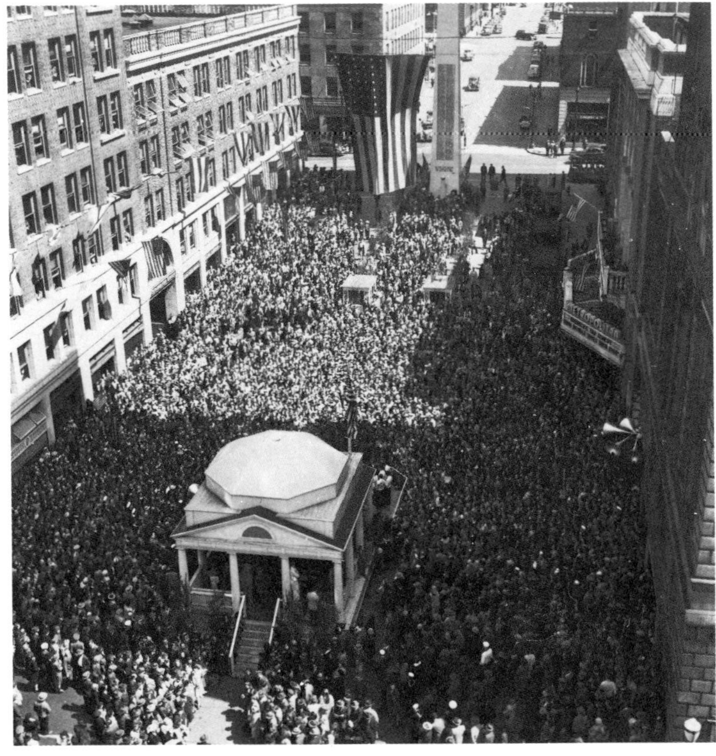

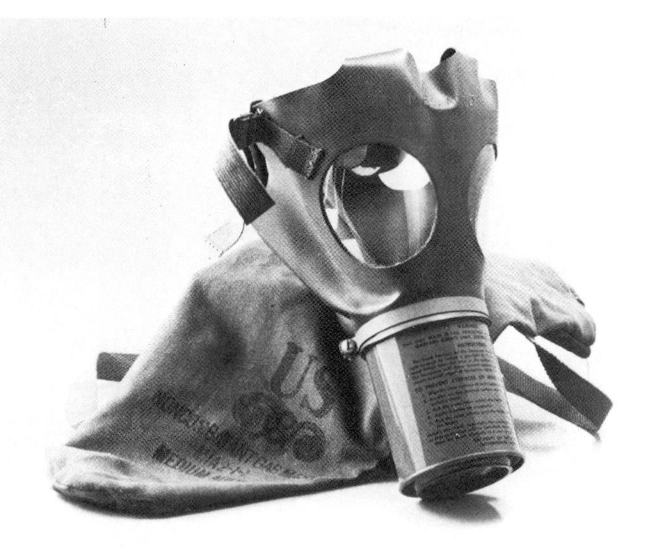

quor ration was a fifth a week, to be picked up once every two weeks. Clothing clinics showed women how to make over discarded clothing. War Ration Book No. 2 was issued with red points for meat and blue points for processed foods. "Victory gardens," in which people grew produce for themselves, abounded. For several months in 1942 and 1943, butcher shops in many cities were without meat. Restaurants, too, felt the squeeze, just as their business was booming from families in which both parents worked and from people without facilities or inclination to cook. Furthermore, members of the armed services on leave in Seattle consumed from 35 to 40 percent of all restaurant output.

Transportation systems were taxed to the fullest. Seattle's new trackless trolley and bus system, which in 1940 had replaced the old streetcar system, carried an average of 12.5 million passengers per month in 1943, more than double the 1940 average. Problems of transit maintenance were multiplied by shortages of mechanics and replacement parts as factories switched to producing war materials. Diesel fuel and gasoline quality deteriorated and became scarce, automobiles wore out, and more and more people rode public transportation.

In the overcrowded cities, recreational facilities were often open 24 hours a day to handle the swing- and night-

Opposite
Top
During World War II, Victory Square on University Street was the center of activity for the war effort. Paper, aluminum, and bond drives as well as fashion shows were conducted in the square, where movie stars and other celebrities helped to draw crowds like this. Courtesy, Post-Intelligencer Collection. (MOHAI)

Bottom
This noncombatant gas mask was carried during World War II. (MOHAI)

Above
Members of the Women's Army Corps parade during World War II. Serving in the armed forces for the wars duration were some 89,000 King County residents. (MOHAI)

shift crowds. The most popular entertainment was seeing movies. A Seattle motion-picture chain had reported in 1938 that weekly attendance averaged 62,000; by 1943 it had increased to 116,000—an 85 percent jump. Taverns, notably those with a bar, cafe, and dance floor, were crowded, especially on weekends after paydays. On those Friday and Saturday nights, the crowd was swelled by servicemen on weekend leave. Seattle, at the time, had 507 taverns. Dancehalls, too, were popular. Seattle's 10 dance emporiums were packed to the rafters on weekends, and the average-sized hall took in around $1,900 on those two nights.

Delinquency, strangely, did not accelerate during these times, even though children were often left on their own. Though family control and moral standards relaxed, as usually happens in wartime, juveniles were partially controlled by stringent curfew ordinances.

Crime did not increase significantly, in spite of the larger population, perhaps mainly because almost everyone was busy with war work. Arrests were most often for drunkenness in public places. The number of inmates at the State Reformatory at Monroe and the State Penitentiary at Walla Walla actually declined, though the city and county jails were full, usually with persons picked up on minor charges.

Early in the war, prostitution proliferated with organized brothels doing a thriving business. Then a rigid program of repression inaugurated by the armed services and Public Health officials chased most of these illicit activities underground. Venereal disease increased markedly.

In 1942 William F. Devin was elected Seattle's mayor. Since he had been a police judge, he knew firsthand the dark underside of the city. Choosing George Eastman as his police chief, he bluntly told him to clean things up. The lid was clamped on Seattle, and it was time. Seattle was close to being called off limits by the nearby military bases. With the assistance of Dr. Ragnar Westman of the U.S. Public Health Department, the mayor organized a V.D. treatment center.

At last, the long war began to reflect the might of the Allies. Victory followed victory in Europe. When Germany and Italy surrendered, the Pacific became the focus of attention.

After the A-bombs had been dropped on the Japanese of Hiroshima and Nagasaki in early August of 1945, the workers at the Hanford Engineering Works in southeast Washington learned that they had been producing plutonium for the bombs.

The year of victory, 1945, was dimmed with the death of President Roosevelt just a few days before the war in Europe ended. But V-J day was celebrated mightily in King County as it was all over the free world. The world once more was at peace—for a while.

PEACETIME LIVING

Peace, however welcome, brought its problems. Changing from a wartime to a peacetime economy was not easy. Boeing, for example, suffered a decline in annual sales from over $600 million to $14 million. Their employment roster dropped from 40,000 to 11,000. William Allen, the new president who took over when Philip Johnson died in 1945, attempted to renegotiate a contract with the aerospace mechanics' union but the union struck. Dave Beck entered the arena and tried to reorganize the union under Teamster control, which caused great animosity in several circles. The strike was finally settled in 1948 on Allen's terms, in good part because unemployment had once again become a problem in the Seattle area. Two years later, the aerospace workers managed to evade Teamster control.

The outbreak of the Korean War again found Boeing busy with government contracts. The company came out with the B-47 and B-52 bombers, both outstanding planes. Boeing also received orders to build KC-97 tanker transports with swept wings and jet engines, and the Bomarc guided missile project was progressing. In 1952 Boeing moved back into commercial airline business by manufacturing the 707, a jet transport. On July 14, 1954, it flew for the first time. Soon the airlines were ordering the 707. Boeing was about to win the battle for commercial jet orders. When it became fully operational in 1959, the 707 paid off far beyond even Boeing's highest estimates and optimistic expectations. Yet there was danger in this reliance upon a single major industry for employment and the whole area's economic well-being. In 1947 one out of every five King County employees worked in aerospace manufacturing connected with Boeing. By 1957 the figure approached one in two.

Peacetime meant declines in shipbuilding, the lumber industry, and mining. But booms came in other areas of the economy as Americans, deprived during the war of both necessities and conveniences, went on a grand buying spree—acquiring new cars, homes, appliances, and furniture. There was also that new communication marvel, the television set. Along with the plethora of consumer goods, there were the building of superhighways and the repair of worn-out roads, the construction of new office buildings and the expansion of government facilities—all of which offered employment. Colleges burgeoned as the discharged servicemen took advantage of the GI Bill—and the GI Loan program helped them finance decent housing. World War II had exerted a democratizing effect on a younger generation, who expected, and often demanded, new opportunities for advancement and comfort.

As the GIs married and settled down to raise families,

Opposite
V-J Day on Fourth and Pike streets was a frenzy of elation and excitement. Courtesy, Post-Intelligencer Collection. (MOHAI)

Right
Women picket the downtown Frederick and Nelson department store on April 1, 1946. The women are protesting sex discrimination in the employment of elevator operators and janitors. Courtesy, Post-Intelligencer Collection. (MOHAI)

they took to the growing suburbs. Northwest-style "ranch" homes were being efficiently built by the thousands in housing tracts. New streets, water mains, utilities, and the other needed services expanded at a startling rate. The baby boom which followed the war swelled school enrollments to bursting. Small school districts suddenly grew large, requiring several new buildings to be added each year, often temporary prefabricated structures. In all, the metropolitan area in and around Seattle was expected to accommodate the population's needs as rapidly as possible, sometimes resulting in an unplanned spread that was both expensive to sustain and ugly.

During the 1950s Seattle gained the reputation as the place to live—where people weren't too crowded and the amenities of civilized living were readily available at an affordable price. It had no ghettos, except for perhaps what might be called a small one in the Central Area, and it had plenty of good water, little smog, and beautiful scenery. In winter, one could ski in resorts less than an hour away. In summer, the mountains beckoned to hikers and fishermen and campers, while boaters using sail or power could explore the seemingly endless waterways around Puget Sound. As for its notorious rainfall and gray days . . . you could even learn to appreciate them.

Above
In 1947 a group of pioneers founded Group Health Cooperative of Puget Sound, a consumer-owned and operated plan offering comprehensive, prepaid medical care. Today GHC is the largest consumer-controlled health maintenance plan of its kind, with over 270,000 enrollees, two hospitals, and 11 medical centers. Courtesy, Group Health Cooperative.

Left
Nellie Cornish, born in 1876, founded the Cornish School in the Booth Building on the corner of Broadway and East Pine. The school, from the beginning, was a center for the arts in Seattle. Its early faculty consisted largely of Russian immigrants. To this day it hosts many major gatherings in the arts. Courtesy, Historical Photography Collection, U of W Libraries.

AN ERA OF ILL WILL

The distrust of Communism that had built up during the period after World War I and then the Depression years occupied the forefront again as the "Cold War" with the Soviet Union began. The paranoid mood came partly as a reaction to the Soviets' development of their own atomic weapons, partly as a fearful response to the takeover of the Republic of China by the determined Chinese Communists. Middle America felt vulnerable, unable to fully enjoy the peace it had so recently fought for. It resulted in the formation in 1947 of the state legislature's Joint Fact-Finding Committee on Un-American Activities. For the first time since the 1932 election sweep of President Roosevelt, the Republicans had gained control of the state legislature. Combining with conservative Democrats, they developed what was commonly called the Canwell Committee, after its chairman, Albert Canwell, of Spokane. This group of legislators was charged with scrutinizing organizations known or suspected of including members who were Communists. The Canwell Committee was to expose those people who had belonged to the Communist Party or were closely affiliated with it. They did not attempt to determine if any subversive activity had actually taken place. Their investigations led them to the Building Service Employee Union, the Washington Pension Union, the Seattle Repertory Theater, the University of Washington and other organizations.

Protestors outside the Canwell Committee hearings of 1948 carry signs voicing their opposition to the hearings. Three of the six accused faculty of the University of Washington were dismissed and the other three were put on probation. The resulting bitterness which swept the campus lasted until the generation of faculty involved retired. Courtesy, Post-Intelligencer Collection. (MOHAI)

Early in 1948 the committee held a series of stormy hearings in Seattle, during which five witnesses from the university were convicted of contempt of the legislature. The names of suspects at the university were handed to its board of regents in September of 1948. A committee of professors chosen by the faculty senate held lengthy hearings and sent their recommendations to President Raymond Allen, who in turn sent them on to the regents with his own interpretations. The regents—including Dave Beck—decided to dismiss three faculty members and place three on probation. They also prevented renowned but "pink"-tainted scholars such as J. Robert Oppenheimer from speaking on campus.

The legal aspects of this action lingered into the '50s, concerned with loyalty oaths, constitutional rights, and academic freedom. Many people in the state consider these hearings as previews of the HUAC-McCarthy era that followed two years later, affecting the entire nation. Bitterness on campus lingered for a generation. The University of Washington hearings were but an example. Many innocent persons found their livelihoods jeopardized, their reputations ruined, and their bankrolls depleted as a result of "witch-hunting" tactics of the seemingly all-powerful state and federal investigating committees. In the end, all convictions were thrown out by the U.S. Supreme Court. Canwell and others who ran for reelection on the record of the committee were defeated in the 1948 elections, and the State's Joint Fact-Finding Committee on Un-American Activities was allowed to die.

METRO

As Seattle and King County became home to an ever-expanding population, with suburbs ringing Lake Washington, the once sparkling waters of this large inland lake became dirtier and more polluted. As each suburban town grew, the amount of both raw and treated sewage flowing into the lake steadily increased. As unincorporated lands were developed, septic tanks fed into streams which fed into the lake. Soon algae were developing into thick masses, and beaches had to be closed to swimmers. When driving across the lake on the Lacey Murrow floating bridge, one could smell the lake—not a pleasant aroma.

These suburban municipalities and governmental units, developing at a rapid pace, resulted in a patchwork of cities, towns, county land, and private developments with overlapping governmental jurisdictions. Some communities installed their own sewer systems and developed their own city services. But the interlacing lines of the various boundaries and responsibilities made an almost impossible situation in attempts to remedy environmental and civic problems.

As early as 1951, James Ellis had campaigned for a new charter for King County that would offer better urban planning mechanisms, but it was defeated in 1952. At a Municipal League meeting, Ellis proposed a metropolitan government similar to the innovative Toronto system then much in the news. Mayor Gordon Clinton in 1956 named Ellis chairman of a group of 48 citizens to draft proposed legislation. A Metropolitan Municipal Corporation Act was successfully lobbied through the 1957 legislature and a $145

FINDING A HOME FOR HISTORY

The members of the Seattle Historical Society, forerunner of the Historical Society of Seattle and King County, pose in costume, circa 1911. For years they met annually on Founders' Day at the Carkeek mansion. Mrs. Emily Carkeek, the founder, is the second woman from the right in the front row, wearing a large, flat hat. (MOHAI)

One measure of a city's cultural worth is its relationship with its past—how it preserves, displays, and explains to new generations the relics and mementos of their famous or nameless predecessors. The frontier town of Seattle took 60 years for an appreciation of its heritage to develop, and another 40 years of continuous struggle by a handful of Seattle citizens, mainly women, to establish a worthy home for this legacy.

The pivotal person in this effort was an attractive, adept woman, Emily Carkeek, the wife of Morgan Carkeek, a famous contractor and land developer. Emily arrived in Seattle in 1879 from Bath, England, to join her husband, who had come to Seattle from Cornwall in 1871. During the next 30 years, Mrs. Carkeek became increasingly concerned about gathering together the rich heritage of Seattle and King County.

On November 13, 1911, the 60th anniversary of the Alki landing, Mrs. Carkeek acted. She scheduled a luncheon at her home on First Hill at which guests were asked to wear historical attire, and she served a chowder made from Puget Sound butter clams. They discussed the need to create an organization devoted to local history.

For the next three years, these Founders' Day parties became an annual event, and on January 8, 1914, they finally resulted in the formation of the Seattle and King County Historical Society. It was incorporated by Emily Carkeek, Cannie Ford Trimble, Charlotte Haller McKee, Virginia McCarver Prosch, and Flora Thornton Prosser. Among the first trustees were three judges: George Donworth, C.H. Hanford, and R.B. Albertson. Lawrence J. Coleman, Edmond S. Meany, and Miss M.L. Denny were also trustees.

At the Founders' Day party the succeeding November, the new historical society's activities began in earnest. Mrs. Prosser was appointed chairperson of a committee to gather historical data, and Mrs. Prosch began listing acquisitions in a small red book. Research projects were outlined. Other women were assigned writing tasks relating to the history of music and art in Seattle.

Housing the society's growing collection became a problem. In 1914 Professor Edmond Meany secured a room at the University of Washington for meetings, as well as space in a fireproof building to store books, manuscripts, and artifacts. From that time on, the society sought to find a permanent museum structure worthy of its purposes. Meanwhile, new members were added to the board, such as Rolland Denny and Vivian Carkeek. In 1919 Seattle's first fire bell, weighing 5,000 pounds, was presented to the society; it was transported to the original Carkeek Park on Lake Washington, where Morgan had set land aside for a museum. However, in 1926 the society relinquished the land, which was deeded to King County, so that Sand Point Naval Air Station could be erected on the site.

On December 29, 1926, Emily Carkeek died. Having lost its guiding light, the historical society nearly ceased to function for the next four years, until Mrs. George Donworth and Mrs. N. H. Latimer called a meeting on March 4, 1930. With the help of Mrs. Vivian Carkeek, Mrs. D. W. Bass, Mrs. Edmond Bowden, Mrs. George Heilbron, Mrs. Paul Watt, Mrs. L. N. Chamberlain, Mrs. Frederick Swanstrom, and Miss Margaret Prosser (who attended for her mother, Mrs. William Prosser), the society began searching for a new museum site. A year earlier, Morgan Carkeek had dedicated a new Carkeek Park and again had reserved a place for a history museum. But most of the society's members considered the location at 110th Street too far from the city.

In 1935, two new names appeared on the trustee list—E. B. Holmes and Philip G. Johnson. During that same year the Founders' Day celebrations were revived at Rolland Denny's home, with Ben Petit showing historical slides. In 1936 Morgan Carkeek passed away, leaving a $5,000 bequest to apply toward building the museum that had been for so long the dream of his late wife. In 1940 the collections were moved to the home of Mrs. Theodore (Guendolyn) Plestcheeff, the daughter of Morgan and Emily Carkeek. The drive began in earnest for funds to erect a museum, with the women of the society actively searching for a suitable site.

Philip Johnson donated $5,000 for the museum building fund in 1942, and in that year too the society acquired one of his company's first prototype airplanes, the Boeing B-1. Mrs. Johnson agreed to continue keeping an aviation scrapbook, begun in 1925, for the society. In 1945, after Mr. Johnson's death, the Boeing Company donated $50,000 in his memory. (Mrs. Johnson later left $100,000 for the benefit of the museum's aeronautical section, in her husband's name.)

A short time later, an ideal location was discovered at the north end of the Arboretum, just east of Montlake Boulevard, and the city park board backed the plan to erect the museum on the site. At the time, however, the University of Washington was in charge of the property, and its regents refused to allow the museum to be built there. But Mrs. Frederick Swanstrom would not give up. Discovering that some of the Arboretum property was under federal ownership as part of the old canal right-of-way, Mrs. Swanstrom and Mrs. Plestcheeff, now the society's president, flew to Washington, D.C. to attempt to secure the site. The U.S. Army Corps of Engineers declared the property surplus, then deeded it to King County, who in turn gave it to the city of Seattle. Later an agreement was signed for its use by the Historical Society.

Meanwhile, plans were approved for architect Paul Thiry's design of a modern museum structure. Fund-raising activities flourished. By the end of 1947 more than $40,000 had been collected, and membership surpassed 1,000. Collections of artifacts and art continued to accumulate, including the Early American glass collection of Mrs. Nathan Eckstein, purchased through the efforts of Mrs. Dietrich Schmitz and her associates. The Sophie Frye Bass estate gave her collection of rare Northwest books—the foundation of today's extensive museum library.

Emil Sick, with the help of Governor Arthur B. Langlie and Mayor William F. Devin, developed a "Spirit of Seattle" Committee, which collected $130,000 for the building fund. And Mrs. Plestcheeff, aided by volunteers, presented a museum preview in the penthouse of the Olympic Hotel to garner further support.

In September of 1950 bids were opened, and the Kuney Johnson Company was named general contractor. On February 15, 1952, after band music, speeches, and ribbon cutting, the key to the Museum of History and Industry was presented to Mayor Devin by the president of the Historical Society, Mrs. Plestcheeff. After more than 40 years of planning and effort, Seattle and King County had finally obtained its museum free and clear, including not only buildings but one of the West Coast's largest collections of historical memorabilia and artifacts. Guendolyn Carkeek Plestcheeff saw her mother's dream come true.—**James R. Warren and Bob Cole**

The BOMARC rocket, a product of the Cold War, was rolled out at Boeing in 1957. Courtesy, Post-Intelligencer Collection. (MOHAI)

million bond issue was placed on the King County ballot in 1958. The plan called for a Metro council of eight members from Seattle and seven from suburban areas, to supervise building of sewers, develop rapid transit, and begin concerted area-wide planning—the only solution for the complex multiplicity of problems. The vote required a majority in the city of Seattle and another majority in the suburbs. The city passed the measure, but the more conservative voters outside of Seattle refused the plan.

Nevertheless this defeat did not stop the action. Ellis and others went to work revising the plan. With removal of the area-wide planning and transit system itself, and limiting the issue to sewers only (estimated to cost about $80 million), the measure passed in 1958. Soon treatment plants and new sewer lines were under construction. Lake Washington began to clear up, the fetid aroma vanished, and the swimming beaches reopened.

The regional cooperation required for the Metro sewer system plan was a monumental accomplishment. It was a crucial first step toward solving problems of a metropolitan area nature. Even though limiting their support to the cleaning up of the waters of King County, the forward-looking citizens had agreed to tax themselves to achieve a common goal.

Had the voters been able to foresee the shortage and escalating costs of fuel for automobiles, they might have passed rapid transit too on that first ballot—and perhaps also coordinated planning in municipalities and the county—still badly needed at times.

But the citizens were not through. Seven years later they would be considering Forward Thrust bond issues that would carry them further toward mutually beneficial goals. Meantime, they had a world's fair to sponsor.

CHAPTER 12

THE RECENT PAST: 1961-1980

The decade of the '60s arrived with a world's fair on the horizon and ended with the protests against war, racial prejudice, sexism, and other injustices.

In the next decade, with the Viet Nam War ended, youth seemed to quiet down and to concentrate on traditional success efforts but still kept a wary eye on business, government, education, and society in general.

When 1980 arrived, other events dimmed before a white-topped mountain called St. Helens—which literally blew its top in one of the most devastating and picturesque eruptions of modern times.

CENTURY 21 EXPOSITION

According to the late Nard Jones, four men happened to gather at the Washington Athletic Club bar in January 1955, and in their conversation planted the seed for a world's fair to take place in their city. The four: Don Follett and Denny Givens of the Chamber of Commerce; Al Rochester, a city councilman; and Ross Cunningham of the Seattle *Times*, who had known a former city editor instrumental in dreaming up the Alaska Yukon Pacific Exposition of 1909. Aware that Seattle had experienced a decade of postwar prosperity, and that business now seemed to be hitting the doldrums, they felt a focus was needed. Furthermore, tourism was proving a lucrative local industry. Seattle lacked a cultural center. And Seafair, the annual summer festival, needed a new boost.

From that meeting, Al Rochester conceived of another fair, perhaps to be held in 1959, a half-century after the A-Y-P. He and others promoted the concept. The idea slowly spread through downtown business groups. Jerry Hoeck, an advertising executive, and a colleague, Marlow Hartung, dreamed up a title for this fair-to-be—the Century 21 Exposition. The name seemed appropriate, since in 1957 the Russians had sent Sputnik I skyward and the U.S. was entering the Space Age, with the Boeing Company closely involved. Seattleites liked the possibility of creating an image of itself as a city leading the way toward the new century.

But the proposed fair needed a site, financing, and organization. The Seattle City Council memorialized the state legislature to appoint a world's fair study commission. Governor Arthur Langlie—completing his third term and about to run unsuccessfully for the Senate—signed the bill and appointed Edward Carlson as chairman of the World's Fair Commission. Several groups quickly began to shape the exposition: the World's Fair Commission, Century 21 Exposition, Incorporated, and finally a group of architects who created what some would call "a fair in a jewel box." The civic center was chosen as the site, largely because the exposition would provide several permanent buildings there. Some of the property adjacent to the center that was needed to increase the area to 74 acres proved difficult to obtain, but eventually the location was ready for building.

Plans began to form in the larger Century 21 Exposition, Incorporated group chaired by William S. Street, who was later assisted by Joseph P. Gandy. Paul Thiry, a local architect with a national reputation, was chosen as supervising architect, and Lawrence Halprin as landscape architect. Minoru Yamasaki, with the cooperation of Naramore, Bain, Brady, and Johanson, was asked to design the United States Science Pavilion.

Though the public initially seemed largely indifferent about the plan for the fair, when the city council placed a $7.5 million civic center bond issue on the ballot, it passed three to one. On the other hand, when two pleas for state involvement were carried to Olympia, neither received positive response from governor or legislature. However, after Albert D. Rosellini took the oath of office as governor early in 1957, Eddie Carlson went to call on him. He emerged with the promise that the state would provide an amount equal to Seattle's investment, and later that year the legislature did authorize a $7.5 million bond issue for the world's fair in Seattle—which would now become a reality. From this money, $4.5 million was set aside for the Coliseum, which was to house the Washington State Exhibit and later to provide exhibit space and a performing arena.

Though several hundred hardworking and highly dedicated Seattle businesspeople, civic leaders, and public officials were involved, the fair was postponed twice. Ewen Dingwall was made project director of the fair; as the plans progressed, he was promoted to vice-president and general manager. A gratifying number of nations began to sign up as participants.

Jim Faber, who took over as public relations director in

Photograph by Victor Gardaya
(MOHAI)

1957, visited the Brussels exposition and on his way home stopped off to visit Washington's noted Warren Magnuson, one of the Senate's most powerful members. In the end, thanks largely to "Maggie," the U.S. government provided $12.5 million, including the costs of the Science Pavilion, which would concentrate on demonstrating the promise of scientific endeavors.

With $15 million now in the till for basic construction and preparation costs, the fair was still in need of financing for promotion. A few of Seattle's more successful business concerns took out notes of debenture; the Boeing Company was not among them because of its policy against involvement in promotional ventures, but it did something even more appropriate. In the Science Pavilion it installed the Spacearium, a short and exciting simulated journey to the stars. It took viewers on a 60,000-billion-billion-mile round trip in space, traveling at 10 trillion times the speed of light.

Transportation posed a problem until Alweg of Sweden offered to build a monorail from the downtown Westlake Mall to the fairgrounds, a distance of 1.2 miles. Their two ultramodern cars running on concrete pillars and tracks above the street would travel the route in 95 seconds.

After some effort, in November of 1960 the Bureau of International Expositions in France agreed that Century 21 should be sanctioned as a legitimate world's fair. Now the exposition in common parlance became the Seattle World's Fair, with the Century 21 Exposition almost a subtitle.

About this time, Carlson, who had seen the revolving television tower in Stuttgart, conceived of a combination high-rise restaurant and observation platform for the fair. John Graham and Associates were awarded the design contract. The eventual result was the Space Needle, 600 feet tall and crowned with a great gas flame. Built with private funds, as the futuristic structure rose on spidery legs into the Seattle sky, it announced to local citizens that the fair was really coming. It remains an enduring symbol of the city's commitment to succeed as an international city aimed at the future.

The fair's plan originally called for educational exhibits dedicated to science, technology, and culture, but as with the A-Y-P, that strict concept didn't last long. Soon a Show Street and a Gayway were added. Gracie Hanson's Paradise International, a theater-restaurant with 700 seats, headed the Show Street offerings.

At 3 p.m. EST on April 21, 1962, President John F. Kennedy pressed the same gold nugget key that had opened the A-Y-P Exposition back in 1909. This time, however, instead of a direct telegraphic impulse by wire, the signal to open Seattle's 1962 Exposition went through a computer in Maine that focused a radiotelescope on the star Cassiopeia A, some 60,000 billion-billion miles away. From that star, the telescope picked up a vibration that had begun its journey about 10,000 years earlier and instantly relayed it to Seattle. The fair was officially open.

The six-month exposition proved a great success, financially and otherwise, due in part to funding by local, state, and federal taxes. People from all over the world attended, contributing to the city's prosperity through various services provided. Unlike the experience at the A-Y-P, the fine arts outdrew Show Street and the Gayway. And as a permanent legacy, the city was left with Seattle Center, which includes a new Opera House built in the shell of the old Civic Auditorium, a Coliseum, a refurbished Arena, the Science Center, the Space Needle, the Monorail, theaters, a handsome fountain, and attractively landscaped grounds.

Since the fair closed, local citizens have voted bonds to refurbish and improve the Center, which has become the cultural heart of the Puget Sound country and draws millions of visitors each year.

A DECADE OF CHANGES: 1965–1975

For a few years after the fair, Seattle basked in the progress it had brought. But by 1965, things were again stirring.

King County was prosperous, healthy, growing, and complacent. Seattle's skyline increasingly grew heavenward. Regional planners presumed that the transportation needs for Puget Sound in 1990 would call for more of the same—cars and freeways. The R.H. Thomson Expressway was being cut through the Central Area and Northeast Seattle. The city council appointed Edward Riley, a 66-year-old former state legislator, to fill the vacancy left by the death of Wing Luke, a progressive young Chinese leader killed in a plane crash.

On August 22, 1965, Peter Raible, pastor of the University Unitarian Church, unhappy with the Riley appointment, thundered "Shame on Seattle!" Seattle must begin planning

Opposite
The Century 21 Exposition, given from April 21 to October 21, 1962, permanently changed Seattle's skyline. "Man in the Space Age" was the theme of the Science Pavilion. (MOHAI)

Above
This aerial view of the University of Washington was shot circa 1957. Courtesy, Post-Intelligencer Collection. (MOHAI)

its future before it is too late, he warned. Five days later, Camden M. Hall, Kenneth M. Shubert, Gary M. Little, and Christopher T. Bayley formed Citizens for Charter Reform, which for a time stirred some public interest as Cincinnatus had once done.

Not since the war years had so much agitation been heaped upon city council members and other leaders. The council had grown old—the youngest in 1967 was 55. Furthermore, the city had for decades operated under a strong council/weak mayor concept of government, which seemed to succeed when pressures were not too great.

But now Seattle was waking up again. The World's Fair had been a success, Forward Thrust was being planned, the blacks were agitating, and the young were growing increasingly uneasy.

The 1967 elections brought three new and younger faces to the council—Phyllis Lamphere, Tim Hill, and Sam Smith. Soon after, an organization called Choose an Effective City Council (CHECC) came into existence and with a flair for publicity overcame its lack of funding. CHECC helped elect George Cooley, John Miller, and Bruce Chapman to the council and Chris Bayley as county prosecutor. By 1971 the city was largely being governed by a new generation of people who urged change—all sorts of change. They advocated public support of the arts, the renewal of Seattle's unique neighborhoods, preserving historic buildings, and developing greater citizen participation in local government's decision making. And they were against extending freeways over valuable city land, bridging Lake Washington a third time, and other programs that a few years earlier would have been

supported with little question.

County government also was taking its lumps. By 1968, King County was becoming too complex for three county commissioners to handle. Population had grown by more than 220,000 in the previous decade. By 1970 92.5 percent of King County's population lived in urban settings. The matter of changing the form of administration was taken to the people by the Municipal League and the League of Women Voters, who carried petitions around the county and explained the need to develop a new kind of government. In November of 1968, the people responded with a vote to form a new charter and elected freeholders to write it. John Spellman, a Seattle attorney, became the first county executive and the King County Council was formed to replace the old commissioner style of governance.

As with other American cities, a move was afoot to retain Seattle's special identity. One way to do so involved saving some of yesteryear in the form of old, historic structures. To accomplish this, the city returned to the populism that has so frequently come to play in its history. And the people chose.

Pioneer Square by the 1960s had deteriorated into a ghost town, with 80 percent of the rental space vacant. It was home to derelicts and alcoholics and most of Seattle ignored it. Yet it was, after all, the site of Seattle's oldest structures, those built after the fire of 1889 had swept over the area.

But citizen action began to take effect. In 1965 an architect named Ralph Anderson moved his office into a grimy, three-story 1902 Pioneer Square building, the former home of Capital Brewing Company. Having purchased the struc-

Opposite
Looking west to the Olympic Mountains in 1962, the United States Science Pavilion and the Ford Motor Company exhibits in the Seattle World's Fair can be seen. (MOHAI)

Top, right
Seattle City Councilmen Sam Smith, left, and Tim Hill were elected in 1967. Courtesy, Post-Intelligencer Collection. (MOHAI)

Middle, right
The Mercer Island Floating Bridge, built in 1940, is one of two main thoroughfares used by commuters between the east side of the lake and Seattle.

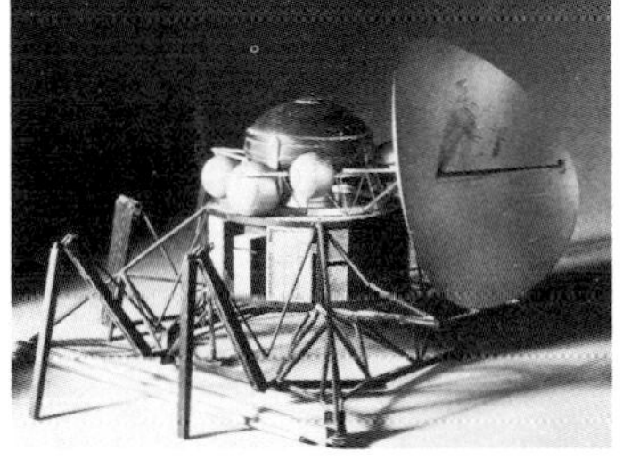

Bottom, right
By designing and building the Boeing Lunar Landing Module (shown here as a model), the Boeing Company participated significantly in the United States' entry into the Space Age. (MOHAI)

Right
Historic cobblestone streets lead to Seattle's Pike Place Market, one of the last remaining farmer's markets in the country. Courtesy, Seattle-King County Convention & Visitors Bureau.

ture for $30,000, he sandblasted the exterior and refurbished the interior. The handsome and comfortable result proved some of the advantages of preserving historic buildings. Equally telling was the important issue of economy: in an age of rapidly escalating construction costs and real-estate prices, the venture was a bargain. Furthermore, many banks—backed by federal funds—would begin to make low-interest, long-term loans for renovating acknowledged cultural "landmark" structures by private companies or parties. And there were tax breaks to add still more incentive.

By 1970 the Pioneer Square area was dramatically different. With federal and local money, a $2 million landscaped cobblestone mall, street improvements, and median planting strips were installed. Within four years private investors had spent $8 million in renovating the old buildings. The police department added a historic touch by assigning mounted police and patrolmen attired in uniforms of the 1890s. Suddenly what had been dark, dank, and unwanted became a very popular part of town. Hundreds of restaurants, small shops, and professional offices sprang to life.

Equally deserving of preservationist attention was the old Pike Place Market, a fading, unpretentious complex of stalls and loft buildings along the waterfront. It was scheduled for demolition and rebuilding under Urban Renewal, but in 1964 architects Victor Steinbrueck, Fred Bassetti, and Ibsen Nelson, along with others, established a "Friends of the Market" group that fought to retain the original buildings. The new people in city hall were not averse to the concept, and the matter was referred to the voters. As the magazine *Progressive Architecture* reported in November 1972:

> The downtown area may yet be saved from suicide by dullness through two preservation efforts—Seattle's only two—one the rehabilitation of a ragtag market complex dating from 1907; the other, re-use of commercial buildings from the 1890's clustered around the world's original Skid Road. Pike Place Market is being preserved for reasons that have nothing to do with style, craftsmanship or historic associations, but as a setting for a lively mix of functions—food-sellers, flea markets, craft shops, cafes, rooms to let. . . .

Today suburbanites as well as Seattle citizens travel to the Pike Place Market to buy directly from the growers. Colorful and bustling, Seattle's Market abounds in fresh produce, small shops, and eateries.

PROTEST TIME

Seattle's black population had increased more than 70 percent during the decade of the '50s, but they were still only 5 percent of the total population. Most were forced to live along the Madison Street corridor, hemmed in by more affluent neighborhoods and their unemployment rate double that of whites. They rebelled during the mid-'60s.

Opposite, top
Washington State Ferries are one of the state's top visitor attractions for both pedestrian and car travelers. Courtesy, Seattle-King County Convention & Visitors Bureau.

Opposite, middle
Fresh vegetables, fish, and crafts can be bought in stands like this at Pike Place Market. Photo by Jonathan Ezekiel.

Opposite, bottom
The second Lake Washington floating bridge, the Evergreen Point Bridge, is shown here during construction in March 1963. This view faces east, toward Bellevue. Courtesy, Post-Intelligencer Collection. (MOHAI)

Top, right
University of Washington President Charles Odegaard meets with students during the campus strikes, circa 1970. Centered around the Vietnam War, this strike was part of a nationwide student protest movement. One of the major demonstrations was a freeway march staged by thousands of students and other sympathizers. Photo by John A. Moore. Courtesy, Office of Information Services, University of Washington.

Bottom, right
This aerial view of Seattle in the mid-1960s, looking north from above downtown, shows the new freeway, Interstate Five (I-5), being cut through town. Lake Union is on the upper left. Courtesy, Post-Intelligencer Collection. (MOHAI)

Several of President Lyndon Johnson's Great Society projects, such as the Central Area Motivation Program and Headstart, were gaining some successes in moving minorities and poor whites toward mainstream America, but at the same time Seattleites defeated an open-housing ordinance.

The summer of 1968 was a hot one for Seattle. Central Area stores were largely boarded up, and those windows still visible were screened as protection against rocks. Police cars constantly and cautiously patrolled the area; occasionally a helicopter throbbed overhead. Though the Central Area was tense, unlike the center of black population in many other cities, it did not explode—probably because the city had a few advantages. The black "ghetto" was not a large blighted area, though many examples of poor housing could be seen. And the percentage of truly destitute families of all races was comparatively low.

The nationwide unrest in the mid-1960s reached the University of Washington, where an Upward Bound program had started to recruit students from poverty-level families—youth with potential but lacking in achievement. In 1967 the Black Student Union emerged on campus from the previous "Afro-American Student Society" and that spring took over part of the administration building, for awhile holding members of a faculty senate committee hostage after presenting them with demands.

As a solution to the situation, University President Dr. Charles Odegaard told the students to go out into the larger community and recruit any students interested in attending U.W. He organized an Office of Minority Affairs under a minority vice-president. In 1969 and 1970, the tense situation was exacerbated by the marching and rioting over the Viet Nam War and its escalation, especially the Cambodian incursion. Faculty, students, and citizens became involved in the confrontations and they were headlined incessantly in the mass media. Young people of all races marched by the thousands, usually accompanied by increasing numbers of supporting older citizens. They even used the freeway, cleared for the event, to march from the University District to the heart of Seattle.

Charles Odegaard was able to tell the militants that Viet Nam was beyond the university's power to correct, but minority education was not. Many respected his stand. He also kept the campus police in charge on the university grounds, with the city police to be called only if needed.

For the most part, these rebels and agitators were allowed to carry their message to the people, but when property or life was endangered, the forces of law stepped in. Several young leaders were arrested and tried. A few even spent some months in prison. A decade later, many of the young activists of those days have become Establishment leaders and are even running for political office.

Seattle and King County did witness some violence in that period of strong social protest. Homes of two state legislators, the university's ROTC building and a City Light substation were bombed.

Those were tumultuous months in Seattle as elsewhere. But during that time Seattleites became aware of local problems they had believed belonged only to other cities. Some citizens frowned on the liberal-tending responses of the university, fearing that the militant and sometimes furious encounters would result in anarchy. But the Viet Nam War did eventually end. And as a result of the university's opening its gates more widely to the underprivileged, more minority students were graduating, eventually to enter professions. Soon the more affluent minority families were finding it easier to buy homes in the suburbs. Blacks were accepted in Rotary and other civic and social clubs, appeared on television screens as news reporters, and found that more doors were swinging open to able minority men and women.

In the decade between 1965 and 1975, Seattle became a more cosmopolitan, more caring metropolis. More citizens knew of the Central Area, the larger percentages of unemployed black youth, the lower living standards; they tried to comprehend the disenchantment of the young. In the process, they began to realize that minorities did not always enjoy the same rights and privileges as themselves. As new laws backed them, middle-class families of all races and creeds were moving into previously segregated neighborhoods, and for the first time, perhaps, a majority of the white neighbors agreed that as Americans, they had that right.

RECESSION AND RECOVERY

Projections that air travel would increase in the 1970s as it had between 1955 and 1960, resulting in continued demand for the Boeing 747, proved to be an overestimate. This, coupled with the decision of Congress to shelve plans for the supersonic transport, resulted in a financial crisis for the Boeing Company. In the two years following January 1970, it had to dismiss about 65,000 employees—a two-thirds reduction of its work force. Since the region's economy leaned heavily on the aerospace industry, a severe recession ensued. A billboard saying, "Will the last person leaving Seattle please turn out the lights?" received national attention.

However, most of those who had been laid off, not just Boeing personnel but those in allied industries, refused to leave Seattle; fewer than 15 percent migrated elsewhere. As a result, local unemployment went up to 12 percent and remained high longer than would have been the case if Seattle had not been such a good place to live.

Seattleites suddenly found themselves setting up food banks manned by volunteers. The citizens of the city and county began discussing the need to diversify industry and get involved in communal activities and goals.

Neighborhood activity blocked completion of the Thomson Freeway midway in its construction, stopped high-

PORT OF SEATTLE

The basic philosophy and specific actions of the Port of Seattle have aroused considerable controversy throughout the 20th century. Significant changes in its philosophy and actions, though, have been reflected in the altered nature of the opposition. Creation of the Port in 1911 by the voters of King County, resulted from a long struggle to assert public control over the Seattle waterfront. This struggle dated back to the 1890s and focused on the belief that ownership of wharves and control of tidelands by railroads and other private interests curbed economic expansion and competition. During the progressive era after the turn of the century, municipal reformers concentrated on this issue and celebrated the founding of the Port of Seattle as a major triumph for progressivism in the city.

Under the direction of reform-minded commissioners Hiram Chittenden (designer of the Lake Washington Ship Canal) and Robert Bridges, the Port acquired tidelands and docks and began the improvement of the Duwamish Waterway. A public grain terminal and a cold-storage facility were constructed and creation of a public market was endorsed by the port commission. These actions and the guiding philosophy of the Port—that the public interest should prevail on the waterfront—earned Chittenden and Bridges the enmity of Seattle conservatives and business leaders.

Ultimately, progressivism waned, Chittenden and Bridges resigned from the commission, and, during the 1920s, the Port allied itself with the shipping industry. Terminals were leased to private firms at advantageous rates and the Port became a promoter of trade. Three decades of unimaginative administration combined with the stifling impact of the Great Depression and competition from other Pacific Coast ports to bring the Port of Seattle to the low point of its history by the mid-1950s.

Critical studies sparked a renewed debate over the future of the waterfront and led during the 1960s and the 1970s to a major revitalization of the Port. Facilities along the Duwamish were modernized with the introduction of container technology, a new grain terminal was constructed, and the Port-operated Seattle-Tacoma International Airport was transformed into one of the most modern airports in the country. The Port became a major shipping point for wheat from east of the Cascades and for automobile imports from Japan.

Controversy, however, continued, albeit from different quarters than during the progressive era. Seattle inhabitants complained that the new grain terminal spoiled the view from Queen Anne Hill and worried about further expansion into residential areas. Taxpayers, especially in rural parts of King County, questioned the wisdom of public support for an institution that seemed to exist for the benefit of private waterfront interests. Since the Port was both a public agency and a big business, the basic controversy remained: whether public concerns or business considerations should be paramount in the determination of policy.—**Robert E. Ficken**

◆

Top
Seattle's waterfront circa 1919, showing Pier 9 (known as Gaffney Dock) and Pier 10 (known as Virginia Street Dock). Photo by Webster and Stevens. Courtesy, Williamson Collection, Puget Sound Maritime Historical Society.

Middle
Longshoremen unload freight with hand trucks, circa 1920. (MOHAI)

Bottom
The Kitsap County Transportation Company's "White Collar Line," circa 1910. Photo by Webster and Stevens. Courtesy, Williamson Collection, Puget Sound Maritime Historical Society.

rise apartments going up on Queen Anne and Capitol hills, and saved the Pike Place Market.

In spite of the recession, building construction in downtown Seattle continued and the Port of Seattle was experiencing one of the greatest upsurges in its history with its $250 million improvement program and installation of containerized cargo equipment. Smaller businesses were launched in large numbers, many succeeding as the unemployed sought new outlets for their talents.

In 1972 a citizens' commission called "Seattle 2000" developed strong themes for Seattle's future. Included were preservation and enhancement of the natural environment, strengthening the diversity and quality of neighborhoods, enhancing the role of the downtown as a center of the Puget Sound region, support for increased social and economic equality among residents, and a commitment to quality in design, education, health care, the arts, and the administration of justice.

An outgrowth of this futuristic exercise was the formation of the Seattle-King County Development Council, designed to explore ways to achieve a more diversified business and industrial base.

FORWARD THRUST

In 1965 the Seattle Rotary Club, second largest in the world, heard member Jim Ellis, attorney and father of the Metro plan that had cleaned up the waters of King County, explain a new dream. Called "Forward Thrust," it included plans for rapid transit, a domed stadium, new parks, a world trade center, and street and other improvements.

A 200-member citizens planning committee was put to work culling through 2,000 project ideas. They recommended to the voters 13 separate bond issues totaling $819 million and two state bond issues worth $65 million. In February 1968 King County citizens at the polls approved local programs totaling $333.9 million and in November both state issues were approved. The Forward Thrust package became the nation's largest per capita public improvement plan ever approved. Even projects the voters turned down were, in some instances, made possible under Forward Thrust.

Clearly, Seattle and King County had begun to stir. A few years later, Walter Hundley, then Seattle's budget director, observed: "When you're living with great change, it doesn't impress you at all."

Opposite
Pollution made Lake Washington unsafe for bathing before the Metro plan to clean up King County waters and construct sanitary sewers was implemented. Courtesy, Metro.

Above
Attorney James Ellis advocated "Forward Thrust," a plan for rapid transit, new parks, a stadium, and other Seattle city improvements. He also is responsible for the Metro plan that cleaned up the waters of King County. Courtesy, Metro.

Right
The Public Health Hospital, formerly the Marine Hospital, is open to all who need its services. (MOHAI)

The 1980 final Forward Thrust report lists the following accomplishments:

The Kingdome. While the voters approved $40 million, the stadium cost $60 million. However, property taxpayers will pay only about $13 million. It opened in March 1976. By the end of 1979, 12 million persons had attended events in the Kingdome, generating an estimated $315 million for county businesses.

Parks and Recreation. By 1980, 4,776 acres of land had been acquired, including more than 300 parks and 53 miles of waterfront. The Seattle Aquarium was built, the zoo modernized, Marymoor Park's 486 acres were developed, Freeway Park was built downtown, conservancy areas were established, more than 200 neighborhood parks and playgrounds were developed or improved, and 102 sports fields, 98 tennis courts, and 23 swimming pools were provided. More than 90 miles of trails for bicycles, hikers, and joggers were installed.

Arterials. More than 200 miles of improved or new road systems were built. Of the 326 projects planned, 266 were completed by the end of 1979.

Metro Transit. While the voters failed to approve Metro transit funds in the Forward Thrust package, legislative initiatives by the Forward Thrust Committee in 1967, 1969, and 1971 made Metro transit possible. In 1972 King County voters authorized a county-wide public transportation system and a levy of a .3 percent addition to the sales tax to match other vehicle excise tax receipts to fund the system.

Per capita transit ridership increased 67 percent between 1973 and 1979, which saved an estimated 110 million gallons of gasoline. King County Metro had the largest per capita increase in ridership growth of any major bus system in the nation in 1979.

Port of Seattle. The Forward Thrust Committee, at the request of the Port, included port improvements in their studies but the funds were not in the package presented to voters. Airport expansion costing $175 million and a $14 million grain elevator were undertaken as a result.

Youth Service Center. With $6.1 million of Forward Thrust bond monies, additions and improvements were made to the Center, which includes the Juvenile Court facilities.

Neighborhood Improvements. A total of $12 million was voted for 20 Seattle neighborhoods. About 130 community-planned improvements were made, including stairways, landscaping, alley paving, and street lighting.

Fire Protection. Thirteen new fire stations were built and equipped for $6.2 million, lowering response time and reducing damage and deaths due to fire.

Sewer Improvements. Seventy million dollars went to construct sanitary sewers and to separate sanitary and storm drainage systems. This reduced backups and the amount of sewage spilling into recreational waters of King County.

DEMOGRAPHIC CHANGES

Between 1965 and '75, population shifts within city and county became more noticeable. There were fewer children and fewer people aged 40 to 50 in Seattle. But there were more 25- to 35-year-olds and ethnic groups. In the early '60s, for the first time in nearly 30 years, the number of deaths in Seattle outnumbered the births. This, combining with the exodus of families to the suburbs, caused the population of the city to fall by 55,000 during those 10 years, while the population of King County itself increased by 24 percent.

Seattle, though one of the younger cities in the U.S., was experiencing what older cities were going through in the same period. The city's economic base was slowly being eroded by businesses moving to the suburbs. Manufacturing employment within the city limits decreased from 82,500 in 1958 to 54,900 in 1972.

The Puget Sound Council of Governments predicted Seattle would continue to shrink until the 1980s, when its population would fall below a half-million—which is what happened. However, the number of households continued to grow, though each held fewer individuals. Enrollment in the city's public schools dropped sharply, from 95,000 in 1966 to 66,000 in 1975. Meanwhile, the number of minorities increased to constitute almost 30 percent of public school enrollment.

A sure symptom of urban stress, crime increased through the decade. Manslaughter doubled, murder more than doubled, and rape quadrupled. The number on welfare and the number of divorces proliferated.

The Equal Rights Amendment, written by Congress in 1972, was ratified by the Washington State legislature the following year. The anti-discrimination law in 1971 was broadened to cover sex discrimination.

The air we breathe was cleaned up in the decade from the mid-'60s to the mid-'70s. In the 1960s, on smoggy days, people downtown found breathing almost intolerable. The number of days when carbon monoxide pollution levels exceeded legal limits in downtown Seattle decreased from 131 days in 1973 to only 39 days in 1975. Although the weather had a lot to do with it, industrial and commercial air pollution abatement proceedings also had their effect.

Seattle's ring of water benefited when raw sewage was pumped to Metro plants instead of being dumped into lake and bay. Metro's regional approach to handling the wastes of the populated areas in King County was taking effect.

The Green and Duwamish River valleys early in the settlement of King County had attracted farm families. The major problem of the area was periodic flooding, sometimes so severe as to demolish homes and barns, as well as to ruin any crops in the ground. To prevent this flooding, Mud Mountain Dam was built in the 1940s to control the White River and Howard Hanson Dam was completed in 1962 to tame the Green.

Now another problem developed. As with the Duwamish Valley before it, the fertile acreages of the Valley of the Green became increasingly valuable as Seattle and the suburbs grew. Truck farming and other agricultural pursuits began giving way to urban spread. Highways, shopping malls, industrial parks, and housing projects—built on tons of rock, gravel, and poor soil excavated from bench lands—buried much of the most valuable farmland.

In 1979, after two previous defeats, a farm preservation measure was passed by King County voters that would raise $50 million to purchase development rights to valuable farmland. Private landowners would voluntarily sell their development rights but would retain ownership and management of the farmlands. However, with interest rates above the maximum allowed in sale of such bonds, the process was slowed.

A city's heart is important to the region it serves. Downtown Seattle had managed to remain comparatively youthful. As further evidence of Seattle's impetus toward change and growth, during the decade 1965–75, more than a dozen major buildings containing in excess of three million square feet of office space were built in the downtown area.

In 1965 the arts in Seattle were limited to little more than the Seattle Repertory Theater, the Seattle Symphony, Seattle Opera, the Seattle Art Museum, and A Contemporary Theater (ACT). During the succeeding years, the existing theaters expanded and new theaters were founded, such as Empty Space, Skid Road Theater, and others. Two dance companies also formed—Pacific Northwest Dance and First Chamber Dance.

In the visual arts, dozens of new galleries emerged. A number of first-run movie theaters opened. Allied Arts, PONCHO, and other groups were formed to support the arts. And under Lyndon B. Johnson's presidency, the National Endowment for the Arts (NEA) was born, to pump millions of dollars into local arts groups.

During the decade, the new Kingdome attracted professional sports teams to the area, including the Sounders, the Sonics, the Seahawks, and the Mariners.

REPRISE

In 1976 Dr. Dixy Lee Ray, former University of Washington professor and director of the Pacific Science Center,

Above, left
The Kingdome Stadium, a sports arena built in March 1976, had generated approximately $315 million for county businesses by the end of 1979.

Above, right
Seattle Supersonics in tip-off action with the Denver Nuggets in the Seattle Kingdome, circa 1980. Courtesy, Russell Johnson, Silverlight Studio.

was elected Washington State's first woman governor. Serving one frequently stormy term, she lost in the primary in her bid for reelection. In 1976 popular and influential Washington Senator Henry M. (Scoop) Jackson, an Everett native, was a serious contender for the Democratic nomination for the presidency of the U.S., but his party chose Jimmy Carter as their candidate. In 1980, John Spellman, King County executive, assumed the governor's chair.

There was a serious drought in 1977, which left the usually snowy peaks of the Cascade range mostly bare all winter. Millions of dollars in losses accrued to agriculture, fish runs, and forestry, and unemployment rose. Another consequence of the drought was a shortage of electric power, rare in the Northwest. That same year the first Alaskan oil flowed from the North Slope to Valdez, where tankers took it aboard and some was delivered to refineries on Puget Sound.

A big wind storm in 1979 caused part of the Hood Canal floating bridge to sink, cutting off the major access from Seattle to the Olympic Peninsula, but ferries were soon reinstated for cross-canal operation. And in 1979 the U.S. Supreme Court upheld the Indian fishing rights decision of five years previous.

The big story of 1980 was the eruption of Mt. St. Helens, located about 100 miles south of Seattle. Prevailing winds kept all but a light sprinkling of ash from King County. That year also, the Washington Public Power Supply System developed severe problems, the result of ballooning costs, labor strife, and opposition to nuclear power. Though billions of dollars had already been spent, additional billions were needed to finish the five nuclear power stations. The effect was bound to cause higher electrical rates in the Northwest region, which long has boasted the nation's lowest. A big question arose as to how many, if any, of the proposed plants would be completed.

The Puget Sound Council of Governments predicts King County's population will grow by 300,000 between 1980 and 2000 A.D. More than half this growth will occur in unincorporated King County areas. In the future, the county could become a sprawling Los Angeles-type development or it could be an area that retains its Northwest identity.

The county has a Growth Management Program Group, created in 1978, which plans land use patterns and growth strategy. There is some talk of three categories of land use—urban/suburban for present heavily populated areas, growth reserve areas, and, farthest from the cities, rural area zoning.

If the past is any measure, the enlightened populace will keep the area among the world's most livable. In spite of the increased complexities of 20th century urban life, the great majority of those who reside in King County want to preserve its special way of life while continuing the growth and development of the area.

◆

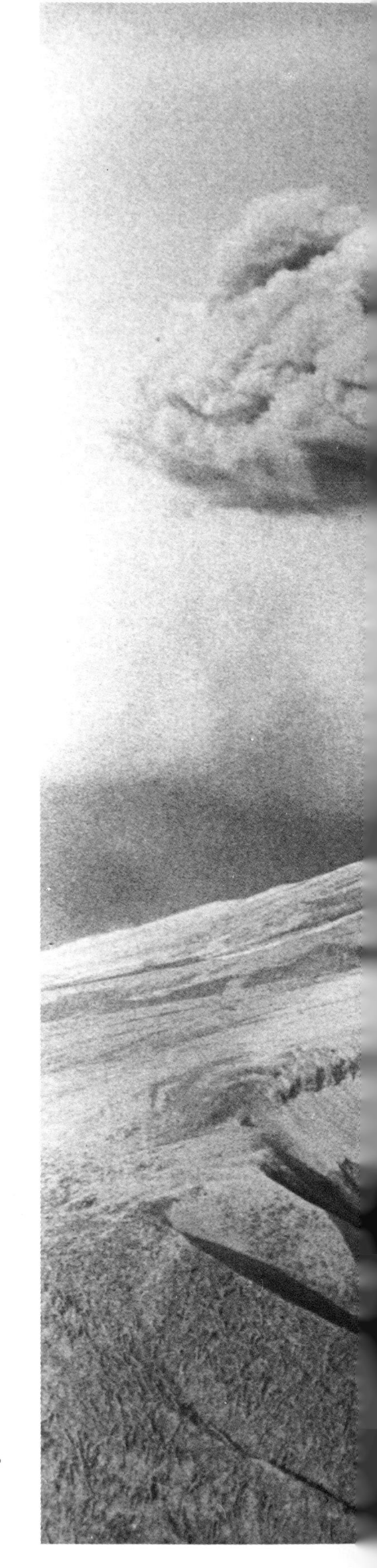

An angry mountain: staggering, costly toll of fish and wildlife. Photo by Rick Perry, Courtesy, *Seattle Times*.

CHAPTER 13

SEATTLE'S NEIGHBORHOODS

Seattle grew by neighborhoods. During recent decades the city has made efforts to maintain the particular identity of each of those neighborhoods, to enhance their livability, and to encourage citizen participation in the management and development of the areas in which they reside.

At the base of such activities must come a knowledge of the history of the areas, a respect for the endurance of topography, buildings, transportation systems, and culture. Here are briefly told histories of some of Seattle's main, "close-in" neighborhoods.

BALLARD

In 1887 Captain William Ballard, Thomas Burke, John Leary, and Boyd Tallman platted 720 acres north of Salmon Bay and called the settlement Farmdale Homestead. Captain Ballard persuaded the Stimson Mill to relocate from the Midwest to Salmon Bay and soon the waterfront was a long row of lumber and shingle mills. This drew employees and their families to the town that became known as the "Shingle Capital of the World."

A railway company connected its line with Ballard in 1890, and by 1904 it was home to 10,000 persons. Three years later Ballard was the seventh largest town in Washington State. With the rapid growth came such problems as an inadequate water supply. In 1907 the people of Ballard decided it was time to annex to Seattle.

On July 4, 1917, the Ballard locks were first opened and the flagship *Roosevelt* of Admiral Peary's expedition to the North Pole led a flotilla through the new canal. Ballard initially was a fishing village, but after the locks were finished, the fishing fleet began mooring at Fisherman's Terminal, as it does to this day. Many of the early settlers were Scandinavians; their descendants continue to give Ballard a distinct ethnic flavor.

Today, new multifamily apartments are replacing some of the older houses, although single-family dwellings ranging from Victorian farmhouses to new ranch-style ramblers can be seen. Old Ballard retains many of the colorful turn-of-the-century brick structures, most of them now renovated. The industrial area along Salmon Bay includes warehouses, and many water-oriented industries. Along the Ballard waterfront are the government locks and gardens, fish ladders and Shilshole Bay.

FREMONT

In the 1880s the area was just a small clearing with a mill. Then in 1888, platted as the Denny-Hoyt Addition, it became populated. By 1891, the year it was annexed to Seattle, Fremont was a town of 5,000 people.

The town was named after the Nebraska hometown of two of Fremont's three founders: L.H. Griffith and E. Blewett. (The name originally honored John C. Fremont, an early American explorer of the West.) The third founder, Dr. E.C. Kilbourne, named Aurora Avenue after his Illinois hometown.

At the northwest corner of Lake Union, Fremont occupied a strategic location. In 1888 a ditch big enough for small boats was dug between the lake and Salmon Bay. In 1916 the present Fremont drawbridge was built over the newly completed ship canal.

Fremont's sawmill burned four times; the last fire, in 1932, caused it to be closed permanently. Other early businesses were ironworks, a tannery, machine works, and many small retailers. Many of Fremont's early homes, including some Victorian-style houses, still exist.

The neighborhood has long held a reputation for being close-knit and active. Recently a concentration of arts and crafts studios and stores have taken over many of the original business district structures, helping to revitalize Fremont.

Though its early dependence on fishing, logging, and community businesses has been replaced and Fremont is now primarily a residential area for commuters, the neighborhood retains much of the diversity of its early days as a small town.

FIRST HILL

First Hill, rising 344 feet above downtown Seattle, was the first of Seattle's slopes to attract residents. Tree-covered and abounding with sweet-water springs, in the early 1880s the hill drew the interest of the likes of Colonel Granville Haller and Morgan Carkeek. Many other well-known families lived on First Hill—the Terrys, Minors, Hanfords, Burkes, Lowmans, Fryes, Pigotts, Malmos, and Dennys, among others. In the early 1960s First Hill was cut off from

TWENTY-FIVE CENTS

JANUARY 18, 1963

TIME

THE WEEKLY NEWSMAGAZINE

ARCHITECT MINORU YAMASAKI

VOL. LXXXI NO. 3

LIFE

Fabulous Fair in Seattle

ALSO THIS WEEK:

Citizens Guide: Right Wing Who's Who

The Flying Wallendas, Heroes in a Tragedy

Durable Movie Queens, Still Going Great

Bargain: 3 Way Blouse for $4

Photograph by Victor Garda
(MOHAI)

SEATTLE SCULPTOR

Richard S. Beyer, born in Washington D.C., and a Seattle resident since 1957, has sculptures in public areas and private collections throughout the United States, as well as in Japan, England, and Switzerland. Beyer strives to debunk the mystique that art is not part of our time by advocating cooperation between artists and citizens in the community where the piece of art is to be located.

Rich Beyer's public sculptures have the unusual quality of focusing neighborhood energy. Most notable for this quality is *People Waiting for the Interurban*, located in Seattle's Fremont area. The *Interurban* sculpture evolved in the national movement towards redevelopment of inner cities. The sculpture's theme is the quality of life in the urban community. Growing out of the impulse toward community self-help, ultimately the sculpture aroused the interest of the whole city, to become a symbol not only of Fremont, a working-class community, but of all of Seattle. Perhaps a thousand people contributed funds for its construction.

The Belltown Dogs are scampering along in downtown Seattle at Belltown Park, an area which was a parking lot until the city bought it. The sculptured canines carved out of local sandstone, "have a rat under the lip of the first stone," Beyer says. "They are looking for it everywhere."

The Sasquatch, an Indian motif indigenous to the Puget Sound area, "suggests the accepting dependence of the Indian on the generosity and terrifying power of the thick forest in the mountain and along the sea."

Rich Beyer says that even though the Sasquatch has been trivialized in popular culture, there are enough of us around in the borderline who need the real story and keep it circulating. The sculpture stands in an abrupt corridor on the lower level of the Public Market—"lurking, as if to take by surprise, the giddy explorer who ventures through the maze of the Market."

The Transient, located in the Broadway district of Capitol Hill and made of cast aluminum, was commissioned by the community design agency, Environmental Works. The man at his journey's end sleeps on a bench, in an area which was formerly a village of garbage cans. The newspaper, which so often screams of politics and war, keeps the sun off the man's face. And he seems content, lying there.

McGilvra's Farm in Madison Park occupies a playground. The project was put together by architect Art Skolnik of the Conservation Company. Rich Beyer was commissioned for the work—"because I have a reputation for telling stories, and children like stories."

Beyer chose to portray McGilvra as an old-time farmer in whose farm the children could play. But since the original farm stood in a dangerous wilderness, an old and young bear are scheming to grab one of the sheep. McGilvra's faithful dog is guarding the sheep, but his horse is unaware of the great cougar sneaking up behind him. Adding to the confusion are beavers, rats dancing on the top of a tree, snakes, crows and alligators' heads. McGilvra himself, with his pitchfork in the clouds, stands as a weathervane on top of the barn. Beyer feels McGilvra would want to be remembered this way.

The Fool Killer, larger than life, is a legendary figure from the mountains of the southeastern U.S. He comes into town now and then and stands, ax in hand, on a Fremont street. He asks people who come by who the fools are in the town. If common agreement points to certain people, no matter what their status, "The fool killer cuts them up with his chopper, gets back in his truck, and drives on."

General Fremont, the Explorer resides appropriately in Fremont. "It is said less reverently now than in the past," says Beyer, "that the cities of the West are built on the ashes of Fremont's campfires." This and other statues of General Fremont are Beyer's memorial to the irony of his and our history of the American West.—**Margaret Beyer and Carol V. Davis**

People Waiting for the Interurban

The Belltown Dogs

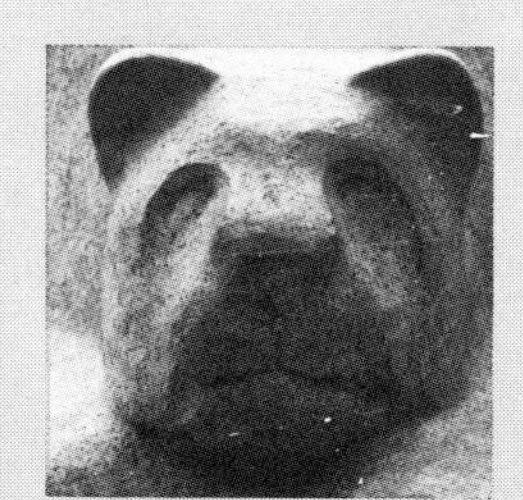
McGilvra's Farm (detail)

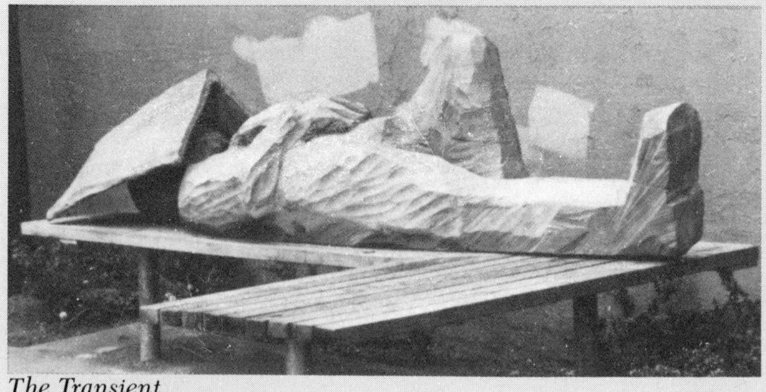
The Transient

General Fremont, The Explorer

The Sasquatch

Above
Many of Seattle's earliest homes were built in what is now the downtown area. Among them was the John Leary residence, built in the late 1870s and situated at Second and Madison. (MOHAI)

Top
Tower Grove, home of Edward F. Wittler, was erected in 1888–1889 at Melrose Avenue and John Street. The First Hill property had five fireplaces, a billiard room on the third floor, and a yard with more than 1,000 choice rose bushes. It was demolished in 1957. (MOHAI)

downtown by the freeway, until Freeway Park was built atop Interstate 5. The famed Yesler Terrace Housing Project was completed in 1941 and remains an outstanding low-income housing complex.

Located on First Hill is Seattle's most important medical and hospital center, and many important churches. High-rise apartments and condominiums stand on the western slopes, overlooking downtown and Elliott Bay, and older lower-rent structures are found further up the hill.

CENTRAL AREA

The Central Area of Seattle has long served as a melting pot of nationalities and races. Logged early, it was among the first areas settled, and contains some of the oldest sub-neighborhoods—Yesler/Atlantic, Judkins, Mann/Minor, and Stevens.

William Gross, a black pioneer, secured considerable property in the Central Area in 1890. After he acquired a large section of land between 21st and 23rd near Madison, in settlement of a debt, he moved his family to this locale despite the opposition from existing white residents; other black families soon followed. Their homes occupied the nearby blocks, including the area around Jackson and Cherry streets. Thus the Central Area became the most important and stable black neighborhood in Seattle.

In 1916 Japanese families began living along Yesler Way and until they were forced to leave during World War II, their numbers increased. In the Judkins neighborhood, German and Italian communities developed and several synagogues attest to a once-significant Jewish population.

Through the years, most middle-class residents moved away, leaving aging houses to low-income minorities and the elderly. Increasing arterial traffic further fragmented the neighborhoods.

Beginning in the middle 1950s, various planning and community action efforts have been made to improve the Central Area's living conditions. The Yesler and Atlantic Urban Renewal projects were started and the Model Cities program was funded in 1968 to improve economic and social conditions in the Central Area. The locale is home to schools, community centers, hospitals, and many mini-parks.

THE INTERNATIONAL DISTRICT

A large part of the history of the International District is given to efforts by ethnic groups to build a stable community despite opposition from dominant segments of society.

Seattle's original Chinatown was centered at Second and Washington in the Pioneer Square part of town. In 1886, after the 400 Chinese living in the Puget Sound area were subjected to extreme prejudice, all but 50 left Seattle. Japanese immigrants soon began taking over Chinese dwellings and jobs. The Chinese began to filter back slowly, to be joined by Native Americans, Filipinos, and blacks in the multiracial

International District.

Chinatown continued to grow slowly with new shops, restaurants, hotels, and boardinghouses. During the Jackson Street regrading of 1910, the Chinese and Japanese merchants shifted their businesses to the newly paved King Street area. In 1942, after the Japanese were evacuated and interned, the International District became home mostly to the elderly, the poor, and single men.

In the 1960s, the freeway was cut through the area. More recently, the domed stadium has introduced traffic congestion and land speculation. However, this new influx of people may infuse the International District with additional commercial prospects and a cultural interest that might insure the continuing life of a district that is among the oldest in Seattle.

MT. BAKER

Mt. Baker was one of the first areas planned as a residential community. David T. Denny acquired the property in the 1860s. It was platted in 1907 by the Hunter Tract Improvement Company and they named it the Mt. Baker Park District. The Hunter Company employed the famed Olmsted brothers to lay out streets and lots.

The developers and residents succeeded in establishing an exclusive residential district. However, the Great Depression of the 1930s forced out many of the older, established families. By 1945, the community was no longer upper-class. Construction of the Mercer Island floating bridge disrupted the northern portions of the area.

Nonetheless, the Mt. Baker neighborhood remains a prestigious and pleasant place to live—with fine homes and

panoramic views, only a short distance from downtown.

WEST SEATTLE

The birthplace of the city, and therefore the longest continuously inhabited neighborhood, is West Seattle. Made up of several communities, this peninsula across Elliott Bay from downtown Seattle still retains an identity of its own.

In 1902 West Seattle was incorporated and an electric rail line to Seattle was built. Growth continued, and in 1907 the area was annexed to Seattle. In that same year, Luna Amusement Park opened, becoming a popular attraction for years. It burned down in 1913, and in 1945 the site became a public park. In 1908 Ferdinand Schmitz donated Schmitz Park to the city with the stipulation that it remain a natural setting. Hiawatha Playfield opened in 1911.

In the early years of the century, speculators found the level portions of the Admiral district atop the hill ideal for middle-income homes development. The Depression slowed private investments but federal projects continued.

To this day the steeper slopes around Duwamish Head remain in forested condition, a natural green belt. The commercial strip along California Avenue, centrally located, acts to unify the community. West Seattleites are proud of their special identity and heritage.

QUEEN ANNE HILL

Queen Anne Hill rises 450 feet between Lake Union and Elliott Bay. Some of the precipitous hillsides remain natural, with scenic viewpoints located conveniently for visitors to look out over the bay to the Olympics. Many a vivid sunset

Opposite
Members of the Norwegian-American Lutheran Synod congregation gather outside the church in Ballard, a predominantly Scandinavian community, in May 1908. Photo by F. L. Meyer (MOHAI)

Above
The Sholem Synagogue, torn down in 1913, was located at Eighth and Seneca. It is shown here circa 1900. (MOHAI)

Right
In this 1935 photo, Seattle's Japanese Bon Odori dancers celebrate a festival that dates back to the sixth century. The 10-day dance festival includes visits to local cemeteries and the remembrance of ancestors. Courtesy, Post-Intelligencer Collection. (MOHAI)

has been enjoyed from these slopes.

Queen Anne is a dominant topographic feature near to and visible from downtown Seattle. Atop the crest, warning lights blink airplanes away from television and water towers.

The first homes on Queen Anne were built on the south slope overlooking the city. Thomas Mercer had filed a claim there for 320 acres, calling the place "Eden." By the early 1870s Mercer was selling homesites successfully.

The west side of Queen Anne Hill was logged off first because of its proximity to Smith Cove, which allowed logs to be floated to the mills. In 1882 a sawmill was established on the south shore of Lake Union, which was fed the trees from the eastern slopes. By 1891 Queen Anne had been annexed to Seattle. Because many of the first builders used the late Victorian Queen Anne style of architecture, the community was called Queen Anne Town, later becoming Queen Anne Hill.

Many beautiful parks grace Queen Anne Hill, and some of the magnificent homes, built during the Alaska Gold Rush, still remain as showplaces.

UNIVERSITY DISTRICT

The University District was once known as "Brooklyn." Its growth has paralleled that of the University of Washington. Prior to 1885 it was considered too far from the city center to attract many settlers. In 1887 the Seattle, Lake Shore and Eastern tracks reached the area. But the region was still difficult to get to. This isolation resulted in development of a self-sufficient community.

Then in 1890 David Denny and Associates built the first electric trolley line over the old Latona Bridge to Brooklyn and in 1893 the University of Washington received a gift of land between Union and Portage bays and two years later moved to the area.

From 1890 to 1920, the community drew many working-class families. Small truck farms and minor industries provided employment. In 1902 the first seven fraternity houses in "Greek Row" were founded, and in 1906 the first bank (University National) was begun. The Alaska-Yukon-Pacific Exposition of 1909, located on the campus, started a real-estate boom. In 1889 Ravenna Park was started and then purchased by the city in 1911. Cowen Park was given to the city in 1909.

During the Depression years, development slowed temporarily. In 1939 the 45th Street Viaduct was completed, encouraging development to the east. After World War II, the veterans' housing spread over the flat around Union Bay and University enrollment soared.

In the early '60s the University District went through another building boom when many of the contemporary apartments were built. Then the Northlake Urban Renewal Area at the south end of the district was taken over as part of the university campus. The Interstate Freeway swept through the western reaches of the district.

Top
The Stockade Hotel at Alki Point in West Seattle was the site of the first settlers' landing. This photograph was taken on Founders' Day, November 13, 1905, by Theodore Peiser. Courtesy, McDonald Collection. (MOHAI)

Above
In 1980 the remodeling of Summit School neared completion. This First Hill institution, once a public school, became a private school of the arts. Photo by Jonathan Ezekiel.

Above
In this 1946 view of the University Bridge, Eastlake Avenue is in the foreground, and the University District is in the distance. Courtesy, Post-Intelligencer Collection. (MOHAI)

Left
In 1932 children crowd on the street in front of the Yook Gee Drug Company to watch the beginning of the Dragon Parade, part of the Chinese New Year celebration. Courtesy, Post-Intelligencer Collection. (MOHAI)

In the 1970s, building continued and residents have been well organized into two community councils strongly committed to preservation of present housing and maintenance of living standards.

EASTLAKE/CASCADE

These two communities along the southern and eastern shores of Lake Union were originally two of the oldest residential areas. To this day there are Victorian houses and cottages mixed among the manufacturing and commercial buildings. These may not be neighborhoods in the conventional terms but they do have a special identity in relation to Lake Union.

At first both Eastlake and Cascade were settled as small farms and homesteads. Cascade originally attracted Norwegian and Swedish immigrants and later became the transportation exchange site where the streetcar met the Lake Union boats.

Eastlake still retains considerable residential character, although light industry has moved into the area. Eastlake also is the base for many houseboats ("floating homes") and new apartment buildings are going up.

GREEN LAKE

Green Lake is a unique area. Erhart Seifried, known as "Green Lake John," first settled on the northwest shore in 1869. A few years later other homesteaders arrived, and on the east shore A.L. Parker built a sawmill and a logging railroad to Fremont. In the late 1880s a 10-acre amusement park was built in what is now West Green Lake. A trolley car line was extended from the park around to the sawmill site on the east shore, then on to Fremont, where it met the boat, which ran across Lake Union to the trolley car that took passengers on to Seattle.

While Green Lake development was under way, Guy Phinney was developing "Woodland Park," his estate at the south end of the lake. There he built a zoo, conservatory, and boating and other facilities. The city purchased the Phinney estate in 1900 as Woodland Park—still the site of the zoo.

The Green Lake area was annexed to Seattle in 1891. By 1900 about 1,500 people lived near Green Lake and the shopping area started to build. In 1905 Green Lake itself was given to the city as a park and the Olmsteds recommended the park plan to include lakeshore property all the way around. With some difficulty, the city acquired the shore property and lowered the lake by seven feet. They diked and filled to improve the shorelines and beaches, but in so doing reduced the size of the lake further and cut off its outlet to the Ravenna ravine. Stagnation problems ensued as creeks and springs were eliminated by construction. Algae clumps began to float around the lake. The shore was cleaned in the 1930s, but during the '40s and '50s, however, as the algae reappeared, Green Lake became famous for "swimmers' itch." During the 1950s Green Lake was closed to swimming periodically because of sewage contamination.

Finally it was decided to pump surplus water from city

The George Kinnear residence at 819 Queen Anne Avenue, shown here circa 1900, is a fine example of the architectural style for which Queen Anne Hill was named. Although the mansion was torn down, it can still be found in the logo of the Queen Anne Historical Society. Courtesy, Anders B. Wilse Collection. (MOHAI)

The Ballard-Howe mansion is located on Highland Avenue on Queen Anne Hill. Photo by Jonathan Ezekiel.

reservoirs into Green Lake on a daily basis, which cleared up the problem. Today the lake attracts swimmers, joggers, bicyclists, and picnickers. It also serves as the focal point for the Green Lake Community.

MONTLAKE

The land between Union Bay and Lake Union in 1869 was called Union City, but there were few homes there. Well before canals and bridges, freeways and arterials, it was a potentially large and pleasant site. Union City was annexed to Seattle in 1891. By 1908 the area was renamed Montlake.

In 1885, a small canal to accommodate log rafts and small boats was dug between the two lakes. Then in 1917 the Lake Washington Ship Canal was opened and today forms the northern boundary of Montlake. The Puget Mill Company in 1900 deeded 62 acres to the city in exchange for water extensions. This acreage became Washington Park, which grew in size when the city purchased more land.

When the University of Washington moved to its present site in 1895, Edmond Meany had proposed his concept of an arboretum on the campus. However, for the A-Y-P Exposition of 1909 the campus was cleared of forests. Finally, the arboretum dream came into actuality at Washington Park when garden clubs raised money to hire the Olmsted Brothers to design a master plan. WPA labor was used for much of the landscaping.

Montlake has been populated by families of young professionals, drawn to the area by its pleasant qualities and proximity to the university. That same university expansion, along with freeway construction and commercial interests, appeared to threaten the community, and the residents united to form a politically active community lobby.

Montlake remains a residential community well-endowed with public open spaces and one small commercial area, and within its confines are such institutions as the Seattle Yacht Club, the Fisheries Bureau Laboratory, and the Museum of History and Industry.

WALLINGFORD

The Wallingford community spans the hill on the north shore of Lake Union, with easy access to the University District, Seattle Center, and the downtown business district. Earliest platting occurred around 40th and Meridian in 1883. The location around Ashworth and 36th was platted in 1889 by Corliss Stone and William Ashworth and named "Edgewater." James A. Moore platted and promoted the eastern part of Wallingford as "Latona." John Wallingford's division just east of Woodland Park eventually gave the name to the entire neighborhood, which was annexed to Seattle in 1891.

The small-boat canal which opened in 1885 gave Wallingford a direct water link to downtown Seattle, and in 1887 the Seattle, Lake Shore and Eastern Railroad extended along the north shore of Lake Union. In 1893, where the freeway bridge now stands, the wooden Latona bridge was built. By 1900 a wooden trestle bridge at Stoneway gave direct streetcar access to downtown Seattle. This transportation potential

Above
Transportation between distant neighborhoods was convenient on the steamers of the "mosquito fleet." The sternwheeler shown here at Alki Point in West Seattle, circa 1900, is the *Fairhaven*. Courtesy, Williamson Collection, Puget Sound Maritime Historical Society.

Right
The *Bainbridge* passes under Montlake Bridge's open span, with the tug, *J.E. Boyden*, circa 1949. There are three other moveable-span bridges on the Lake Washington Ship Canal: the Ballard, the Fremont, and the University. Courtesy, Puget Sound Maritime Historical Society.

WOODLAND PARK.
Laurelhurst
of Seattle

Opposite, top left
This was the entrance in 1900 to Woodland Park, part of Guy Phinney's estate before it was purchased by the city. To promote the land and to attract potential real estate buyers, Phinney ran a trolley line out here and kept exotic animals on his property. The area is now a city park and zoo. (MOHAI)

Opposite, top right
At the turn of the century, Assistant City Engineer George F. Cotterill developed a 25-mile system of bicycle paths which ran from Montlake to Green Lake and Woodland Park. Here the bicycle path at Lake Washington passes by a lunch room. (MOHAI)

Opposite, bottom
The *Laurelhurst*, circa 1910, was used as a passenger steamer between Madison Park and Laurelhurst when the latter area was first being developed. Courtesy, Williamson Collection, Puget Sound Maritime Historical Society.

Above
Madison Park Theatre was built in 1895 and operated until 1898. Shown here in 1900, it was eventually destroyed by fire. (MOHAI)

attracted industry to the north Lake Union shore, including a number of sawmills, shingle mills, and a sash and door factory. After an asphalt company, a gas plant, a tar plant, a garbage incinerator, and other enterprises were located there, residents became concerned about the smoke and pollution.

In 1956 the gas plant was closed because of the availability of natural gas from Canada and is now a city park—Gas Works Park. The population began to change in the 1950s as more families moved to the suburbs, but in the 1970s the Wallingford Community Council and Chamber of Commerce began activity, working to maintain Wallingford as a pleasant residential community.

MADISON PARK/MADRONA/LESCHI

Madison Park, Madrona, and Leschi have separate identities, but all three share an orientation toward Lake Washington, an abundance of wooded parklands, and a predominantly residential character.

The Lake Washington shoreline was considered an ideal residential site ever since the Indian right to the land was taken by treaty. But before they would become popular, the plats, some distance from the city center, needed transportation facilities. A cable car line was built along Yesler Way from Pioneer Square to the Lake Shore.

To the north, Judge John J. McGilvra established an estate on land he had purchased from the University of Washington for $5 an acre. In 1864 a road was built from downtown, along the route of present Madison Street, to a 21-acre Madison Park set aside by McGilvra. By the end of the '80s, amusement parks were built at Madison and Leschi.

The Madrona area was homesteaded by the Randall family, and by 1899 a small community had developed. Land speculation followed, and a cable car line was built to the shore.

During the first decade of the 20th century, the Park Department acquired a number of areas scattered throughout the city. A plan was developed by the Olmsted brothers to link these parks and green belts with broad boulevards. Successors of the Olmsteds included Madrona, Leschi, and Madison parks into the scheme, which continued from Seward Park through the Arboretum, the university campus, and Ravenna, Green Lake, and Woodland parks to Magnolia Bluff and Fort Lawton. This greenbelt combination remains one of Seattle's most accessible, beautiful, and unique resources.

When the level of Lake Washington was lowered nine feet after the ship canal was opened, Seattle residents demanded more swimming beaches and recreational facilities. Some of these were established on the Madrona shore in 1919. The Broadmoor Country Club opened in 1927 as a private residential park for Seattle's wealthy.

In 1940, when the first floating bridge was built across Lake Washington, citizens became concerned how lakeshore

neighborhoods were developing. Since 1958 activist groups have reviewed problems and worked to maintain the residential image. They were helped by Model Cities Programs in the 1960s and the Central Area Motivation Program undertook a neighborhood renewal in Madrona.

The State of Washington Shoreline Management Act of 1971 and development of the Lake Washington Regional Shoreline Goals and Policy help maintain the natural characteristics and private residential nature of the areas.

CAPITOL HILL

James A. Moore is credited with the platting of the Capitol Hill addition to the east of the growing city shortly after the turn of the century. How the hill received its name is not clear. Some say Moore named it after a hill of the same name in Denver. Others insist the name stuck after a real-estate firm offered a site there for the state capitol.

By 1908, Capitol Hill along with First Hill had become the most fashionable district in Seattle. The wealthy lumbermen, bankers, shipping tycoons, and the newly rich from Alaska built great homes there, employing artisans from around the world.

Volunteer Park became the focal point of the hill. The 140 acres were purchased from J.M. Colman in 1876 and Lake View Park was established there in 1887. The name was changed later to honor volunteers in the Spanish American War. In 1932 Dr. Richard Fuller and his mother built the Seattle Art Museum in Volunteer Park.

Capitol Hill is the home of many fine churches and schools, and active neighborhood groups continue to work for the preservation of this unique community.

◆

Opposite
John J. McGilvra built cottages, a boathouse, piers, and a promenade on his Madison Park estate, shown here circa 1900. The *Xanthus*, the steamer at dock, was used for excursions around the lake. Eventually such steamers were superseded by the ferry system and then the bridge. Courtesy, Puget Sound Maritime Historical Society.

Above
The Denny Hotel on Denny Hill was built in 1890–1902, but it long stood idle because of financial difficulties. After J.A. Moore Investment Company bought the hotel in 1903, it was renovated and renamed the Washington. It burned in 1906 during the Denny Hill regrade. Photo by Anders B. Wilse. (MOHAI)

CHAPTER 14
KING COUNTY COMMUNITIES

BY CHARLES PAYTON

King County was established in 1852 when the Oregon territorial legislature demarcated its boundaries. It was named for William R. King, elected Vice-President of the United States during the administration of Franklin Pierce.

With an area of over 2,200 square miles, King County is larger than the state of Delaware or Rhode Island, and has an economy surpassing many foreign countries. The county is a manufacturing, educational, residential, shipping, and transportation region second to none in Washington State. The cultural and recreational facilities of the county, the "boating capital of the world," are internationally celebrated and acclaimed.

Although King County's fascinating history is relatively short, its achievements in forestry, mining, agriculture, and maritime and urban development comprise one of the more unique stories in the United States. Settlers and immigrants by the thousands came to the Puget Sound country, attracted by magnificent opportunities and rich natural resources.

The varied river valleys, hill districts, and islands of King County each have their own distinct heritage, any one of which makes a complete and fascinating story in itself. The brief accounts presented here can only suggest the county's part in the great drama of America's westward expansion. In fact, much of the story of King County has yet to be written.

WHITE RIVER

Renton

At the southern shore of Lake Washington is Renton, one of Seattle's major neighboring cities. This residential, commercial, and manufacturing city is situated on what was a century and a half ago several encampments of the Coast Salish Indian group, the Duwamish.

The earliest settlers in the area found the heavily wooded Black River site an ideal place to carve out farms and homesteads. As early as 1853, Henry Tobin homesteaded here and helped establish a small water-powered sawmill. Upon his death in 1857, Tobin's widow Diana married Erasmus Smithers, who became a large landowner and influential pioneer, helping in 1876 to plat the town of Renton. The pioneers named their new town for Captain William Renton, a financier of the Renton Coal Company, founded in 1873.

The small community at Black River pioneered formal education in King County in 1853 by opening its first school on nearby Earlington Hill with Adelaide Andrews as teacher.

It was during these early years too that a truly significant event in county history occurred. In the process of clearing land on his donation claim near Black River, Dr. R.M. Bigelow discovered an exposed coal seam. Renton became the gateway to the King County coalfields and the hub of the local coal industry.

The key to Renton's continued development was its centralized location. It was one of the few towns in the county to be connected with Seattle by passable wagon or military roads. For years, the Black River passage to Elliott Bay also served as an artery of commerce. Eventually Renton was blessed with access to three major rail lines.

In addition to coal and agricultural production, Renton developed industries such as lumber and shingle mills, terra cotta brick and tile plants, a glassmaking factory, a cigar factory, and a railway car manufacturing plant.

The face of the city is today much changed from a century ago. With the opening of the Lake Washington Ship Canal in 1916, the Black River ceased flowing, and has virtually disappeared. The Cedar River, once a tributary to the Black River, has been diverted through the city and into Lake Washington. Although most vestiges of coal production have vanished, Renton is an industrially strong community with a host of major producers, not the least of which are Pacific Car and Foundry and the Boeing Company. Longacres racetrack located nearby is a popular recreational site.

Tukwila

The city of Tukwila is located on former Duwamish tribal land, first settled by whites in 1853 when the Joseph Foster family claimed a 640-acre tract along the Duwamish River.

Before the Interurban years from 1902 to 1928, the Tukwila vicinity seemed a desirable residential and agricultural community. Real settlement of the area, however, began with the development of the Seattle-Tacoma Interurban rail line through the community. In 1902 a section of the area was platted. The budding community was at first called

Photograph by Victor Gardaya
(MOHAI)

Garden City or Garden Station, but a contest to name the community produced the name Tukwila, after Indian words meaning "land where the hazelnuts grow."

After World War II had ended and an attempt to disincorporate had been defeated, the city looked forward to its future under a succession of progressive mayors. Tukwila successfully fended off the land acquisition plans of the Port of Seattle and attracted the interest of Allied Stores, who in the late '50s and early '60s developed Southcenter, a regional shopping center at the junction of the newly constructed I-5 and I-405 highways. The neighboring Andover Park Industrial District, which was developed in the 1960s, is an awesome assemblage of manufacturing and distribution.

Modern Tukwila is a unique complex of fine homes, recreational facilities, major regional shopping centers, and massive industrial development. It has evolved from a quiet river and interurban junction to King County's "Crossroads of Commerce."

Kent

The foundation for the future city of Kent was laid when in 1853 the Samuel Russell family established themselves on 320 acres in the southeast section of the present town. In the ensuing decades, they were followed by many others.

A settlement in the area, then known collectively as White River, began in the 1850s. Small produce farms flourished, as did dairy farms. In the 1880s, hop farming was introduced to the area. And in 1881 the first of many lumber mills opened in the community.

In the late 1880s some controversy arose over the naming of the townsite. Although Seattle pioneer Henry Yesler platted a town on the site in 1884, James H. Titus, a local pioneer, platted the boundaries of a town called Titusville on adjacent property. By 1890 the populace had adopted the name of Kent for their newly incorporated city, named for a prominent hop-growing county in England.

The city experienced another surge of growth after the Puget Sound Electric Railway built its interurban line through the city in 1902. Kent became the operating base for the line, where all trains originated and ended.

In 1906 a devastating flood changed the course of rivers in the vicinity, with the result that the channel formerly known as the White River was renamed Green River, a change which has resulted in much confusion over the years.

Many industries have found a home in the Kent area, including a chemical plant, a milk condensery, and a vegetable packing plant. The surrounding valley became a large lettuce-producing region, and the base for poultry breeding and exporting.

In recent years, the "Kent Valley" has attracted such industries as a manufacturer of fiberglass sailboats and the Boeing Company's Space Center research facility. So much industry has located there that much of the once fertile farmland has been replaced by industry. It is not uncommon to see a dairy herd pasturing beside a modern manufacturing or distributing plant. In a little over a hundred years, the valley has gone from forest to farm to factory, a remarkable transition.

Auburn

In the middle 1850s settlers began clearing farms along a section of the White River, which was later to become the city of Auburn. The homesteaders were barely established when news of Indian hostilities in other parts of the state forced them to flee to the relative safety of Seattle. Of those who remained behind, a number were killed in 1855, the event now known as the White River Massacre. Another attack shortly thereafter on an encampment of soldiers resulted in the killing of Lt. William Slaughter and several of his men. Out of respect for the young lieutenant, the community that formed there was originally called Slaughter.

Among those establishing claims after the hostilities had ended were Dr. Levi Ballard and his wife Mary, William Faucett, Dr. Alexander Hughes, George Hubbard, and Gottlieb Treager. Dr. Ballard platted the town of Slaughter in 1886, and the town was incorporated in 1891. The future development of the community was assured by Dr. Ballard and his son Charles. In 1893 a delegation of local citizens petitioned the state legislature to change the rather unbecoming name of Slaughter to Auburn.

The farms around Auburn were largely hop producers in the 1880s. After the decline of that crop, producers developed dairying, vegetable farming, and fruit growing into major concerns. In the early 1900s many Japanese-Americans established farms in the area, and became prominent until their internment in World War II.

The first interurban line, the Puget Sound Electric Railway, was completed through Auburn in 1902, and was later followed by others.

Industries that dominated the community included a sawmill, a dairy products company, and others.

The Boeing Company and subsidiary industries figure largely in the economy of modern Auburn, as do lumber-related concerns like Weyerhaeuser and Palmer G. Lewis Co. The city has many recreational facilities, a modern airport, and excellent educational institutions, including the Green River Community College.

The Muckleshoot Reservation, located just to the southeast of Auburn, is King County's only recognized treaty land. As one of the recognized "tribes" of the Point Elliot Treaty of 1855, the Muckleshoots—comprised of bands of the Stkamish, Skopeamish and Smulkahmish—were first given reservation land around Ft. Muckleshoot, lands later increased in 1874. In 1934 the Muckleshoots adopted a tribal constitution, and in 1975 a new Tribal Center was built.

White River's Other Communities

Other less known historic communities of the Green (formerly White) River Valley are the towns of Orillia, O'Brien, Thomas, and Christopher. These unincorporated towns have been largely absorbed into neighboring cities or went into decline after the demise of interurban service through the valley in 1928.

The town of Orillia was settled in 1853, and named in 1889 by Malcolm McDougall after his birthplace, Orillia, Ontario. The town was known for vegetable growing, dairy farming, and logging. After 1959 what remained of Orillia was partitioned, with sections annexed by Renton, Kent, and Tukwila.

The town of O'Brien was named for Terence and Morgan O'Brien, who pioneered there in 1868, and the community was settled principally by persons of Irish Catholic descent. It was known for its hops and later for a pickle, kraut, and vinegar plant run by the William Hunt Company. What is left of the community has been annexed into the northern section of Kent.

Just south of Kent was the town of Thomas, named for John Thomas, pioneer of 1853, but was formerly called Bialshie, from an Indian word signifying fighter. Fort Thomas, a standard log blockhouse, was constructed there by the U.S. Army in 1855–1856, and later the Standard Milling and Logging Company also had an operation there.

Just to the north of Auburn was Christopher, named for Thomas Christopher, a Norwegian immigrant who settled there in 1863 and developed a sizable dairy farm.

On the Pierce-King County line is the small community of Pacific, a development of real-estate promoter C.D. Hillman, platted in 1906 and incorporated in 1909. Just to the north of it is Algona, a small farming community formerly known as Valley City, which incorporated in 1955.

SNOQUALMIE VALLEY

Duvall

Along the Snoqualmie River's most northerly course through King County is situated the rural community of Duvall. Once the domain of the Snoqualmie Indians, this territory was traversed by volunteers of the Northern Battalion during the Indian War of 1855–1856.

The community, which took form in the 1870s and 1880s, was called Cherry Valley, and James Duvall, for whom the present city is named, was the first to claim land there in 1875.

By the 1890s a swing bridge had been built over the river and was being operated by the pioneer Dougherty family. Overland transportation was possible but slow, and was less often used than was the Snoqualmie River, where steamboats called regularly at farmers' landings and towns along the banks.

In the 1900s the Chicago, Milwaukee and St. Paul Railroad surveyed the valley for development of a line and, after some negotiation, convinced the community of Cherry Valley to relocate in order to accommodate a railroad grade. About 1909, a store, church, and other buildings were uprooted and moved. During the transition to the new townsite, John and Ida Bird platted the town of Duvall in 1910, and by the time the community was incorporated in 1913, the Great Northern Railway had also laid rails through the town.

The Cherry Valley Townsite Company, after some legal maneuvering, was instrumental in promoting and developing the boom town of Duvall, and new businesses and hotels sprang up in the new location. A bank, a utility company, and a number of new homes were quickly added. In addition to successful farming and dairying operations, the economic mainstays of the community were timber-related businesses.

Although most vestiges of the timber industry are now gone, Duvall has maintained viable farming activities and is becoming an increasingly attractive site for residential development. The city has pleasant shops and stores, as well as one of the country's fine "down-home" restaurants.

Tolt-Carnation

Prior to historic times, Tolt (now Carnation) was the site of a sizable Snoqualmie Indian longhouse village and the principal home of Pat Kanim, chief of the Snoqualmies. The Snoqualmies befriended settlers, and Pat Kanim and his warriors served beside the rangers of the Northern Battalion. The name Tolt is an anglicized abbreviation for an Indian word meaning "swift running waters."

James Entwistle, formerly of the Northern Battalion, first claimed land at Tolt in 1858 and "proved up" his homestead in the 1860s. Others followed, establishing farms in the area. Tolt farmers shipped their orchard and garden produce, grain, and dairy products downriver to Snohomish City (then called Cadyville), and on to Everett.

An older section of the townsite was platted as early as 1894, and newer sections were added in 1911. All were incorporated in 1912. The community remained primarily agricultural, but several shingle and logging companies were established.

In 1909 E.A. Stuart established the Carnation Milk Farms there. Stuart created an outstanding dairy complex where he bred and raised a number of world record-holding Holstein cows. In 1917 the town elected to change its name to Carnation, and despite some misgivings, has retained the designation since. The town is still in the heart of dairy country.

Preston

The town of Preston, located along the Raging River, a tributary to the Snoqualmie, was settled in the early 1890s. The community, which was for a short time called St. Louis, was named for William T. Preston, an official of the Seattle,

Lakeshore and Eastern Railroad which pushed through the Valley in 1889–1890.

In the early 1890s the village of Preston was a sawmill town but later acquired a shingle mill. In 1896 August Lovegren and his brother Emil organized the large and long-lived Preston Mill Company and induced Elaf Edwins to come from Sweden to manage the mill's sawing, planing, and shingle-cutting facilities.

The company town of Preston was largely of Swedish descent, and many of its inhabitants had emigrated there directly from the old country. It was said that anyone in Preston who wasn't Swedish was considered a foreigner.

Present-day Preston is a small community along the I-90 route to Snoqualmie Pass. The long-running Preston Mill is silent, but its machinery is still visible, a reminder of an earlier and more prosperous era.

Fall City

Three miles below Snoqualmie Falls, at a site close to the Snoqualmie Indian village of Chief Saniwa, James Taylor and the Boham brothers, Edwin and George, filed land claims in 1869. Taylor and the Bohams opened a trading post and store on the site of Fall City, and in 1873 Watson Allen built the valley's first sawmill. Others soon followed.

From the middle 1870s onward, steamboats began to navigate the river as far as Fall City. In the early 1880s transportation across the river was by cable ferry, but by 1888 a bridge connected Fall City with the town of Tolt.

Hops were the major crop of the area, and a number of logging camps and lumber mills operated around the town. The town was initially bypassed by the Seattle, Lakeshore and Eastern Railway, but since the construction of the railroad and the development of the hydroelectric station at the Falls, the excursion and tourist trade has helped to maintain the economy of Fall City. Agricultural production and dairying also continue to keep the local economy viable.

Although the town remains unincorporated, it is a residential, trading, and agricultural center, which has retained much of its tradition amidst one of King County's most beautiful valleys.

Snoqualmie Falls

The first white man to explore Snoqualmie Falls was Washington Hall in 1848, though it had been a sacred place for the Native Americans for generations. The picturesque waterfall, 268 feet high, is formed of an erosion-resistant outcrop of andesite lava.

In early 1869, Territorial Governor William Pickering laid claim to 640 acres of land encompassing the Falls, which his descendants later farmed there. In 1898 Charles Baker began the construction of a hydroelectric power station there, parts of which were built into the solid rock beneath the Falls. The following year, the Snoqualmie Falls Power Company was generating current for Seattle and Tacoma. For its time, the Falls generation station was an amazing feat of science and engineering. Today hundreds of thousands of people visit the Falls and generating facilities each year. A second plant was added below the Falls in 1910 and enlarged in 1957. This facility remains a highly functional energy source for 16,000 homes in the Puget Sound area and is operated by Puget Power Company of Bellevue.

Snoqualmie

In 1858 young Jeremiah Borst scouted the fertile prairie adjacent to the present city of Snoqualmie. Borst was so taken with the farming potential of the valley soil there that he laid claim to a tract of land around Fort Alden, a log blockhouse built during the Indian War of 1856.

Borst found several squatters on the prairie who had served as rangers in the Northern Battalion, but they were men without families and departed in a few years, leaving Borst the first permanent settler. Through the 1860s and 1870s only a few widely scattered pioneer families lived in the Snoqualmie Valley. During these early years, Borst gradually acquired hundreds of additional acres on the prairie and produced vegetables, fruit, and pork, which were shipped to market on the river.

Hops became the major crop of the area and provided jobs for transient and local labor.

Stores, shops, and hotels were built, and the major hop ranch had its own hotel, a favorite retreat of prominent Seattle citizens such as Dexter Horton, Henry Yesler, and the David T. Denny family.

The Snoqualmie Land and Improvement Company platted the town in 1889 and the city was incorporated in 1903. The community of Snoqualmie is now most often associated with Snoqualmie Falls, one of the state's foremost tourist attractions, and the city's Victorian train depot has been beautifully restored by the Puget Sound Railway Historical Association, which operates the county's last steam train and railway excursion line.

North Bend

Located at King County's primary eastern gateway to interstate commerce is the city of North Bend. Danish-born Matts Peterson claimed 160 acres of land in the vicinity in 1865 and was soon joined by others.

Mt. Si, which towers over the town, was named for Josiah "Uncle Si" Merritt, a handicapped pioneer who came to the valley in 1862, establishing his farm at the foot of the peak named for him. Lucinda Fares, who homesteaded the Toll Gate farm on Snoqualmie Prairie with her husband Joseph, was the valley's first pioneer woman, and the daughter of Luther Collins.

The district was at first primarily agricultural, and the hop growing boom of the 1880s brought many new settlers to

Top
Wildwood Station was on the Seattle, Renton and Southern line, which was reputed to be the fastest street railway in the world, circa 1900. (MOHAI)

Above
William Rufus Devane King was elected Vice President when he ran with Franklin Pierce in the Presidential election of 1852. In the same year, the northern portion of Thurston County in Washington Territory was divided into four counties, two of which were named for Pierce and King. (MOHAI)

Top
Miners posed at the entrance to the Renton Cooperative Coal Company mine, circa 1896. The company was organized by a group of laborers who were tired of being out of work. Photo by Kinsey and Kinsey. Courtesy, Renton Historical Society.

Above
This view of the Black River near Renton was taken circa 1898 by Anders B. Wilse. The river dried up when Lake Washington was lowered by the canal construction. It was filled in gradually and became the home of Renton Airport and Boeing Commercial Airplane Company. Courtesy, Anders B. Wilse Collection. (MOHAI)

the community. A trail through the Snoqualmie Pass brought cattle from Kittitas County to Seattle. Roadbuilding efforts had commenced in the 1850s, spurred on by the discovery of gold east of the Cascade Mountains. After decades of effort and many false starts, in 1914 a good auto road was built over the pass.

Prospecting in the nearby hills and mountain pass resulted in a number of claims being made, including Arthur Denny's Snoqualmie Lode iron ore mine. Lumber milling, however, became the major industry.

Mary and Will Taylor platted the town as Snoqualmie in 1889 but the town several miles downstream was named Snoqualmie Falls, after the railroad's depot. The name of Mountain View was advocated for awhile, but the railroad eventually named it North Bend after the northerly turn of the Snoqualmie River, and the city was incorporated in 1909.

Today the city of North Bend is a picturesque mountain community on the threshold of King County's major snowsport recreational facilities. The nearby entrance to the Snoqualmie National Forest is a reminder of the region's historic dependence on forestry and the wood products industry.

Cedar Falls

The small community of Cedar Falls grew up around a hydroelectric generation station established on the Cedar River by the city of Seattle in 1906. The town, which had been called Moncton (after a settler who arrived there about 1909), was also a station on the Chicago, Milwaukee and St. Paul Railway. In 1912, at the urging of J.D. Ross, the railroad was convinced to change to the more becoming name of Cedar Falls, and added an electrified sign to its depot.

The town was flooded in 1915, creating Rattlesnake Lake in the process. Though no one was injured, the town was nearly destroyed. A devastating fire in 1922 also created havoc and today little is left of the once sizable town.

Cedar Falls was not only the birthplace of Seattle City Light's Cedar River Watershed project, but it was also one of the first publicly owned hydroelectric generating facilities in the U.S. The facility today furnishes enough power for about 8,000 Seattle homes.

SAMMAMISH

Issaquah

Issaquah, located just south of the highly popular recreational site at Lake Sammamish, had its beginnings when settlers L.B. Andrews and David Mowrey discovered coal there in 1859. As other homesteaders, such as the Casto, Bush, and Welch families established themselves there in the 1860s, the community began to take form. In the early days, budding Issaquah as well as the adjacent valley, lake, and river now known as Sammamish, were called by the name Squak, an anglicized form of an Indian word of uncertain meaning.

When L.B. Andrews carried a sample of his newly discovered coal to Seattle in 1862, it was found to be of high quality. By 1864 Andrews had delivered a load of five tons more to Seattle by means of a scow down the Sammamish River. Since Andrews' route took 20 days and was accompanied by high transportation costs, his coal could not remain

This view shows the city of Kent in the 1910s. The large Carnation Milk Condensery is in the white complex of buildings at right. Once cleared of timber, the flat valley floor became immensely productive farmland. Courtesy, White River Valley Historical Society.

competitive on the Seattle market. It was not until 1888, when the Seattle Lake Shore and Eastern Railroad put a line through to the community, that mining coal here became practical. The Seattle Coal and Iron Company shipped its first coal in 1888 and produced continuously until 1904.

The community of Squak was incorporated and renamed Gilman, in 1892, in honor of Daniel Hunt Gilman, an officer of the railroad. Since there was already a town by that name, the Post Office forced a change to Olney. It was not until 1899 that the current name of Issaquah was adopted.

At about the same time that the coal mines were being developed, several lumber and shingle mills were built in the area.

The first farm produce, consisting of such items as potatoes, eggs, oats, butter, and pork, were shipped to Seattle markets in 1867. The pioneer Wold family of Norwegian immigrants was the first to plant acreage in hops on the valley farm in 1886.

Even before the turn of the century, dairy farming was being established here on a large scale. The Anderson, Tibbets, Pickering, and Prentice farms were among the heavy producers, and the Thomas Wilson Guernseys were featured at the Alaska-Yukon-Pacific Exposition's Model Dairy Barn at Seattle in 1909. The Meadowbrook Condensed Milk Company and the Northwest Milk Condensing Company were established in the 1900s, and the dairy industry has flourished to the present day.

After the turn of the century, coal production at major Issaquah mines was irregular. Even after reorganizations and an influx of foreign capital, production was inconsistent, although many smaller operations continued to produce for decades.

In 1940, the opening of the Lake Washington Floating Bridge made access to Issaquah much easier, and today's commuters find it relatively easy to live in Issaquah and work in Seattle. Issaquah has become a highly desirable residential and marketing community with charming shops on Front Street and at Gilman Village, but it still retains much of its rural charm.

Redmond

After a hitch as sheriff of Kitsap County, Irish-born Luke McRedmond, together with Warren W. Perrigo, settled in the Sammamish (then called Squak) Valley in 1871. Perrigo and his wife, who had arrived in Seattle with the Mercer Girls in 1866, was joined by his brother William, who proceeded to establish a series of trading posts in the area as well as the first store at Redmond in the 1890s.

For a time the settlement now known as Redmond was known as Salmonberg, after the abundant dog salmon in the creeks and river, but was later changed to Melrose, after the Warren Perrigo homestead. The town was finally named Redmond in honor of the widely respected pioneer, first mayor, and postmaster, Luke McRedmond.

Over the years, logging became the primary industry in the Redmond area. By the 1890s Redmond had developed into an important trading and transportation center. A western-style stagecoach connected it to the Snoqualmie Valley

Auburn was a marketing and manufacturing center at the heart of King County's most productive agricultural lands. In this view taken of Main Street, looking west from Division Street, circa 1908, the Green River Hotel can be seen in the background. Courtesy, White River Valley Historical Museum.

Mt. Si towers over the flourishing hop fields on the prairie near the town of Snoqualmie, circa 1905. At peak production the hop ranch shown here operated 83 kilns and employed over 1,200 people. Photo by Darius Kinsey. Courtesy, Snoqualmie Valley Historical Society.

and to Kirkland, and steamers to Seattle. The growing city incorporated in 1912.

After the original straightening of the Sammamish slough in 1912, much land in the valley was reclaimed for farming. Poultry, vegetable, and dairy farming flourished, providing produce for Seattle's Pike Place Public Market. Many fine dairy farms prospered in the valley climate. Nearby Willowmoor Farm produced world class Ayrshire cattle and sleek Morgan horses.

Today, Redmond is a booming city, greatly increased in size, with major new industry, shopping centers, and a growing population. Greater Redmond is one of King County's major growth areas.

Woodinville

The greater Woodinville area, though presently unincorporated, has a distinct heritage of its own. The "town" was named for Ira and Susan Woodin, who preempted a claim here in 1872, and later set up a general store in partnership with Thomas Sanders.

Several sawmills and shinglemills began operating in the 1870s and other small industries such as a desk factory and brick and tile yard appeared, but without continued success. Woodinville became an important railway junction town for the Seattle Lakeshore and Eastern Railroad, which arrived there in 1877 from Seattle.

Located on the site formerly known as Derby, Fred Stimson's Hollywood farm developed between 1910 and 1912 and was noted for its Holstein-Friesian Cattle and its Duroc-Jersey swine. The community that grew up around the farm included a poultry farm, nursery, and a brick schoolhouse, which today houses a collection of shops.

The area is still farmed, and has beautifully wooded residential expanses, but is probably best known for its Bryant boat manufacturing industry and the Chateau Sainte Michelle Winery. Located on the site of the old Hollywood Farm, the varieties of wine produced are becoming recognized and appreciated worldwide.

Bothell

The city of Bothell is named for David C. Bothell and his wife Mary Ann, who filed the first plat of land for the community in 1888. Their son George is credited with founding the town where he and his brother John began logging in 1889, operating a shingle and lumber mill there until 1892.

The early years along the Sammamish (then called Squak) River saw only a few pioneers, but by the late 1880s there were several mills functioning.

When the Seattle Lakeshore and Eastern Railroad reached Bothell in 1877, it helped open the region to further development. Steamer service from Madison Park to Bothell was inaugurated in 1884 with the flat-bottomed steam scow Squak, which made twice weekly runs up the Squak River.

Bothell area farms produced dairy products, produce, and poultry. The prosperous City of Bothell was incorporated in 1909, but suffered a disastrous fire in 1911. By 1912, though, the Pacific Highway between Everett and Seattle was completed through the city, and the modern era of transportation and commerce had begun.

Kenmore

The adjacent community of *Kenmore*, now a sizable residential and marketing district was developed somewhat later. Territorial governor Watson C. Squire leased acreage there to John and Annie McMasters, who took over the Fir Lumber Mill in 1903. The McMasters named the community which grew up along the Pacific Highway Kenmore after their former home near Ottawa, Canada.

EASTSIDE AND LAKE

Juanita

The unincorporated residential community of Juanita was originally named Hubbard, after a logger who worked the area in the 1870s. Mrs. Charles Terry renamed the settlement Juanita. Timber was logged in the area and a water-powered sawmill was built by Dorr Forbes in the 1880s, which shipped lumber and shingles. Finns were one of the ethnic groups that settled Juanita. The ferry dock, which had its own confectionery, was served by the steamer *Urania* until 1916, when Lake Washington's water level was lowered. Forbes is also credited with building the original bridge over Juanita Slough to Kirkland at the time of the steel mill boom in the early 1890s.

In the 1930s, Juanita Beach became a popular recreational site with swimming, canoeing, picnicking, and dancing facilities. St. Edwards Seminary, built on the Juanita lakeshore in 1931 on property once owned by capitalist Marshall Blinn, has since been transformed into a state park facility, one of the attractions of the community.

Kirkland

Just below the Houghton district of the city of Kirkland, Mrs. Nancy Popham McGregor and sons located a homestead in 1870 on Pleasant Bay, now the residential district of Yarrow Bay. Samuel and Caroline French homesteaded on the site of present day Kirkland in 1872, and others followed in the 1870s and 1880s.

The community on Pleasant Bay was named for Sarah Jane Houghton of Boston, whose generous contribution furnished a bell for the town church about 1880.

Among the wealthy Seattle investors attracted to property on the East Side was Leigh S.J. Hunt, owner of the Seattle *Post-Intelligencer*, a promoter of uncommon ability. About 1887, Hunt conceived the idea of locating a steel mill at the site just above Houghton, which he envisioned as the "Pittsburgh of the West." Hunt attracted the interest of Peter

Top
David Thomas Denny, shown here by his cabin, supervised repair work on Snoqualmie Pass wagon road from south of Lake Keechelus to the foot of Grouse Ridge in the summer of 1899. (MOHAI)

Above
Looking north on Front Street, this view shows Issaquah circa 1912, when the town was on the verge of an economic boom generated by the Issaquah and Superior Coal Mining Company. Courtesy, Marymoor Museum.

Top
This view of the mountain town of North Bend, circa 1910, shows Mt. Si in the distance. After the arrival of the Seattle, Lakeshore and Eastern railway in 1890, logging became a primary industry in the area. Photo by Siegrist. Courtesy, Snoqualmie Valley Historical Society.

Above
Storefronts line the west side of Leary Way in Redmond, circa 1910. The Redmond Trading Company, to the left, a classic country general store complete with bins, hardware, and pot bellied stove, operated into the 1950s. Courtesy, Marymoor Museum.

Kirk, a wealthy English industrialist. Hunt and Kirk, along with Seattle interests, organized the Kirkland Land and Improvement Company and the Moss Bay Iron and Steel Works of America in 1888, with the intention of developing an integrated industry capable of processing ore into steel rail for the world market.

This speculative effort managed to erect several buildings, attract a spur line of the Seattle, Lakeshore and Eastern Railroad, and partly furnish a mill, which was among several industries that collapsed as a result of the depression of 1893. More fortunate was the state's first woolen mill, organized at Kirkland in 1892 by Edward Eyanson. The mill, later sold to George Matzen, supplied woolen goods to outfit Seattle's Gold Rush trade. By the mid 1930s fires and a declining market forced an end to the mill's production.

A building boom spawned by the land company and steel works, managed to build a number of fine brick homes and business buildings at the townsite, although surrounding stump lots remained into the 20th century. The city of Kirkland was platted in 1888 and was incorporated in 1905.

Agriculture around Kirkland was based largely on berry, fruit, and bulb farming, and chicken ranching was also significant. A cannery was built at Kirkland in 1922, but was out of operation by the early 1930s. In 1936 a WPA cooperative project revived the cannery industry in Kirkland, supplying state institutions and needy local residents with foodstuffs.

Ferry docks were active at Kirkland by the late 1880s, and in 1900 King County and a private steamboat company were providing ferry service on the lake. The *Leschi*, the last boat on the Madison Park-Kirkland run, ceased operations in 1950. At one time 10 auto stage lines radiated to surrounding towns on the East Side from the Kirkland Docks.

The community of Houghton, which had remained relatively aloof from their neighboring town's steel mill scheme, developed a thriving industry of its own. Beginning with the early shipbuilding efforts of the Curtis family, who built the steam scow *Squak* on their ranch in 1883, and continuing with the Bartch and Tompkins Transportation Company shipyard on the same site in the 1900s, shipbuilding emerged as the town's major activity.

John L. Anderson acquired control of the facility about 1907 and it was known thereafter as the Lake Washington Shipyard. The expanded facility produced or repaired hundreds of boats, yachts, and defense contract vessels during the World Wars, though Anderson himself had sold his interest in it in the 1920s. Peak employment at the yard during World War II was about 6,000 persons, but by 1950 the shipyard was idle.

The city of Houghton, which incorporated in 1947, merged with the city of Kirkland in 1968. The Kirkland-Houghton area is presently a growing residential city with excellent marinas and shoreline properties and is home to the Seattle Seahawks Football Organization.

Bellevue

Since the end of World War II, Bellevue, the "Contemporary City" has emerged as the fourth largest municipality in Washington State and has won recognition as one of the nation's All American Cities.

The area's earliest settlement was Aaron Mercer's claim

The milking barns at Fred Stimson's Hollywood Farm near Woodinville were filled with Stimson's Holstein-Friesian cows, top producers that won many awards. Sammamish Valley was one of several in King County ideally suited to dairy production. Photo by Asahel Curtis. Courtesy, Washington State Historical Society.

Many varieties of wine issue from the main building of the Chateau Sainte Michelle Winery in Woodinville.

along the Mercer Slough in 1864, and in 1869 Seattle pioneer William Meydenbauer established a cabin on the bay later named for him. In the eyes of the county's earliest settlers, the heavily forested terrain of Lake Washington's eastern lakeshore lacked the strategic location or fertile prairie lands of the more remote sections, and the area was bypassed for more than a decade. In the 1870s, however, a small number of settlers began to fell timber and carve out homesteads on the East Side. During those formative years of the community, James Northup, the King Brothers, Clark Sturtevant, Alvin and Mary Goff, Isaac Bechtel, and Patrick Downey were among the early arrivals, and in 1882 Albert Burrows opened the area's first school and post office.

The community was named for pioneers Matt and Lou Sharpe's hometown of Bellevue, Indiana, and the first section of land was platted in 1891 as the Cheriton Fruit Gardens Tracts. Oliver Frantz and William Raine platted the Bellevue townsite in 1904.

For many years the only way to reach Bellevue was by boat. Small steamers began to serve the numerous lakeshore docks in the 1890s, and in 1913 the King County ferry *Leschi* began regular service. The Johnson brothers' *Ariel* provided feeder service to the main landings beginning about 1916.

Parts of Bellevue were logged with ox teams by the Peterson Logging Company, and the Shiach Brothers operated with horse teams in the eastern sections of Bellevue adjoining Lake Sammamish. About 1895, another logging company established a mill at Wilburton Hill, and a booming company town sprang up around the mill. By 1916, much of the area had been logged off and the opening of the Lake Washington Ship Canal had lowered Mercer Slough by 9 to 12 feet, leaving the mill with so little water access to Lake Washington that it shut down in 1918.

In the 1880s and 1890s, Bellevue had established itself as a productive agricultural area. Fruit and vegetable gardens, orchards, and vineyards furnished considerable produce for Seattle markets and local canneries. Bellevue's prized Marshall strawberries were readily marketed in the city. Starting in 1918 and continuing until World War II, the annual Strawberry Festival was a major social event for the East Side. Poultry, bulb, and blueberry farms were important to the local economy in later years.

In 1916 William Schupp located a winter port and scotch drydock for six vessels of the American Pacific Whaling Co. at Meydenbauer Bay. During World War II, however, the Coast Guard leased the company's vessels as patrol craft and the port as a repair base, but a declining market and increased restrictions on the whaling industry caused them to cease operating after the war.

After the opening of the Mercer Island Floating Bridge in 1940, Bellevue experienced rapid population growth. In 1946, Kemper Freeman began the development of the town's key Bellevue Square, and in the same year the Bellevue Arts and Crafts Fair, now one of the nation's largest, had a modest beginning. The city was incorporated in 1953, and in 1955 was voted the nation's All American City.

In 1963 the completion of the Evergreen Point Floating Bridge provided further access to the city and aided the expansion of the industrial, marketing, and distributing base.

continued on page 215

This view of Bothell looking north across the Sammamish River dates from about 1915. At peak spring runoff seasons, much of the land along the river became inundated. The opening of the Lake Washington Ship Canal lowered the river nine to 11 feet. Photo by Asahel Curtis. Courtesy, Washington State Historical Society.

This view shows the waterfront at Kirkland, looking south toward Houghton, circa 1909. In the background the county-operated ferry *Washington of Kirkland*, launched in 1908, is stationed at the dock. Courtesy, Marymoor Museum.

VISION OF THE NORTHWEST

◆

Since the Pacific Northwest landscape lends itself remarkably well to aesthetic interpretation, through the years artists and photographers have flocked to the Seattle area, delighting in the impressive setting of water, forests, and mountains. Much of urban Seattle, in fact, seems built with picturesque vistas in mind.

The following pages abundantly display the variety and sheer beauty in the region in both its natural and man-made aspects. Here are period paintings, historical photographs on hand-tinted lantern slides on glass, and contemporary color photographs taken mostly by resident photographers.

The distinctive Northwest "school of art," also known as the "Northwest tradition," originated in the Seattle environs around 1940. The best-known artists were Mark Tobey, Morris Graves, Kenneth Callahan, and Guy Anderson; others included Ambrose Patterson and Clayton Price. Many were born in the Northwest in the first decade of this century, and during their childhoods Seattle began a dramatic cultural awakening.

Callahan summarized the main characteristics of the Northwest "school" as broken form and grayed color, a preference for tempera, and "leaning towards symbolism and expressionism; and the influence of Oriental art . . . a mystic essence." The artists also studied Asian philosophy and both Eastern and Western mythology, seeking alternatives to the increasingly restrictive national mode of regarding and representing reality.

For all their involvement with mysticism and a stylized depiction of the natural world, however, some of these artists—Tobey, notably—also took interest in the human sphere, and portrayed people caught up in city living. Remarkable also was the prolific Depression-era work of a self-taught "urban primitive" artist named Ronald Debs Ginther, a dedicated "Wobbly." His paintings, combining watercolors and India ink, depicted scenes of Skid Road with its down-and-outers and flophouses, union parades and brawls, and jail inmates.

The artists whose work, in a variety of media, is represented in the last six pages of this section have certainly been influenced by their surroundings. These pictures reflect the richness of color and subject matter available to artists, and, indeed, to all who dwell in the region.

Floral designs, symbols, and writing combine in this brightly colored quilt, made in Ohio in 1849. It crossed the continent, as most early King Countians did. It now belongs among other pioneer artifacts at Seattle's Museum of History and Industry. (MOHAI)

Top
The warship *Decatur* fired cannon balls, grapeshot, and mortar shells on January 26, 1856, during the Indian attack on Seattle. (MOHAI)

Bottom, left
The ship *Lucille* loads at Seattle during the Alaska Gold Rush, circa 1898. (MOHAI)

Bottom, right
Indians used adzes, fire, water, sandstone, and sharkskin (as sandpaper) to carve canoes from cedar logs. (MOHAI)

Opposite
Concentric rings of diamonds pattern this piecework quilt. Sometimes called the Blazing Star, this is one of many quilts which found their way to Seattle's Museum of History and Industry. (MOHAI)

Top, left
Flames and smoke engulfed the Grand Trunk dock in 1914. (MOHAI)

Top, right
The sky reflected a brilliant red as the Frye Opera House burned in the Seattle fire of 1889. Fire fighters hoped that the brick building would act as a fire-stop, but it, too, was finally taken by flames. (MOHAI)

Middle
H. Eastman's July 4, 1874 watercolor portrays a view of Seattle, looking toward Puget Sound. Courtesy, Phelps Stokes Collection, New York Public Library.

Bottom
The side-wheeler *Alida* stands in the foreground of this 1870 view of the Seattle waterfront. Seattle's second church, the "Brown Church," is on the left. (MOHAI)

Opposite
Looking north to Lake Union from downtown Seattle, this view was captured in 1915. (MOHAI)

Left
Visitors watch as boats make the transition from the fresh water of Lake Washington and Lake Union to the salt water of Puget Sound through Hiram M. Chittenden Locks in Ballard, Seattle's Scandinavian neighborhood. Courtesy, Seattle-King County Convention & Visitors Bureau.

Bottom
Brightly painted houseboats are often permanently moored on Lake Union. Once an inexpensive and offbeat kind of housing, they have increased in popularity and price.

Opposite
The downtown Seattle skyline continues to expand, and new buildings now crowd the horizon since this photo was taken in 1980. (MOHAI)

Top, left
The light of sunset reflects in the water surrounding fishing boats moored at Fishermen's Terminal. Photo by Russell Johnson, Silverlight Studio.

Top, right
University of Washington's Drumheller Fountain is in "Frosh Pond," which was constructed for the A-Y-P Exposition of 1909.

Bottom
Built during Seattle's World Fair in 1962, the Monorail runs from the site of the fair, Seattle Center, to downtown.

Opposite
The Arboretum, home to many indigenous trees and flowers, borders the University of Washington and Union Bay in Montlake.

Top
From a Washington State Ferry enjoy spectacular view of downtown Seattle the Cascade Mountains. Courtesy, Seattle-King County Convention & Visitors Bureau.

Bottom
Boating, when weather permits, is a popular local sport. A spinnaker, shown here, catches the wind, with the Space Needle in the background. Photo by Jonathan Ezekiel.

Opposite, top
Wet Wharf, a watercolor by the Seattle painter Jess Dan Canthorn. Puget Sound is an ideal area for watercolorists. Courtesy, West Seattle Art Club, Seattle Art Museum.

Opposite, bottom
Traditional Colours, an acrylic painting, is one of a thematic series by Donald J. Barrie. It depicts a Native American craftsman with blankets at Pike Place Market. Courtesy, Donald J. Barrie.

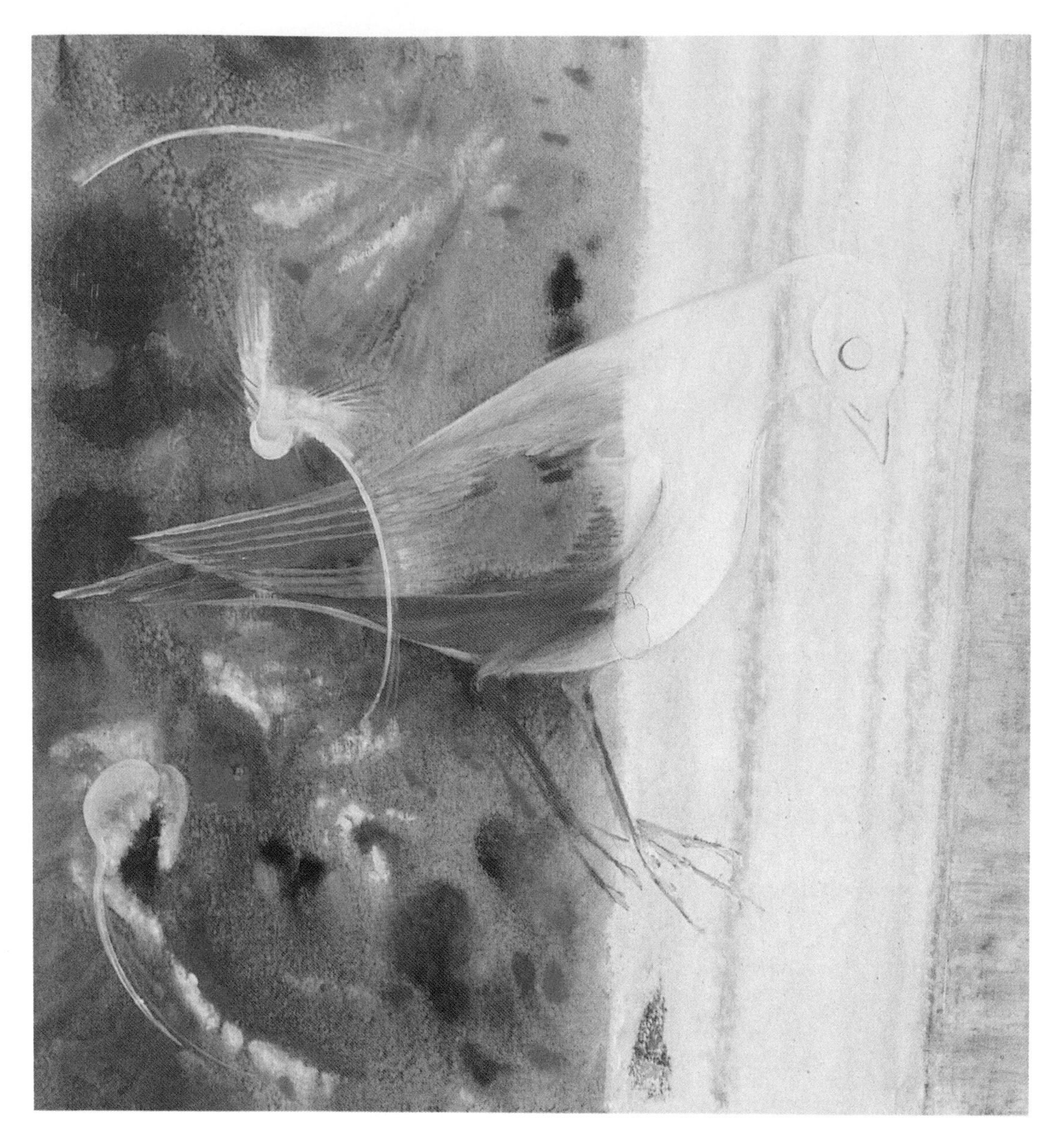

Top
Bird #4, The Multicolored One is a 1969 tempera on paper painting by Morris Graves. Graves worked toward simplicity and mysterious symbolism, often using birds or other small animals. His work grew increasingly abstract in 1950s and 1960s. Courtesy, Eugene Fuller Memorial Collection, Seattle Art Museum.

Bottom
Moss on the Trees, an oil painting, was done by Harold Wahl in 1959. His art often deals with the dynamic force of nature as manifested in natural details. Courtesy, Seattle Art Museum.

Opposite
Northwest Landscape was painted in oil on board by Kenneth Callahan in 1934, when the artist was 28 years old. Courtesy, Eugene Fuller Memorial Collection, Seattle Art Museum.

Top
McGilvra's Farm, a sculpture by Richard S. Beyer, is located at Madison Park. (See sidebar, page 174.) Photo by James Miller.

The Fool Killer, a wood sculpture in Fremont by Richard S. Beyer. (See sidebar, page 174.) Photo by James Miller.

Bottom, right
Mark Tobey's 1941 *View of Figures by Stalls* belongs to a series of paintings of Pike Place Market, entitled *Public Market Types*. Tobey used "white line" or "white writing" in many of his paintings, a form derived from a synthesis of Oriental brushwork and American abstractionism. Courtesy, Eugene Fuller Memorial Collection, Seattle Art Museum.

Opposite, top
Portage Bay was painted in 1954 by Australian-born artist Ambrose Patterson. He established the School of Painting and Design at the University of Washington in 1919. Courtesy, Eugene Fuller Memorial Collection, Seattle Art Museum.

Opposite, bottom
Boats, a 1930 oil on panel by Clayton S. Price, vividly captures the Northwestern milieu. Courtesy, Eugene Fuller Memorial Collection, Seattle Art Museum.

Top, left
Breadline on Western Avenue, Winter of 1934–5.

Above, left
The Great Depression Tapering Off, 1935–36, Shacktown.

Top, right
The Great Depression. Unemployed Battle Police.

Above, right
End of the Line—'Dehorns' Drinking Denatured Alcohol and Rum.

Paintings of Depression-era Seattle by R.D. Ginther. Courtesy, Washington State Historical Society.

continued from page 198

In 1966 the Bellevue Community College opened, further enhancing the city's already excellent educational facilities.

Medina

In 1876 Thomas L. Dabney purchased property on the site of the present city of Medina encompassing the point of land now named for him. Some of the other early pioneers of the area in the late 1880s and early 1890s were the families of Samuel Belote, M. Gigy, George Baum, and Thomas Burke.

Floyd Croft came to the area in 1894 and operated a shingle mill and raised tobacco on his farm. Dabney built a dock on his property in 1891, which later was used for the town's ferry dock. He also promoted the name "Flordeline" for the town, but lost out to Adelaide Belote, who named it Medina, after the sacred Moslem city of Saudi Arabia.

George Trapp started the town store in 1908, but it was soon sold. A telephone exchange was also an early feature of the town. After the 1900s, the lakeshore section of Medina became known as the "gold coast" for its many wealthy landowners and residents.

The community was platted in 1914, and in 1919 the Overlake Golf Course was established. The city of Medina, which also includes Evergreen Point, over which SR 520 approaches Seattle on the "new" floating bridge, was incorporated in 1955. The historic ferry dock building, which once housed a restaurant and waiting room, has become the city hall.

Yarrow Point

William Easter was the first to patent a claim on the little peninsula of land called Yarrow Point in 1886 and was followed in the same year by Ole Hanks. A small steamer named for Mrs. Easter, *The Edith E,* was built and launched from the Easter ranch in 1886.

Seattle financiers Bailey Gatzert and Jacob Furth established summer homes there in the late 1880s. Leigh S.J. Hunt also had a beautifully developed estate on the Point he named Yarrow, after a poem by William Wordsworth.

In 1888 Hunt helped establish the county's first municipal water district. Much of the point was logged off by Isaac Bechtel in 1907 for George Meacham, whose real-estate firm promoted and developed the Point in subsequent years.

Much of the Point was taken up with summer homes, but in 1902 a holly farm, which exported products across the United States, was established. Truck farming and chicken ranching once were undertaken on the Point. The town of Yarrow, now a gracious residential area, was platted in 1901 and incorporated in 1959.

Hunt's Point

The small peninsula of Hunt's Point (Evergreen and Yarrow points are located on either side) was named for Leigh S.J. Hunt, Seattle publisher and east side promoter, who purchased property there first secured by Marshall Blinn, Kitsap County lumberman in 1871.

In 1892 Francis Boddy and family built a house, sawmill, and greenhouses there. In 1906 William Meydenbauer purchased a home on Cozy Cove along the Point's west side. In 1955 the residents of this small but wealthy community voted to incorporate.

Clyde Hill

The city of Clyde Hill, believed to have been named for the Clyde River of Scotland, was first settled in 1884 by Hans Nicholson, whose acreage was later owned by Soren Sorenson and Adolph Peterson. Prior to World War II, much of the land was farmed by Japanese truck gardeners on leased land, but after the war the eastside population and development boom made residential development inevitable. The town was incorporated in 1953 in response to pressure from real-estate developers. In addition to having a scenic outlook on Lake Washington, the community had one industry, the Summit Winery.

Beaux Arts

Several members of Seattle's Western Academy of Fine Arts, founded by Sidney Laurence in 1908, came to the East Side the same year to establish an "artistic community," an active environment in which artists could develop their specialties. Frank Calvert and Alfred Renfro organized the village near the site of the George Miller pioneer farm of 1883. Although the dream of an art colony has faded, the community has become a fine residential community, incorporating in 1954.

Mercer Island

The beautiful residential community of Mercer Island, with an area of some six and a half square miles and situated in Lake Washington adjacent to Seattle, was named for Judge Thomas Mercer.

Although the island had attractive stands of timber, many potential homesites, and was opened to homesteading as early as 1861, permanent settlement began only in 1876. It was then that Vitus Schmid, a wagonmaker's apprentice from Baden, Germany, and John Wenzler, a cobbler from Chicago, filed the island's first donation land claim of 160 acres. After a series of misfortunes, the pair departed, but Schmid returned several years later to settle and establish a family there.

Charles Olds, an early settler, helped to establish the island's first school, and his daughter Alla became one of its early teachers. Olds also aided in the development of a local road improvement district in 1890.

Logging crews came to Mercer Island in the 1880s and by about 1900 most of the island's virgin timber had been taken. Although time has effaced most of the companies, their skid roads were evident for years.

Another early resident of the island, C.C. Calkins, who homesteaded on the island in 1887, purchased an additional 700 acres of land on the island's west side in 1888. Calkins had a magnificent vision of development for the community of "East Seattle," and proceeded to construct a ferry dock and a grand resort hotel on his property. Ferry service was provided from Leschi Park, on the Seattle side, to "East Seattle" and Bellevue's Meydenbauer Bay.

Calkins' ornately constructed hotel became the focus in the late 1880s of the blossoming of the "East Seattle" community into the cultural center of the island. Summer cottages, permanent homes, a store, post office, school, and telephone and water systems were all developed there.

Unfortunately the national panic and depression of 1893 ruined Calkins' business and dreams for development. After the structure was sold in 1902, it was used as a parental home for boys, a sanitarium, a boarding house, and a summer hotel, before it finally burned down in 1908.

While "East Seattle" was becoming a developed site, island pioneers were creating homesteads, dairy farms, and resorts. A series of ferry docks built around the island were left unused when the Lake Washington Ship Canal was opened in 1917. The water level of Lake Washington dropped by more than 11 feet, creating new waterfront for many islanders but property disputes for others.

A succession of steamers provided transportation in the early years.

One of the more interesting ferry landings was that of Fortuna Park with its dance hall pavilion, boating facilities, picnic grounds, and bathing beaches. The Park was well known to islanders and mainlanders alike, and was operated privately by Captain John L. Anderson, master for many years of the Lake Washington ferry fleet.

The east channel bridge was completed to the east side in 1924, and the islanders' long standing demand for a bridge connection to Seattle was realized in 1940.

Following years of debate over parallel administration of the island by a city and a town government, the island's citizens voted in a unified administration in 1970.

Today, one of the island's chief concerns is the widening of the I-90 corridor across the island. Despite the difficulties presented by the expansion, Mercer Island continues to be one of the finest residential communities in the area, known for its relaxed atmosphere, fine homes, and excellent schools.

SOUTHEAST

Newcastle

The Newcastle-Coal Creek area, located between Renton and Bellevue, is a historic district which was once of great economic importance to the development of Seattle and King County.

In 1862 William Perkins secured two claims in the area,

The old Bellevue school, located at 100th and Main, was built in 1892. The building, shown here in 1893, expanded in the 1910s and was used in later years for municipal offices. Courtesy, Marymoor Museum.

The lavish C.C. Calkins Hotel, built in 1890, was the focus of a magnificent resort complex at East Seattle on Mercer Island. The beautifully furnished hotel, equipped with its own electrical lighting system, had its own dock and steamer service as well as a 100-vessel boathouse with turkish baths and dozens of dressing rooms. (MOHAI)

and in the following year Edwin Richardson came upon a coal seam while surveying a townsite. When news of the discovery got out, a number of men rushed to file claims.

About 1866 Daniel Bagley, George Whitworth, P.H. Lewis, John Ross, Selucius Garfielde, and others organized the Lake Washington Coal Company that opened the "Seattle Mine" and shipped out 150 tons of coal in 1867.

Coal became the major industry of the region and remained so until the 1920s. A number of small companies continued to produce until after World War II.

A few board and batten miners' houses and the old community cemetery above Lake Boren are all that remain of the once productive town. The press of population will in a few short years completely envelop the once historic site of Newcastle.

Maple Valley

In 1870 John McCoy left Seattle to look for a homestead and found a suitable spot in the Cedar River Valley a few miles east of Renton. Later that year James Maxwell came to live with the McCoy family and stayed until 1873 when both families moved upriver and established farms in the heart of what is now Maple Valley.

In the late 1870s the three pioneer families of George Ames, C.O. Russell, and Henry Sidebotham located farms in the area and in 1882 started the community's first sawmill on the Maxwell farm. Ames, Russell, and Sidebotham selected the name Vine-Maplevalley for the community, but in later years this was shortened to Maple Valley.

C.O. Russell was instrumental in establishing the town's first schools on his land, laid out the townsite in 1887, and became the first postmaster in 1888.

Anticipating the arrival of the Columbia and Puget Sound Railroad in 1885, James Colman organized the Cedar Mountain Coal Company in 1884. The mine was worked until 1907 when the mineshaft encountered an impassable rock fault. It was not until 1920 that the coal seam was relocated and worked again. The mine was permanently closed in 1940.

Logging camps and lumber mills were established in the late 1880s. Dairy farming, poultry raising, and fruit growing were small but widespread activities throughout Maple Valley.

Although there is still some farming activity in the area, Maple Valley is today an exceptionally beautiful residential and lake resort community.

Hobart

Hobart, the area adjacent to Maple Valley, was first settled in the late 1870s by the families of Charles Peacock and Henry Sidebotham. At one time the area was heavily forested, but farmers cleared the land establishing produce, fruit, and dairy farms.

In 1895 a group of farmers built and operated a cooper-

This photo of Mercer Island homes was taken from the Lake Washington Floating Bridge.

This mining crew worked at Coal Creek in 1909. The mine, located just over a mile east of the Old Newcastle Mines, is sometimes referred to as "New Newcastle." Coal Creek was productive through World War I, but the main shafts closed forever in 1920–1921. Photo by Asahel Curtis. Courtesy, Washington State Historical Society.

ative sawmill on part of the Sidebotham property, and in 1898 the Columbia and Puget Sound Railroad extended its line through the area. The community was granted a post office in 1900 and adopted its name from Garett Hobart, vice-president under William McKinley. The English settled the area early on, as did the Swedes and Finns.

The Maple Valley Lumber Manufacturing and Loggers Supply Company was established there in 1899, and at one time Weyerhauser operated a lumber camp in the area, later donating five acres of its land for the town's school.

In 1912 William Wood and Iver Iverson established a successful lumber mill at Hobart, which logged large tracts of timber, hitting peak production about World War I. The company coined its own aluminum disc money called "hickeys," which were accepted as legal tender as far away as Seattle. The Wood and Iverson Mill continued into the 1930s when it sold out to the Baldridge Company. The last logging in the area ended in the 1940s, when the community reverted to an attractive farming and residential area.

Taylor

In the late 1890s the town of Taylor, now merely a site in the Seattle's Cedar River Watershed, was developed by the Puget Sound Fireclay Company on land purchased from pioneer Sam Galloway.

In 1892 Arthur A. Denny's Denny Clay Company was organized and took over the holdings of the Fireclay Company, and in 1903 a plant was established at Taylor to produce building and paving brick, roofing and drain tile, clay conduit, and other holloware. In 1905 the Denny-Renton Clay and Coal Company took over the plant and adjacent coal mines. Taylor's other industry was a saw and shingle mill built by Joe Donlan in the late 1900s and which operated until 1920. In the town's boom years of around 1910, the ethnically rich population soared to almost 1,000, and as many as 22 carloads of lumber, coal, and clay products were shipped from Taylor per day.

After the United Mine Workers' general strike in 1921–1922, the coal mine was closed, and subsequent efforts to mine coal ended in 1928. In 1927 the Gladding McBean Company took over the Denny-Renton operation, and continued it until 1947 when the city of Seattle condemned the townsite, by then part of its watershed. The clay plant machinery was moved to Renton, and the buildings of the town demolished, leaving only a pile of bricks to mark the site of the once prosperous town.

Black Diamond

In 1880 P.B. Cornwall, president of the Black Diamond Coal Company, began looking for a new source of high-grade coal to satisfy the company's markets. Attracted by reports of earlier successes in the Cascades, Cornwall sent V.E. Tull to investigate western Washington. He found the enormously rich deposits around Black Diamond, Franklin, and Ravensdale. Samples of coal sent to San Francisco for analysis proved to be of high quality, and thereafter the company began to purchase land and develop the site in earnest.

Over the many years of production at Black Diamond, the town was often the largest coal producer in King County. Miners at Black Diamond's Morgan Slope worked at a depth of 6,200 feet, or well over a mile below ground, lower than any other miners in the country. Working conditions were always hazardous, due to the inclines of mineshafts, black lung, and explosive gasses, and accidents occurred, including one in 1910 when 16 men were killed at the Lawson Mine.

Although there is still coal to be mined in the district, production costs and the availability of cheap competitive energies has meant minimal output in the coalfields.

Among the ethnic groups who settled in Black Diamond were Italians, Austrian-Slovenians, and Poles. The town of Black Diamond has, overall, fared better than many of its neighboring communities. Although the bustling hotels and shops are no longer evident, the town has held its own, and incorporated in 1961. Among the town's attractions are the Black Diamond Bakery and the Old Confectionery, now refurbished into one of the county's fine art galleries. The ancient train depot is being restored as the Black Diamond Historical Museum in order to preserve the unique heritage of the Green River Coalfields.

Ravensdale

The rich coal deposits of the McKay seam underlying the town of Ravensdale, a small community once located just north of Black Diamond, were first explored in 1880 by Victor Tull of the Black Diamond Coal Company. In 1885 a small village was established there around logging and farming activities. In 1890 the Leary Coal Company opened a mine there, which was taken over by the Northwest Improvement Company.

The original community had been named Leary, after the coal company, but was called Georgetown in later years when the Northwest Improvement Company laid out the town of Ravensdale just to the south in 1914. The combined communities proved to be the region's recreational center. Ravensdale was an ethnically diverse community with many Yugoslavian, Polish, Italian and Welsh families.

A tragic gas explosion in the mines killed 31 men in 1915, thoroughly disheartening the town and destroying its social fabric. Following the explosion, the Northwest Improvement Company closed the mine. The town, which had been incorporated in 1913, was dismantled and finally disincorporated in the 1930s.

In the late 1920s the Continental Coal Company worked several seams, and the town experienced a brief revival, but through the '30s the population again declined. In the late '30s another company acquired the mines and

Top
This residential area is located by the Sammamish River in Bothell.

Above
The Wood and Iverson Mill, erected at Hobart in 1912, became one of King County's major mills. After moving from Snohomish County, logging operations continued at the mill, shown here circa 1915, until the 1940s. Courtesy, Marymoor Museum.

Top
The *Millard T. Fillmore* docks near apartments built at the Kirkland Marina.

Above
A mining crew stands at the entrance to the Denny-Renton Clay and Coal Company Mine at Taylor, with the mine superintendent's offices to the left, circa 1911. Much of the coal mined here was used to fire the kilns which produced brick and clay tile for Seattle buildings. Courtesy, Renton Historical Museum.

worked them through World War II, but declining demand for coal, coupled with several additional fatal accidents in the 1950s, sealed the community's fate. The once prominent coal town is today little more than a memory.

Franklin

In 1884 the Oregon Improvement Company began to mine the rich McKay vein at Franklin on a steep hillside overlooking the Green River Gorge. By 1885 the first 7,000 tons of coal had been shipped, and the company town of Franklin was forming. That year, a masked and militant mob, organized by the Knights of Labor, drove from Franklin a small number of Chinese laborers who were brought in to work the Oregon Improvement Company's rail line.

The mines went through several major natural and social disturbances. By 1900 the mines reached peak production. Even though there was some mining activity through World War I, the community experienced a continuous decline.

Like other towns in the coalfields, the populace of Franklin was largely ethnic. In addition to blacks, there were Scots, Irish, English, Welsh, Belgians, and Italians at work in the shafts.

By the late 1920s, when coal production had declined drastically, Franklin was virtually reduced to a ghost town. The site of the mines, the beautiful Green River Gorge, is now a major state park.

A number of similar company towns in the Cedar and Green River valleys met a parallel fate. Bayne, Kummer,

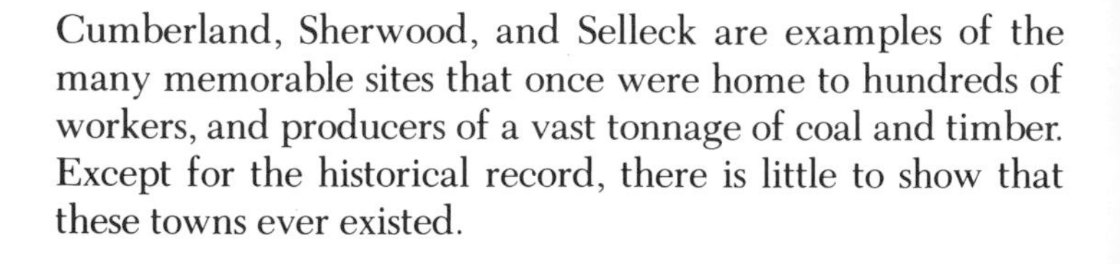
Cumberland, Sherwood, and Selleck are examples of the many memorable sites that once were home to hundreds of workers, and producers of a vast tonnage of coal and timber. Except for the historical record, there is little to show that these towns ever existed.

Enumclaw

In 1853 Allen Porter homesteaded on the prairie adjoining the upper White River near the site of the present city of Enumclaw. In the same year, a number of settlers, including a 36 vehicle wagon train led by James Longmire crossed the Naches Pass, which traverses the Cascade Mountains to the immediate south and east. Downriver at Muckleshoot Prairie, Dominic Corcoran and James Riley established homestead claims in 1853. Other settlers followed in the 1870s.

In 1884 Frank and Mary Stevenson platted a townsite called Enumclaw, after the ridge referred to in local Indian mythology as the place of thunder or the home of evil spirits. The Columbia and Puget Sound Railroad completed their extension to the townsite in 1885, utilizing land donated by the Stevensons, and soon businesses were established along the rail line.

The late 1880s were boom years for the development of the town and neighboring communities. Lumber mills and dairies were soon operating. Some of the local farmers were even caught up in the hop-growing craze of the late 1880s and early 1890s.

Among the ethnic groups that influenced the commu-

A visitors' cabin was located at Chautauqua (Ellisport) on Vashon Island's eastern shore, circa 1890. After 1888 the site was Chautauqua's permanent home. Residents, proud of their young community, improved their homes and gardens. (MOHAI)

This view of the town of Enumclaw facing the Cascades was taken in the 1900s. At that time Enumclaw had a vigorous economy of its own based on lumbering and agriculture. (MOHAI)

nity were the Austrian-Slovenians at Krain, and the French, Poles, Germans, and Scandinavians. The Danes, who arrived in the late 1880s, brought with them their preference for forming cooperatives. Among those formed were the Enumclaw Creamery Company, the Small Fruit Growers' Cannery and Farmers' Mutual Insurance Company.

After the depression of 1893, the White River Lumber and Shingle Company was purchased by Charles Hanson and associates and was renamed the White River Lumber Company. This became the primary industry of Enumclaw and one of the largest mills in King County, until consolidating with Weyerhauser in 1930.

After the town's incorporation in 1913, the city of Enumclaw became a major gateway to the Cascades along the Chinook Pass highway, and is also an entry to Mt. Rainier National Park. Since World War II, Enumclaw has become the home of the Farman's Pickle Company and the site of the annual King County Fair. The Crystal Mountain Ski Resort, Federation Forest State Park, and many other fine recreational facilities are located nearby.

SOUTHWEST

Greater Burien-Highline

The greater Burien-Highline area was first scouted for homesteading when young Mike Kelly climbed up over the Riverton Hill from the Duwamish River in 1869 to view the land below. Kelly returned in 1872 with his wife and newborn child to a newly built cabin and farm, where they grew vegetables and later planted acreage in hops. Their hop house was used for dances and social events by the community, which was named Sunnydale for Kelly's farm, and the first school class was taught in the Kelly cabin kitchen in 1874.

German immigrant Gottlieb Von Boorian, for whom the adjacent community of Burien was named, established himself southeast of Lake Burien in 1880. Many families followed the Kellys and Von Boorians, clearing land and establishing small farms. Promotion of the area initiated a land boom in the late '80s and greatly inflated land prices.

The earliest means of travel between farms and villages was the Military Road connecting Steilacoom and Seattle, which was begun in 1853 and completed in 1860. In 1905 Charles Schoening purchased the Von Boorian property on Lake Burien and constructed a hunting lodge on it, later developing a productive farm on the site. In the 1910s Stock Bros. Logging Co. was active in the Sunnydale area. In 1911 the Highland Park and Lake Burien Railway was organized to promote development of the area. This nine mile stretch of irregular, meandering road supported more or less regular electric railcar service from 1912 to 1929. The line was known affectionately as the "Toonerville Trolley" or the "Galloping Goose" for its many idiosyncrasies but its service succeeded in contributing to the development of the community.

In the early decades of the century, the region was principally devoted to residential development and farming. The Three Tree Point Community (as the area was popularly known) began to attract permanent residents as well as numerous picnickers and weekend vacationers. Poultry farms

Passengers disembark, circa 1912, from the steamer *Vashon* at Tree Point and head for the popular picnic grounds and resort homes in the vicinity. Courtesy, Williamson Collection, Puget Sound Maritime Historical Society.

Shown here are a post office and business buildings at Richmond Beach in 1906. Accessible by interurban railway and steamer, Shoreline became a favorite hunting and fishing area. Courtesy, Shoreline Historical Museum.

were common in Burien and Japanese-Americans established productive truck gardens there.

The adjacent city of Normandy Park began as a planned residential development of the Seattle Tacoma Land Company in 1929 and grew into a community of fine homes, incorporating in 1953.

Many new residents were attracted to the area during World War II to work in the nearby Boeing plants, and many remained after defense production came to an end. Today the Burien-Highline area is famous for the Seattle-Tacoma International Airport, which began development here in the late '40s on lands homesteaded over a century ago.

White Center

Directly to the north of the Burien area is the town of White Center, named at the toss of a coin by George White and Hiram Green in 1918. White won the toss and named the town.

The Edward Solomon family began farming in the community in 1870, but met with little success, and development of the area did not begin until the late 1880s, when Sam Carr and Tom Hood began logging there with oxen teams. Gottlieb Green established a mill there in 1888, which was succeeded by the Washington Lumber and Logging Company Mill in 1905.

Further development of the community was dependent upon improvement of the roads and transportation, so pioneers like Jacob Ambaum cleared roadbeds with horse teams. Ambaum aided George White and others to build the Highland Park and Lake Burien Railway, which brought many new residents in the 1920s. The town's location at the southern city limits of Seattle made it a desirable place for homesites, which were close to industries in the Duwamish Valley. World War II brought an unprecedented boom to the local economy, with White Center becoming a popular recreational spot, but the area today has reverted to residential pleasantries.

Des Moines-Zenith

The first settlers arrived in the Des Moines area in the 1870s. Among them was John Moore, who claimed land there in 1872 but later relinquished it. F.A. Blasher, who arrived in 1888 from Iowa, convinced other Midwesterners to follow him to the area, which was duly named Des Moines after their home town. The Des Moines Improvement Company was organized in 1889 to develop the community, and it platted the townsite and established the area community's first sawmill.

Despite considerable promotion and speculation, the community began to decline after 1890. This trend was reversed in 1903, however, as property once again was avidly sought by people seeking retreats from city life in Des Moines' pleasant country surroundings. In 1908, Annie and Herman (known as "Daddy") Draper established their home for children in the former Hyatt Hotel, built at Des Moines in 1890. Their barn was later converted into an "opry" house where children, raised by the Drapers, displayed their musical talents.

Beginning in the 1880s, a succession of small steamers served the community for several decades, ending their runs in 1919. Other access to the community could be gained by walking or riding to the Interurban stations at neighboring Kent or O'Brien. Even before the rutted mud or gravel roads to Des Moines were replaced by brick-surfaced roads in 1916, bus service was inaugurated to Seattle.

Although there were several attempts made to establish small industries, the community depended primarily on its lumber and shingle mills, chicken ranches, and truck gardens. During World War II, defense plants south of Seattle attracted a sizable number of new residents to the area.

The city of Des Moines, incorporated in 1959, is a residential city known for its fine marina and retirement facilities.

Vashon-Maury Islands

One of the earliest regions of King County to be discovered is that of Vashon and Maury islands, a short ferry ride to the southeast of present day Seattle. Captain George Vancouver of the British Navy discovered the islands on May 28, 1792, and named it for a friend, Captain James Vashon, later an admiral. Lieutenant Charles Wilkes of the United States Exploring Expedition of 1838–1842 charted Maury Island in 1841 and named it for William L. Maury, a member of his survey team. Although Vashon and Maury islands appear today to be a singular land mass, the two sections were apparently once separated by a shallow channel or a muddy land bridge depending upon the tides. Landfill was later deposited on the "portage" in order to allow a passable road between Vashon and Maury.

The islands were initially inhabited by the Shomamish, a Coast Salish speaking group related by culture and tradition to the other indigenous groups of Puget Sound. After the enforcement of the Point Elliot Treaty of 1855, the Duwamish, Suquamish, and allied tribes were relocated to their present reservation on the Kitsap Peninsula. Little remains of their presence on the islands.

After intermittent visits to the islands by ships seeking to harvest spar poles from the virgin forests of Douglas fir, occasional attempts to develop logging operations, an experiment in sheep grazing, and transient homesteading efforts, the first permanent settlement on the islands occurred in 1877. After an exploratory tour of the islands in the summer of that year, S.D. Sherman returned with his wife and four children to find shelter at "Ft. Necessity," an abandoned logger's shack. Sherman purchased a sturdy boat for transportation to and from Tacoma, the nearest marketing center. From the late

'70s onward, settlement of the islands proceeded continuously. Regular ferry service, which was predominantly oriented to Tacoma in the early years, commenced with the *Harry Lynn* and improved steadily over the years. Ferry service from Portage to Des Moines on the Seattle side was established in 1916, and regular island service has been maintained ever since.

The 1880s saw the development of the first saw and shingle mills, stores, schools, brickyards, and commercial boat service to Tacoma. About 1885, the Puget Sound Chautauqua Assembly was held here, and after several years of meetings, a permanent site was chosen on the east side of Vashon Island. Chautauqua was the island's first town to be formally platted. A wharf was constructed as well as cottages and a pavilion.

The '90s saw the large-scale cultivation of berry crops, especially strawberries, and greenhouses were constructed to furnish produce to Seattle and Tacoma markets.

In 1891 a floating drydock was towed to Quartermaster Harbor between the islands. The Puget Sound Drydock Company operations gave rise to the town of Dockton on Maury Island with its "piano row" of supervisors' homes.

In 1892 Vashon College was organized. In its heyday the college attracted more than 200 students, but in 1910 the main building on the campus was gutted by fire. Competition with other schools made rebuilding the college impractical.

The Martinolich Shipyard of Dockton completed its first vessel, *The Vashon*, a passenger steamer in 1905. Over a span of 25 years, this yard produced a series of purse seiners and other fishing boats, schooners, and mosquito fleet steamers. At its peak, the shipyard employed 285 people. Other industries developed over the years; among these were a fish cannery, a linoleum plant, and a canning company.

The remoteness of the islands has at times, over the years, produced the feeling that King County government cared little about the islands and their people. At various times there have been movements afoot to secede from King County, but none of them have succeeded.

The island developed the modern amenities such as telephone service in 1905, and electric light and power transmission was begun in 1915. A Campfire Girls camp was established on Vashon in 1921 and is still in operation.

Today Vashon-Maury Islands is probably best known for its world-famous K-2 skis. The island has retained much of its historic charm, and its relative isolation from the mainland allows it to maintain the atmosphere of an island retreat.

Federal Way-Poverty Bay

The populous but unincorporated district known today as the Federal Way-Redondo area was a region that developed relatively late. Before the advent of settlers, this area was intersected by Indian trails stretching from shoreline clam beds and campsites on Poverty Bay, to the interior of the White River Valley, where hop and vegetable farming attracted large numbers of seasonal laborers.

As early as 1870, Ernst F. Lange settled in the area, and in the following year, Sam Stone established a homestead on Poverty Bay, around which a small community called Stone's Landing formed in the following years. The vicinity around the Landing had already become a popular retreat for vacations and excursions, and regular steamer service was established by the mid 1880s.

The first school was established in the district in the early 1880s at French (now Mirror) Lake, and by 1890 T.T. Webb had settled at the crossroads later called Webb Center. That same year, the community of Buena was the first area of present-day Federal Way to be platted.

Beginning in the late 19th century, a number of sawmills and lumber camps worked the area. Today, the Weyerhaeuser Company has their impressive corporate headquarters just west of Interstate 5.

Weston Betts is credited with platting and improving the site around Stone's Landing in 1904, and by 1911 the community had a population of about 200, where stores, churches, and a post office were soon operating.

Although there are many attractive little communities in the area adjoining Poverty Bay on Puget Sound such as Lakota, Star Lake, Woodmont, Adelaide, Buena, Redondo, Harding, and Sacajawea, the region became known as Federal Way, after a school district named for the Pacific Highway, which was completed through the area in 1930 with the aid of federal funds.

The opening in 1955 of the Federal Way Shopping Center was followed by other large marketing centers, and in 1975 the remarkable Seatac Mall began serving the public. Although Federal Way is now one of the most rapidly developing areas of the county, its beautiful stretches of shoreline and recreational park facilities make it a desirable commuter community for nearby Tacoma and adjacent areas of King County.

NORTH

Shoreline

The Shoreline District is a large and well populated residential area located south of the King-Snohomish County line, and stretching from Puget Sound to Lake Washington.

George C. Fisher was the first homesteader to patent a claim in this heavily forested district in 1872, but because overland access to the area was extremely difficult, Shoreline remained sparsely settled for decades. Norwegian-born Mikel and Anna Lund pioneered here in 1883, and sponsored a number of their countrymen in farming, fishing, and logging.

In the late 19th century, a number of lumber and shingle mills worked the vicinity, and as they retreated, settlers began to improve the stump lots into workable farms.

Although much of Shoreline remains unincorporated, a "City of Richmond" was platted in 1889 adjacent to the Sound and named for George Fisher's ancestral home of Richmond, England. In 1910 the government added to the name, making it Richmond Beach. Through the 1900s much of Shoreline remained undeveloped, the forests alive with game and predators, and the lakes and streams an angler's delight, attracting many Seattleites.

As population increased, key improvements were made in transportation, including a dock at Richmond Beach, a line of the Great Northern Railway, and an auto road to Seattle. In 1915 the Pacific Highway was finished from Seattle to Everett through Bothell along Shoreline's eastern margin.

After logging operations had begun to clear the timber, other small industries operated in the area around Richmond Beach. In 1909, the fireboat *Duwamish* was built at Point Wells, where Standard and Shell oil companies later erected tank farms.

The most important activities in the local economy, however, were in agriculture. Richmond Beach, the Highlands, and vicinity were known for their magnificent strawberry crop, which supplied the neighboring cities of Seattle and Everett. Other farmers were involved in dairy, egg, and poultry raising.

Among the other notable communities in Shoreline, Lago Vista was developed in the late '20s and early '30s, Echo Lake was developed as a bathing beach after 1917, and the Boeing Company cleared and developed the Innis Arden section beginning in the early 1940s. Lake Forest Park, Shoreline's only incorporated community, owes its name, presumably, to Ole Hanson, former mayor of Seattle who is credited with naming it after a city near Chicago.

The Seattle to Everett Interurban, which had been completed in 1910, played a large part in developing Shoreline. The Shoreline community is presently a noted residential district with excellent lake and forest view properties and is the home of Shoreline Community College.

Stevens Pass

One of the most scenic highways in Washington State follows the course of the Skykomish River through Stevens Pass in Northeastern King County. Engineer John F. Stevens, for whom the Pass was named, surveyed a difficult section of railway grade through this Cascade route for the Great Northern Railroad in 1890–1891.

Railroad construction attracted large numbers of laborers, some of whom remained to settle the area. From the outset, the local economy was tied to development of the railway, and during various construction periods, the small station towns boomed. During peak construction periods, the hotels and saloons of Skykomish were said to have run 24 hours a day. Further exploration of the area led to the development of several lumber and shingle companies that produced shakes and ships lumber. Several mining operations were also organized to produce gold, silver, copper, lead, coal, and iron. The Baring Granite Works, located near Skykomish, produced granite used in constructing the main buildings at the State Capitol in Olympia and office buildings at Seattle and other cities. Baring Granite also furnished many of Seattle's curbstones and memorial markers.

Other communities sprang up along the rail and river route, among them Alpine and Berlin, the latter called Miller River after World War I, which spawned several mining and milling concerns.

The small community of Wellington achieved unpleasant notoriety in 1910 when a freak storm precipitated a catastrophic avalanche, destroying two stalled trains at Windy Point and killing 96 passengers and crew. A new tunnel, nearly eight miles in length, was cut through the Cascades in 1929, eliminating the dangerous grades and switchbacks that plagued the railway in earlier years. This tunnel remains the longest in the Western Hemisphere.

The community of Scenic Hot Springs was the site of a delightful resort hotel operated by J.V. Prosser. This remarkably beautiful location attracted many tourist and sport fishermen in the early part of the century.

The Stevens Pass communities are now perhaps best known as waypoints to one of Washington State's fine recreational skiing complexes, the western gateway to the region, often referred to as the "American Alps."

Above
This view along Railroad Avenue in Skykomish, circa 1911, shows new buildings erected after the fire of 1904. The tallest building in the center is the Sky Hotel, built in 1904, which was later renamed the Molly Gibson. (MOHAI)

Opposite
Men ride on tracks at the Black Diamond Mine in the 1920s. Photo by Asahel Curtis. Courtesy, Renton Historical Museum.

NEIGHBORHOOD AND COMMUNITY DEVELOPMENTS 1981-1996

UNIVERSITY DISTRICT

Construction has continued year after year, mainly on the University campus and in the district business center.

WHITE RIVER

The site of the former Longacres racetrack in Renton was purchased and is being developed as training and office space by the Boeing Company.

Recently Emerald Downs Race Track was opened near Auburn, a replacement for Longacres, which was closed and in the 1990s the Muckleshoot tribe opened a large gambling casino.

SNOQUALMIE VALLEY

Dairy farms are still found near Carnation but large suburban home tracts are also being developed nearby.

The once quiet sawmill town of Preston is located near suburban developments and its population is expected to increase in the years ahead.

Though once considered distant from Seattle, North Bend is beginning to attract many suburbanite families.

SAMMAMISH

Residents of Issaquah may travel up Highway 405 which now extends up the east shore of Lake Washington and north to Everett.

Once a rural village, Redmond today is a booming suburb, home to the huge Microsoft campus and various other modern technology companies. It also has large residential developments within its city limits and the population has nearly quadrupled in the last 25 years from 11,000 to more than 40,000.

Within the last decade, recently incorporated Woodinville has attracted shopping centers, residential developments and several new and thriving businesses.

Bothell, which straddles the King-Snohomish County line, is thriving, its population near 50,000 and a branch campus of the University of Washington is being built there.

EASTSIDE AND LAKE

The shipyard has now completely vanished from Kirkland-Houghton, replaced by Carillon Point, a large business park that includes restaurants and a hotel.

Bellevue has expanded through annexations and new construction. The number of residents continues to increase rapidly. At latest count (1997) the population was estimated to be about 104,000.

The most expensive home in the Northwest is being build in Medina by Bill and Melinda Gates (of Microsoft fame). This modern mansion is replete with technological advances and with part of it constructed underground on a slope above Lake Washington. The cost is anticipated to be in excess of $40 million.

Hunts Point, Yarrow Point, and Medina are contiguous and are now jointly referred to by locals as the "Gold Coast" because of the wealthy families who reside there.

Clyde Hill, on the scenic hillside overlooking a golf course, Lake Washington, and in the distance Seattle and the snow-capped Olympic Mountains, scores of new homes have risen during the past two decades.

In the 1980s, Interstate 90 that crosses Mercer Island was widened and landscaped concrete lids built over parts of the highway. The island thus gained parks, gardens, and walking paths.

Opposite page
Despite a regional recession, work was well under way in October 1982 to transform the skyline of Bellevue. A downtown core of low-rise buildings surrounded by parking lots grew with great energy and sophistication into an energetic commercial district of distinctive architecture and polished retail centers. Photo by Skip Howard Photographs (neg # 82100X)

Microsoft headquarters in Redmond has expanded dramatically over the last 15 years. Photo by Rich Andrews, Microsoft.

SOUTHEAST

Developers of homesites have discovered Newcastle, now incorporated and with a population already in excess of 8,000.

A growing number of middle class families have been attracted to Enumclaw, within commuting distance of various Boeing plants, Microsoft, and several major new businesses. During World War II, its population was about 2,600. Today it numbers more than 10,000.

SOUTHWEST

During the late 1980s in Burrien-Highline, part of the area incorporated as the City of Sea-Tac, is now home to more than 23,000 persons.

Federal Way, now incorporated, is one of Seattle's largest suburbs, with a population of about 75,000 residents.

CHAPTER 15

CHANGING TIMES: 1981-1996

Mt. Saint Helens, dormant since 1857, helped celebrate the dawn of a new decade. On March 28, 1980, this symmetrical peak began spewing steam, ash, and small boulders from its crater. Geologists warned a more violent eruption was likely. Their prediction came true at 8:39 a.m. on May 19, when an explosion blew the top and side off the 9,677-foot peak. Flood waters, mud slides, ash and forest fires resulted. Several persons who had not evacuated the area were killed. The eruption made headlines around the world.

THE ECONOMIC SEESAW

The Seattle-King County newspapers published during the 1980s frequently headlined the economic situation of the area. Mirroring the country as a whole, at first the news was sour for the most part, but then turned sweeter as the decade progressed and unemployment figures dropped as production figures escalated.

Articles about the "worst recession since the 1930s" framed front pages in 1982 along with reports of interest rates as high as 17% and rising inflation figures. The number of unemployed equaled 10% of the State's work force. This sick economy resulted in insufficient tax dollars to provide for the social agencies attempting to assist record numbers of hungry and homeless families. A $144 million state deficit in 1982 caused headaches for Governor John Spellman and legislators. To help balance the budget, the legislature in July approved a state lottery. Critics called it a game that victimized the poor and compulsive gamblers, but the popularity of the lottery exceeded everyone's expectations. Before Christmas, a month previous to predictions, a total of 45 million $1 tickets had been sold.

A couple of examples indicate the seriousness of the recession:

During the late 1970s the Boeing Company had unveiled two new jet liners but then their orders for new planes fell to the lowest level in 20 years, forcing a 1982 reduction of 8,900 in their work force.

Seattle First National, the largest bank in the state, suffered severe image problems during 1982. Causes included a heated feud over employee unionization, a consumer boycott, and a threat to move credit card operations to South Dakota if voters approved an interest-rate lid. The bank lost $165 million when Penn Square Bank in Oklahoma failed, and suffered more losses when a $1.2 billion loan to oil and gas producers was defaulted after energy prices plummeted in late 1981. The Bank's debt rating fell and three top executives took early retirement. Then, on July 1, 1983, BankAmerica of California acquired the historic Seattle financial institution for $250 million in cash and preferred stock and $150 million in capital investment.

At the same time, the timber industry faced an economic downturn. This was due to many causes, among them declining timber prices after sky-high interest rates reduced construction, a declining Japanese demand for finished lumber, and increasing competition from Canadian and Southern forests. Several small timber companies declared bankruptcy and even the industry giant, Weyerhaeuser, announced plans to close four Washington State mills.

By 1983, the financial picture was brighter. Layoffs at Boeing were reversed with an increase of 3,000 employees. Military and space contracts that year in the Boeing Aerospace Division totaled a record $2.3 billion.

During 1985 Boeing reported a record $13.7 billion in jet orders. The next year the giant aeronautical company landed orders for 341 planes worth $19 billion. Many of these orders were for the new 747 jumbo jet, each worth $100 million or more. Great Britain ordered six 707s equipped with airborne warning and control systems (AWACS), an order worth $1 billion. In 1988, Boeing sold more than 630 jets, 100 of them to Lease Finance Corporation of California, a $4.6 billion order. That year the Boeing payroll grew by 7,500 jobs to a total of 96,600.

Photograph by Victor Gardaya (MOHAI)

Photographs (above) made during a Boeing employees open house, 7/21/91. We see inside the largest building in the world, the 747 plant in Everett. Interior views show the main assembly line for the 767 and the 747. The Everett plant is located north of Seattle just outside of King County, but Boeing is an economic force throughout the region. Arden Gordon Collection (MOHAI) (Roll 14-28,14-11)

Historic Pioneer Square is Seattle's oldest residential area, now a major visitor attraction with restaurants, galleries and lively clubs. Courtesy, Seattle-King County Convention and Visitors Bureau.

The latter half of the 1980s saw the importance of Microsoft's successes being widely recognized. And not only Microsoft, but an increasing number of other advanced technology companies developed in King County. In 1989, the year Washington celebrated its centennial of statehood, the economy boomed. Microsoft's Bill Gates gained national fame as the country's youngest billionaire. This highlighted the point that Seattle and King County, so long dependent on Boeing and allied companies, were developing diversified economies. Boeing suffered a severe strike at the end of the decade, but the development of business diversity diluted the effects on the economy of Seattle and King County.

CRIME STORIES

During the decade crime generated almost as many headlines as the economy. Throughout this period the "Green River killer" was at work. In 1982, six bodies of strangled prostitutes were found along the forested banks of the Green River. The next year six more were discovered and in 1984 four more, not all of them near the Green River. From time to time in years that followed, more women were found murdered and added to the Green River list. Then the killer seemed to stop and so far has not been found.

The top crime story of 1983 was the murder of 13 persons at the Wah Mee gambling club in Seattle. This, the worst mass murder in the city's history, was the work of three young men who were sentenced to long prison terms or, in one case, the jury decreed death, a sentence which was appealed.

In 1984 Robert Baldwin owed $110 rent on his Yesler Terrace apartment. King County Detective Michael Raburn, an eviction notice in hand, knocked on Baldwin's apartment door. The door opened, a sword cut down viciously, and Raburn fell mortally wounded. After a 17-hour standoff, police stormed the apartment and shot Baldwin 21 times in the back. A jury ruled the shooting was justified, a result that angered many in the black community.

White supremacists became active in the Seattle area in 1986 and 23 of them were indicted on rack-

Nurse is first $1 million winner! Million-dollar lottery winner Jana Page hugs her husband, Bob, as second-place winner Mark Freeman, left, and KING-TV moderator Dick Klinger look on. Photo by Mike Siegel , *Seattle Times.*

eteering charges by a Seattle grand jury. Eleven pleaded guilty, one was convicted of the earlier killing of a Missouri state trooper, and ten eventually were convicted of racketeering charges in a federal court trial in Seattle. Richard Scutari, the organization's security chief, avoided capture until March 1986, then pleaded guilty to charges of racketeering, conspiracy and armed robbery. A federal judge sentenced him to 60 years in prison.

By far the largest crime story of 1986 was the conviction of David Lewis Rice for the stabbing and bludgeoning deaths of attorney Charles Goldmark, his wife, and two young sons on the previous Christmas Eve. Rice, posing as a delivery man, forced his way into the home. He was believed to hold a grudge against Jews and Communists but the Goldmarks were not Jewish. Twenty years earlier Goldmark's late father and mother had been involved in a much reported libel case in which they successfully sued to clear themselves of charges that they were Communist sympathizers.

During the late 1980s, several news items reported on the Los Angeles gangs that were moving to Seattle and environs to seek new markets for drugs. Drive-by shootings, gang-related murders, and sales of cocaine became more common in the inner city. The concern increased that this gang activity was attracting increasing numbers of local young people to become members. This activity branched into some of the suburban cities and law enforcement throughout the county began to combat the problem.

MEDICAL ADVANCES

AIDS struck in Washington State in 1982. During the decade about 1,600 cases were diagnosed in the state and about half of whom died before 1990. University of Washington scientists began working to develop a vaccine for humans.

After 20 years of successful kidney and cornea transplants, the University Medical Center in 1985 began performing heart and bone transplants. About 55 heart transplants had been performed by 1990. The region also aided in the development of artificial-heart technology. Barney Clark, a Burien dentist, on December 2, 1982, became the first long-term recipient of a Jarvis artificial heart. He survived for 112 days. The device is used primarily today to keep patients alive while they await heart transplants. Seattle employers were among the leaders in the nation to ban cigarette smoking from the work place because of the health hazard. By the end of the decade, restaurants, theaters, bars, and other gathering places were posting no-smoking signs.

GOVERNMENT

New names making political headlines in 1982 included Booth Gardner, chosen by voters as Pierce County Executive and in 1984 elected Governor of the state. Norm Rice, Seattle City Councilman, would serve as mayor of the city in the 1990s. Brock Adams, former Congressman and Cabinet secretary, began his campaign to become a senator with polls showing him far behind incumbent Slade Gorton but when the votes were counted, he took the seat from Gorton by two percentage points. Charles Royer, Seattle's mayor in 1986, was rebuffed by a reluctant Metro Council when he tried to convince them to locate the new sewage plant on the Duwamish River rather than expanding the plant at West Point. Garbage and sewage disposal problems continue as the population increases.

Washington voters during the 1980s rotated the two major parties in and out of control in Olympia. In March 1988, conservative state Republicans engineered a Pat Robertson victory in their party caucuses. This shocked

Senator Henry M. Jackson, left, and Senator Warren G. Magnuson are shown together in 1980 photograph. The two Democrats formed a powerful team for the 28 years they served together in the U.S. Senate, and gave Washington state considerable clout in Washington D.C. Photo by Barry Wong, *Seattle Times.*

Newly-elected Seattle Mayor Norm Rice greets a young constituent with a hearty handshake during festivities at the Seattle Children's Museum in February, 1990. Next to Mayor Rice is young Aram Herschenson, who headed the special campaign committee "Kids for Rice". Photo by Skip Howard Photographs (neg # 900202-12).

many moderates who preferred George Bush or Bob Dole as a candidate. In November, the majority of Washingtonians joined voters in nine other states in supporting losing Democratic presidential candidate Michael Dukakis.

During the decade, Washington State lost its two most effective and popular Democratic Senators, a team that had served the state well for nearly 30 years—Warren G. Magnuson and Henry "Scoop" Jackson. In 1980 Slade Gorton defeated Magnuson who died a few years later. Jackson died of a ruptured aorta on September 1, 1983, while still in office. Governor John Spellman appointed former Governor Dan Evans, a moderate Republican, to the vacant Senate seat until a special primary election. The popular Evans was handily elected and served out the remaining five years of Jackson's term. However, he found no joy in the other Washington and refused to run for re-election.

King County government also was busy during the decade. To illustrate the sort of activity in the county courthouse, consider the year 1984. Randy Revelle was County Executive. He included in his goals the passage of a long-awaited comprehensive land use plan and the opening of the new city jail. The County Council made several changes in the land use plan and the new state-of-the-art jail, at Fifth Avenue and James Street, still sat empty six months after it was to have opened because of trouble with the locking system. During the year, the county bought development rights to more than 2,000 acres of farmland in order to preserve it as open space. Also King County purchased several hundred acres east of Issaquah as part of the planned Cougar Mountain Regional Wildlife Park.

WPPSS FIASCO

At the outset of the '80s, The Washington Public Power Supply System, known as WPPSS, (pronounced WOOPS) was in trouble. By 1982, the system was attempting to persuade utilities to pay for mothballing two of five nuclear plants then under construction. Instead, projects 4 and 5 were abandoned and the court was asked to decide who should pay the $7 billion debt for their partial construction.

The next year WPPSS defaulted leaving investors holding $2.25 billion in nearly worthless bonds. It was the biggest municipal default in U.S. history. WPPSS, because of its financial dilemma was later forced to mothball projects 1 at Hanford and 3 at Satsop. However,

Above
Seattle has gained an international reputation as a city supportive of art and artists. Here, at the Pratt Fine Arts Center opened in 1976 by the City of Seattle Parks and Recreation Department, renowned glass artist Dale Chihuly (right) demonstrates the talent and teamwork that have made him famous. Photo by Skip Howard Photographs (neg # 0X830Y).

Right
Seattle's Pike Place Market is world-famous for its fresh seafood and produce, and its lively arts and craft scene. Courtesy, Seattle-King County Convention and Visitors Bureau.

after 10 years of construction, Nuclear Project 2 at Hanford received a federal license to generate electricity in 1984, only to have the Department of Energy shut the plant down the following year because of safety concerns. Permanent closure, which followed in 1988, caused the loss of 16,000 jobs in the Hanford area.

WPPSS appeals reached the State Supreme Court in 1984 where the judges refused to reverse their earlier ruling that the State's public utilities had no authority to sign construction agreements with WPPSS. In separate cases, several employees of WPPSS contractors were convicted of fraud.

THE ENVIRONMENT

Washington residents care very much about their natural surroundings. Residents of Seattle and most suburbs, aware of the mountains of garbage on soon-to-be-filled dump sites, took advantage of large-scale and innovative recycling programs being started in their cities. These programs are touted as some of the most successful in the country.

Environmentalists were active on many fronts throughout the decade. Their most publicized effort was the battle to preserve what little old-growth forests remained. They argued that these few forests provided shelter for many living creatures including the spotted owl that could not survive elsewhere. Furthermore, these forests, hundreds of years in the developing, were irreplaceable.

Above
Would-be captors of a sea lion check their net while supporters of the mammals display their signs at the Ballard Locks. Photo by Betty Odeser, *Seattle Times*.

A California sea lion enters a specially designed trap installed on a floating platform in Shilshole Bay. State and federal officials hope to capture sea lions, which are gorging themselves on wild steelhead trout, and move them to the Washington coast. The sea lions are endangering a run of fish that gather at the Ballard locks to begin their spawning journey into fresh water. Photo by Jim Lott, *Seattle Times*.

Sea lions, after discovering that steelhead salmon congregated at the foot of the Ballard locks fish ladder had decimated the salmon runs. Several futile attempts to keep the sea lions away, especially the largest male leader, named Herschel, cost nearly $320,000 in the late 1980s. These attempts, including shipping the worst offenders to California, failed to control the voracious appetites of these large beasts. Another area-wide problem resulted when too many commercial fisherman went after not enough fish. The state's fishing fleet, most vessels moored in Seattle, were facing lean years. Managers tried to balance survival of the salmon with the needs of the fishing industry. They further reduced the days of the commercial fishing season and the Fisheries Department and Puget Sound Indian tribes reached agreement on joint management of South Sound chinook salmon stocks.

Nature went to extremes during the mid-'80s, offering the driest January on record in 1985, then in November cascading 17.4 inches of snow in Seattle, which often receives none over a winter. Temperatures sank to a record low for Seattle of 10 degrees Fahrenheit and thick fogs snarled traffic. The summer of 1987 brought one of the driest summers on record. Only two inches of rain fell between the beginning of June and the end of October, months when average rainfall is 9 inches. As a result, many Cascade Mountain lakes, sources of water supplies, shrank to puddles and use of water was restricted. Eventually the watering of lawns was entirely banned. Then in mid-December, heavy rains quickly refilled mountain reservoirs and restrictions were lifted.

Concern over possible water shortages would continue into the future. At the end of the decade, the population in King County stood at about 1.5 million, an increase of 250,000 during the '80s. About one-third of these were Seattle residents and it was the Seattle water system that supplied the needs of several burgeoning suburbs. Different solutions to anticipated water shortages were being researched.

Four major oil spills occurred in Washington waters during the decade, which reminded residents of why the state had rejected the Northern Tier Pipeline Company's efforts to build an oil pipeline under Puget Sound.

Fear of environmental disaster was focused on nuclear waste during the 1980s. The Hanford Nuclear Reservation was named the nation's most polluted site. Documents indicated the plutonium reactor had released high levels of radiation, especially in the early years of plutonium production. The Federal Government funded health studies on residents who lived nearby and some efforts were made to clean up the reservation.

Another major story concerned pollution of Puget Sound. Ernesta Barnes, regional head of the Environmental Protection Agency, and the national director, William

Left
The downtown Seattle Art Museum, designed by architect Robert Venturi, opened to rave reviews in 1991. Courtesy, Seattle-King County Convention and Visitors Bureau.

Below
Opening day ceremonies at the newly remodeled Key Arena, formerly the Coliseum, at the Seattle Center. "The Key" is homecourt to the Seattle Sonics. Arden Gordon Collection (MOHAI) (Roll 59-7).

Seattle's lively and dynamic waterfront offers sightseeing, dining and shopping galore. Courtesy, Seattle-King County Convention and Visitors Bureau.

Ruckelshaus, described toxic sediments, unhealthy bottomfish and contaminated shellfish, problems that had been worsening for years. Ruckelshaus offered $1.6 million for studies, which he called a down payment to show EPA's concern. A new environmental group called the Puget Sound Alliance, was formed and pollution of Washington's waters was one of the top issues in the 1984 gubernatorial campaign which resulted in the election of Booth Gardner.

THE SEATTLE CENTER

The Seattle Center, site of the world's fair of 1962, was wearing out. In 1983, city officials felt they had to begin repairing leaking roofs, painting and creating new uses for unused meeting rooms, and planning for proper uses for the modern age. City Hall grudgingly supplied funds to take care of some of the problems. Mayor Charles Royer called Ewen Dingwall out of retirement to assist. Dingwall, a board member during the Seattle Center's best years, had also acted as consultant before being named Director. He convinced the City Council they were too stingy and soon had funds to properly maintain the buildings and grounds, but the $90 million convention center he hoped would be sited on the Seattle Center grounds went downtown. And the new Seattle Art Museum he hoped would replace Memorial stadium also was sited downtown. But the new Bagley Wright Theater opened at the Center and soon other new buildings would be added, including the completely renovated Coliseum, now called Key Arena, and the Children's Theater. The Pacific Science Center developed new programs and brought in popular traveling attractions such as an exhibit of Chinese science and history through the centuries. Soon the Seattle Center was as popular as ever.

TRANSPORTATION

With increasing population and more and more vehicles using the streets and highways, traffic gridlock was being experienced almost daily at certain hours of the day. There were more and more discussions concerning the need for light rail. In 1988, voters of King County, by more than two to one, approved a proposition calling for an accelerated development of a rail-transit system. The measure was advisory and did not consider financing nor location of the system. The proposition urged local officials to provide a light rail transit system by the year 2000—a decade earlier than the plan previously adopted by the Puget Sound Council of

Inside Metro's underground bus tunnel in downtown Seattle, April, 1994. This is the Westlake Center station, one of 5 sophisticated, uniquely designed transit stops under the city streets. After nearly 5 years of difficult construction, the tunnel was finished in 1990. Arden Gordon Collection (MOHAI) (Roll 29-10).

Many new buildings were added to the skyline of downtown Seattle during the 1980s, including the major development known as Westlake Center. A nighttime view in December shows this busy retail and commercial center decorated brightly for the holiday season. Photo by Skip Howard Photographs (neg # 881202-21).

Governments. Still, no light rail services existed in the mid-1990s, largely because of the high costs of construction, though "final" plans were being developed.

Even the State's reliable ferry service hit rough waters in 1985. After parts of the Hood Canal Floating Bridge sank in a severe windstorm, tolls were re-imposed to pay for the repairs. But a judge declared these tolls were illegal, and the State suffered a $5.2 million revenue loss. Ferry users were asked to take up the slack. A few months later, an out-of-court settlement on a controversial $106 million contract for building new ferries provided more worry. A new chief officer was hired and ferry fares were increased. Later, new-style smaller and faster water craft to use on Sound crossings were being considered.

This 1994 holiday season view from the balcony of Westlake Center takes in the pedestrian plaza created by the closure of Pine Street to through traffic between 4th and 5th Avenues. Holiday shoppers in downtown Seattle shared the street with delivery vehicles, bicycles, and horse drawn carriages. A carousel offered free rides for everyone. In 1996, under pressure from some retailers, Pine street was reopened to through traffic. Arden Gordon Collections (MOHAI) (neg # 960647-17).

EDUCATION

The two biggest stories of the decade involved a teacher's strike and a branching of university services.

The Seattle Schools strike of 1985 was the longest in history. It dragged on for 19 days as students and parents grew increasingly frustrated at the delay. Finally Governor Booth Gardner called both sides to Olympia, insisted on a settlement, and stayed with the negotiators until 5 a.m. to gain an agreement. The strike cost about $1.1 million, pushed the end of school for 43,000 students back into July, and resulted in resignations or retirement of 26 teachers.

Two years later, Governor Gardner proclaimed 1987 to be "The Year of Education" and asked for a $1.5 billion improvement package. The legislature did not provide all that he requested but did agree to increase teacher salaries and to fund smaller class sizes.

The Higher Education Coordinating Board presented an ambitious plan to create four new branch University campuses in the State by 1995. One of these called for a large University of Washington branch campus in Bothell.

In 1988 the Seattle School District board, after a year of planning and hearings, voted to end its ten-year desegregation plan by substituting a "controlled choice" system to allow most parents to send their children to their first or second choice of school. This allowed more students to enroll in schools near their homes.

NEW SKYLINES

Seattleites complained in 1987 about downtown's mammoth construction projects that complicated driving in the area. The most obvious distractions were the Metro bus tunnel which opened in 1990; the Washington State Trade and Convention Center over Interstate 5, the first section of which opened in 1988; and the Westlake Mall project which included building an office tower and retail complex in the city's heart.

Also in February 1987, the University of Washington Husky Stadium was being enlarged. Construction of the 20,000-seat addition on the north side of the football field had proceeded quickly. But when some temporary guy wires stabilizing the heavy roof were prematurely removed, the entire cantilevered structure folded earthward like a bellows. Luckily, no one was killed or injured.

Building boomed throughout the decade. Sally MacDonald, a *Seattle Times* reporter, described it this

Above
The 1985 skyline looking east to Mt. Rainier. Photo by Paul Miller, *Seattle Times*

Opposite above
Some days you can see forever, as in this view of downtown Seattle and beyond. Enclosing Elliott Bay in a protective embrace is the West Seattle peninsula tipped by Duwamish Head, and across Puget Sound are the dim outlines of Vashon Island, the Kitsap Peninsula and the south end of Bainbridge Island. Photo by Matt McVay, *Seattle Times.*

Opposite bottom
High above Elliott Bay from the Admiral Way viewpoint in West Seattle could be seen a history lesson in the downtown skyline in 1985. To the far left, finished in 1962 for the Seattle World's Fair was the Space Needle. To the far right was the bright terra cotta of the Smith Tower, the tallest building west of the Mississippi when it was built in 1913. To its left was the brand new holder of that honor, the 76-story Columbia Center. Photo by Skip Howard Photographs (neg # 850804)

way: "Capital amassed in the '80s helped build Seattle's new crystal skyline and the chateau-styled suburbs sprawling east to the Cascades, south to Tacoma, and north to Everett." Bellevue built its own skyscrapers. Young families moved to newly incorporated suburbs such as Federal Way, Mill Creek and SeaTac. Single adults and couples tended to move the other way, opting to live in high rise condominiums close to downtown. Joining the area's population were many Californians coming north to make homes in the area, touted time and again as the most livable in the country. Added were a mix of immigrants from Vietnam, Cambodia, and Central and South America. A few statistics prove the point. In 1980, King County was home to about 62,000 Asians; a decade later nearly 119,000 lived here. The Hispanic numbers also increased from 27,000 to 44,000. The population would continue to develop a more international flavor.

By the end of the decade, the suburbs had increased their populations to where seven of the fifteen largest cities in Washington State—Seattle, Bellevue, Renton, Kirkland, Kent, Redmond, and Auburn—were located in King County. This growth would accelerate during the 1990s.

Opposite top
From 1980 thru 1989, downtown Seattle has added 10 million square feet of office space—the equivalent of 17 towers the size of the Seafirst Building, the 50-story "black box" now the 1001 Fourth Avenue Plaza. Another 5 million square feet of office space, as of April 1989, equal to 8 1/2 Seafirst buildings–were under construction or received city permits. Photo by Barry Wong, *Seattle Times*

Below
Taken from the end of the Alaskan Ferries pier in downtown Seattle, this 1986 panorama gives us some familiar landmarks and a few new arrivals on the waterfront skyline. In the foreground, at the edge of Elliott Bay, is the Washington State Ferries' Colman Dock; to its right is Ye Olde Curiousity Shop. Behind Colman Dock, the Seattle Trust Tower was under construction; at far right, seeming to sprout from the bridge of the *Malaspina*, was the Smith Tower, for many years the tallest building in Seattle. When the Columbia Center opened in 1985, its dark 76-story profile just to the left of the Smith Tower took over the prize for height. Photo by Skip Howard Photographs (neg # 860X00-B2-B5).

THE 1990s

At the outset of the decade, Mother Nature once again decided to show Puget Sounders who was boss, providing weather that caused all sorts of problems in 1990. Major culprits: January and November floods, and major snowfalls in February and just prior to Christmas. A wind and rain storm on November 25 combined with human error to sink some pontoons on which the original I-90 bridge across Lake Washington floated. The structure was being enlarged at the time and fortunately the newly constructed lanes were completed and could serve two-way traffic while the damaged portion was rebuilt.

At the outset of the 1990s, King County's economy, despite record sales for Boeing planes, seemed headed for another recession. During 1992, Boeing went through another cycle of downsizing, a result of competition from Airbus and lagging sales combined with protracted labor negotiations. The difficult retail economy, resulting in part from increasing unemployment and from growing competition from new stores, caused two historic retailers—Frederick and Nelson and Pay'n Pak—to close their doors. A shortfall in state revenue reflected the recession and by the end of 1992 the State's unemployment had surpassed the national average.

In 1990 Boeing twice made the headlines. It purchased Longacres Race Track in Renton as a site for company expansion and is building offices and a training center there. And it introduced a new airliner, the 777, which immediately became a popular new addition to the fleets of many airlines.

A few months later, competition forced some of these airlines to announce unprecedented losses and to cancel or delay orders for new planes. This caused

Boeing to eliminate more than 16,000 jobs during 1993 and more during 1994. But the situation proved not to be as dire as predicted. Layoffs slowed as '94 came to an end. An increase in state income surprised the legislature by producing a $439 million dollar surplus by year's end.

Boeing made news again on October 6, 1995, when the machinists' union went on strike for 69 days. Thousands of employees were without salaries until a contract agreement was signed in December.

Also that year, Microsoft's long-awaited *Windows '95* software came on the market and quickly gained popularity the world over.

Education made headlines when 21,000 school teachers from Western Washington walked out for 11 days in April, held mass rallies in Olympia, and demanded greater state support for education.

The 1990s were filled with sports' headlines. The Goodwill Games brought international sporting events to Seattle but the expected tourist onslaught did not arrive, leaving Seattle hotels, restaurants and founder Ted Turner disappointed.

In 1991, the financially strapped Seattle Mariners baseball team was for sale. By 1994, falling tiles from the Kingdome ceiling forced the Mariners and the Seahawks football team to seek temporary fields on which to play. The ceiling was soon stabilized but the experience gave both professional teams the opportunity to demand new fields. The Mariners, who surprised everyone with an amazing season finish in 1995, now seem certain of a new stadium with a retracting roof. And incidentally, their center fielder Ken Griffey, Jr., has developed into one of the most popular and finest players in the country.

The major crime headlines of the decade were generated in 1995 when the Pang warehouse in Seattle resulted in the death of four firefighters. Martin Pang, son of the owners, after being charged with murder and arson, fled to Brazil, which agreed to extradite him on the arson charge but not if the charge was murder.

The debate over how much of the state's forests should be harvested continued well into the decade. Environmentalists hailed the designation of the northern spotted owl as a threatened specie which resulted in the setting aside of several million acres of timberland. This caused the timber industry to react heatedly. A group calling themselves the "God Squad" was formed to try to find compromises. In 1993, newly elected President Clinton announced plans for a timber summit. Over time, the debates cooled and plans developed to allow some harvesting of timber while at the same time protecting endangered species. But neither the timber companies nor the environmentalists seemed satisfied with the compromise.

The 1990s were rife with partisan politics. Several politicians left office under a cloud and others survived allegations from the opposition. Mike Lowry was elected Governor in 1992 after a campaign that limited contributions and conceded tax increases in 1993. Early in 1995 he was accused of sexual harassment by a former press aide. An investigation found the governor's actions did not constitute sexual harassment in the legal sense but his actions had obviously offended the aide. He reached a settlement out of court with Susanne Albright, but the rumors followed him. He later decided not to seek another term.

Meanwhile the state's Republicans had swept into power with the 1994 election, sending seven Congressmen to Washington where before there was only a single Republican. State officials struggled with health care reform, but Congressional inaction in the nation's capital kept most of it from becoming reality.

The 1995 Olympia session found Republicans in control of the House and nearly so in the Senate. The new legislators touted their "Contract with Washington." The new majority discarded most of the landmark state health-care law, cut taxes, and criticized many state regulators.

Fishermen's Terminal on Seattle's Salmon Bay was extensively remodeled during the 1980s. It is the home port for many of the vessels in the commercial fishing fleet, and features the Fishermen's Memorial, a dramatic landmark listing the names of those whose lives have been lost at sea. Photo by Skip Howard Photography (neg # 89090X).

The 1996 elections were hotly contested and on the national level most contestants won by only a few votes. Republicans lost one seat in the U.S. Congress but retained the majority. They ended with thinner majorities in the State house but gained control of the Senate by a few votes. The Democrats retained the Governor's chair when Gary Locke was elected as the first Asian-American to govern a mainland state.

The initiative is a political factor in many Washington elections and the early '90s saw it frequently used to force items onto the ballot. In 1991, two emotional issues were on the ballot as initiatives. Voters narrowly rejected term limits for state public officials, but the next year supporters forced it onto the ballot a second time and it passed, though the vote was close. The second initiative of 1991 concerned euthanasia. Voters turned down a plan called "Death with Dignity", thus preventing terminally ill patients from receiving medical assistance in ending their lives. However, in March 1996, the 9th Circuit Court of Appeals struck down this state law barring doctor-assisted suicide.

Other major events of the '90s: Several hundred Washingtonians were involved in the 1991 Gulf War in Kuwait and in 1994 hundreds began hooking their computers to the Internet.

Perhaps the event for which the 1990s will be best remembered is the rapid increase in the population of the Seattle-King County area (see table page 293). In 1990, the legislature attempted to alleviate the concerns about growth, but the results were insufficient to satisfy many. Voters rejected a ballot measure that would have set up stringent controls on statewide growth, but the campaign brought promises of action from officials. The switch in party control of the legislature in the mid-'90s added to the difficulty of coming up with meaningful legislation.

Susan Douglas gets into the Caribbean beat listening to a steel-drum band play at Bumbershoot activities at the Seattle Center. Photo by Peter Liddell, *Seattle Times*.

Below
Seafair Pirates successfully storm the beach at Aiki, capturing the city (again) to kick off fun season. Photo by Natalie Fobes, *Seattle Times*.

Meanwhile the towns and cities and county were encountering the many problems of rapid population growth including: traffic gridlock, crowded schools, the need to enlarge parks and playfields, the demand for more police and fire protection, the need to expand utilities, to extend streets and transit services, to find new sources of potable water, and to maintain the Northwest environment that had been praised all across America. How much larger can our cities grow and still retain the quality of life desired by Washingtonians? No one seems to be able to answer the question, though efforts are being made to control the urban growth. The Growth-Management Act passed in 1990 attempts to control urban growth and to preserve some rural areas, steering development away from major farmlands, preserving wetlands and remaining forested areas of the county, to control the concentration and types of buildings, and in other ways to maintain the environmental standards and life style of the region.

Most Washington residents are very proud of and concerned about maintaining the Pacific Northwest life style: fishing in rivers an hour or two from home, ski slopes beckoning within fifty miles, scenery free of forest clear-cuts, mountains visible through smog-clear air, towns and cities safe and livable, good schools, and the opportunity for every citizen to succeed. With the anticipated continued rapid increase in population, this dream is difficult to maintain, but most citizens of Seattle and King County are working to keep the dream alive.

CHAPTER 16

CHRONICLES IN LEADERSHIP

BY BOB COLE

The saga of Seattle's commercial history is largely unknown, for while history books have painted broad images of the city's economic ups and downs, little has been written about individual businesses—how they came to be, who their founders were, what they experienced, and what their successes and failures were.

Here, in the following pages, are fascinating tales of these early businessmen, of their innocent striving to make a better living for themselves and their families, of their desire to escape poverty, of camaraderie with their workers, of sacrifice and hardship during the lean years, of pride in their work, and of courageous and bold endeavors.

In Seattle, this legion of entrepreneurs came from all over the country and the world. Many were first- or second-generation immigrants from northern and central Europe. Of these, most brought with them the European work ethic and sense of craftsmanship. Each in his own way sought an opportunity to make a name for himself and start a new life.

Many arrived penniless after wandering the country in search of steady work or after attempting to strike it rich in the Klondike. A few, the privileged, arrived with an entourage, their names and reputations preceding them, to play a life-size game of Monopoly® with the region's productive assets and resources.

In the end, they formed the mosaic that became the business fabric of the city—the prosperous to retire in the splendor that wealth and success can give and the failures to drop from sight into history's oblivion. Those who survived a goodly portion of the city's life did so through successive generations of good luck, adept management, and knowing how to ride the crest of favorable economic tides and avoid the eddies of recession and panic.

The following vignettes offer but glimpses of their stories.

IMPROVED EIGHT DAY
CLOCKS
MADE AND SOLD BY THE
N.
Mfg. Co.
CONN., U. S. A.

BALLARD SHEET METAL WORKS, INC.

At the turn of the century Ballard was booming. The area that Captain W.R. Ballard had reluctantly taken in settlement of a debt came to life when it was discovered that it could supply Seattle, burned out in the Great Fire of 1889, with badly needed shingles and lumber. More than 20 sawmills lined the placid shores of Salmon Bay and everyone needed sheet metal work, blowpipe, dust collectors, and roofing metal.

In 1907 two sheet metal workers from Renton, commuting to Ballard each day on the interurban, decided to start their own firm. Oscar Simpson, a 24-year-old Scotch Irishman from Indiana and a friend, Oscar Ranes, formed Ballard Sheet Metal Works. That same year Oscar Simpson's first son, Harold Simpson, was born.

From their first shop, at 5114 Ballard Avenue, near what is now the Washington Ship Canal, they made their rounds and served the mills. By the mid-teens, the mill work had slowed but the fishing industry was beginning to grow and the firm began building fuel tanks, water tanks, and providing other metalwork for Alaska fishing vessels.

In 1919 Oscar Simpson bought out Oscar Ranes, and moved the company to a larger facility, in the now-historic St. Charles Hotel building, one block south of the company's present location. In the '30s, Oscar Simpson died and his son, Harold, assumed management of the firm. By then, the business had changed. The mills had closed, but the fishing industry had continued to grow. Harold Simpson shifted the emphasis of the business to the area's small shipyards, such as the old Sagstad Shipyard, and the canneries of Alaska. This portion of the business has continued to grow through the years. During World War II, Ballard Sheet Metal fabricated and installed ventilation systems and other parts for the U.S. Navy

In 1957 Donald H. Simpson, grandson of the founder, graduated from the University of Washington and joined his father in the firm. They worked together until Harold Simpson died in 1971. Donald Simpson assumed control of the company at that time.

Today, 1997, the fourth generation of the Simpson family has assumed control of the company. David B. Simpson, 36 and Douglas A., 34 are now operating the business, and Donald is in the process of retiring.

Ballard Sheet Metal Works, is a complete job shop, but has always specialized in the marine and industrial fields. The company has also become very well known for the fabrication of high quality stainless steel range hoods and counters for residential use.

The company's office is at 4763 Ballard Ave., still in historic Ballard.

Oscar Simpson and a partner formed Ballard Sheet Metal Works in 1907.

His son, Harold Simpson, assumed management of the company during the 1930s.

THE BEMIS BUILDING

Courtesy MOHAI.

For nearly a century the towering letters of the Bemis Bag Company sign have dominated the skyline south of Pioneer Square, marking the edge of Seattle's industrial district. Erected over a fifty year period the massive five story 150,000 square foot factory mirrored Seattle's growth during the first half of the century. Judson Moss Bemis established the company in St. Louis three years before the Civil War with only one press and two sewing machines. It was revolutionary in that cloth bags had always been sewn by hand, but the enterprise flourished and expanded rapidly.

In 1904 Robert McAusland, traveled out of the Omaha plant, soliciting bag orders sufficient to fill out a rail car. These would be shipped to Seattle and broken down for delivery. It is said he managed to sneak a desk into one of these shipments and rented a small office at First and Madison streets for five dollars a month. This became Bemis's first Seattle sales office. Albert Farwell Bemis, company president, followed this expansion into the Pacific Northwest with great interest. In a letter he outlined the factors he considered germane to expansion in Seattle, concluding: "If, after studying, you think it desirable to establish a plant, go ahead." Compare that with the endless committee meetings, financial analyses, and stacks of reports prerequisite to any such venture today! Reginal Parsons, the founder's son-in-law, transferred from the San Francisco plant to join forces with McAusland. A building designed by Bemis's engineers was erected off Atlantic Street, near the waterfront. Operations commenced in 1905, with Mr. Parsons as the plant's first manager. Much of the early production went to the milling and export trade, carrying flour to the Orient. Burlap fabric imported from India was converted to "Jute 140s", cotton bags were also produced.

By 1915 the plant could no longer keep up with demand. Thomas Scruggs was dispatched from St. Louis to design and construct a new addition. The imposing brick facade fronting Atlantic Street was completed in 1917, doubling the size of the original factory. Scruggs designed an incredibly solid structure with seismic reinforcement well ahead of its day. In 1941 plant production was expanded to include paper bags for a wide range of uses. The huge presses ran round the clock as demand increased.

The 7.1 earthquake of 1949 that wreaked havoc throughout Seattle also brought down a section of the old south wall at Bemis, while the 1917 addition "Never lost a brick" to quote the local press. To rectify the damage Bemis expanded again in 1949 demolishing the walls of the 1904 building, extending the perimeter and constructing a new reinforced concrete addition. The plant continued operation, employing as many as 450 workers running 3 shifts. Textile bag production was phased out in 1978 as the paper operation expanded. By 1990 The Bemis Company had grown to a large international corporation with 28 production plants. The Seattle facility was obsolete for the companies needs so operations were consolidated with its Vancouver, Washington plant. In 1993 the presses and machinery fell silent.

Courtesy MOHAI.

Somerset Properties, lead by Seattle artist David Huchthausen, purchased the Bemis Building in 1994. Huchthausen, a former University Professor with an extensive background in architecture designed a mixed use redevelopment incorporating light manufacturing, warehouse and offices with 30 residential artists lofts. Interior demolition produced over 47 tons of debris, from the top two floors alone. Crews refinished 25,000 square feet of maple flooring producing 3 tons of sawdust. The project included over a mile of new interior walls creating studios from 1500 to 3000 square feet. Overhead beams in the 12 to 17 foot ceilings remain exposed, retaining the industrial feel of the spaces. Windows were replaced with thermopane incorporating interior grids to match the look of the original factory windows, maintaining the historic integrity of the structure.

The Bemis Building is the largest professional arts development in Seattle, adding a vibrant component to Seattle's South Downtown District. Tenants include architects, graphic designers, sculptors, painters, photographers, and other artists.

BAUGH CONSTRUCTION

Baugh Construction was founded over 50 years ago in 1946. Seattle was just coming into its own due to Boeing's involvement with World War II and because of the proximity of the Puget Sound to the war in the Pacific arena. New companies shot up everywhere shortly after the war. In the midst of the company's start-up years, Bob Baugh joined the burgeoning construction company and, with his uncle Larry Baugh, formed the philosophy and work ethics that are still practiced today. Baugh Construction had the right formula for starting what was to become the Northwest's largest employee owned construction company.

Over the last 50 years, the company has seen many positive changes. Baugh has consistently been a builder who takes on the most difficult projects and succeeds. Since the start of the post-war era, this contractor has performed work in virtually all major market segments in the Northwest. Baugh has renovated, consulted on, or constructed a good deal of downtown Seattle and downtown Portland including many of these cities' proudest landmarks. They are also the contractor for some of the biggest industrial names in the Northwest region.

Baugh's philosophy from its inception has been that its people are the company's true strength. Each individual is an asset —highly qualified people who realize the importance their work has on their clients and their clients' customers. With this value, Baugh continues to build its reputation on service, the ability to build high-quality, efficient projects, and a belief in the importance of establishing long-term relationships. These relationships have resulted in Baugh becoming a regular builder for many of the Northwest's most prominent companies.

◆

Baugh's largest job to date $195,000 in 1950, four years after opening.

In 1950, Baugh built Seattle's first Safeway store. It was the largest project at that time for Baugh at a value of $195,000. By 1959, Baugh achieved its first $1,000,000 job with the completion of Ballard High School. Following these significant benchmarks in Baugh's history, they regularly contracted for some of Washington and Oregon's better known names including: Boeing, Seattle University, Nordstrom, Intel, Weyerhauser, Georgia Pacific, Microsoft, Portland Airport, AT&T, Seattle Pacific University, Virginia Mason, Group Health, Starbucks, Kemper Freeman's Bellevue Square, The Bon Marché, Seafirst Bank, Kimpton Hotels and many more well known names in the region.

Throughout the Pacific Northwest, Northern California, Idaho, Wyoming, Montana and Alaska, the construction firm has demonstrated expertise in every job and every phase of construction—commercial, industrial, interior and renovation work.

Baugh's first million dollar job–Ballard High School 1959.

Recent regional projects include the Ashgrove Cement Plantin Leamington, Utah, RIBI Immunochem Production facility in Hamilton Montana, the Coeur d'Alene, Idaho Target store, and the four star hotels–The Benson Hotel, and Heathman Hotel (historical renovations) in Portland, Oregon.

Baugh is presently involved in what could arguably be noted as some of their most exciting projects to date. Baugh recently completed St. Ignatius Chapel at Seattle University and the renovation of the Frye Art Museum, a beloved Seattle landmark. Currently under construction is the $109 million Benaroya Concert Hall in the heart of downtown Seattle and the major Portland International Airport expansion. Each of these projects poses unique challenges in their historical significance, unique locations, and requirements of absolute perfection from foundation to finishing craftsmanship. With the inclusion of hi-tech into all phases of construction, this all-employee owned company is proudly meeting the challenges of building into the 21st Century.

Benaroya Concert hall, 1997–$109M value.

BOGLE & GATES P.L.L.C.

Lawrence Bogle

Cassius E. Gates

Two men of greatly differing personal styles guided the growth of a law firm formed in Seattle in 1926 which became, in the succeeding years, one of the most successful in the West and among the largest north of San Francisco. Lawrence Bogle was a classic Southern gentleman—elegant, gracious, soft-spoken. A complementary personality, Cassius Gates, was colorful, ambitious, and hard-driving. The two leaders worked well together and the unique combination of their divergent personalities provided the key to the early success of the firm now known as Bogle & Gates P.L.L.C.

While the modern firm dates from 1926, its origins go back to 1891 when Judge W. H. Bogle, Lawrence's father, opened an admiralty law practice in Tacoma. In 1898 he moved to the Colman Building in Seattle and in 1906 was joined by his son Lawrence. When Gates joined the Bogles in 1926, the firm's name became Bogle, Bogle & Gates and remained so for nearly 40 years. Judge Bogle died in 1927, leaving his son and Cassius Gates as leaders of the firm.

Bogle & Gates and its predecessor firms served numerous clients in the maritime industry and handled some of the most colorful and tragic cases on the West Coast. These included litigation relating to the *Princess Sophia*, which sank in 1916 with 350 lives lost, and the collapse of the Tacoma Narrows Bridge in 1940.

To complement the firm's maritime practice, Cassius Gates encouraged the development of specialists in fields most useful to the business community, such as antitrust law, banking, taxation, securities, acquisitions, and mergers. Major civil litigation continued and the firm participated in cases such as the landmark General Electric antitrust cases, the controversial Boldt decision regarding Indian fishing rights, and more recently, the Exxon Valdez oil spill litigation.

But times have changed, and so has Bogle & Gates. Its clients range from some of the world's largest corporations to individual entrepreneurs, spanning a wide spectrum of industries. While the firm is known for its representation of companies with deep roots in the Pacific Northwest, it is also proud of its role in launching new businesses and protecting their new ideas. Today, Bogle & Gates has nearly 200 lawyers and maintains the largest litigation practice in the Northwest.

Headquartered in Seattle, the firm also maintains offices in Anchorage, Bellevue, Portland, Tacoma, and Vancouver, B.C.

THE BON

In the late 1870s, Edward Nordhoff, a German emigrant working in the Paris Louvre Department Store, admired the integrity, service, and attitude of a famed rival store, the Maison à Boucicault au Bon Marché. He often dreamed of opening a store modeled after this fine retail establishment.

Ten years later, in 1890, after immigrating to Seattle via Chicago, he and wife Josephine invested their life savings, $1,200, to buy merchandise to open their own store, which they proudly named The Bon Marché. This first store was in Belltown, north of the city's early business district, in a brick veneer building which they leased for $25 a month. The building is still standing today.

Mrs. Nordhoff, not yet 20 years old and a mother, helped stock shelves, keep books, clean, and mop. Often she measured dry goods with a baby on her hip. The Nordhoffs kept the doors open from 7 a.m. to 9 p.m. Mrs. Nordhoff learned the Chinook language so she could better wait on Indian customers. Although the store was blocks from the downtown area, customers began to trade with the hard-working couple.

The Bon Marché survived the depression of the 1890s, and in 1896 moved closer to the heart of the city to a one-story building at Second and Pike streets. With the advent of the Gold Rush, The Bon Marché boomed. But in 1899, the company suffered a brief setback with the death of Edward Nordhoff, who had suffered for years from consumption. Mrs. Nordhoff, then 27, took over, and in 1901 expanded the store to include all the frontage on the Second Avenue block. That same year she marred a dynamic 31-year-old merchant tailor, Frank McDermott, who took over as president and manager.

Under his leadership, assisted by Mrs. Nordhoff and Edward's brother Rudolph, the store grew in leaps and bounds, from sales of $338,000 in 1900 to $8 million in 1923. More than 135,000 persons attended the grand opening when The Bon moved to its present site in 1929.

World War II brought thousands of people to the Seattle area, and in 1949 the company opened an Everett store. In the 1950s The Bon again began expanding when Allied Stores pioneered a new concept in retailing with the opening of the Northgate Mall, in which The Bon was the anchor store. Other stores were opened in Tacoma, Yakima, and Bellingham, and the downtown Seattle store added four stories, making it the largest store west of Chicago. In 1960 a 10-story self-parking garage was constructed and a "sky bridge" was built connecting it with the store.

Today, The Bon operates 42 stores, employing 7,000 people and serving customers in Washington, Oregon, Idaho, Montana and Wyoming.

◆

Below
The first Bon Marché, which was located at First Avenue and Cedar streets, opened in 1890. The store was owned and operated by Edward Nordhoff and his wife Josephine.

Bottom
Thirty-nine years later, in 1929, The Bon Marché built a completely new store covering one city block between Third and Fourth on Pine Street. It was the first Seattle store to have automatic elevators and escalators.

CALLISON ARCHITECTURE, INC.

Born and raised in Seattle, entrepreneur Anthony Callison opened his first architecture office as soon as he graduated in 1960 from the University of Washington. As an architect and business person, he concentrated on building his firm through strong interpersonal relationships and project diversity. By 1975, his small firm expanded into The Callison Partnership as it forged its first links with Nordstrom, a family-owned fashion specialty store which was just beginning the growth and expansion that has turned it into a retail giant.

Perhaps the key to Callison Architecture's success is what the firm has derived from Nordstrom: a new kind of customer service that is still rare in the architectural profession, creating a design synergy out of the retail world's balance of quality products, uncompromising service and customer satisfaction.

The result is a firm based on client relationships and the value of people. Callison encourages its designers to demonstrate their commitment to the client in unprecedented ways, learning as much about what the client needs as the client knows about what its customers want. Although the firm has grown significantly during the last twenty years, that desire is the hallmark of work with all of its clients.

Tony Callison died in 1988, but he lived long enough to mentor his small Puget Sound firm into one of the most successful architectural practices in the world. Today, with offices in Seattle and Hong Kong, Callison Architecture's 320 employees serve some of the most prestigious and successful corporations in the world–Nordstrom, Microsoft, Nike, Eddie Bauer, Samsung, Starbucks Coffee and Bank of America–throughout North America, Latin America, the Middle East and Asia.

Managed today by a three-member board of directors and 21 shareholders, Callison is the largest architectural design office in the Pacific Northwest and the fourth-largest firm in the United States. The firm provides comprehensive planning and design services in specialty areas that include high-rise and mixed-use developments, retail and entertainment facilities, financial institutions, corporate office environments, hospitality and residential buildings and healthcare facilities.

US BANK CENTRE "Of all the recently built downtown towers, Pacific First Centre (now US Bank Centre) is worth singling out as a work of collaborative design, applied at a variety of scales and in a variety of approaches: a melding of art, architecture, graphics and marketing." -Don Canty, The Seattle Post Intelligencer

◆

Callison continues to be the primary architect for Nordstrom–including 83 stores across the United States–as well as the design of more than 30 shopping centers (new and renovation/expansions), entertainment facilities, and specialty shops. Their expertise in retail is matched by their hotel, resort and multi-family residential projects throughout the world. Callison is also a design expert for office buildings and interiors, with more than 30 million square feet of headquarters, corporate campus, high rise and high-technology facilities in the firm's portfolio.

In addition to the new Downtown Seattle Nordstrom store, set to open in late 1998 in the historic former Frederick & Nelson Building, Callison has designed a number of other significant projects throughout the Puget Sound-area, including A Contemporary Theater's new home in the renovated Eagles Auditorium; Seattle Repertory Theater's second performance space; Eddie Bauer's new corporate headquarters in Redmond; more than a dozen buildings at Microsoft's World Headquarters in Redmond; Boeing's Customer Service Training Center in Tukwila; Carillon Point in Kirkland; Downtown Seattle's U.S. Bank Centre; the Inn at Semiahmoo in Blaine; Harbor Steps in Seattle; and renovations to the famed Pacific Science Center.

◆

Since 1984, Callison has provided architectural design and land planning services for more than 3 million square feet of offices at Microsoft's World Headquarters in Redmond.

THE CHEMITHON CORPORATION

The Chemithon Corporation was established in 1954 by brothers Burton and Richard Brooks, graduates of the University of Washington in Chemical Engineering, along with three other original founders. Today Burt Brooks remains Chairman of the Board and actively involved in new product development. According to Burt, there weren't many jobs for Chemical Engineers in the Pacific Northwest in 1954. However, the brothers knew they wanted to stay in the area because of the quality of life the Northwest offers.

The group created Chemithon to commercialize the continuous oleum sulfonation process Burt invented and developed while working on his master's thesis. Sulfonation is an industrial chemical process used to manufacture a diverse range of products, including the active ingredients in laundry and dish washing detergent, shampoo, toothpaste, oil additives and industrial cleaners. The majority of sulfonates produced throughout the world are used as surfactants in laundry detergent and other cleaning products.

Household detergent production in the United States began in the early 1930s, and then skyrocketed after World War II. The wartime shortage of fats and oils used to make soap further stimulated detergent research. In addition, the close of World War II left the U.S. petrochemical industry with a large excess capacity for production of high octane aviation gasoline. This technology was adapted to make raw materials used in the sulfonation process.

The availability of these raw materials, custom tailored for detergent production, resulted in rapid sulfonation process development. Chemithon researchers replaced early "batch" processes and developed continuous sulfonation processes using oleum. Two of these early patents formed the foundation on which Chemithon was created.

In the late 1950s, Chemithon began development work on an improved sulfonation process using sulfur trioxide, a gas, rather than oleum, which is a liquid. This new process yielded higher quality surfactants and, unlike the oleum process, did not produce contaminants requiring disposal. Chemithon has been awarded a number of patents on this technology.

Chemithon's original target market was U.S. manufacturers of surfactants, detergents and specialty chemicals. Soon, they found there was a worldwide need for quality sulfonation equipment to meet demand for detergent created by the expanding post-war economy. Chemithon now has supplied more than 300 plants in almost every area of the world, including Asia, Africa, North and South America, Europe, the Middle East, Australia and the Pacific Rim. Customers range from major multi-nationals such as Procter & Gamble, Lever Brothers, Chevron and Witco to small independent businesses.

The Chemithon Corporation is under the umbrella of Chemithon Enterprises, Inc., a privately held group of international companies offering process development, engineering, plant equipment manufacturing, and mechanical construction. Chemithon also supplies air pollution control systems for the power generation industry and is a key supplier of equipment, processes and supplies to the surface finishing and printed circuit board industries.

Because on-going product development is critical in Chemithon's effort to remain on the leading edge, Chemithon maintains its own laboratory and pilot plant to develop and improve processes and equipment. A complete analytical laboratory in support of process equipment and surface finishing customers enhances Chemithon's capabilities.

Chemithon's diverse product offering has made it possible for them to expand markets at home, and at the same time strengthen their position in the global market.

◆

Original Chemithon founders, from left, Burt Brooks, Phil Hebner, Cy Richardson and Dick Brooks.

CANLIS RESTAURANT

A massive stone fireplace welcomes you when you arrive. An open copper grill faces the dining room. Candlelight twinkles on the tables, and the lights of the city sparkle on the lake outside the windows. Friendly and efficient servers attend your every need. There is music; there is magic. This is Canlis, the birthplace of northwest cuisine, a restaurant where deals are made, dreams are born, and where state of the art dining has been defined and redefined over five decades of continuous award-winning service.

Before Peter Canlis opened his restaurant at the foot of the Aurora Bridge in 1950, Seattle was not the food lover's mecca that it is today. Visitors to the city were dubious about dining opportunities in what had so recently been a frontier town. While the city could boast a handful of hotel dining rooms offering the standard continental cuisine, there were no restaurants serving northwest regional cuisine, for there was no northwest style to speak of. Terms like Pacific Rim and The Ring of Fire had no culinary meaning.

Forged from the fiery imagination of Peter Canlis and architect Roland Terry, Canlis was unlike anything the city had seen before. Seattle historian Bill Speidel called it "A bold experiment." Cantilevered into an east-facing slope overlooking Lake Union and the rugged Cascade mountains beyond, the new building cut a bold façade. But the perspective that made Canlis unique was the restaurant's orientation toward the Pacific, for the seeds of Canlis were flown in from Hawaii where Peter Canlis already owned and operated the successful Canlis Broiler on Waikiki.

Whereas east coast restaurants looked to Europe for inspiration, Canlis the first great restaurant of the Pacific northwest turned to Asia and the Pacific islands. This shift initiated a whole new way of cooking and dining, and Seattle wholeheartedly embraced it. With exotic game fish grilling over an open broiler, tropical wood accents, and kimono-clad waitreses, Canlis brought romance and food from the Pacific into the city. Drawing inspiration and many of the key ingredients for its signature dishes from the lands that touch the great ocean, Canlis pioneered Pacific Rim Cuisine.

More than that, Canlis became for Seattleites a kind of "Third Place," neither home nor work, but a meeting ground where milestones in both of those arenas could be celebrated and honored. For, in spite of all its exotic elements, Canlis never lost touch with its regional roots nor with the mainstream American diners who constitute its clientele. Perfectly grilled salmon and midwestern steaks have always been as much a part of the menu as grilled mahi mahi with passion fruit butter. The food has always been contemporary and exciting, but never trendy or intimidating. Canlis drew its first customers from the many loyal followers of the Hawaii restaurant who lived in Seattle and spent winter vacations on Oahu. It wasn't long before Seattle society claimed Canlis as its own and made it the first choice for special events. By the time Chris Canlis and his wife Alice assumed responsibility for the restaurant in 1977, Canlis was more than a restaurant, it was a vital Seattle landmark.

The philosophy of the restaurant is symbolized at its entry by a Kura door from a seventeenth century Japanese treasure house. A treasure house, built to secure a family's most valuable belongings, was constructed more substantially than the light residential buildings that surrounded it. It had three doors, the inner most being the Kura door. Canlis is a treasure house, and Seattleites trust Canlis with their most valuable treasures—the special times of their lives. Here, in the city's most beautiful restaurant, milestones are carefully safeguarded.

The Kura Door

◆

In the Penthouse, perched above the main dining room, rehearsal dinners, receptions, and retirement parties are celebrated in an atmosphere that is simultaneously refined and familiar. In the Executive Dining Room, tucked discretely behind the main dining room, more intimate gatherings are fostered by the residential feel captured by designer Doug Rasar. The room was expanded and the feeling was enhanced by Jim Cutler during a makeover in 1996. During the renovation, a third private dining room was added to the building, the tiny Caché, an intimate space with a view, a fainting couch, and one table for two.

From a private marriage proposal to the formal reception of Deng Xiaoping at his only public dining experience in the United States, Canlis is where Seattle celebrates the passages of life. The businesses that shape Seattle's character have made the private dining rooms at Canlis their celebration headquarters. Families who have relied on those businesses for their livelihoods know they can trust the restaurant's professional staff to enhance their special occasions, public or private.

Canlis employees, a culturally diverse group with more than ten different languages spoken between them, are a significant part of the Canlis story. At other restaurants, workers move from property to property almost as frequently as the customers do, but in five decades of continuous operation, this kitchen has had only two executive chefs. When original chef Joe Ching retired, he was replaced by Rocky Toguchi, who had already been with the company for a decade. Employees stay with the company because the restaurant is more than a place to work. The crew is an extended family, and each employee knows that the company cares.

Decades before other restaurants provided basic benefits, Canlis inplemented a wonderful program of perks for its staff, including full health care coverage, paid vacations, profit sharing, and use of a vacation home on Whidbey Island. The family style staff meal at five o'clock is a gathering of thirty or more workers. Every evening, as dinner winds down in the executive dining room, the gathering becomes a business meeting where management prepares the staff for the upcoming evening. The extraordinary service that results is one reason that Canlis is the most award winning restaurant in the northwest.

And Canlis gives as much as it gets. From hospital wings to symphonies, from restoration of homeless shelters to a mock Canlis dining room at a recovery center for stroke victims, recipients of Canlis' generosity are many and diverse. The owners strive to make their giving count; and fundraising events are always tailored to the cause for which the funds are raised. When Caché was opened, proceeds from the private dining room for two went to a counseling center to mend broken relationships. Oscar night generates funds for a young actors' guild.

Canlis continues to break new ground every year, winning national recognition, holding benefits, and generally setting the standard for excellent food and service. Canlis is traditional, but its tradition is innovation. The stone pillars and the dramatic architectural lines may evoke the stability of the Eisenhower era; but the passion that spawned Seattle's most beautiful and most celebrated restaurant still burns. The fire that lights the massive fireplace warms the heart of this great city.

Above: The Executive Room

Below: The Main Dining Room

CHEVRON PRODUCTS COMPANY

Chevron, formerly Standard Oil Company of California, has been selling its products in Seattle for over 110 years. The first Seattle operation opened in 1886, while Washington was still a territory, as part of Frederick Taylor's Pacific Coast Oil Company, the grandfather of Standard Oil Company of California. Taylor, an early industry wildcatter, had discovered oil in the Pico Canyon of Los Angeles and together with other investors formed the company in 1879.

But the real growth of the Seattle office began with the Gold Rush in 1897, when the company played a key role in supplying Klondike miners. Its pearl-illuminating oil, kerosene, naphtha, and lubricating oil were valued commodities as far north as the Arctic Circle, where miners often purchased them with gold dust. At the height of the Gold Rush, the company's stern-wheeled steamer, *Oil City*, sailed from Seattle to the Klondike with her hold full of valuable oil cargo products.

In 1899 Standard Oil of California acquired the Pacific Coast Oil Company and expanded its facility in Seattle. In those days the company ship, *Loomis*, supplied the city's new marine terminal and bulk station from its depot at Redondo Beach in Southern California.

Chevron built the first service station on the West Coast in Seattle in 1907. John McLean, a local Standard employee, fastened a 30-gallon water tank on a platform a few feet above the ground and attached a garden hose with a control valve. He then dispensed gas directly into the customer's tank, measuring the flow with a simple glass gauge.

Today, Chevron is a leading marketer of petroleum products in the state of Washington. Chevron's vision is to be the motorist's choice for quality gasoline, quick service food and other convenience goods. Currently, Chevron operates over 150 modern service stations in the greater Seattle area. These stations incorporate the latest technology in motor fuel dispensing and underground storage systems. In addition, card readers built into the dispensers satisfy a strong customer preference to pay at the pump.

As the city grew, Chevron acquired property at Richmond Beach, 12 miles north of the city. Situated between the Great Northern Railroad tracks and deep water, the site is now occupied by Chevron's 5,000 barrel-per-day asphalt refinery. In its early days, the company created a lovely residential tract of six cottages for employees and implemented an active social program of dances, horseshoe tournaments, and crystal-set listening, which kept the employees happy and close to home.

During the many years of Chevron's operation in the Northwest, the company has developed a strong commitment to the Seattle community. In keeping with the desire to remain a responsible corporate citizen, company contributions help fund numerous community organizations, such as the Nature Conservancy of Washington and the Seattle Symphony. Environmentally, Chevron strives to lead the industry in safety and reliability.

Today Chevron Products Company employs about 12,500 people worldwide and is one of the largest industrial concerns headquartered west of the Mississippi. To learn more about Chevron please visit their website at www.chevron.com.

◆

Below
The Standard Oil Marine Plant on Elliott Bay, circa 1907-09.
Bottom
"Gassing up" at the West's first service station-Seattle, 1907.

CHILDREN'S HOSPITAL AND MEDICAL CENTER

At the turn of the century, Anna Clise, a prominent and influential Seattle woman, suffered a tragic loss: the death of her five-year-old son to inflammatory rheumatism. Her grief brought with it the recognition of this region's great need for medical care for children, and compelled her to establish a legacy that we know today as Children's Hospital and Medical Center. The words and work of her cousin, Dr. John Musser, president of the American Medical Association and founder of a hospital ward for children in Philadelphia, validated her insight. His advice: "There's nothing so important to be done as service to children. Look about and see what is being done for them in your state. Find out what is not being done that is necessary and worthy, and do that."

Nine years later in February, 1907, Anna Clise and 23 women friends established the first orthopedic facility for children on the West Coast, Children's Orthopedic Hospital Association Ward in a wing of Seattle General Hospital. From its inception, Children's served as a regional hospital. Mary, a nine-year-old from Alaska suffering from tuberculosis, was one of Children's first patients.

For Children's Hospital to become a reality, the first Board of Trustees was faced with an urgent need for community support. The trustees believed that given the opportunity, women from surrounding neighborhoods and communities would respond as passionately as they had to the medical needs of children, and be willing to give their time and money to support such a purpose. Modeling a membership plan after a hospital in Toronto, Canada, Children's Hospital Guild Association was founded. It consisted of neighborhood guilds where friends gathered once a month to support specific projects needed by the patients and donated annual dues to the hospital.

In October 1907, the Board of Trustees established Children's underlying mission—of providing health care for children—and the essence of its philosophy ever since: To accept any child regardless of race, religion, or the parents' ability to pay.

Children's moved to its own facility in 1908, a 12-bed cottage on Queen Anne Hill. In 1911 Children's moved to a self supporting, 40-bed facility next door. In 1953 Children's moved to its present site in the Laurelhurst neighborhood of Seattle.

Above
Trustees and patients pose on the back porch of the 12-bed "Fresh Air Cottage," Children's first stand-alone facility on Queen Anne Hill. Women trustees founded Children's; today the all-women board continues its leadership role as it helps direct the hospital into the next century.

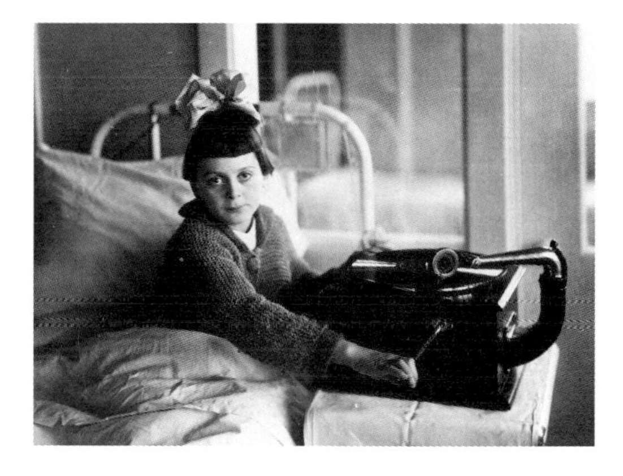

Right
Children's understood that being hospitalized was more than providing medicine and rest. To this day, patients who are able can choose from a variety of recreational activities to help pass the time.

Since then, the medical center has updated its facilities and technology regularly to provide a state-of-the-art environment for children.

Nineteen ninety-seven marks Children's 90th anniversary, a milestone based on a strong legacy. Today, as both a community resource and a regional referral center for the states of Washington, Alaska, Montana and Idaho, Children's scope of care includes a multitude of specialty services provided by nationally known experts in disciplines such as cancer, heart disease, birth defects, genetics and infectious diseases. Our long-standing affiliation with the University of Washington School of Medicine, as one of the finest medical schools in the country, has enabled us to attract faculty who focus on patient care, teaching and research, the basic tenets of our mission. This relationship allows us to stay close to current developments, new technology and the best and brightest talent in our mutual goal to care for children and to work toward the goal of eliminating the need for them to ever be hospitalized.

CONTINENTAL SAVINGS BANK

In the summer of 1921, during financially uncertain times and a period of bank failures, a small real estate finance company was founded in Seattle's University District. Continental Mortgage and Loan Company would grow during the next 75 years into one of the largest mortgage lenders and strongest financial institutions in the state of Washington, as it anticipated the needs of the Northwest and met those needs with service and integrity. Ralph W. Green, who was connected with the King County State Bank, and other University District business men saw the potential for growth in the University District and other parts of Seattle and the state of Washington and determined that there was a need for financing this growth.

The first employee was a young man named W. Walter Williams, who had graduated from the University of Washington five years before and was to be paid $100 a month. He quickly took on the day-to-day management responsibilities, and in June of that year, when there were openings, he was elected to Continental's Board of Trustees.

The first several years were very difficult ones, with stock sales far slower than had been hoped, bonds sales more difficult than anticipated, and some of the early mortgage loans ending in losses (including an uninsured sawmill which burned down). Mr. Green resigned as president in 1923. However, during the 1920s, Continental was very active financing the construction of many apartment buildings and other commercial properties in the University District, Capitol Hill and other parts of Seattle. These included the University Methodist Temple and Seattle Repertory Theater in the University District. Continental provided a variety of additional financial and real estate services, including financing single-family homes, bonds and other investments, insurance, property management, and real estate sales. Continental represented several life insurance companies as their mortgage loan correspondent. W. Walter Williams became president of Continental in 1927.

The Depression years were very difficult for Continental as they were for most businesses and individuals in the Seattle area. Even during these times, however Continental continued to look for new ways of meeting the needs of the communities. It moved its office to downtown Seattle and changed its name to Continental, Inc. to better reflect its diverse real estate and financial services. W. Walter Williams was elected to be president of the Mortgage Bankers Association of America and met with former President Herbert Hoover and President Franklin D. Roosevelt. After the Federal Housing Authority was formed, Continental was

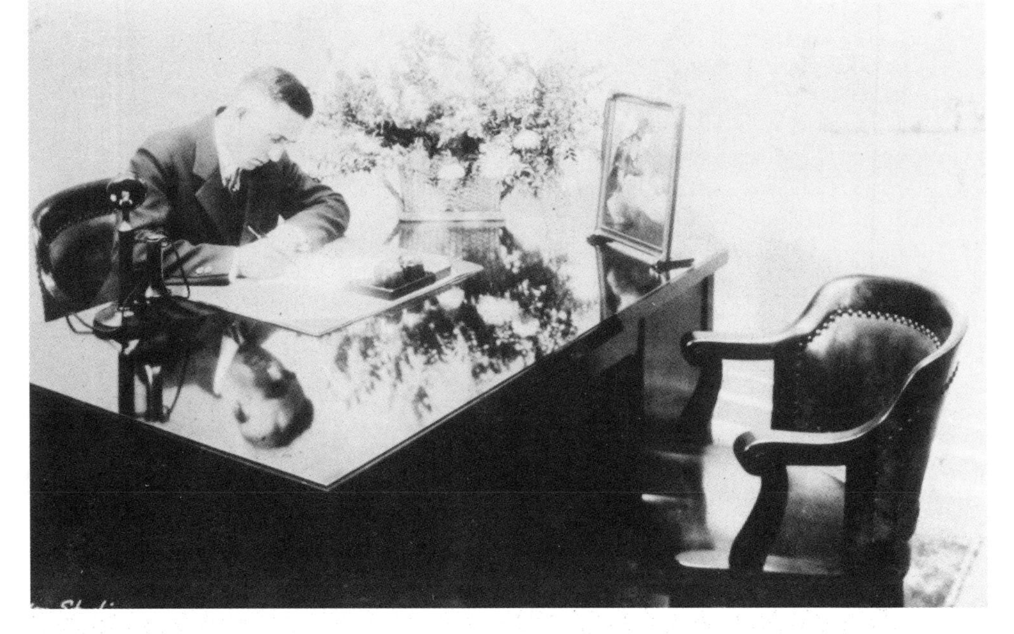

W. Walter Williams, 1925

◆

◆

Early 1920's family home.

approved to make FHA home loans for the life insurance companies and, later, for the Federal National Mortgage Association.

When World War II broke out, building materials were scarce and rationed, but Continental teamed up with builders who were to construct homes for the "war workers" flooding Seattle. New communities of moderate-priced homes were built in Magnolia, Beacon Hill and north Seattle. By 1944, Continental was ranked the third largest mortgage lender in King County, providing both construction and permanent financing.

During the "post war years", Continental responded to the new needs of young families. It added "VA" loans for the returning soldiers to its other loan programs, and Continental continued to finance the construction of new homes and new communities. During the 1950s and 60s, these communities were frequently in the suburbs on the east side of Lake Washington. Continental continued to finance apartment and commercial buildings, but it also saw new patterns to the Northwest life. Continental was an early partner in the development of Northgate, one of the first shopping centers in the nation, and then went on to develop University Village, Aurora Village, and Westwood Village.

Today's Pacific Northwest family home.

In 1964, Walter B. Williams, the son of W. Walter Williams, took the leadership of Continental as its new president. In the 1960s and 70s, the real estate and financial needs continued to evolve and Continental did so, too. Branch offices were opened from Lynnwood to Olympia and from Bellevue to Silverdale. In the mid-60s, Continental became involved with life insurance companies in what was called "The Billion Dollar Program" to provide loans for inner city development, and Continental handled the financing for Group Health Hospital. It also developed the first "mini-storage" facilities in the Pacific Northwest. When Boeing had its major "downturn" in the late 60s and early 70s, times again were quite difficult for Continental as well as for its customers and builders, but Continental was able to weather through it.

Walter B. Williams

Continental continued to grow in the 1980s, opening more branches in Washington State and in Oregon, as well. In order to meet the increasing and changing financial needs of the community as well as Continental, itself, in 1986, Continental Savings Bank was started. In an era of bank mergers and "mega-banks", Continental felt that there was a strong need for a regional bank which could provide personal service, a variety of financial products including checking accounts, C.D.s and ATM access, and competitive rates. Since then, Continental has been one of the fastest growing financial institutions in the state of Washington, indicating that once again it was meeting the needs of its Northwest communities' customers.

In 1990, Richard S. Swanson, was elected Continental's president, and Walter B. Williams became chairman. Continental continues to grow in ways that serve Northwest communities, through more branches (now in Washington, Oregon, Idaho, and Hawaii), more products, and more services, but always with the tradition of high standards of service and integrity.

GROUP HEALTH COOPERATIVE

In 1947, a few hundred Seattle-area citizens—members of granges, labor unions, and consumer cooperatives—joined a group of idealistic physicians to form Group Health Cooperative of Puget Sound. As Group Health celebrates its 50th anniversary in 1997, it has grown into the nation's largest not-for-profit, consumer-governed healthcare organization.

Today the Northwest's largest managed healthcare system, Group Health provides more than 700,000 residents of Washington state and North Idaho with comprehensive, coordinated healthcare for a fixed, prepaid fee. The Cooperative offers care through its health maintenance organization, through self-funding health insurance options, and through the region's first point-of-service plans—which allow patients to choose doctors from a managed-care network (with minimal copayments) or from any community doctor (for a slightly higher fee).

The Cooperative's nearly 850 staff doctors provide care in more than 40 Group Health–owned medical centers and hospitals, and with patients in their home or workplace. In addition, its affiliates, subsidiaries, alliances, and partners offer care to patients in a variety of settings. Group Health also contracts with an additional 2,400 community doctors and group practices for primary care and consulting specialty services.

No matter the plan or the setting, the Cooperative's doctors and nurses focus on prevention-oriented, coordinated care.

Over the past 50 years, Group Health has come to be regarded by many national experts as a model for the future delivery of healthcare. Along the way, the Cooperative's initiatives, innovation, research, and community outreach have advanced prevention, health promotion, and the treatment of disease. From studies on women's health issues and the management of chronic diseases, to community partnerships against violence, Group Health continues to break new ground in health research and care delivery:

- The Cooperative, with the University of Washington, developed one of the first programs in the country to train family practice doctors.
- Group Health pioneered a proactive breast cancer screening program.
- Group Health was the first health plan in the region to receive full accreditation by the National Committee for Quality Assurance.
- The Cooperative is in the forefront of developing evidence-based clinical guidelines — an effort still in its infancy in the United States.

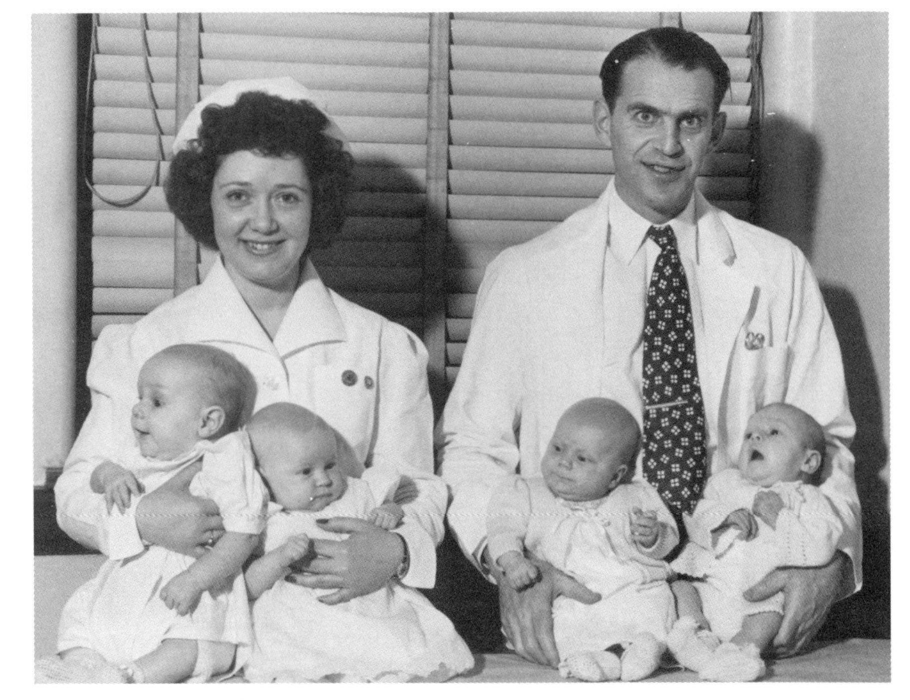

Nurse Elise Cook and Dr. Sandy MacColl show off the first Group Health Cooperative babies in 1947: Trygve Erickson (left), Wendy Lou Hougen, Joanna Marie Jenner, and Roger Paulsen.

St. Luke's Hospital (Group Health's first), is shown shortly after its expansion in 1950.

Group Health's dedicated staff and visionary members believe that health is everybody's business and everybody's right. Its member-elected Board of Trustees works with administrators to devise new ways to make quality healthcare more affordable and efficient for its members.

At the same time, the Cooperative reaches out to improve the health and well-being of the community... through partnerships with local health agencies, community groups, employers, and schools. Group Health has implemented preventive programs to deal with common public health issues such as teen smoking, infant mortality, vaccine-preventable disease, and violence.

Through the years, Group Health has demonstrated the role that a socially responsible healthcare organization can play in improving the quality of life for its members and the community. That spirit will continue to guide Group Health's evolution through its next 50 years.

KIBBLE & PRENTICE

When Ted Kibble and Arnie Prentice boarded the same flight to attend an industry conference 28 years ago, little did they realize that their chance encounter and ensuing friendship would create one of the earliest and largest fully integrated financial services firms in the United States. Founded in 1972 in a shoebox office and with only one employee, Robbie Ferderer, Kibble & Prentice, Inc. now employs more than 100 individuals who provide comprehensive financial services to clients throughout the Pacific Northwest.

Initially trained as life insurance agents, Ted and Arnie were well versed in providing business and estate planning-related life insurance products to the owners of privately held businesses and wealthy individuals. Yet, they realized that their clients' needs for financial services were much broader. Time and again, the goals of *building net worth and managing risk* were mentioned. Ted and Arnie chose to adopt this as their credo. While providing business and estate planning life insurance, property and casualty insurance, employee benefits, pension administration and investments, Kibble & Prentice has found that clients' goals are achieved while saving those clients significant time and money. As the Puget Sound region's economy recovered from Boeing layoffs of the late 1960s and into the early 1970s, Kibble & Prentice added an employee benefits practice. Dale Cowles, an employee benefit specialist, joined the company in 1974 to build an independent group medical, dental, disability, life insurance and flexible benefits business. This component of Kibble & Prentice's business is one of the largest of its kind in the Pacific Northwest, currently serving more than 500 corporate clients with employers ranging in size from 10 to 5,000 employees.

As their employee benefits department grew, Ted and Arnie sought additional and innovative strategies to help their estate planning and life insurance clients transfer wealth and manage risk. In the early 1980s, the company joined the M-Financial Network, a nationwide consortium of companies like Kibble & Prentice, providing its members greater buying power and access to a diversity of innovative life insurance products. Today, M-Financial is the leading provider of estate planning and management compensation-related life insurance products to America's fortune 1,000 companies and their owners.

As a response to client investment needs, Kibble & Prentice initiated its investment consulting services in the early 1980s. Today, through its strategic relationships with the Frank Russell Company of Tacoma and the Charles Schwab & Co., Inc., Kibble & Prentice continues to provide financial strategies and investment opportunities to wealthy individuals and the trustees of qualified retirement plans.

During this same period of growth and expansion, Arnie and Ted pursued the goal of helping clients build net worth by assisting entrepreneurs with the financing of small, privately held businesses. As businessmen, they invested and helped raise capital for then emerging companies such as Northland Cable Communications (now the 30th largest cable business in the United States) and the Northwest franchise of the Drug Emporium. Most notably, in 1986, a young entrepreneur named Howard Schultz approached Arnie and Ted for help in raising the initial funding of Il Giornali, which was later to acquire the Starbucks Coffee Company. Many of Kibble & Prentice's clients invested in Starbucks and continue to invest as other opportunities arise. The company's reputation as a leader in sources of capital for privately held Northwest ventures continues. Today, more than 20 different companies employing more than 10,000 people and generating revenues in excess of two billion dollars have benefited from their efforts.

The last two components of Kibble & Prentice's financial services were in place by the mid 1980s. After the company's investment business was launched, Ron Sheron joined the company to develop a fully integrated property and casualty insurance brokerage for Kibble & Prentice clients. Ron and his staff developed a leading regional brokerage which in 1988 purchased Bellevue's Western Insurance Company. This merger created one of the largest independently-owned property and casualty businesses in the Northwest. Today, this division of Kibble & Prentice employs 45 people who provide commercial and individual property and casualty brokerage services. It is now one of the three largest privately and locally owned property and casualty businesses in the Northwest.

Finally, as a response to client interest in defined contribution retirement plans, Kibble & Prentice developed its pension administration division. This division, headed by Craig Stuart, provides record keeping, reporting and administrative services to the trustee and participants of qualified plans. In 1991, Kibble & Prentice purchased the pension administration services of Security Pacific Bank. This division, among the first to offer electronic record keeping and true daily valuation of participant accounts, currently serves more than 300 clients.

Time and outside influences can have a dramatic impact on the goals and aspirations of young entrepreneurs. In the case of Kibble & Prentice, the company has developed into the complex and comprehensive financial services firm envisioned by Ted and Arnie. The company continues to grow and be a positive force in the emergence of the Pacific Northwest as a major center of commerce in the United States. Today, as in 1972, the company remains committed to *building net worth and managing risk.*

HOWARD S. WRIGHT CONSTRUCTION CO.

The name Howard S. Wright is synonymous with construction in the Northwest and has been since 1885. For more than a century, Wright has virtually shaped the skyline of Seattle. In fact, the very symbol of Seattle, the Space Needle, was built by Howard S. Wright Construction.

Some of the other more visible landmarks the company has constructed include the 76-story Columbia Seafirst Center (one of the tallest buildings west of the Mississippi), the Washington Mutual Tower, Westlake Center, Westin Hotel's twin round towers, the Sheraton Hotel, Northgate Mall (the first covered shopping center in the nation), the Seattle Art Museum and the Monorail.

In more recent years, under new leadership, the company is also shaping the character of surrounding communities that are home to many high-tech companies, including Microsoft where new construction is continually underway. These new buildings join other Wright-built Eastside landmarks such as One Bellevue Center and the Rainier Bank Plaza in Bellevue, the Physio-Control Corporation complex in Redmond and the Ste. Michelle Winery in Woodinville.

Meanwhile, the Seattle core continues to reflect Wright Construction's handiwork. One of the more recent high visibility projects is the Meridian Block, which was instrumental in revitalizing that part of downtown because it includes such prominent names as Niketown, Wolfgang Puck's ObaChine restaurant, SEGA Gameworks entertainment facility, the Original Levi's Store and 16 movie theaters for Cineplex Odeon.

The firm's influence is not limited to the Northwest, as evidenced by its expanding geographic reach, built around customer service. So far the company has opened offices in three other locations–Portland, Sacramento and Phoenix–to support existing customers.

In Portland, for example, Wright Construction has done projects for such customers as Nike, U.S. Bank, Rouse Development and Wright Runstad. Sacramento projects include work for AT&T, MCI, Price Costco, and Forest City Developers. While from Phoenix the company customer list includes Rouse Development, Electric Lightwave and Hilton Hotels.

With all of this activity, the company's annual revenues now exceed $200–million.

Howard S. Wright, founder of the company bearing his name.

◆

The origins of this influential building firm can be traced to a draftsman, cabinetmaker, and framing superintendent named Howard S. Wright who was born in Nova Scotia. In 1885 he established himself in the frontier town of Port Townsend as a homebuilder.

Wright moved the business to Everett in 1893 and expanded it to include schools, apartments, and other commercial struc-

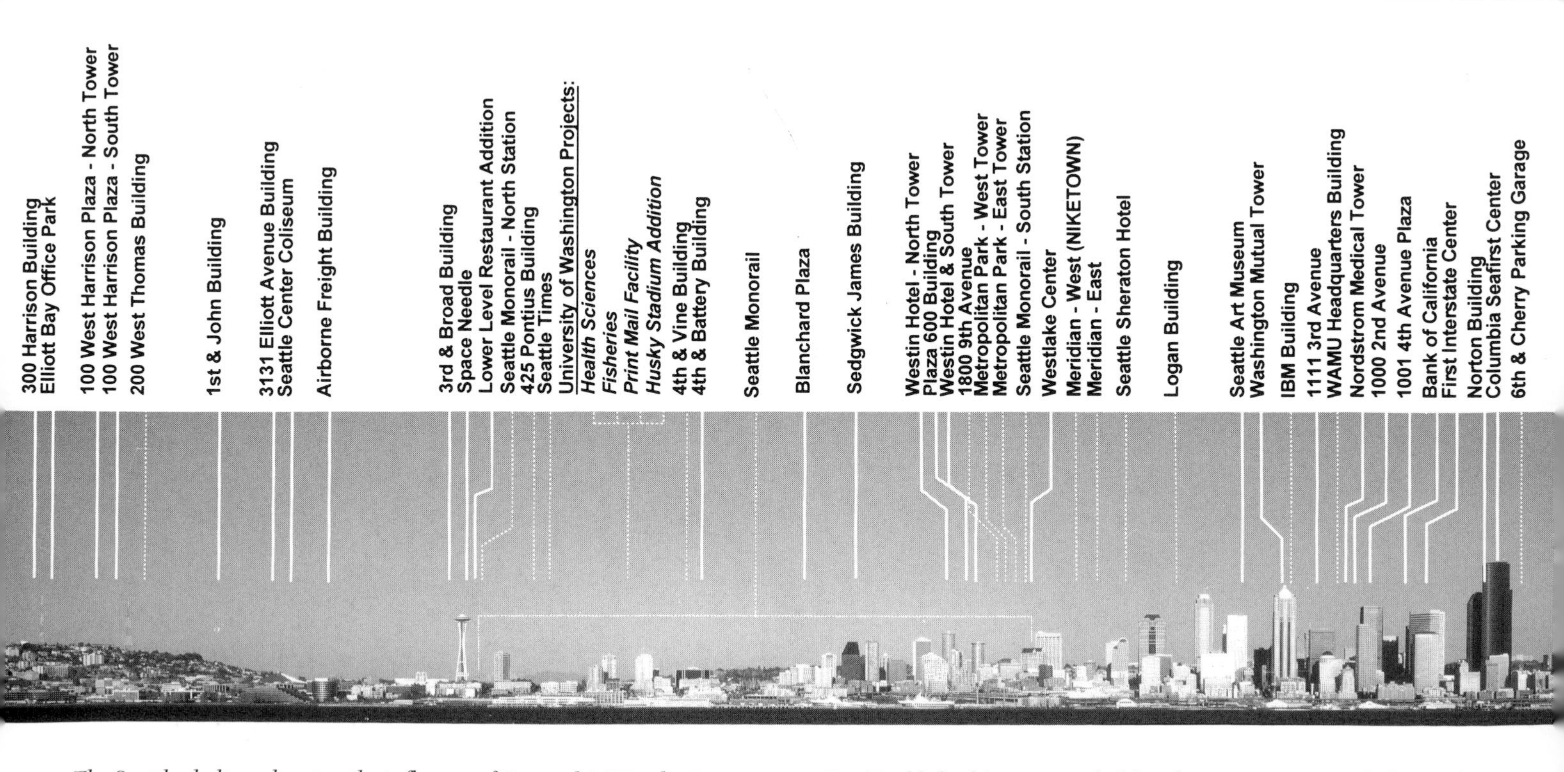

The Seattle skyline, showing the influence of Howard S. Wright Construction Co. (Visible buildings are in bold and unseen ones are in light type).

tures. Around the turn of the century, he took time away from his business to work as a framing superintendent on the elegant Del Coronado Hotel in San Diego.

Wright's son, Howard H. Wright, was born in 1899 and went to work for his father in 1923. About the same time, his brother-in-law, George J. Schuchart, joined the firm. Wright moved the company to Seattle in the mid-1930s and gave control of the business to his son and George Schuchart. In the 1930s, the company built the Gainsborough Apartments, the Cascadian Hotel in Wenatchee, the Aberdeen World newspaper building, Cougar Stadium in Pullman, and their first pulp and paper mill, a line of work that would become a cornerstone.

The war years gave the business a needed boost. Between 1941 and 1944, nearly all of Wright's work was war related. They built projects for the Puget Sound Naval Shipyard and, in joint venture, constructed the city of Richland.

After the war, they returned to private construction and built numerous structures, including the *Seattle Post-Intelligencer* building, Children's Orthopedic Hospital and the largest concrete structure in the world at that time, a hangar at Moses Lake that housed eight B-52s with its doors closed.

Howard H. Wright was a dynamic leader in the construction industry, fostering many innovative construction techniques. He insisted on close team work between the contractor, architect, and engineers. That philosophy resulted in almost unbelievable records for fast construction, a legacy that continues to this day and explains why the firm does predominently negotiated work.

By 1955, annual revenues exceeded $18 million. Twenty some years later, that figure has increased eleven-fold to more than $200-million.

When Howard H. Wright became seriously ill in 1956, the firm was reorganized. Wright and his brother-in-law, George J. Schuchart, gave up day-to-day management of the company to their sons, Howard S. Wright II and George S. Schuchart. This third-generation partnership made the company one of the leading construction firms in the West.

The Space Needle, the symbol of Seattle, was built by Howard S. Wright Construction Co. for the 1962 World's Fair.

◆

Several companies grew out of, or became affiliated with, the original Howard S. Wright Construction Company. They include: Wright Schuchart Harbor Company, General Construction Company, Schuchart Industrial Contractors, Inc., Harbor Electrical, Inc., Commercial Plumbing and Heating Company, HUICO, Inc., and Arctic Slope Alaska General. They also had affiliate companies in Canada.

Although the Wright family has not been involved in running the business since it was sold in 1988 to the huge New Zealand conglomerate, Fletcher Challenge, the name of the founder is back on the door, thanks to a more recent change in ownership.

In late 1996 Fletcher decided to exit the North American construction market and sold the company to the local management team.

President/CEO Brad Nydahl and Executive Vice President Mark Johnson lead the new team of owners. Their first act was to put the most venerated name in the Northwest construction industry back in the title. And, just like the namesake, they also put their emphasis into building long-term relationships with some of the best customer names in the Northwest—Boeing, Microsoft, Wright Runstad, Rouse, Nike, the U.S. Navy and many more.

More than one skyline has been shaped by the company. The majority of the buildings shown in this aerial view of the Microsoft campus were built by Howard S. Wright Construction Co.

LOOMIS, FARGO & CO.

From his youth to his later days as founder of the Loomis Armored Car Service Company, Lee B. Loomis was a true American pioneer. Throughout his life he always sought opportunity. Despite risks and uncertainty, his mettle and persistence moved him to face the frontiers of his day.

Lee B. Loomis was born on June 24, 1870 in Elm Hall, Michigan. At the age of ten, his family moved to the Dakota Territory where he helped his father, George H. Loomis, run a general store in the prairie. In his teens, he rode the range at his father's ranch in Ipswich, Dakota Territory. The Loomis family was caught up in the Indian uprising of 1883 and 1884, which included the Custer Massacre. In 1890, at the age of twenty, Lee married and in the same year was present at the last Sioux uprising, the Battle at Wounded Knee.

Lee tended stock until 1894, when he moved to Seattle, Washington with his brother-in-law Charlie Jones. Sending his wife and three children ahead of him by paying their fares with fifty dollars he borrowed, Lee "worked" his way across the country. In Bozeman, Montana he punched cattle and broke horses for several months. He sent most of his earnings to his wife in Seattle, building up a reserve that enabled him to join her later that year.

During his first few years in Seattle, he operated a stock seed business. In 1896, he staked a claim on the old channel of Canyon Creek in Whatcom County, Washington. After just three trips earned him about ten dollars a day in gold dust, the pioneer spirit gripped him once again.

On July 24, 1897 Lee B. Loomis left for Alaska aboard the S.S. Mexico, the second ship to leave Seattle for the Klondike gold rush. The nine-hundred mile passage brought Lee and hundreds of others to Dyea, Alaska. He and his partner, Billy Hensell, then packed over grueling Chilkoot Pass to Lake Bennett. It was here that all of their supplies and the boat they had just purchased was stolen. Without supplies or funds, Lee worked as a boat builder and packer in order to acquire more gear.

During the winter of 1897-88, Charlie Jones rejoined Lee in Skagway, Alaska. They each got jobs caring for horses that winter and in the spring of 1898 went to Dawson City, Yukon Territory and operated a general store. In 1903 Lee left for Nome, in the far western part of Alaska, where stories of gold strikes aroused his interest. Panning for gold, he instead amassed a debt of $4,000. He then borrowed another $5,000 when he had the chance to purchase used outfits and provisions from men who gave up on the gold rush to return to the States. He resold the goods to incoming prospectors at a 100 percent profit. The next year Lee moved to Fairbanks where rich gold strikes were making headlines. With his earnings from these gold fields and other odd jobs, he was able to get himself completely out of debt. He now owned four saddle horses, a one-half interest in a pack train of ten mules and a one-third interest in a store.

The first Loomis armored car, September 10, 1925. Lee Loomis is at left.

◆

In 1905 he started the Cleary Creek Commercial Company near Fairbanks. Known there as the "Four C's", they established the first free delivery on Cleary Creek, thirty miles north of Fairbanks. Their main business became dog sled transport service to nearby mines, carrying supplies directly to customers. Because of his personal integrity and reliability, Lee was then entrusted to transport gold safely back to town on behalf of his customers. It would be another twenty years until he started a similar service with armored cars.

In 1906, Lee returned to Seattle where he earned a living shipping horses to Alaska. Two years later, in charge of the "Julia B.", a

Yukon River boat, he left Seattle pulling two barges destined for St. Michael, Alaska. During the two-month trip to the Yukon River he lost one of the barges in the ocean due to stormy seas.

Lee spent the next fourteen years in Seattle where he owned Westlake Sales and Livery Stables and was the main supplier of horses sold and shipped to Alaska. He also furnished horses for the city of Seattle, the Fire Department, department stores, commercial houses and the U.S. Army at Fort Lewis. Following the death of his first wife in 1920, he returned to Alaska once again.

In 1922 Lee took a position with the Northern Commercial Company in the Kuskokwim district. He headed two trading posts, Tokotna and McGrath on the Kuskokwim River, shipping out six hundred tons of goods annually, trading with trappers for their furs and with miners for their gold dust at sixteen dollars an ounce.

In 1923, as postmaster in the Kuskokwim country, Lee hired Grace A. Anderson as clerk. She became his second wife, and has the added distinction of handling the first airmail ever received or dispatched in Alaska.

Lee bid farewell to Alaska in 1925 to settle down in Portland, Oregon. He took his entire $8,000 savings and commissioned a Portland carriage works to build an armored body on a new White chassis. The first armored car west of St. Louis, it was put into service in Portland on September 10, 1925.

Lee B. Loomis (fourth from left), son Walter(second from right), remainder of his family and his partner in front of the cabin he built in Fairbanks, Alaska, circa 1904.

His first customer was the Federal Reserve Bank, followed by several area banks. Other businesses showed little interest in the car until a violent crime wave hit Portland in the late 1920s. A well-publicized robbery of the city's biggest department store was the turning point. They signed up, followed by the theaters, newspapers, mercantile firms, electric, steamship, motor and railway companies.

After his startup of this new industry proved successful, Lee persisted with its early growth. Over the next fifteen years armored car service was established in Vancouver (Canada), Seattle (company headquarters), Tacoma, Spokane, San Francisco, Oakland and Sacramento. His sons, Walter and Leon, were instrumental in the development of the Loomis Armored Car Service Company.

Lee B. Loomis never lost interest in the affairs of Alaska. He served as president of the Oregon-Alaska-Yukon Society, president of the International Sourdough Reunion and was chairman of the international convention of the Alaska-Yukon Society. His name was prominent in connection with Presidential appointments to the Alaska International Highway Commission formed to administrate the construction of the Alaska Highway. With respect to the nominations, an editorial in a Northwest newspaper wrote of him: "Loomis is a practical, hard-headed business man of good judgment who is in the transportation business and is thoroughly familiar with Northern conditions, is well known and trusted in Canada—a thoroughly good man for the position".

Lee was also elected president-emeritus of the National Armored Car Association, but soon after passed away on April 1, 1949 at the age of 78. Walter Loomis immediately succeeded his father as president of the company and in 1960, grandson Charles became president. Loomis Armored Car Service became a prominent national company under continuous family leadership for five decades.

Founder, Lee B. Loomis.

The Loomis, Fargo & Co. of today maintains the same status as the premier service provider in the armored car industry. The 1997 merger of Loomis Armored Inc. and Wells Fargo Armored Service Corporation brings service coverage to all fifty states. Strategically, the future looks bright as the company continues to pioneer better ways to serve its customers just as Lee Loomis did.

Loomis, Fargo & Co. fully embraces the proud heritage of the Loomis name—the rugged tradition of Lee Loomis' first dog sled carrying miner's gold safely out of the wilderness to his vision in 1925 of a fleet of modern armored cars.

MARKEY MACHINERY CO., INC.

In 1957 a small blue book, "The Markey Story," opened with these simple words: *The log of the Markey Machinery's first 50 years...not so much to look back, as to remind ourselves, our customers and our other friends that progress is made by looking ahead.* The story has always been a true "Log" because MARKEY began as a waterfront firm and remains so today.

Charles Henry Markey went to sea in 1902 at the age of 24. With two partners, C.H. built the power schooner "Alice," trading as far north as Nome in 1905. In 1907 he came ashore and began the C.H. Markey Machinery Co., located at Weller and Occidental, moving to Smith's Cove in 1910 with John Wilson to build cannery vessels and fishing craft as "Markey & Wilson." The name changed to "Markey Machinery Co.," just before WW-I.

Demand for steam cargo winches, windlasses & steering gear required the 1917 erection of the present "Plant I" on Horton Street. In 1925 C.H.'s son, Bill Markey, joined as a truck driver, draftsman, and engineer. With his time at the U of W, with a 2nd Engineer's ticket, and with his years around the shipyard and shop, William Charles Markey began his 63 year career.

The depression demanded diversity. MARKEY's did ship repair, built the equipment for the lead mill on Harbor Island, hot water tanks, and even its own line of Markey diesel engines — the "Viking." The firm survived because manufacturing integrity and financial independence were the core of C.H.'s beliefs. The Markey's lived closely, with available funds going back into the firm.

As the thirties ended, the war build-up required enlargement on Horton Street and the construction of a steel fabricating shop on 8th Avenue South — "Plant II." A second machine shop was built and then enlarged at the new site, becoming "Plant III." The firm's involvement in the second war included 400 men, seven days around the clock. In 1943 the "Army-Navy E" award ceremony in Victory Square honored that work.

When C.H. Markey died in 1948, Bill Markey became President. "Hell For Stout" and "Build What You Know You Can Build Right" were two of his core beliefs. These were absorbed by his sons, Donn and Michael, along with "Don't pay interest on other people's money," and "Pay your bills on time." Growth was secondary to readiness for the next slow period.

In 1996 Markey employees gather by Oceanographic Traction Winch—one of 3 shipsets for AGOR class R/V's assigned to Scripps, Woods Hole & NOAA.

Donn Markey left lumber hauling to join the firm in 1957, shoring up the fabrication operations. His younger brother, Michael, came west in 1958 after four years with G.E. to start over as a draftsman.

In 1988, Bill's health ended his Presidency after 40 years of leading one of the country's most respected deck machinery producers. He was welcomed in nearly every Naval Architect's office, shipyard and tug fleet on the salt water coasts. Until his passing in May of 1996, he visited his office and made the rounds regularly.

Mike Markey moved from Chief Engineer to President in 1988. He accelerated the computerization of the firm, pushed the department heads to freshen the shop equipment, and began the change from W.C.'s successful one-man rule toward team management.

In 1996, Mike saw the need to speed the process and to move the younger men into the point jobs. Engineering Manager, Blaine W. Dempke with 18 years as a draftsman and designer, and studies at the U.W. business school, became the 4th president of MARKEY. Several others from Blaine's generation stepped up to tackle today's hard management issues. The Markey brothers and their senior peers could now focus on doing what they do best. Several father-son teams have made careers with the firm including three generations of LeCoques running the shop operations.

From 2 partners to 400 men during WW II and back to the present 50, the MARKEY MACHINERY story has remained one of good people doing what they enjoy—and doing it right.

In 1943 Bill Markey(left) and C.H.Markey (far right) at the Army-Navy "E" presentation.

PACCAR INC

In 1905, William Pigott, Sr. founded Seattle Car Mfg. Co. to produce railway and logging equipment at its plant in West Seattle. The company later merged with Twohy Brothers of Portland to become Pacific Car and Foundry Company, a name retained for the next 55 years.

In 1924, William Pigott sold control of the company to American Car and Foundry Company. During the Depression of 1929, business declined and the Renton plant fell into disrepair.

Products from Seattle Car Manufacturing Company roll along the shores of Puget Sound, circa 1907.

Paul Pigott, son of the founder, acquired a major interest in the company from American Car in 1934. Under his leadership, the company expanded its products and introduced the Carco line of power winches for use on crawler tractors in the logging industry. This product line later became the basis for PACCAR's Winch Division which now includes Braden, Carco and Gearmatic.

In 1941, America went to war, and the company's Renton plant built Sherman Tanks and tank recovery vehicles for the military. Pacific Car and Foundry also constructed dry docks and steel tugboats during the conflict.

The company entered the heavy-duty truck market in 1945 with its first major acquisition, Kenworth Motor Truck Company of Seattle. Pacific Car and Foundry greatly expanded its heavy-duty truck capability with the purchase of Peterbilt Motors Company in 1958.

In 1960, PACCAR became an international truck manufacturer. Kenworth moved into Mexico with 49 percent participation in an affiliate company, Kenworth Mexicana S.A. de C.V., now a wholly owned subsidiary. In 1966, PACCAR entered the Australian truck market with the establishment of a Kenworth Truck assembly plant near Melbourne.

In 1960, Carco Acceptance Corporation, currently PACCAR Financial Corp., was launched to facilitate domestic sales of trucks, and in 1967, the Dynacraft division was formed to provide belts, hoses, adapters, and other accessories for Kenworth and Peterbilt truck plants.

Believing "Pacific Car and Foundry Company" no longer accurately reflected the company's products and activities, directors and shareholders voted to adopt PACCAR Inc as its new name in 1972.

In 1973, PACCAR International was formed to consolidate the sales and service of company products abroad, and PACCAR Parts Division was established in Renton to supply aftermarket parts sales.

PACCAR Leasing Corporation was established in 1980 to offer full-service leasing and rental programs. A year later, PACCAR became an European truck manufacturer with the acquisition of Foden Trucks in Sandbach, U.K.

PACCAR's new Technical Center opened in July of 1982. Located approximately 65 miles north of Seattle, the multimillion-dollar center underscored the company's commitment to technical excellence, quality and value in the products it manufactures.

In 1986, PACCAR became a recognized world leader in manufacturing oil field pumps and accessories with the addition of Trico Industries, Inc.

PACCAR acquired Washington-based Al's Auto Supply, an aftermarket retailer and wholesale distributor of auto parts and accessories in 1987. A year later, it added Grand Auto, Inc., a California-based retailer of auto parts and accessories, to its PACCAR Automotive subsidiary.

The acquisition of DAF Trucks N.V. in 1996 solidified PACCAR's position as one of the top three heavy-duty truck manufacturers in the world. DAF Trucks is a Netherlands-based truck company with production facilities in Eindhoven, the Netherlands and Westerlo, Belgium.

Today, PACCAR Inc is a worldwide manufacturer of heavy-duty trucks under the Kenworth, Peterbilt, DAF and Foden nameplates. It also provides financial services and distributes truck parts related to its principal business. In addition, the Bellevue, Washington-based company manufactures industrial winches and oil field extraction pumps and sells automotive parts and accessories.

This is a view of the Pacific Car & Foundry plant in Renton, about 1920.

PHYSIO-CONTROL CORPORATION

Physio-Control's North Building was dedicated in May 1981, completing a 25-acre campus development.

Perhaps one day we will live in a society in which no person dies suddenly from cardiac arrest. So envisions Physio-Control, the Redmond-based company that pioneered portable defibrillation technology and is today recognized as world leader in acute cardiac care devices.

This Northwest success story began more than 40 years ago when Dr. Karl William Edmark, a Seattle cardiovascular surgeon, developed a machine that could stop the uncoordinated contractions of a fibrillating heart, allow it to resume normal activity: the first direct current (DC) external defibrillator. He patented his device and in 1955 formed a company which he named Physio-Control.

A sideline business, there were lean years for Edmark's small enterprise, then in 1965 he hired W. Hunter Simpson, head of IBM's Northwest District office in Seattle, to provide company direction. Simpson established a financial base and working environment infused with motivation and determination for success.

His expectation was realized. In 1968 Physio-Control developed a product that changed emergency medical care: the first portable defibrillator/monitor, a lightweight, battery-powered device which enabled paramedics, for the first time, to defibrillate patients at the scene of a cardiac event, *before* transport to a hospital. Then in 1976 the company introduced the LIFEPAK 5 defibrillator/monitor, which, because of its durability and small, interchangeable batteries, was a paramedic standard for many years.

As Physio grew, so did the scope of its products. Defibrillator/monitors for hospitals and emergency medical systems utilized the latest technology, added external noninvasive pacing to the LIFEPAK products.

During the 1980s Physio pioneered semi-automatic defibrillators, specifically designed for emergency medical technicians (EMTs) trained to defibrillate. A decade later the American Heart Association embraced automated external defibrillators (AEDs) such as the LIFEPAK 500 AED for first responders, police officers, firefighters, security guards, flight attendants and others generally first to reach the scene of a cardiac arrest.

Because cardiac care doesn't end with first response, Physio develops products that connect the health care system, from management of cardiac arrest on the street or in the home, through transport to a hospital, to care in the hospital, to follow up data management.

One product that exemplifies this connectivity is a diagnostic cardiac monitor developed in the mid-1990s that enables paramedics to take a 12-lead electrocardiogram at the scene of a suspected cardiac arrest and via cell phone and modem transmit diagnostic information to the hospital prior to the patient's arrival. A trend for moving care to the patient rather than moving the patient to care favors development of such devices.

Known as a humanitarian company, Physio donates equipment to organizations that provide medical assistance to underdeveloped countries and to U.S. disaster teams for rescue operation during earthquake, hurricane, and other catastrophes. Physio also sends LIFEPAK products to the Olympic Games, Goodwill Games, Tour de France, and other major events. The company's defibrillators are in the White House, aboard Air Force One, and support the U.S. military during peace and conflict.

Physio is frequently recognized by industry and civic organizations as an outstanding corporate citizen and a superior place to work for its 1,000 team members. Awards run the gamut from commendation for its environmentally sensitive campus to accolades for programs that employ the physically and developmentally disabled. Physio has been featured in *The 100 Best Companies to Work for in America* and in 1996 was named by *IndustryWeek* magazine as one of "America's 10 Best Plants."

Although Physio retains an entrepreneurial spirit, it recognizes the value of sharing its technology and resources. Alliances have formed with like-minded medical instrumentation companies, such as Marquette Medical Systems, Inc., and relationships strengthened with key research laboratories dedicated to defibrillation technology such as the University of Alabama, Birmingham.

Physio has known change: under Simpson a public company, it was acquired by Eli Lilly and Company in 1980, sold to Bain Capital, Inc., in 1994, then once again became a public entity in 1995. But the company's mission has remained consistent: *"We make lifesaving tools for lifesaving teams, unique medical devices of the highest quality which predict or urgently intervene in life-threatening, cardiorespiratory events."*

Somewhere in the world right now an ambulance weaves in and out of traffic, medics on board working to save a life. More than likely it's cardiac arrest. More than likely a LIFEPAK defibrillator/monitor is at the scene.

PRESERVATIVE PAINT COMPANY

In Georgetown, a small village adjacent to Seattle, Asphaltum Products Company began selling asphalt and coal tar products in 1908. Six years later, in response to increasing public demand for bright, colorful paints, it rechartered as Preservative Paint Company. But the story of the company's success and growth began the following year and involved some courageous decisions by a talented young woman.

In 1913, 19-year-old Carrie West exaggerated her age to 25 to get a job as the firm's bookkeeper. Eleven years later when Cash Williams, the company's owner, died, the business was near bankruptcy. Carrie West bought the company, went to San Francisco, and made payment arrangements with the firm's creditors to prevent foreclosure. She brought in her brother, Frank, who was then a student at the University of Washington, and the two of them instituted cost and production controls that resulted in turning the business around and keeping it solvent.

The firm had fully recovered by the late '20s, and Carrie's other brother, Robert, joined the venture. For the following years, even through the Depression, the company prospered, selling retail products at its factory outlet and wholesale to dealers, shipyards, and local industries. It prided itself then, as it does today, on being a Northwest company catering to the Northwest.

In 1938 Carrie sold her interest in the business to her brother, Frank, so that she could enjoy retirement with her husband. In the 1940s, the company began opening stores in the Puget Sound area to serve customers directly and continued to grow. In the 1950s, it extended its distribution to Alaska.

Frank West passed away in 1969 after nearly 50 years with Preservative Paint. For several years the ownership of the firm was tied up in probate and held in trust. In 1972, eight key employees of the company and Ron West, Frank's nephew and Robert's son, who had started his own business processing waste chemicals, bought the firm. In 1975 the company expanded the employee-ownership concept by extending ownership to eligible employees via an employee stock ownership trust.

In 1994, Preservative Paint Co. was acquired by Kelly-Moore Paint Co. Kelly-Moore Paint Co. was established in 1946. In addition to its success, the company takes great pride in its heritage, in that it still manufactures and sells paint in Georgetown, and in that the same building in which it started business 74 years' ago remains a part of its headquarters facility.

The original plant, 1908.

Free monorail rides, 1962.

PSF INDUSTRIES, INC.

In 1900 the promise of a new century inspired men like David W. Bowen to found new companies. Bowen started Puget Sound Sheet Metal Works in rented offices in the Hoge Building to provide sheet metal and roofing for Seattle's booming lumber mills and new buildings. His first plant was located at 1328 Western Avenue.

Today under the name PSF Industries, Inc., the firm serves customers in the western states, utilizing the most modern equipment in heavy metal fabricating and erecting, sheet metal contracting, and engineered air-conditioning systems.

In the early 1900s, Seattle was growing and by 1906 Bowen's success required a move to a larger plant on Railroad Avenue, now Alaskan Way

When Harry S. Bowen, son of the founder, joined the firm at the beginning of World War I, he helped launch the company's war effort—building and fabricating lifeboats, rafts, ventilation and duct equipment, and providing metal fabricating for the area's shipyards. During these hectic years, the company bought land and built a new plant at 3631 East Marginal Way, a site that served as its home for many years.

In the '20s and '30s, when the pulp and paper industry was growing, Puget Sound Sheet Metal supplied complex sheet metal and roofing configurations for plants throughout the Northwest.

During World War II, virtually all of the company's work was again war-related. For several years it leased a large plant at the north end of Boeing Field and provided 1,000 aircraft workers to assemble fuselage sections, wings, bulkheads, pilot floors, and other aircraft parts for the B-17 and B-29 bombers.

The firm's plant was completely destroyed by fire in 1949. Puget Sound Sheet Metal continued operating in rented facilities with rebuilt and rented machinery while a new 70,000-square-foot plant and office were constructed on a newly purchased 5-acre site adjacent to the destroyed plant.

In 1965 a group of key employees headed by James Beardsley Jr., acquired the remaining Bowen family interests in the business. The new owners changed the name to PSF Industries, Inc., and moved the plant to its present home at 65 South Horton Street.

By 1980 PSF Industries had a $2-million annual payroll and two major operating divisions. The Metal Fabricating Division custom fabricates heavy steel alloys and exotic metals for a variety of uses, and erects tanks, towers, and process and pressure vessels on industrial project sites throughout the western United States. The Sheet Metal Division fabricates and installs architectural sheet metal, engineered air-conditioning systems, and roof deck structures for commercial buildings p marily in western Washington. Much of the Division's work can be seen in the buildings that make up Seattle's skyline.

◆

Below
Puget Sound Sheet Metal, forerunner of today's PSF Industries, at 1328 Western Avenue in 1900, the year it was founded.
Bottom
Ventilator cowlings made by the company for military use during World War I.

Top left
Autoclave,one of three, weighing at 1 million pounds, field fabricated and moved into the production facility at Fredrickson, Washington.
Bottom left
Continuous Digester, weighing in excess of 1 million pounds, along with an Impregnation Vessel, Flash Tanks and 3 Bleach Towers fabricated in PSF's Seattle Shop and Erected at Longview, Washington.

◆

In the late 1980s the Custom Metal Fabrication and Construction Division shifted its emphasis to more on-site erection projects while maintaining its heavy steel plate and alloy fabrication facility. This provides a single source responsibility for design, fabrication and erection of process and pressure vessels, heat exchangers, stacks, tanks, towers and erection and maintenance of boilers.

During the 1990s, PSF Industries has taken on increasingly large and more complex fabrication and erection projects. This work has been a major contribution to fiber board bleach plant modernization projects in the Pulp and Paper industry.

In 1991, the Sheet Metal Divsion was sold to Warren Beardsley. It continues to operate today as PSF Mechanical.

At the end of 1995, James Beardsley, Jr. retired, selling the Beardsley family interest in PSF Industries to Vice President Stanley R. Miller.

PSF Industries continues to move forward under the leadership of Stanley R. Miller and his team of skilled and experienced employees. The office and fabricating plant is still at 65 South Horton Street with an annual payroll averaging $5 ½ Million. Field crews travel throughout the twelve Western States and British Columbia performing field fabrication, erection and maintenance at industrial sites for the Aerospace, Brewing, Mining, Petroleum Refining, Pulp & Paper and Utilities Industries.

Their knowledge and creative talent has enabled PSF to be a leader in ASME code design, engineering, fabrication welding of special materials and construction techniques. Their accomplishments in the industry allows them to be one of the largest heavy steel plate fabricators and erectors in the Northwest. PSF Industries is looking forward to celebrating their 100 year anniversary in the year 2000!

RAINIER BREWING COMPANY

Just over 100 years ago, in 1878, a German immigrant brew-master, Andrew Hemrich, founded a small brewery along Airport Way in the south of Seattle. He called the brewery Seattle Brewing and Malting Company and named his premium beer Rainier. By 1916 this modest brewery which produced only 200 barrels its first year, became the largest brevvery in the state and the sixth largest brewery in the world. The company built its reputation satisfying the legendary thirsts of frontier loggers, miners, farmers, and fishermen, and grew to serve the tastes of the genteel as well as the hearty in the gold fields of Alaska, in California, the Orient, and throughout the Pacific Northwest. The company outlasted many competitors with colorful names—Lorlei, Aero Club, Washington Viking, and Tacoma Pale.

Prohibition in the state of Washington in 1916, however, turned the Georgetown brewery into a feed mill. The buildings survive today, living out a sedate and useful old age as warehouse and icehouse. When the brewery shut down, the Rainier brand name was sold to a brewery in San Francisco. It was not until the 1930s that the name was finally restored to the Northwest by Fritz and Emil Sick, a father and son with extensive brewing interests in Canada. The Sicks acquired the brewery and renamed it Sicks Century Brewing Company and, in addition to Rainier, began bottling Rheinlander, which they billed as "The Beer of the Century" in reference to the firm's new name. The Sicks further celebrated the return of the name by purchasing the Seattle Indians baseball team of the Pacific Coast League and renaming them the Rainiers. In the process, they built Sicks Stadium, which was long regarded as the premier minor league ball park in the country. The Rainiers were an instant success, winning pennants in 1939, 1941, and later, in 1951 and 1955 before being sold to the Boston Red Sox. In the years to follow, the Sicks became involved in many civic, cultural, charitable, and community activities. Emil Sick died in 1964.

Over the years, Rainier has undergone many changes in corporate structure. In 1977 the company was purchased by G. Heileman Brewing Company of La Crosse, Wisconsin. All Heileman assets, including the Rainier brewery and the popular Rainier brand, then were purchased in 1996 by The Stroh Brewery Company, the nation's fourth largest brewing company. Stroh continues to uphold the tradition of brewing excellance established by Andrew Hemrich and the Sick family, and continues to market and distribute Rainier beers across Washington State and throughout the Pacific Northwest.

Top
After the turn of the century, woman played a key role in the production line of the fast-growing enterprise.

Above left
Seattle Brewing and Malting Company, predecessor of today's Rainier Brewing Company, was founded in 1878.

Above right
Still located on Airport Way in the south of Seattle in 1900, the firm's production had greatly increased.

RYTHER CHILD CENTER

For more than 110 years, the name "Ryther" has meant a place where children can find safety, guidance, compassion, and love. In 1883, Olivia Ryther, a recent transplant from the plains of Iowa, took three homeless children into her home. From that first magnanimous step, "the Ryther Way" was born. Through the years this phrase has meant something very special to thousands of children in the Pacific Northwest.

Today, "the Ryther Way" continues at Ryther Child Center. The Center is a nationally recognized and accredited leader in providing vital services for children and their families. The Center cares for some of the most severely damaged and disturbed children in the entire state. Physical and sexual abuse, emotional neglect, and drug and alcohol dependency are the life experiences children bring with them to Ryther. The children who come to the Center are the ones others have given up on and in some cases, forgotten.

Last year, the Center provided services to nearly 2,000 children and their family members. It is not just the number of children and their families that is growing. The severity of the issues which the children bring is increasing in an alarming way. More younger children are needing care and treatment. The staff of Ryther are seeing more and more children and young people coming for care and treatment, not just with 'dual-diagnoses,' but with 'multiple diagnoses.' The extreme emotional and psychological damage inflicted on the children is greater than ever before.

The services the Center provides to the Pacific Northwest community include:

- therapeutic day treatment for children 2 1/2 to 6;
- intensive residential care for children 6 - 12 with significant sexual behavior problems;
- chemical dependency treatment for adolescents including in-patient, out-patient, transitional living and aftercare;
- residential care for children 6 - 12 in a major, traumatic life crisis; residential care for boys 14 and younger transitioning back to the community from the juvenile justice system;
- chemical dependency services to 6 youth agencies; and
- out-patient child and family mental health counseling.

"The Ryther Way" would not be possible without the support of others. In the early days, neighbors shared food and other necessities. As time went on, the community built "the Ryther Home." Today, the special kind of care so vital for thousands of young lives would not be possible without the generosity of thousands of people who believe in and support "the Ryther Way."

Ryther provides almost $1 million a year in uncompensated care. In order to "make ends meet," community support is more crucial than ever. This support comes from individuals, businesses, corporations, foundations, and volunteer organizations like the Ryther Child Center League. As Seattle, King County, and Ryther Child Center move into the 21st century, many things will change. One thing that will not change, thanks to the on-going support of the Pacific Northwest community is–**the Ryther Way...for the children.**

In 1883, Mother Ryther's care, concern and compassion became the foundation for one of the nation's leading child welfare agencies...Ryther Child Center.

Today, Ryther Child Center continues its work to build brighter, more positive futures for thousands of children and their family members.

ROTTLER MANUFACTURING

In 1922 Clarence T. Rottler started the ROTTLER BORING BAR CO. in order to manufacture machine tool equipment for the automotive after market.

This start was not the financially organized beginning of a business as we often see it today. C. T. Rottler worked in a machine shop located on First Avenue South in Seattle. The first machine sale resulted from construction of a portable type machine during off hours, then hand-carrying that machine on a street car to an "automobile row" automotive repair shop to demonstrate it and to sell it.

In the early day of the automobile when travel was mostly on gravel roads, repairs were required frequently. If an automobile journeyed from Seattle to Portland and back, some engine repairs were likely needed.

In this climate, the ROTTLER BORING BAR CO. became an independent entity and increasingly prospered through the roaring twenties. The company occupied larger quarters on 8th Avenue North, across the street from where the Marina Mart is now located, and this became the center of manufacturing. As the depression began, the company moved to a fine manufacturing plant located on West Spokane Street. There were approximately one hundred employees during this early successful period.

Later, at the outbreak of World War II the Spokane Street plant was sold and automotive equipment production for the U. S. Government continued with a smaller work force building portable machines for the typical automotive machine shop generally associated with auto parts sales throughout the United States.

During this time a substantial marketing effort was not implemented, and ROTTLER BORING BAR CO. did not enjoy the same prosperity that existed in the twenties.

Important key people in the company through this first era were, of course, Clarence Rottler and his wife Helen. Florence McLaughlin, a close family friend was Controller. Shop management included Tom Samson, Charles Bailey and Starr Peterson.

An interesting sidelight was C. T. Rottler's avid interest in private flying. Although he was not a pilot, he developed a sales agency active in Washington, Oregon and California for the WACO aircraft and sold a number of airplanes during the mid 1930s.

Company headquarters and manufacturing plant on Spokane Street in the 1930s.

◆

Clarence T. Rottler died in 1956 and his son Don Rottler, already active in the company, assumed the leadership. At that time Don had considerable experience and education in the metal manufacturing field. However, the automotive line had really dwindled and the marketplace changed to fewer but larger shops that economically performed complete automotive engine remanufacturing.

Don Rottler steered the company into building equipment more suitable for these shops. The machines were larger and no longer portable, and although these machines were much more expensive, they were much more productive and more easily operated by lesser trained personnel. Other machine products were added to the line and appropriately the company name was changed to ROTTLER MANUFACTURING CO. Sales volume slowly grew to multi-million dollar numbers as new innovative and patent protected products were added to the company's catalog.

After two plant relocations, first to rented quarters on First Avenue South and then to an owned property on Poplar Place, the company constructed a thirty-five thousand square foot manufacturing facility on a four and one-half acre site in Kent, Washington. The company continues to operate this plant today.

Among the important key people that contributed to the company's success in addition to Don Rottler, were Starr Peterson, Larry Shogren, Lance Dalton, Mike Walker, Gene Shawley, Larry Pistoll and Gary Stein. Ann Baller and Becky Burdine played an important role in administration and Dave Engnell contributed to product engineering. Outstanding early field

Company headquarters in Kent, Washington.

sales roles included Max Temple and Bill Mansfield. The company has employed between fifty and eighty people during this thirty-five-year era.

An interesting fact is the mirrored interest of Don Rottler in private aviation. Don has piloted a company aircraft extensively, eventually accumulating 12,000 hours while efficiently providing contact with customers located throughout the United States and Canada. The airplane made possible the effective visitation to shops in smaller communities and contributed to the establishment of new ROTTLER products.

In 1985 a transition was marked as the company's products changed from strictly mechanical controls to electro-mechanical systems that were soon coupled to micro-processors providing automated work cycles. This transition was essentially completed throughout the product line by the end of 1996.

And now, in 1997, Don's son Andy Rottler is at the helm, and again the avid interest in aviation is in Andy's blood too. Andy brings his many talents and experience in manufacturing to the scene. Don had traveled world-wide to establish a market for his products in many countries and Andy ably continues this responsibility. About one-third of current sales are shipped overseas and annual sales have grown to seven million dollars.

Generally, Rottler products enjoy a fine, if not the best, reputation for quality and integrity in their field. The enterprise has a rich heritage and a fine group of men and women will continue to prosper with it in the future.

EXCELLENCE IN MANUFACTURING IS GROWING TOWARD THE CENTURY MARK

SCHUCK'S AUTO SUPPLY, INC.

Harry Schuck, 1921.

Harry Schuck, the founder of Schuck's Auto Supply, was fond of of saying, in his private moments, that his business got its start in Uncle Adolph Liska's backyard. Harry had a difficult life as a child. Raised in a children's home after his mother died, he was a fourth grade school drop-out who had lived in the streets as a teenager. But out of this hard life was forged an ambition and kindness which became his personal trademark. By the late teens of this century, when Harry was not yet 20 years old, he was working at two jobs–one by day in the city's shipyards and the other at night and on weekends in his uncle's backyard selling motorcycle parts.

When his business grew, he opened a small storefront shop at Ninth and Blanchard streets, not far from his uncle's house. In the mid-1920s, he moved to a larger shop at 1922 Westlake, and a short time later started selling auto parts.

In 1928, with the business still growing, he hired Erna Jorgensen, a graduate with a degree in English from the University of Washington, to help out. From a rolltop desk in the balcony of the store, she learned the business, made collections, bought merchandise, and helped him manage the company. In the process, they became close friends.

Within a year, she talked Harry into going into the auto wrecking business. With $500 "seed money," she rented an old livery stable on Ninth and Roy streets and started Schuck's Auto Wrecking.

In 1935 Harry Schuck made Erna Jorgensen a partner and together they opened auto parts stores around the city–in Ballard, the University District, on Broadway, and on First Avenue South. In those days, as was the custom of the time, they worked 12 hours a day with no overtime and no vacations. In their words, "we loved every minute of it."

In 1940 Schuck's purchased its first property at Seventh and Bell streets and opened a store. The site still has a Schuck's store today. By 1967, the company's 50th anniversary, Schuck's had eight stores and 42 employees, and was well-respected by both customers and suppliers.

In that same year, Sam Stroum, head of one the Northwest's leading industrial electronic distributorships, bought the company. A longtime acquaintance of Harry Schuck and Erna Jorgensen, he had, years before, expressed an interests in buying the business. Stroum invited his son-in-law, Stuart Sloan, to help him. Under Sloan's leadership and personal commitment to maintaining the company's reputation, Schuck's continued to grow. Today the firm is a highly sophisticated auto parts business with 51 stores in Washington, Idaho, and Oregon, and more than 500 employees.

Schuck's Auto Supply opened this store in Ballard in 1935.

SEATTLE BOILER WORKS

The crew of the original Seattle Boiler Works plant at Ballard. The child is Herman F. Hopkins, 3-year-old grandson of PaulHopkins (left) founder. The child's father, Frank F. Hopkins, is sitting above.

In the spring of 1889, Paul Hopkins purchased three lots on Ballard's Shilshole Bay and erected a small building with lumber that he and his assistants carried on their backs from the beach. He planned to develop a modest general boiler manufacturing company the Ballard Boiler Works, using his many years of experience in boilermaking with the Illinois Central Railroad Company and his own company in Manistee, Michigan. He couldn't have known that the company would flourish and grow to become one of the Northwest's leading boiler and pressure vessel manufacturers, run by successive generations of his children. His boilers have provided power for ships from the gold rush to modern times.

Just after the turn of the century Paul's son, Frank, leased the business from his father for $20 a month for the property and $20 a month for the tools. Shortly thereafter, he acquired the business and changed the name to the Seattle Boiler Works.

The company's business grew, and in 1912 it moved to another location at 1128 West 45th Street in Ballard. In 1918 that facility was enlarged to 30,000 square feet, approximately double that of the original location.

By the mid-1930s, the company needed even more space and acquired another plant at 5237 East Marginal Way. Both plants were operated until the end of World War II, when they were consolidated at the latter location under the direction of Frank's son, Herman Hopkins.

Just after the end of World War II, the great-grandsons of Paul Hopkins, twins Frank and Fred, took a hand in the business. In the ensuing years, they have guided the firm to its present 4.5-acre site on Myrtle Street on the Duwamish River. The plant is one of the most modern heavy-fabrication facilities in the West, and is serviced by rail or barge. Paul's great-great grandson, Craig R. Hopkins, is now active in management. Over the years Seattle Boiler Works has served many prestigious marine and industrial customers, and the company's products are now in use in many parts of the world and particularly around the Pacific Rim area.

The company's second plant was located at 1128 West 45th Street in Ballard.

SEATTLE POST-INTELLIGENCER

The *Seattle Post-Intelligencer* was publishing a newspaper even when Washington was still a territory. In fact, the paper led the territory's successful drive for Washington's admission as the 42nd state. But the newspaper goes back to 1863 when Seattle was a frontier town.

The *Puget Sound Gazette*, then published in Olympia, was floundering and nearly defunct when a San Francisco printer moved it to Seattle in 1867 and rechristened it *The Weekly Intelligencer*. Seven years later, in 1874, he sold it and the new owners published the paper as a daily for the first time. In the following years it absorbed another paper, *The Pacific Tribune*, and in 1878, Thaddeus Hanford, a Seattle pioneer, bought *The Weekly Intelligencer* and absorbed yet another newspaper, *The Puget Sound Dispatch*.

An agricultural monthly, *The North Pacific Rural*, had simultaneously evolved into a newspaper called *The Post*. In what was to be looked upon in later years as a historic moment, the two merged, and on October 1, 1881, the combined owners published the first edition under the name the *Post-Intelligencer*, affectionately known ever since as *"The P-I."*

Under the management of Thomas Prosch, and later Leigh S.J. Hunt, the *P-I* became the most powerful paper in Washington Territory, and it gained a reputation as the voice of the Northwest.

When the Great Seattle Fire destroyed the *P-I* plant in 1889, Hunt, the publisher, dispatched and published news of the fire from his home.

Hunt lost control of the paper in the Panic of 1883 and for several years the *P-I* had a succession of owners, including John L. Wilson, who later became a U.S. senator and who purchased the *P-I* with money loaned him by railroad magnate James J. Hill.

In 1921 William Randolph Hearst purchased the *P-I* at a time when he was acquiring papers throughout the country. Through a series of publishers, The Hearst Corp. has maintained ownership to this day.

In 1983, Hearst and The Seattle Times Co. entered into a joint operating agreement which allows *The Times* to manage both newspapers' production, marketing, advertising and distribution, while responsibility for news and editorial content of the *P-I* remain with Hearst.

In 1986, the newspaper's staff moved into a modern newsroom in the Seattle Post-Intelligencer Building, at 101 Elliott Ave. West. The building is easily spotted on the Seattle skyline because of the P-I Globe, a Seattle icon. One of the world's largest moving neon signs, the globe was designed by a reader who fashioned this promotional message at the globe's equator, "It's in the *P-I*." And so it is.

In 1898, crowds gathered at Second Avenue and Cherry Street to read bulletins on the Spanish American War.

The newspaper's editorial offices are in the Seattle Post- Intelligencer *Building overlooking Seattle's Elliott Bay.*

UNICO PROPERTIES, INC.

Territorial University of Washington in 1870, located in what is now downtown Seattle.

In 1860 the territorial legislature of Washington passed an act establishing a university, "Provided, a good and sufficient deed to ten acres of land, eligibly situated in the vicinity of Seattle, be first executed to the Territory of Washington for university purposes."

The following year Arthur Denny, Edward Lander and Charles Terry, original Seattle settlers, donated 10 acres of virgin forest overlooking Puget Sound, and the university's first building opened its doors to 16 students. "Denny's Knoll" later became known as the Metropolitan Tract and is now the heart of downtown Seattle.

When the University moved to its present site in 1895, the regents agreed to lease the property to private developers. In 1904, a 50-year lease was entered into with James Moore, and in 1907 this lease was assigned to the Metropolitan Building Company. By the 1920s they had completed the White Henry Stuart, Cobb, Skinner, Stimson, and Metropolitan Theater buildings as well as the Olympic Hotel. In 1926 the 2,400 seat Fifth Avenue Theatre opened, stunning audiences with its replica of the throne room of the Forbidden City in Peking.

In 1953 a new company was organized by Roger Stevens, an investor from Detroit with a long-standing interest in real estate and the theater. Steven's University Properties, Inc. won a 35-year lease under competitive bidding with other developers and took up the challenge of rehabilitating and further developing the Tract.

In 1960, the new Washington Building was built, followed by the IBM Building in 1964 and the Financial Center in 1972. In 1975, the company was renamed UNICO Properties, Inc. and started building the 42-story Rainier Tower located on the former site of the White Henry Stuart Building. Rainier Tower was completed in 1978 and UNICO's lease was extended by the University until the year 2014. In 1980, UNICO completely refurbished and restored the 5th Avenue Theatre, on behalf of the 5th Avenue Theatre Association, a non-profit organization. Today the 5th Avenue Theatre is on the National Register of Historic Places.

In 1978, UNICO acquired the Union Square property located a block to the east of the Metropolitan Tract. One Union Square was built in 1981 and Two Union Square followed in 1989, which contains over 1,700,000 ft. of office space. This property continues to be operated by UNICO on behalf of the Washington State Investment Board.

UNICO Properties is a subsidiary of UNICO Investment Company lead by Chairman Henry Ashforth, Jr. Ashforth also is the Chairman of The Ashforth Company, a full service real estate firm located in Stamford, Connecticut. David C. Cortelyou is the President and CEO of UNICO Properties, Inc. In 1996 UNICO added an investment advisory and brokerage division to its development, leasing, property management and construction capabilities and services clients throughout the Pacific Northwest.

The original 10 acres no longer bear woods or classrooms, but under UNICO's management, the Metropolitan Tract has yielded approximately $192 million to the University in rental revenue since 1954, compared to the $4 million returned to the University during the 1904 to 1954 period. Under UNICO's management the land will continue to support the growth of the University into the 21st century while its buildings provide a bold focal point for Seattle's downtown skyline.

Twenty years later, Rainier Tower remains a focal point in downtown Seattle.

THE SEATTLE TIMES

The Seattle Times is one of the oldest and one of the few remaining family-owned newspapers in America. When Colonel Alden J. Blethen bought *The Times* in 1896, it was a failing enterprise that was merely an adjunct to a printing business. Blethen soon turned it around, establishing a legacy of excellence that his heirs carry on, now into the fifth generation.

Blethen initiated a pattern of growth which made *The Seattle Times* an integral part of Seattle life and eventually the largest newspaper in Washington. But the task was daunting. Blethen's new business had already been struggling for 15 years to become established, reaching a circulation of 5,000 in a frontier town of 45,000.

But the determined newspaperman brought verve, style, opinion, direction, controversy and entrepreneurial spirit to his new acquisition. Blethen immediately took steps to change the status quo. He cut the price, moved it to larger facilities at Second and Columbia, established a new printing plant, convinced the Associated Press to expand its coverage and later published a Sunday edition alive with color and original art.

◆

Seattle Times *founder Col. Alden J. Blethen (with cane) is shown with sons C.B. and Joseph in 1914.*

From the beginning, Blethen's actions produced results. Circulation grew, and by 1901 *The Times* had outgrown its new building. By 1906, it was the largest publication north of Los Angeles and west of Chicago, with a circulation of more than 50,000.

A fire in February 1913 slowed the paper's growth, and staff was unable to move back into the plant for months. But with the help of the rival *Post-Intelligencer, The Times* did not miss a day of publication.

When Blethen died in 1915, his son Clarance B. Blethen took over. Under C.B.'s equally independent leadership, *The Times* took a risk on a progressive, modern new plant, moving to its current location on Fairview and John streets in 1931. C.B. moved the newspaper into the modern age of journalism and guided it as publisher for the next 26 years until his death in 1941.

With subsequent Blethen leadership, *The Times* has grown in news and editorial stature and in circulation. In its quest for excellence, the Blethen family has continued to invest in the newspaper to ensure it remains not only the dominant, but also the most reliable source of information for the diverse community it serves. It begins by providing an environment where good journalism can flourish.

Colonel Alden J. Blethen purchased The Seattle Times *in 1896 and made it into a thriving concern.*

◆

Over the years, *The Seattle Times* has won hundreds of awards for outstanding journalism, photography and design. It is a seven-time Pulitzer-Prize-winning newspaper, two of which were awarded in the same year (1997)–a very rare event among regional newspapers. Three Pulitzer award-winning stories of the 1990s–the Exxon Valdez oil spill in Alaska, rudder safety issues on the Boeing 737 and HUD financial mismanagement of tribal housing–had far-reaching national impact. In providing in-depth regional coverage to a regional audience, *The Times* has served the larger public as well.

The Times has quickly adopted new technologies to facilitate the gathering and publishing of news. Decision-makers recognized early on the importance of using emerging on-line technology to do what it does best: gather, report, analyze, interpret, format and distribute information essential to the lives and interests of its readers. In 1990, the company broke ground on a state-of-the-art production and distribution center, the North Creek plant in Bothell. The facility uses electronic transmission, high tech presses, extensive recycling and automated systems to ensure high-quality color reproduction of the newspaper and efficient delivery. In its mission to remain at the forefront of information technologies, *The Times* has an extensive and growing presence on the World Wide Web at www.seattletimes.com.

The company has become an industry leader in embracing diversity throughout the workplace. People of color at *The Times* are more than double the industry average and the newsroom consistently ranks as one of the most diverse in the country. Over 20% of employees are minority in a county of approximately 15% minority population. The Blethen Family Minority Internships and the Urban Newspaper Workshop actively promote journalism among a diverse population.

The Times is also a good place for women to work. One quarter of company executives are female, the company subsidizes on-site daycare and employs other family-friendly policies. It is consistently named one of the 100 best companies for working women by *Working Mother* magazine.

In recent years, the company has emphasized outreach to the community, sponsoring programs like the annual Fund for the Needy campaign to raise money for the neediest, Books for Kids to put new books into the hands of at-risk children, Hinterberger's Alley to raise money for the Northwest Harvest hunger program, and MAVIA (Mothers Against Violence in America) to recognize youth who make a peaceful difference. These and other efforts, such as sponsorship of art and cultural events, have served the community well in the past–and will continue to serve it far into the future.

Today, *The Seattle Times* remains independent, privately owned and Washington's largest daily newspaper. Since 1985, Frank Blethen, great-grandson of Alden Blethen, has been publisher of *The Seattle Times* and CEO of The Seattle Times Company, which owns a number of subsidiaries including the *Walla Walla Union-Bulletin* and the *Yakima Herald Republic* newspapers. *The Seattle Times* employs more than 2,500 people. Its circulation for the six-month period ending September 30, 1996 was 226,000 daily and over 500,000 for the combined Sunday *Seattle Times/Seattle Post-Intelligencer.*

In 1996, *The Seattle Times* celebrated its one hundred year anniversary of family ownership with considerable pride in its growth, accomplishments, longevity and shared history with the Pacific Northwest. Along the way, *The Times* has been a touchstone for news, information and community life: the events, disasters, triumphs, joys and sorrows, debates and decisions that bind a community together.

The centennial year was an occasion to truly celebrate *The Times'* corporate values, its long-term commitment to the regional community and its vision for the future: to remain the Northwest's best newspaper and leading information provider.

The Seattle Times *North Creek production and distribution facility went on-line in May of 1992, bringing the company into a new era of print and distribution technology.*

The Seattle Times *building in downtown Seattle has been the newspaper's news and publishing headquarters since it was built by C.B.Blethen in 1931.*

UWAJIMAYA, INC.

In 1928, Mr. Fujimatsu Moriguchi, a native of Uwajima City, Japan, began business in Tacoma, Washington. Moriguchi sold fresh fish cakes from the back of his truck to Japanese laborers working in logging and fishing camps in the Puget Sound area. Moriguchi named his business Uwajima-ya, after his home town in Japan ("ya" means "store" in Japanese).

In 1942, World War II broke out and Moriguchi, his wife Sadako, and their children were sent to the Internment Camp at Tule Lake, California. After the war, the Moriguchi family, with its seven children, relocated to Seattle. Here they opened a retail store and fish cake manufacturing company on Main street, in Seattle's Chinatown International District. They continued to serve the Japanese community as they had done before the war. It was during this time that Uwajimaya began importing food and gift items directly from Japan.

In 1962, Seattle hosted the World's Fair and during this period, Mr. Moriguchi's ideas blossomed. Uwajimaya began its outreach to non-Japanese clientele, offering fine gift products, kitchenware and delicacies from Japan. The World's Fair venture was a great success. Sadly, Mr. Moriguchi passed away during that summer.

Uwajimaya continued to develop and expand its customer base by catering to the needs of the shopper, which now included second and third generation Asian Americans as well as non-Asians. This was achieved by offering Asian cooking classes, and expanding its product mix to include items from China, Korea, the Philippines and other Asian countries. Uwajimaya continued to provide Asian foods and gifts to an ever-increasing diversity of shoppers. In 1970, Uwajimaya moved to a brand new 20,000 square feet store at 6th and King Street (the current

Above
Fujimatsu Moriguchi, founder.
Below
Fujimatsu, third from left, in his Tacoma, Washington fish cake factory. c. 1930, courtesy of Frank Kubo.

Uwajimaya location), becoming the first Asian store of its size in the Pacific Northwest and the first full-service supermarket for Asian products in the region. Eight years later, another 16,000 square feet was added to this store, complete with a delicatessen, extensive fresh seafood market with live fish tanks, meat and produce sections, kitchenware and gift arcade featuring fine artwork, books and records, clothing, cosmetics and fabrics. The remodeled store also included a place for the already popular Uwajimaya Cooking School.

Since its inception, Uwajimaya has transcended beyond providing basic grocery staples and evolved into a tourist and destination store known for its premium Asian gifts, groceries, kitchenware, produce, seafood, meat/poultry, and deli. Uwajimaya understands that the strength of its retail division is found among its premiere selection of fresh, high quality Asian groceries and gifts. Uwajimaya believes good customer service is paramount. Its reputation is built on being known as the information specialist on all things Asian and part of its mission is to educate the customer on all aspects of Asian cultures. Uwajimaya's pre-eminence among Asian stores comes from its use of modern technology, its emphasis on cleanliness, and an adherence to its business philosophy.

Uwajimaya not only serves the customer but also the community at large. It serves the public by promoting Japanese and Asian cultures, sponsoring cultural events and shows, distributing educational and informational materials, supporting many local programs and contributing to numerous organizations. The Seattle Uwajimaya retail store serves as an important focal point of Seattle's Chinatown International District and the region's diverse Asian community, which is the fastest growing segment of the area's population.

Since 1928, Uwajimaya, Inc. has grown from a family-operated grocery store to become one of the top 150 privately held companies in Washington state. Uwajimaya, Inc. now includes wholesale, food service, and exporting divisions, as well a second retail store in Bellevue, Washington.

◆

Sadako Moriguchi (front) and six of her seven children, from left, Akira, Tomoko, Kenzo (back), Toshi, Suwako and Tomio, courtesy of Kim Zumwalt.

VIRGINIA MASON MEDICAL CENTER

In January 1920, ground was broken for the construction of a new, six-story eighty-bed private hospital and clinic in Seattle. Eleven months later that hospital admitted its first patient.

Today, Virginia Mason Medical Center is a major nonprofit health care delivery system with a patient and referral base stretching throughout the Pacific Northwest and beyond. It encompasses a specialty-tertiary hospital, a 400-member primary and specialty care group practice known nationally for its integrated patient care, an internationally known research center, a nursing residence and adult day health program for people living with AIDS (Bailey-Boushay House), and 22 satellite clinics located throughout western Washington.

Virginia Mason Medical Center was named for two of the founders' daughters who, coincidentally, both were named Virginia Mason. The idea to build a hospital began with six partners and two associates practicing together in Seattle in 1918. Their practice was known as the Mason-Blackford-Dwyer Clinic. In 1920, with the move to the hospital, the name changed to The Mason Clinic.

The group was inspired and led by Dr. James Tate Mason, a physician and surgeon who came to Seattle from Virginia in 1907, and by Dr. John Blackford, also from Virginia. who was recruited from the Mayo Clinic in 1917. Their vision was to develop a "Mayo Clinic of the West," which would integrate a hospital and a physician group practice. At the time, however, group practice was frowned upon. It was only acceptable for physicians to be in solo practice.

Nonetheless, against great odds and only by using their own homes as collateral, the physicians succeeded. Today the medical center is a leader in a number of clinical areas. It was the first institution west of the Mississippi to use insulin to treat diabetic patients; the first to develop regional anesthesia; the first to use ultrasound to dissolve kidney stones; and the first in the region to perform cochlear implantation, a procedure that enables deaf persons to hear again.

The Virginia Mason Research Center has attracted worldwide attention for discovering genetic markers for diabetes and for the risk of developing rheumatoid arthritis.

During the past several years Virginia Mason has become a leader in the field of telemedicine, utilizing video technology to treat patients as far away as Alaska and Montana. Extending its international reach, the medical center has established an exchange program in Russia through which patients needing specialized care travel to Seattle for treatment. Recently, it established an Asian American Clinical Program, offering bilingual physicians, nurses and office staff to the local Chinese, Filipino and Korean communities.

◆

Artist's rendering of the original Virginia Mason Hospital building at Spring Street and Terry Avenue in Seattle, c. 1929.

BIBLIOGRAPHY

Anderson, Bern. *Surveyor of the Sea*. Seattle: University of Washington Press, 1960.
Babcock, Chester D., and Clare Applegate Babcock. *Our Pacific Northwest, Yesterday and Today*. New York: McGraw-Hill Book Company, 1963.
Bagley, Clarence B. *History of King County, Washington*. Chicago: S.J. Clark, 1929.
History of Seattle. Chicago: S.J. Clark, 1916.
Bass, Sophie Frye. *Pigtail Days in Old Seattle*. Portland: Metropolitan Press, 1937.
When Seattle Was a Village. Seattle: Lowman & Hanford, 1947.
Bogue, Virgil G. *Plan of Seattle*. Seattle: Lowman and Hanford Company, 1911.
Bowden, Angie Burt. *Early Schools of Washington Territory*. Seattle: Lowman and Hanford Company, 1935.
Burke, Edward and Elizabeth. *Seattle's Other History*. Seattle: Profanity Hill Press, 1979.
Burke, Padraic. *A History of the Port of Seattle*. Seattle: Port of Seattle, 1976.
Brambilla, Roberto, and Gianni Long. *What Makes Cities Livable? Learning from Seattle*. New York: Institute for Environmental Action, 1980.
Carey, Roland. *The Steamboat Landing on Elliott Bay*. Seattle: Alderbrook Publishing Company, 1952.
Conover, C.T. *Mirrors of Seattle*. Seattle: Lowman & Hanford, 1923.
Costello, James Allen. *The Siwash*. Everett, Washington: The Printers, 1974 (reprinted).
Denny, Arthur A. *Pioneer Days on Puget Sound*. Seattle: Alice Harriman, 1908.
Denny, Emily Inez. *Blazing the Way*. Seattle: Rainier, 1909.
Droker, Howard Alan. *The Seattle Civic Unity Committee and the Civil Rights Movement*, 1944–1964. Unpublished Doctoral Dissertation, University of Washington.
Drucker, Philip. *Indians of the Northwest Coast*. Garden City, New York: The Natural History Press, 1963.
Escoboasa, Hector. *Seattle Story*. Seattle: Frank McCaffrey, 1949.
Gates, Charles M. *Readings in Pacific Northwest History, Washington, 1790–1895*. Seattle: University Bookstore, 1941.
The First Century at the University of Washington. Seattle: University of Washington, 1961.
Grant, Frederic James. *History of Seattle*. New York: American, 1891.
Haeberlin, Hermann, and Erna Gunther. *The Indians of Puget Sound*. Seattle: University of Washington Press, 1977.
Hanford, C.H. *Seattle and Environs*. Chicago: Pioneer Historical Publishing Company, 1924.
Hines, Neal O. *Denny's Knoll: A History of the Metropolitan Tract of the University of Washington*. Seattle: University of Washington, 1980.
Howay, Frederic W. *Voyages of the "Columbia."* Boston: The Merrymount Press, 1941.
Johansen, Dorothy O., and Charles M. Gates. *Empire of the Columbia*. New York: Harper and Brothers, 1957.
Jones, Nard. *Seattle*. New York: Doubleday, 1972.
Kinnear, George. *Anti-Chinese Riots*. Seattle: 1972.
Kirk, Ruth, with Richard D. Daugherty. *Exploring Washington Archaeology*. Seattle: University of Washington Press, 1978.
Lucia, Ellis. *Seattle's Sisters of Providence*. Seattle: Providence Medical Center, 1978.
Mansfield, Harold. *Vision: A Saga of the Sky*. New York: Duell, Sloan and Pearce, 1956.
McCurdy, H.W., with Gordon Newell. *Don't Leave Any Holidays*. Portland, Oregon: Graphic Arts Center, 1967.
McFeat, Tom, ed. *Indians of the North Pacific Coast*. Seattle: University of Washington Press, 1976.
McWilliams, Mary. *Seattle Water Department History, 1854–1954*. City of Seattle, 1955.
Meeker, Ezra. *Pioneer Reminiscences of Puget Sound; and the Tragedy of Leschi*. Seattle: Lowman and Hanford, 1905. Reprinted.
Montgomery, Elizabeth Rider. *When a Ton of Gold Reached Seattle*. Champaign, Illinois: Garrard, 1968.
Morgan, Murray. *Skid Road*. New York: Viking, 1951.
Mumford, Esther Hall. *Seattle's Black Victorians, 1852–1901*. Seattle: Ananse Press, 1980.
Nelson, Gerald B. *Seattle: The Life and Times of an American City*. New York: Knopf, 1977.
Newell, Gordon. *The H.W. McCurdy Marine History of the Pacific Northwest*. Seattle: Superior Publishing Company, 1966.
Newell, Gordon. *Westward to Alki: The Story of David* and *Louisa Denny*. Seattle: Superior, 1977.
Phelps, Myra L. *Public Works in Seattle: A Narrative History of the Engineering Department*. Seattle Engineering Department, 1978.
Phelps, Thomas Stowell. *The Indian Attack on Seattle, January 26, 1856*. Seattle: Farwest, 1932.
Potts, Ralph Bushnell. *Seattle Heritage*. Seattle: Superior, 1955.
Reiff, Janice L. *Urbanization and the Social Structure, Seattle, Washington, 1852–1910*. Unpublished Thesis, University of Washington.
Sale, Roger. *Seattle, Past to Present*. Seattle: University of Washington Press, 1976.
Sayre, J. Willis. *This City of Ours*. Seattle: J.W. Sayre, 1936.
Schmid, Calvin F. *Social Trends in Seattle*. Seattle: University of Washington Press, 1944.
Seattle Century. (Compiled by Research Committee, Seattle Historical Society.) Seattle: Superior Publishing Company, 1952.
Seattle Public Library. *Art in Seattle's Public Places*. Walking tours pamphlets, 1977.
Selby, Kenneth E. *Histories of the Seattle Public Schools*. Seattle Public Schools, 1951.
Sherwood, Don. *History of Seattle Parks*. Unpublished Treatise.
Shorett, Alice. *History of the Pike Place Marketing District*. Typescript, 1972. University of Washington Northwest Collection.
Snowden, Clinton A. *History of Washington*. New York: The Century History Company, 1909.
Speck, Gordon. *Northwest Explorations*. Portland, Oregon: Binfords and Mort, 1954.
Speidel, William C. *Sons of the Profits*. Seattle: Nettle Creek, 1967.
Spencer, Lloyd, ed. *History of the State of Washington*. New York: The American Historical Society, Inc., 1937.
Steinbrueck, Victor. *Seattle Cityscape*. Seattle: University of Washington Press, 1962.
Washington: A Guide to the Evergreen State. Compiled by workers of the Writers' Program of the Work Projects Administration in the State of Washington. Portland, Oregon: Binfords and Mort, 1941.
Watt, Roberta Frye. *Four Wagons West (Story of Seattle*, 1st ed.) Portland: Bindfords & Mort, 1931.

PERIODICALS: *Washington Historical Quarterly, Pacific Northwest Quarterly, Oregon Historical Quarterly, Sea Chest*: Journal of the Puget Sound Maritime Historical Society Quarterly, *Portage*: Journal of the Historical Society of Seattle and King County, *Northwest Magazine, Seattle Magazine, Western Shore, Puget Soundings*.

NEWSPAPERS: *Seattle Times*, Seattle *Post-Intelligencer, The Weekly*, the *Seattle Business Journal*, the *Argus, Seattle Union Record, Seattle Star*.

Bibliography of King County History (Chapter 14)

Bagley, Clarence B. *History of King County, Washington*. Chicago: S.J. Clark, 1929. Reprinted, by White River Valley Historical Society, 1979.
Cameron, C.E. *History, Kent, Washington, U.S.A. and Its Heritage*. N.P: 1978.
Coast Magazine, 17, no. 6 (June 1909).
Corliss, Margaret McKibben. *Fall City in the Valley of the Moon*. N.P: N.D.
Draper, Melanie. *Timber Tides and Tales: A History of the Des Moines Area*. N.P: 1975.
Eyler, Melba, and Yeager, Evelyn. *The Many Roads to Highline*. N.P: 1979.
Fish, Edwards R. *The Past at Present in Issaquah, Washington*. N.P: Harriet Fish, 1977.
Gellatly, Judy. *Mercer Island, the First 100 Years*. N.P: The Mercer Island Bicentennial Commission, 1977.
Haeberlin, Hermann, and Gunther, Erna. *The Indians of Puget Sound*. Seattle: University of Washington Press, 1977.
Halseth, James A., and Glasrud, Bruce A., eds. *The Northwest Mosaic: Minority Conflicts in Pacific Northwest History*. Boulder: Pruett Pub. Co, 1977.
Hill, Ada S. *A History of the Snoqualmie Valley*. N.P: 1970.
Johnston, Helen and Richard. *Willowmoor: The Story of Marymoor Park*. King County Historical Association (Marymoor Museum), 1976.
Lorenz, Laura. *Historical Sketch of the Greater Maple Valley Area*. The Greater Maple Valley Historical Society, 1975.
Lynn, Howard, W. *Lieutenant Maury's Island and the Quartermaster's Harbor*. Vashon: Beachcomber Press, 1975.
Mazy, Patricia. *From a Little Pialshie Thomas Grew*, N.P: 1959.
Morley, Roberta C. *City of Auburn Bicentennial History*. N.P: 1976.
Noel, Patricia S. *Muckleshoot Indian History*. Auburn School District, 1980.

Polk's King County Directory, Vol, 1, 1911–1912. Seattle: R.L. Polk & Co., 1911.

Poppleton, Louise Ross. *There Is Only One Enumclaw.* N.P: 1976.

Ruffner, W. H. *A Report on Washington Territory.* N.Y.: Seattle Lakeshore and Eastern Railway, 1889.

Shoreline Memories: Richmond Beach, Lago Vista, Lake Forest Park, Ronald, Happy Valley, Echo Lake, Innis Arden, 2 Vols. Friends of the Bothell Library, 1977.

Slauson, Morda. *One Hundred Years on the Cedar.* N.P: 1970. Reprinted, Shorey Bookstore, Seattle.

Renton—From Coal to Jets. The Renton Historical Society, 1976.

Squires, Connie Jo. *The Bellevue Story.* N.P: 1967.

Stickney, Amy Eunice, and McDonald, Lucille. *Squak Slough 1870–1920: Early Days on the Sammamish River (Woodinville, Bothell, Kenmore).* Friends of the Bothell Library, 1977.

Stories About the Pioneers of Tolt-Carnation Area. Carnation Women's Club, recorded by Gurina Hjertoos, N.D.

Tharp, Marilyn. "The Story of Coal at Newcastle." *Pacific Northwest Quarterly,* 48, no. 4 (Oct. 1957).

Thomas, Jacob E., ed. *King County Survey of Historic Places.* Seattle: King County Department of Planning and Community Development, 1979.

Thorndale, C. William. *Washington's Green River Coal Country.* Master's Thesis, University of Washington, 1968.

Turner, Harriet. *Ethnozoology of the Snoqualmie,* 2nd ed. N.P: 1976.

Wandrey, Margaret I. *Four Bridges to Seattle: Old Ballard 1853–1907.* N.P: 1975.

Whiting, Jeanne L. *Yarrow: A Place,* N.P: 1976.

Young, Peg, and Knapp, Mike. *White Center Remembers.* White Center Bicentennial Commission, 1976.

ACKNOWLEDGMENTS

Many people helped prepare this book; so many, in fact, that acknowledgments are difficult. To mention all names would require many pages. So we list here principal assistants, while realizing full well that other generous persons gave time and help.

First, the assistance of members of our board of trustees of the Historical Society of Seattle and King County and its executive committee was invaluable. They immediately recognized the potential for this book. Especially we must acknowledge the assistance of Palmer G. Lewis, past president of the Historical Society, who chaired the meetings when the project was discussed and signed the contract after careful perusal by our trustee and legal advisor John Rupp. Also gratitude to Robert C. Wing, the Society's president during the year of the book's preparation, for continuing support; to trustees Barbara (Mrs. Doyle) Fowler and Margaret (Mrs. George) Corley for proofreading the galleys. To the staff of the Museum of History and Industry (MOHAI) we give credit not only for considerable assistance but for helping to fill in at times when the director and librarian were preparing book contents. Special thanks are due to Helen ("Peter") Constantinides, administrative assistant to the director, who arranged schedules to allow the director time to write, and who typed many a page of rough manuscript.

Several descendants of pioneers helped to identify photos and straighten out historical facts. Among them were H.W. ("Mac") McCurdy, Roy Morse, and Mrs. Victor Denny. The governor, the mayor, and members of the city and county councils and their staffs responded with alacrity to our queries.

Among individuals who provided sidebars and other written material were Howard Droker, the book's history consultant; Bob Cole, business biographer; Charles Payton, community museum advisor, historians Robert Ficken, Jonathan Dembo, Doris Pieroth, and Esther Mumford; Rod Slemmons, curator of exhibits, and William Stannard, curator of collections, MOHAI; Lois Rayne Bark, director of education and curator of costumes, MOHAI; Carol V. Davis; Margaret Beyer; and geologist W. Barclay Kamb. Thanks also to the photographers and artists who contributed to the book's illustrations.

The photographic work could not have been done without the help of photographer Howard Giske and his assistants, Larry and Margaret Hoffman. Gratitude as well to Victor Gardaya for his photographic "still lifes"; to Colonel Manfred R. Wolfenstine for use of several of his sketches; to Dennis Andersen, University of Washington Libraries, Historical Photography Collection; to Kathy Gibson, METRO librarian; to Joanne Sjulson, U.S. Army Corps of Engineers; to Wendy Noritake and Grace E. Hoffman, Group Health Cooperative; to Bruce LeRoy, director of Washington State Historical Society, Tacoma, and Jeanne Engerman, assistant librarian; to Ruth Kirk, author, and David Richardson, author; to Suzanne Katz, Seattle Art Museum; to Sister Rita Bergamini, archivist, Sisters of Providence; and to Jane Boney, Cabrini Hospital. Our thanks also go to Dixie Brimhall, MOHAI assistant librarian and to volunteers Marion Reed, Harry Thurlow, Betty Mansfield, Eleanor Still, Martha Johnson, Gail Fox, Louise Lundin, and photo intern Glen S. Lindey.

Additional appreciation to Andy Johnson, the Pacific Northwest Collection, University of Washington Libraries and Glenda Pearson, library specialist; to Dr. James Nason, chairman of anthropology, and Patricia Blankenship, curatorial assistant, Thomas Burke Memorial Washington State Museum.

Also helpful have been the staffs at the history desk, Seattle Public Library, and at the Government Research Library, Municipal Building; Paul Spitzer, historical services; the Boeing Company; Merrill Lindsley, Seattle-King County Convention & Visitors Bureau, and the staff at the *Seattle Post-Intelligencer,* which in the 1960s turned over its collection of news photo negatives to the Museum.

And finally to those firms and institutions whose histories are found in the last chapter, we say, "It couldn't have been done without you."

INDEX

Italic page numbers indicate photographs.

CHRONICLES IN LEADERSHIP INDEX

SIDEBARS

Selected statistics from the "1995 State of Washington Data Book" illustrate the rapid population increases that occurred over the past 35 years.

	1960	1995
King County	935,014	1,613,600
Auburn	11,933	35,230
Bellevue	12,809	102,000
Carnation	490	1,490
Des Moines	1,987	17,283
Duvall	345	3,490
Enumclaw	3,269	10,170
Issaquah	1,870	9,025
Kent	9,017	44,620
Kirkland	8,451	42,350
North Bend	945	2,925
Redmond	1,426	40,030
Renton	18,453	44,890
Seattle	557,087	532,900
Tukwila	1,804	14,740

PHOTO ATTRIBUTION CORRECTIONS

p. 11A-Photo formerly credited to Thomas Burke Memorial Museum is now: Source unknown
p. 11B E. S. Curtis photo is ca. 1912 and the former credit to MOHAI is now attributed to Special Collections, University of Washington Libraries
p. 51 Photo formerly credited to Archives of Sisters of Providence, Seattle now attributed to Sisters of Providence Archives, Seattle, Washington.
p. 74A, 76-Photos formerly credited to Renton Historical Society now attributed to Renton Historical Society Collection.
p. 121 IWW member formerly credited to Historical Photography Collection, University of Washington is now: source unknown.
p. 191C-Photos formerly credited to Renton Historical Society now attributed to Renton Historical Society Collection.
p. 192- Photo # 354A, 193A- Photo # 158- Photos formerly credited to White River Valley Historical Museum now Courtesy, White River Valley Museum.
p. 219D- Photos formerly credited to Renton Historical Society now attributed to Renton Historical Society Collection.
p. 225- Photos formerly credited to Renton Historical Society now attributed to Renton Historical Society Collection.
p. 144B, 145B-Photos formerly credited to Boeing Historical Services, now attributed to The Boeing Company Historical Archives.
p. 166, 167A-Photos formerly credited to Metro, now attributed to King County Transportation and Natural Resources Library.
p. 192 (Photo #354A), 193A (Photo #158) - Photos formerly credited to White River Valley Historical Society and White River Valley Historical Museum now attributed to White River Valley Museum.
p. 202C-Photo formerly credited to Phelps Stokes Collection, New York Public Library, now attributed to I.N. Phelps Stokes Collection, Miriam and Ira D. Wallach Division of Art, Prints and Photographs, The New York Public Library Astor, Lenox and Tilden Foundations.

All photos formerly credited to Historical Photography Collection, University of Washington are now attributed to Special Collection Division, University of Washington Libraries as follows:
p. 5 Quinault woman credit to C.S. MacKenzie NA 747
p. 7 Tetacu
p. 13 Indians catching salmon credit to A. Curtis NA 711
p. 45 Yesler house
p. 58 Yesler house-UW 12241
p. 63 Clara McCarty-UW 3269
p. 64 Central School
p. 77 Frye Opera house
p. 80 Advertisements-UW 539
p. 96 R.H. Thomson-UW 10842
p. 101 Pioneer Building-UW 12631
p. 111 Waterfront credit W. Hester 10059
p. 112 Pike Place Market credit A. Curtis 23588
p. 113 Hiram Chittenden-UW 8392
p. 114 Henry Building
p. 123 Labor picnic-UW 6633
p. 124 Anna Louise Strong-UW 340
p. 133 1411 Building-UW 8525
p. 139 Seattle annex. map-UW 4105
p. 140 Dave Beck-UW 2653
p. 152 Nellie Cornish-UW 862

The following photo credits are all Courtesy The Seattle Art Museum as follows:
p. 209A-59.157 *Wet Wharf* by Jess Dan Cauthorn, West Seattle Art Club, Katherine B. Baker Memorial Award and the Northwest Annual Purchase Fund.
p. 210A - 70.15 *Bird #4 (The Mulitcolored One)* by Morris Graves, Eugene Fuller Memorial Collection.
p. 210 B - 59.161 *Moss on the Trees,* Harold Wahl, Gift of an anonymous donor.
p. 211 - 34.137 *Northwest Landscape,* Callahan, Eugene Fuller Memorial Collection.
p. 212 C - 41.68 *View of Figures by Stalls,* Tobey, Eugene Fuller Memorial Collection.
p. 213A - 62.32 *Portage Bqy,* Ambrose Patterson, Eugene Fuller Memorial Collection.
p. 213B - 36.38 *Boats*, CS Price, Eugene Fuller Memorial Collection